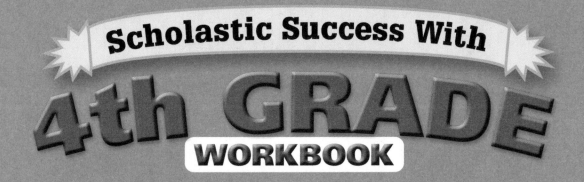

Scholastic Success With
4th GRADE
WORKBOOK

SCHOLASTIC
Teaching
Resources

NEW YORK • TORONTO • LONDON • AUCKLAND • SYDNEY
MEXICO CITY • NEW DELHI • HONG KONG • BUENOS AIRES

Acknowledgments

Maps workbook copyright © 2002 by Linda Ward Beech
Charts, Tables & Graphs workbook copyright © 2002 by Michael Priestley

Cover art by Jon Buller
Cover design by Anna Christian
Interior illustrations by Elizabeth Adams, Jon Buller, Reggie Holladay,
Anne Kennedy, Kathy Marlin, Bob Masheris, and Sherry Neidigh
Interior design by Quack & Company

ISBN 0-439-56972-9

10 08 09

Table of Contents

INTRODUCTION 8

READING COMPREHENSION

Mail Call *(Finding the main idea)* 12

Super Duper Lance *(Finding the main idea and story details)* 14

Honoring Heroes *(Reading for details)* 16

A Very Colorful House *(Using context clues)* . .18

Rattle! Rattle! *(Developing vocabulary)* 20

America's First People *(Comparing and contrasting)* 22

A Difficult Choice *(Comparing and contrasting)* 24

A Real Cool Cowboy *(Sequencing)* 26

Fooled You! *(Sequencing/ reviewing skills)* 28

A Happy Hero *(Analyzing characters/ reviewing skills)* 30

A New Team for Juan *(Analyzing characters/ reviewing skills)* 32

Such Choices *(Making predictions)* 34

A New Start *(Identifying story elements)* 36

A "Peachy" Beach Day *(Identifying cause and effect)* 38

Planet Particulars *(Making inferences)* 40

Guess the State *(Making inferences)* 41

Off to the City *(Following directions)* 42

Food for Fitness *(Classifying/ reviewing skills)* 44

Flower Fun *(Drawing conclusions)* 46

On the Move *(Drawing conclusions)* 47

The Wonderful Whale *(Summarizing)* 48

Climbing Blindly *(Identifying fact or opinion)* 50

Don't Worry, Be Happy *(Appreciating literature)* 52

Improve Learning by Skating *(Appreciating literature)* 54

TESTS: READING

Reading Skills Practice Test 1 57

Reading Skills Practice Test 2 61

Reading Skills Practice Test 3 65

Reading Skills Practice Test 4 69

Reading Skills Practice Test 5 73

Reading Skills Practice Test 6 77

Reading Skills Practice Test 7 81

Reading Skills Practice Test 8 85

Reading Skills Practice Test 9 89

Reading Skills Practice Test 10 93

Reading Skills Practice Test 11 97

Reading Skills Practice Test 12 101

Reading Skills Practice Test 13 105

Reading Skills Practice Test 14 109

Reading Skills Practice Test 15 113

GRAMMAR

Types of Sentences 119

Simple and Complete Subjects and Predicates 122

Compound Subjects and Predicates 125

Compound Sentences .128

Common and Proper Nouns 131

Singular and Plural Nouns 134

Subject and Object Pronouns 137

Possessive Pronouns 140

Action Verbs 143

Verb Tenses 146

Main and Helping Verbs 149

Linking Verbs 152

Scholastic Professional Books

Irregular Verbs 155

Adjectives 158

Adjectives That Compare 161

Pronouns 164

Subject-Verb Agreement 167

Punctuating Dialogue 170

Adverbs 173

WRITING

Sassy Sentences (Writing complete
sentences) 178

Link It Together (Identifying parts of
a sentence) 179

That's Groovy! (Identifying and writing
four kinds of sentences) 180

A Whale of a Fish (Identifying order
in sentences) 182

Number Sentences (Writing questions
from statements) 183

Proofing Pays (Proofreading) 184

Spout Some Specifics (Including details) 185

Make It Interesting (Adding details to simple
sentences) 186

Order the Combination (Combining subjects,
predicates, and objects) 187

A New Challenge (Writing compound
sentences) 188

Hot Subjects (Combining sentences) 189

Sentence Building (Combining details from
several sentences) 190

Applause for the Clause (Combining sentences
using special conjunctions) 191

Triple the Fun (Using commas in sentences) . . .192

Comma Capers (Using commas in
sentences) 193

Show Time (Adding variety in sentences) 194

Keeps On Going (Avoiding run-on
sentences) 195

A Long School Year (Proofreading) 196

Parts of a Paragraph (Identifying the parts
of a paragraph) 197

What's the Topic? (Writing topic sentences) . . .198

Topic Talk (Writing topic sentences) 199

A Lot of Details (Writing topic sentences/
Writing supporting sentences) 200

Drizzle With Details (Identifying supporting
sentences/Writing supporting
sentences) 202

A Musical Lesson (Writing a comparison
paragraph) 204

Is That a Fact? (Writing facts and opinions) . . .205

I'm Convinced! (Writing a persuasive
paragraph) 206

Step by Step (Writing an expository
paragraph) 207

A Sentence Relationship (Writing cause and
effect) 208

What a Mess! (Writing a cause and
effect paragraph) 209

A Vivid Picture (Writing a descriptive
paragraph) 210

Numerous, Spectacular Words (Identifying
overused words) 211

Action Alert (Writing with more
exact verbs) 212

Colorful Clues (Using similes and
metaphors) 213

Adding Spice (Using personification and
hyperbole) 214

Daily Notes (Keeping a journal) 215

Story Time (Writing a story) 216

What Did You Say? (Using quotation
marks) 217

Let's Get Organized (Using an outline to
organize ideas) 218

Read All About It (Writing a news story) 220

CHARTS, TABLES & GRAPHS

MATHEMATICS
Tables 222
Tally Charts 224
Pictographs 226
Bar Graphs 228
Circle Graphs 233
Line Graphs 235

READING/LANGUAGE ARTS
Charts 237
Tables 241

SOCIAL STUDIES
Tables 243
Charts 245
Pictograph 248
Bar Graphs 249
Circle Graph 251
Line Graph 252
Timeline 253

SCIENCE
Tables 254
Charts 256
Bar Graph 258
Circle Graph 259
Line Graph 260

ADDITION, SUBTRACTION, MULTIPLICATION & DIVISION

A Sick Riddle (*Adding 1-digit, 2-digit, and 3-digit numbers*) 262

Blooming Octagon (*Adding 1-digit, 2-digit, and 3-digit numbers*) 263

The Big Cheese (*Using parentheses with addition*) 264

A-Mazing Eighteen (*Using parentheses with addition*) 265

Climbing High (*Adding without regrouping*) 266

Reaching New Heights (*Adding with regrouping*) 267

Wild Birds (*Adding with multiple regrouping*) 268

The American Bald Eagle (*Addition with multiple regrouping*) 269

Funny Bone (*Regrouping with multiple addends*) 270

Canine Calculations (*Identifying missing addends*) 271

Money Fun (*Adding money*) 272

Bathtub Brunch (*Adding 3-digit and 4-digit numbers*) 273

Food To Go (*Story problems, money*) 274

A Penny Saved Is a Penny Earned (*Solving word problems using addition*) ...275

Reach for the Stars (*Using parentheses with subtraction*) 276

Moon Madness (*Using parentheses with subtraction*) 277

Chess, Anyone? (*Subtracting without regrouping*) 278

Checkmate (*Subtracting with regrouping*) 279

Out of the Park! (*Subtracting with multiple regrouping*) 280

Touchdown! (*Subtracting with multiple regrouping*) 281

A Funny Fixture (*Subtracting with multiple regrouping*) 282

Bright Idea! (*Subtracting with multiple regrouping*) 283

Cross-Number Puzzle (*Subtracting greater numbers*) 284

Map It Out (*Subtracting decimals*) 285

Sums and Differences (*Solving word problems*) 286

Follow the Map (*Solving word problems using subtraction*) 287

It's a Circus in Here! (*Learning basic multiplication facts*) 288

Under the Big Top (*Learning basic multiplication facts*) 289

Come to Costa Rica (*Multiplying without regrouping*) 290

The Faraway Country (*Multiplying with regrouping–2-digit top factors*) 291

A Multiplication Puzzler (*Multiplying 1-digit and 2-digit numbers*) 292

The Big City (*Multiplying with regrouping— 3-digit top factors*) 293

A Changing Reef (*Multiplying with zeros*) . . .294

Ship Shape (*Multiplying by hundreds*) 295

Caught in the Web (*Multiplying by thousands*) 296

Purple Blossoms (*Multiplying with regrouping–3-digit top factors*) 297

Stallions in the Stable (*Multiplying with regrouping–4-digit top factors*) 298

Stop Horsing Around! (*Multiplying with regrouping—two 2-digit factors*) 299

Famous Landmarks (*Multiplying with regrouping—two 2-digit factors*) 300

Soccer Balls (*Multiplying with and without regrouping—two 2-digit factors*) 301

In the Wink of an Eye (*Multiplying with and without regrouping—two 2-digit factors*) 302

Monumental Multiplication (*Multiplying with regrouping—3-digit factors x 2-digit factors*) 303

The Music Store (*Multiplying money*) 304

The Corner Candy Store (*Solving word problems using multiplication*) 305

What's on the Tube? (*Learning basic division facts*) 306

Television Division (*Learning basic division facts*) 307

Patchwork Diamonds (*Reviewing division facts*) 308

Mirror Image (*Reviewing division facts*) 309

A Barrel of Monkeys (*Dividing with zeros*) . . .310

No Way! (*Dividing with remainders*) 311

Honeycomb (*Dividing with remainders*) 312

Division Decoder (*Dividing with and without remainders*) 313

Mousing Around (*Dividing with 3-digit dividends without remainders*) 314

Surfing the Web (*Dividing with 3-digit dividends without remainders*) 315

Flying Carpet (*Dividing with 3-digit dividends without remainders*) 316

Poolside! (*Dividing with 3-digit dividends with remainders*) 317

Summer Days (*Dividing with 4-digit dividends with and without remainders*) 318

Bone Up on Division (*Dividing by 2-digit divisors without remainders*) 319

Let's Go to the Show (*Dividing with zeros in the quotient*) 320

Scholastic Professional Books

MATH

Comparing & Ordering Numbers *(Number order and comparisons)* 323

Sign It! *(Number words)* 324

Mystery Number *(Number order and comparisons)* 325

What Number Am I? *(Place value)* 326

A Place for Every Number *(Place value)* 327

Bee Riddle *(Rounding and estimating)* 328

When to Estimate *(Rounding and estimating)* 329

Super Seven *(Patterns)* 330

Pansy's Picture Patterns *(Patterns)* 331

Root for the Home Team *(Ordered pairs)* . . .332

Bewitching Math *(Adding 2-digit numbers with regrouping)* 333

Food Fractions *(Comparing fractions)* 334

Duck Into Action With Fractions *(Comparing fractions)* 335

Into Infinity *(Adding like fractions)* 336

Trefoil *(Subtracting like fractions)* 337

White Socks, Black Socks *(Solving word problems with fractions)* 338

Decimals Around the Diamond *(Decimal place value)* 339

Across-and-Down Decimals *(Adding decimals)* 340

Change Arranger *(Counting money)* 341

Money Magic Puzzle *(Adding money)* 342

Time for Play *(Equivalent measures)* 343

Measure by Measure *(Units of measure)* . . .344

Picnic Area *(Area)* .345

Perimeter and Area Zoo *(Perimeter and area)* 346

Angles for A to Z *(Introducing angles)* 347

Flying Through the Air *(Symmetry)* 348

Shape Up! *(Reviewing geometric shapes)* 349

Terrific Tessellations *(Tessellate patterns)* 350

Kaleidoscope of Flowers *(Decimal place value)* 352

MAPS

What Is a Map? 354

Globes and Hemispheres 356

Map Projections 358

Using a Map Grid and Index 360

Understanding Latitude 362

Understanding Longitude 364

Using a Map Scale 366

Comparing Maps and Scales 368

A Vegetation Map 370

Looking at Landforms 372

A Profile and Contour Map 374

A Physical Map 376

A Product Map 378

A History Map 380

A Road Map 382

A Weather Map 384

A Climate Map 386

A News Map 388

Planning With a Map 390

Maps and Charts 392

Map Review 1 394

Map Review 2 395

Thinking About Maps 396

Glossary 397

Scholastic Professional Books

"Nothing succeeds like success."

Alexandre Dumas the Elder, 1854

Dear Parent,

Congratulations on choosing this excellent educational resource for your child. Scholastic has long been a leader in educational publishing—creating quality educational materials for use in school and at home for nearly a century.

As a partner in your child's academic success, you'll want to get the most out of the learning experience offered in this book. To help your child learn at home, try following these helpful hints:

- Provide a comfortable place to work.

- Have frequent work sessions, but keep them short.

- Praise your child's successes and encourage his or her efforts. Offer positive help when a child makes a mistake.

- Display your child's work and share his or her progress with family and friends.

In this workbook you'll find hundreds of practice pages that keep kids challenged and excited as they strengthen their skills across the classroom curriculum.

The workbook is divided into eight sections: Reading Comprehension; Reading Tests; Grammar; Writing; Charts, Tables & Graphs; Addition, Subtraction, Multiplication & Division; Math; and Maps. You and your child should feel free to move through the pages in any way you wish.

The table of contents lists the activities and the skills practiced. And a complete answer key in the back will help you gauge your child's progress.

Take the lead and help your child succeed with the *Scholastic Success With: 4th Grade Workbook!*

The activities in this workbook reinforce age-appropriate skills and will help your child meet the following standards established as goals by leading educators.

Mathematics

★ Uses a variety of strategies when problem-solving

★ Understands and applies number concepts

★ Uses basic and advanced procedures while performing computation

★ Understands and applies concepts of measurement

★ Understands and applies concepts of geometry

★ Understands and applies properties of functions and algebra

Writing

★ Understands and uses the writing process

★ Uses grammatical and mechanical conventions in written compositions

Reading

★ Understands and uses the general skills and strategies of the reading process

★ Can read and understand a variety of literary texts

★ Can understand and interpret a variety of informational texts

Geography

★ Understands the characteristics and uses of maps and globes

★ Knows the location of places, geographic features, and patterns of the environment

READING COMPREHENSION

Mail Call

*The **main idea** tells what a story or paragraph is mostly about.*

Read the letters Tyler wrote from camp and those he received. Write the main idea for each letter.

Dear Mom and Dad,   Saturday, June 7

Camp is great! I have met a lot of new friends. Jimmy is from California, Eric is from Iowa, and Tony is from Missouri. We have a great time together, swimming, canoeing, hiking, and playing tricks on other campers! Every night, we sneak over to another cabin. We then try to scare the other campers either by making scary noises or by throwing things at their cabin. It's so funny to see them run out screaming! Now don't worry, Mom. I'm not going to get caught like I did last year.

One thing that is different from last year is how many bugs there are! I know that scientists discover 7 to 10 thousand new kinds of insects each year, and I think they could discover even more here! I have at least 100 itchy mosquito bites and about 20 fire ant bites. Every time I go outside, horseflies chase me, too! Other than all these buggy bugs, I'm having the best time!

Love,
Tyler

Main idea _Tyler is at camp and there is lots of bugs_

Dear Tyler,   Tuesday, June 10

Are you sure you are okay? All of those bugs sound awful! Have you used all of the "Itch-Be-Gone" cream I got you? You know how your feet swell if you don't use the cream! How about the "Ants 'R Awful" lotion for the ant bites? You and your Aunt Ethel have always seemed to attract those nasty fire ants.

Now Tyler, I am very happy that you have met some new friends and that you are having fun together. However, you MUST stop trying to scare other campers. Remember, honey, some campers may frighten easily. I want you to apologize for any anxiety you may have caused them and start being the nice, polite boy that I know you are. Do you hear me, Tyler? Please be careful. I want you home safely.

Love,
Mom

Main idea _Tyler's mom is worried about him and doesn't want him to get in trouble_

Dear Steven,   Saturday, June 7

Camp is amazing this year! Our guides help us do the coolest stuff. Like yesterday, we hiked for six miles until we found this awesome spring. Then we used a rope hanging on a tree to jump in the water. I went so high that I made a huge splash! Thursday, our guides took us rowing. We rowed to this little island where we made a bonfire. We roasted the fish we had caught. My fish was the biggest, of course!

Last night, we collected a big bunch of frogs in a bag. Then we put the bag under a bed in another cabin while they were all at the campfire. When they got back, the frogs were all over their cabin. We laughed so hard! I know they're going get us back. I've seen them planning. I can't wait to see what they try. Hey! How's the leg? Sure wish you were here!

Your friend,

Tyler

Main idea _____

Dear Tyler,   Tuesday, June 10

That's great you're having so much fun! I wish I were there. All I do is sit around bumming out, thinking about all the fun you are having. I can't believe I broke my leg two days before camp started. My mom keeps renting me movies and video games, but I think I've seen everything and played everything. I just know I won't be happy again until this cast is off.

Your new friends sound great! Sure wish I was there helping you guys play tricks on the other campers. Remember last year when we smeared honey all over another cabin and all those bees came? That was so funny—except the part where we had to scrub all the cabins clean wearing hot, protective gear. I'm still surprised they let you come back this summer!

Hey! What's up with all the bugs? Your mom called my mom all worried about a bunch of bugs or something. Have fun and write soon!

Your friend,
Steven

Main idea _____

Read a newspaper article about a foreign place. On another piece of paper, write the main idea for each paragraph.

Super Duper Lance

 *The **main idea** tells what a story or paragraph is mostly about. **Details** in a story provide the reader with information about the main idea and help the reader better understand the story.*

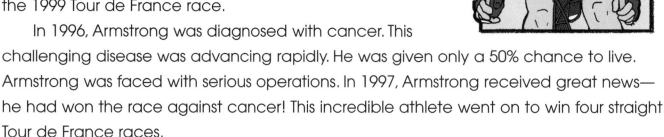

Lance Armstrong is an awesome athlete! This American bicyclist won the Tour de France bicycle race in the summer of 1999. He went on to win it again in 2000, 2001, and 2002. What makes Armstrong's accomplishment even more amazing is that he was battling cancer before competing in the 1999 Tour de France race.

In 1996, Armstrong was diagnosed with cancer. This challenging disease was advancing rapidly. He was given only a 50% chance to live. Armstrong was faced with serious operations. In 1997, Armstrong received great news— he had won the race against cancer! This incredible athlete went on to win four straight Tour de France races.

The Tour de France is the world's premier cycling event. It takes its competitors all over France, even through the Alps and the Pyrenees Mountains. The course changes each year but is always over 2,000 miles long and always ends in Paris.

Circle the main idea for each paragraph.

1. **Paragraph 1:**

    a. Armstrong was the first American bicyclist to win the Tour de France.

    b. Armstrong is an accomplished bicyclist.

    c. Armstrong rides all over France in the summer.

2. **Paragraph 2:**

    a. Armstrong was the first American bicyclist to win the Tour de France.

    b. Armstrong had cancer in 1996.

    c. Armstrong won an important "health" race.

3. **Paragraph 3:**

    a. Riders in the Tour de France get to see all of France.

    b. Tour de France competitors must be very strong to ride through two mountainous regions.

    c. The impressive Tour de France runs all over France and ends in Paris.

Scholastic Professional Books

4. Use details from the story to write why you think Armstrong is an accomplished

   athlete. _____

   _____

   _____

   _____

   _____

   _____

   _____

5. Write a detail about the Tour de France bicycle race on each tire.

6. What are some of the challenges Armstrong has faced? Which one do you think

   was the most difficult? _____

   _____

   _____

   _____

 Read a magazine article about another sports figure. On another piece of paper, write the main idea of the article.

Honoring Heroes

 Details *in a story provide the reader with information about the main idea and help the reader better understand the story.*

Washington, D.C., is the capital of the United States. It is located between Virginia and Maryland on the Potomac River. Washington, D.C., is also the headquarters of the federal government. This incredible city is a symbol of our country's history and the home of many important historical landmarks.

Many of Washington, D.C.'s, famous landmarks are located in the National Mall. The Mall is a long, narrow, park-like area that provides large open spaces in the middle of

the city's many huge buildings. In addition to being home to the U.S. Capitol, where Congress meets, and the White House, the Mall is also dedicated to honoring the history of our nation. Memorials for presidents George Washington, Abraham Lincoln, Thomas Jefferson, and Franklin D. Roosevelt can all be found in the Mall. There are also memorials honoring Americans who fought in the Korean and Vietnam Wars.

Near the Lincoln Memorial another memorial is being built. It is the National World War II Memorial. This memorial will honor Americans who fought and supported the United States during World War II. The U. S. fought in this war from 1941 to 1945.

The new memorial will feature a Rainbow Pool, two giant arches, a ring of stone columns, and a wall covered with gold stars. Each star will represent 100 Americans who died while fighting in World War II.

Bob Dole, a former senator and World War II veteran, has been working tirelessly to get this memorial built. He believes that the memorial will remind Americans of the value of freedom. "Freedom is not free," says Dole. "It must be earned . . ."

More than $175 million has been raised to build the memorial that means so much to Dole and to many other Americans. Many businesses, private groups, and schools donated money to this cause. The memorial is expected to be completed in 2004.

1. **Where is Washington, D.C., located?** Washington D.C. is located between Virginia and Maryland on the Potomac River

2. **Write three facts about Washington, D.C.** _____
   1 many of Washington D.C.'s landmarks are located in the national mall
   2. _____

3. **Which four presidents are memorialized in the National Mall?** _____
   _____

4. **Besides the four presidents, who else is honored in the Mall?** _____
   _____

5. **What is the name of the new memorial?** _____
   _____

6. **Why is it being built?** _____
   _____

7. **How long did the United States fight in World War II?** _____

8. **What are some features of the new memorial?** _____
   _____

9. **Write what the stars represent.** _____
   _____

10. **What World War II veteran has worked hard trying to get the memorial built?** _____
    _____

11. **What remembrance does Dole think the memorial will bring to the minds of people?** _____
    _____

12. **What are the sources of the $175 million that has been raised to build the memorial?** _____
    _____

Read about another memorial in Washington, D.C. On another piece of paper, write five details about the memorial.

A Very Colorful House

 Context clues *are words or sentences that can help determine the meaning of a new word.*

Jackson was excited! He and his family were on their way to the White House. Jackson could not wait to see the President's official **residence**. He had been reading all about it so that he might recognize some things he saw. After standing in a long line, Jackson, his sister, and their parents were allowed to enter the 132-room, six-floor **mansion**. They entered through the East **Wing**. Jackson knew that he and his family were only four of the 6,000 people who would visit this **incredible** house that day.

The first room they were shown by the **guide** was the State Dining Room. Jackson learned that 140 dinner guests could eat there at one time. "What a great place for a huge birthday party!" Jackson thought.

The Red Room was shown next. Red satin **adorned** its walls. The third room the **visitors** entered was the Blue Room. This room serves as the main **reception** room for the President's guests. Jackson wondered when the President would be out to greet him. After all, he was a guest, too.

The Green Room was the fourth room on the **tour**. Jackson and his family were not surprised to find green silk covering the walls in this room.

The last room was the biggest room in the White House. It is called the East Room. Here, guests are **entertained** after **formal** dinners. Jackson wondered if they could **vary** the entertainment by rolling in **huge** movie screens so they could all watch the latest movies. He wondered if kids were invited sometimes; maybe they had huge, bouncy boxes you could jump in. Perhaps they even set up huge ramps so all the kids could practice skateboarding and roller blading. How fun!

Jackson loved his tour of the White House. He was just sorry that he did not get to see the living quarters of the President's family. He wondered if the President had to make *his* bed every day!

Name _____

Write one of the bolded words from the story to match each definition below. Use context clues to help. Then write each numbered letter in the matching blank below to answer the question and learn an interesting fact.

1. following the usual rules or customs in an exact way __ __ __ __ __ __
   <u>1</u>

2. home __ __ __ __ __ __ __ __ __
   12   10

3. a gathering at which guests are received __ __ __ __ __ __ __ __ __ __
   9   17

4. kept interested with something enjoyable __ __ __ __ __ __ __ __ __ __ __
   15   16   8

5. decorated __ __ __ __ __ __ __
   13

6. a leader of a tour __ __ __ __ __
   4

7. a part that sticks out from a main part __ __ __ __
   2

8. a very large, stately house __ __ __ __ __ __ __
   7

9. a trip to inspect something __ __ __ __
   6

10. amazing __ __ __ __ __ __ __ __ __
    11

11. very large __ __ __ __
    5

12. guests __ __ __ __ __ __ __ __
    3

13. to change __ __ __ __
    14   18

How many gallons of paint does it take to paint the outside of the White House?

__ __ __ __   __ __ __ __ __ __ __   __ __ __ __ __ __ __
1 2 3 4   5 6 7 8 9 10 11   12 13 14 15 16 17 18

Rattle! Rattle!

Many kids think Cassidy is crazy! That is okay with her. Cassidy loves rattlesnakes, and that is that. She has every book there is about these fascinating creatures. She loves seeing these animals in the zoo.

Rattlesnakes are extremely poisonous. They often use the rattle in their tails to give a warning sound before they strike. They are classed as pit vipers.

Cassidy has decided her favorite kind of rattlesnake is a diamondback rattlesnake. These snakes can grow to be over seven and one-half feet long! These large rattlesnakes are the most dangerous of all snakes, and they do not always rattle before striking. Like most rattlesnakes, diamondbacks like to eat birds and small mammals.

Part of the fun of being enamored with rattlesnakes is learning all kinds of interesting information about them. For example, Cassidy had always heard that you can tell the age of a rattler by the number of rattles in its tail. This, she learned, is not true. Two to four segments are added to the tail each year, one every time the rattler sheds its skin.

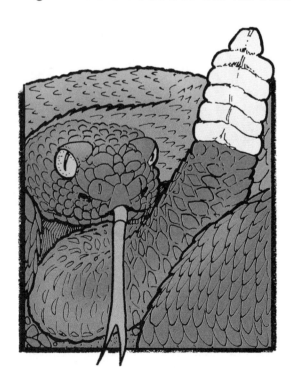

However, once ten have accumulated, they begin to fall off! So you can never be quite sure just how old a rattlesnake is!

Sometimes Cassidy's mom wishes her daughter could love kittens or puppies or ponies instead of poisonous snakes. But actually, Cassidy's love for snakes is definitely what makes her unique.

Scholastic Professional Books

Find a word in the snake to match each definition.

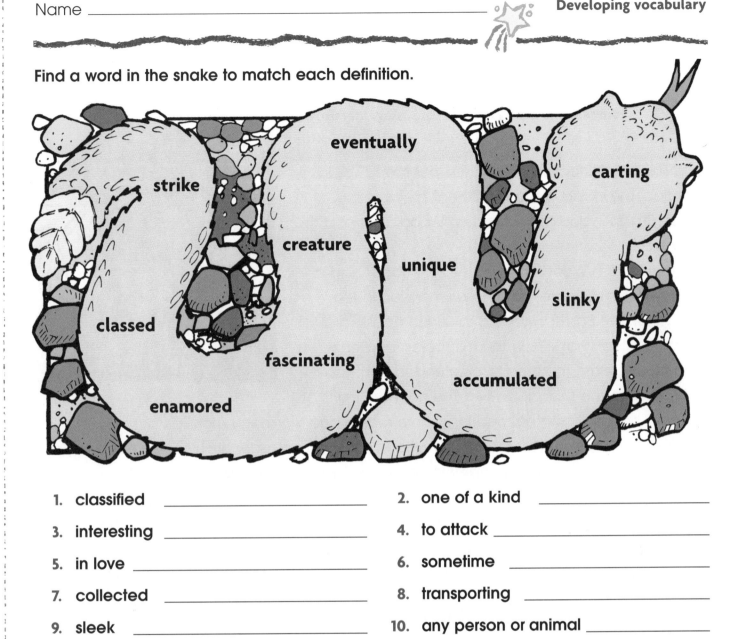

strike

eventually

carting

creature

unique

slinky

classed

fascinating

accumulated

enamored

1. classified _____

2. one of a kind _____

3. interesting _____

4. to attack _____

5. in love _____

6. sometime _____

7. collected _____

8. transporting _____

9. sleek _____

10. any person or animal _____

11. Check the main idea of the story.

☐ Cassidy wants a long snake.

☐ Cassidy loves large, dangerous rattlesnakes.

☐ Rattlesnakes do not always rattle before striking.

12. What kind of snake does Cassidy like best?

_____

Read an article about an animal that fascinates you. Choose five words from the article and write the definition of each on another piece of paper.

Scholastic Professional Books

America's First People

 *To **compare** and **contrast** ideas in a passage, determine how the ideas are alike and how they are different.*

Native Americans were the first people to live in America. They lived in many different areas of the United States including the Eastern Woodlands and the Southwest.

The Eastern Woodlands Native Americans had a much different lifestyle than those who lived in the Southwest. The Eastern Woodlands encompassed all of the area from what is now the Canadian border down to the Gulf Coast. The area also extended from the East Coast to the Mississippi River. The northern parts of this area had cold winters, and the whole region had warm summers.

The Southwest Native Americans lived in a large, warm, dry area. Today, Arizona, New Mexico, southern Colorado, and northern Mexico make up this area. In the northern part of this region, wind and water created steep-walled canyons, sandy areas, mesas, buttes, and other interesting landforms. In the southern part, the desert land was flat and dry.

The Iroquois, Wampanoag, Cherokee, and Chickasaw are just a few of the major tribes that made their home in the Eastern Woodlands. The Southwest was home to tribes such as the Apache, Navajo, and Pueblo.

Housing was very different for the Native Americans who lived in these two different regions. The Eastern Woodlands natives built a variety of homes, depending on their location. Northern dwellers lived in dome-shaped wigwams covered with sheets of bark or in longhouses. A longhouse was a large, rectangular shelter that was home to a number of related families, each living in its own section. Those in the southeastern area often built villages around a central public square where community events took place.

Many of the Native Americans of the Southwest lived in cliff houses or large, many-storied homes built from rock and a mud-like substance called adobe. These adobe dwellings could house many families.

All of the Native Americans living in both regions ate a lot of corn, beans, and squash. Hunting was important in both regions, but fishing was more significant in the Eastern Woodlands.

The tribes living in both regions were excellent craftspeople. Those in the Eastern Woodlands made pottery, wicker baskets, and deerskin clothing. Many tribes in the Southwest also made pottery and were very skilled at spinning cotton and weaving it into cloth. This cloth was made into breechcloths and cotton kilts for the men and a kind of dress for the women.

Learning about these fascinating people is important as they have played, and continue to play, a valuable role in our country's history.

1. **Fill in the Venn diagram using the descriptions below.**

wigwams and longhouses	excellent craftspeople
made pottery	cold winters, warm summers
hunting	buttes
many-storied homes	Arizona, New Mexico, and southern Colorado
steep-walled canyons	corn, beans, and squash
fishing	Iroquois and Cherokee
Apache and Navajo	bordered what is now Canada

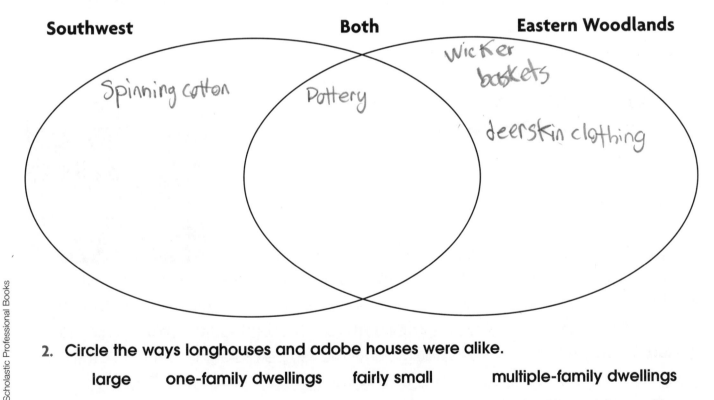

Southwest   **Both**   **Eastern Woodlands**

Spinning cotton   Pottery   Wicker baskets

deerskin clothing

2. **Circle the ways longhouses and adobe houses were alike.**

  large   one-family dwellings   fairly small   multiple-family dwellings

3. **How was the climate in certain parts of the Eastern Woodlands different from other parts in the same region?** _____

_____

A Difficult Choice

Emily and Zach are confused! Their parents told them they could choose between Massachusetts and Arizona for their vacation this summer, and they think both states seem pretty awesome. Emily has always wanted to visit Boston, the capital of Massachusetts. Zach and she both agree that strolling along the Freedom Trail would be pretty neat. Walking the trail would enable them to see Boston's most famous historic landmarks, like the site of the school Ben Franklin attended and the Old State House. It was built in 1713 and served as the seat of the colonial government.

Emily and Zach both love the beach. If they went to Massachusetts, they could spend a few days at the beaches on Cape Cod. Emily loves boogie boarding, and Zach is great at body surfing. They both enjoy building sandcastles with their mom and dad.

Zach finds learning about Native Americans fascinating and has always wanted to travel along the Apache Trail in Arizona. This mountain highway passes Native American ruins in Tonto National Forest. Emily is not as interested in traveling along this trail as Zach, but they both would like to visit Phoenix, the capital, and then travel to Grand Canyon National Park and Meteor Crater. Zach learned in science class that Meteor Crater is a hole over 4,000 feet wide and 520 feet deep that was created when a huge object from space fell to Earth. The object went so deep that it has never been found. Zach would really like to try to locate it. Emily thinks he is crazy! If experienced scientists and researchers cannot find it, Zach might as well not even bother to try.

If Arizona is the chosen state, Emily and Zach would also like to stop at a few other places. Arizona is home to fifteen national monuments. That is more than any other state.

The only drawback for Zach if they choose Arizona would be the heat. It is very hot and dry in this southwestern state. Arizona has a lot of what Massachusetts does not—desert land. Once in July in Arizona, it got up to 127°F !

Massachusetts, on the other hand, is located in the northeastern United States. Here, Zach and Emily and their parents could enjoy mild temperatures of about 75° F. Their parents love hot weather, but Zach and Emily do not really like to sweat. Therefore, both know that they would prefer the climate of Massachusetts.

How will they ever decide to which state they should travel? If only they could take two trips!

Scholastic Professional Books

1. "Pack" each suitcase to describe the two regions.

   Tonto National Forest

   Old State House

   Freedom Trail

   mild climate

   Phoenix

   Boston

   very hot

   Cape Cod

   Apache Trail

   Grand Canyon

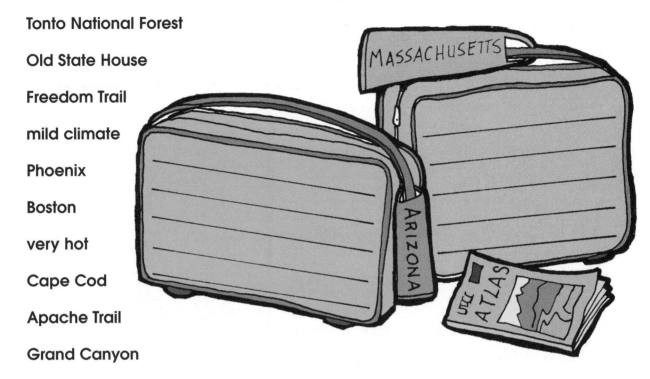

2. Circle things both Emily and Zach like or would like to see.

building sandcastles	Apache Trail	hot weather	beach
Meteor Crater	surfboarding	Freedom Trail	sweating

3. Write one way Zach and Emily are different from their parents. _____

   _____

4. Write one way the Freedom Trail and the Apache Trail are different. _____

   _____

   _____

5. How do Zach and Emily spend their time differently at the beach? _____

   _____

6. How are Zach and Emily's feelings different when it comes to finding the missing

   object at Meteor Crater? _____

   _____

 Read about a state you would like to visit. On another piece of paper, write five differences between the state you chose and the state in which you live.

A Real Cool Cowboy

 *The events in a story take place in a certain order. This is the **sequence** of events.*

Pecos Bill is a well-known character in American folklore. His legend developed from a magazine article written by Edward O'Reilly in 1923. This cowboy hero is often credited for being the creator of branding, roping, and other cowboy activities. It is also said that Pecos Bill taught broncos how to buck and cowboys how to ride.

Legend has it that Pecos Bill was born in the 1830s in Texas. He teethed on a bowie knife and had bears and other wild animals as friends. On a family trip to the West, little Bill fell out of the wagon near the Pecos River. He was found by coyotes that raised him.

Two famous natural landmarks are also amusingly traced back to Pecos Bill—the Grand Canyon and Death Valley. Supposedly, Pecos Bill once made a bet that he could ride an Oklahoma cyclone without a saddle. The cyclone was not able to throw him off, and it finally "rained out" under him in Arizona. This rain was so heavy that it created the Grand Canyon. When he reached California, Pecos Bill crashed. It was the force of his fall that is said to have created Death Valley. In actuality, some rocks in the deepest part of the Grand Canyon date back to about two billion years ago. The Colorado River began forming the Grand Canyon about six million years ago. Over centuries, the water eroded

the layers of rock, and the walls of the canyon were created. More erosion occurred later as a result of wind, rain, and melting snow. Death Valley is a desert in California and Nevada. It contains the lowest point in the Western Hemisphere at 282 feet below sea level.

No one is quite sure how Pecos Bill died. One version says he laughed himself to death after listening to silly questions a man from Boston asked him about the West.

1. Look at each picture. Number the events in the order in which they happened in the story. Write a sentence for each.

_____   _____   _____

_____   _____   _____

_____   _____   _____

_____   _____   _____

_____   _____   _____

_____   _____   _____

2. Four words from the story are hidden in the puzzle. The definition of each word is given below. Shade in the letters for each word, reading left to right and top to bottom. The remaining letters will spell the name of a real cool cowboy two times.

a piece of writing

laughingly

attributed with

a particular form of something

a	p	r	t	e	i	c
c	o	l	e	s	a	b
m	u	s	i	i	n	l
g	l	y	l	c	p	r
e	d	e	i	t	c	e
o	d	v	s	e	b	r
i	s	l	l	i	o	n

Read a story about an imaginary character. On another piece of paper, write five events from the character's life in the order in which they happened.

Fooled You!

Maria decided to have a Prank Party for her friends on April Fools' Day. She invited five of her best friends to come over for the afternoon. Maria and her mom made some delicious "pranks" for her party. They made treats that looked like one food but tasted like another. For example, Maria and her mom made fried-egg sundaes. These sweet treats looked like a fried egg in a bowl, but they were really made of vanilla ice cream topped with marshmallow fluff and a round blob of yellow pudding.

Another treat looked like a thin-crust pizza with vegetables. However, it was really a tortilla with strawberry and apricot jam, a black licorice stick, a green fruit roll, white chocolate chips, and cashew halves. It was so easy to make that Maria's little brother, Juan, even helped.

To make a "pizza," Juan and Maria first stirred the two jams together. Then Maria spread the jam on a tortilla, being careful not to go all the way to the edge. Maria's mom sliced the licorice stick to resemble black olives and the fruit roll to look like green pepper strips. The cashew halves looked like mushrooms.

Next, Maria melted the white chocolate chips at half power in the microwave for one-minute intervals. Juan stirred the chips after each minute to see if they were completely melted. (Maria's mom made sure he had a dry spoon when he stirred because she said that water makes the chocolate lose its creaminess.) Once it was melted, Maria quickly spread the melted chocolate on the pizza. Then she and Juan topped the "pizza" with the "olives," "peppers," and "mushrooms."

Maria's friends loved the delicious pranks she had made. No one dared to play an April Fool's trick on Maria since her pranks were so tasty and fun!

1. **Number the steps in the order Maria and Juan made a Prank Pizza.**

    ___ **Juan and Maria topped the pizza.**

    ___ **Maria's mom created "olives" and "green peppers."**

    ___ **Maria melted the white chocolate chips.**

    ___ **Maria spread the jam on the tortillas.**

    ___ **Juan and Maria stirred the two jams together.**

    ___ **Juan stirred the chips with a dry spoon.**

    ___ **Maria spread the melted chocolate on the pizza.**

2. On the pizzas below, write one way a real pizza is similar to Maria's Prank Pizza and one way it is different from it.

Similar 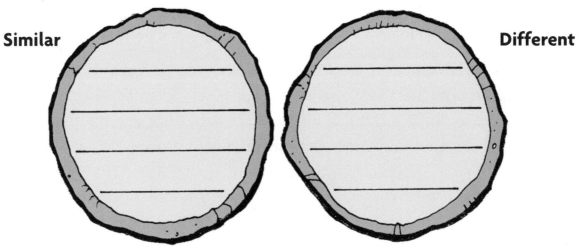 **Different**

3. Write a synonym from the story for each word below.

trick _____

celebration _____

scrumptious _____

4. Why did Maria's mom make sure Juan used a dry spoon to stir the chocolate?

_____

5. Check the ingredients used in making the Prank Pizza.

___ crust   ___ strawberries   ___ tortilla

___ apricot jam ___ red licorice   ___ green fruit roll

___ walnuts   ___ cashews   ___ chocolate chips

6. Circle the main idea of paragraph one.

Maria is a big prankster.

Maria "sweetly" tricked her friends on April Fools' Day.

Maria's mom had great prank ideas for April Fools' Day.

7. What ingredients were in the fried-egg sundaes?

_____

8. If the vegetables on Maria's pizza were real, what would they have been?

_____

Read the recipe of one of your favorite foods. Write each step on a strip of paper. Mix up the strips and then see if you can put them in the correct sequence.

A Happy Hero

*To better understand a character, a reader needs to carefully study, or **analyze**, a character's traits, personality, motivations, relationships, and strengths and weaknesses.*

One day, Lindsay and Erica were sitting at Lindsay's house working very diligently. Fourth grade was tough, and they were working on a science project about weather. Lindsay was a hard worker like Erica, so the two girls were happy to have each other as partners. They were currently writing about rain and were amazed to learn that Hawaii is the world's wettest place. Lindsay found that Mount Waialeale, on the island of Kauai, gets about 460 inches of rain a year! In 1982, Mount Waialeale set an all-time world record when it received 666 inches of rain. The girls knew that their classmates would find all these facts interesting.

The girls were enjoying the fun facts they were finding when all of a sudden, Lindsay saw Erica choking. Erica had been chewing on a pen cap and had accidentally swallowed it! Erica started pointing to her neck. Lindsay asked her if she was choking. When Erica nodded to say yes, Lindsay quickly stood up and did the Heimlich maneuver to try to help Erica stop choking. (The Heimlich maneuver is a way to save someone from choking. This method is named after the doctor who invented it, Henry Heimlich.)

Lindsay was afraid of hurting her friend, so the first time she tried the Heimlich maneuver, she did not do it very hard. She tried a second time, and nothing happened. After trying it a third time, the pen cap flew out of Erica's mouth!

Erica was very grateful to Lindsay. She had been terrified when she realized she had swallowed the pen cap and could not breathe. Lindsay was very brave to try to save her friend. This was one science project that both girls would never forget!

1. Circle each word that describes Lindsay.

   hard worker   boring   brave   fast-thinking

   quick-acting   selfish   timid   lazy

2. Circle each word that tells how Erica might have been feeling when she realized she was choking.

   scared   thankful   enthusiastic   helpless

   courageous   sick   alarmed   friendly

3. What do you think Lindsay might be when she grows up? _____

   _____

4. Write L for Lindsay, E for Erica, or B for both.

   ____ good students   ____ frightened   ____ persistent

   ____ courageous   ____ grateful   ____ appreciative

5. What is the name of the doctor who invented the lifesaving maneuver?

   _____

6. What is the name of the wettest place in the world? _____

7. Circle the average amount of rain Mount Waialeale received each day in 1982.

   almost 3"   just under 2"   just over 4"   about 1"

8. Why do you think this project will be one neither girl will ever forget? _____

   _____

   _____

   _____

Choose a character from a book. On another piece of paper, make a list of ten words that describe this character.

A New Team for Juan

Juan was angry! His mom had signed him up late for baseball, and now he was not on his old team. He would not get to play with Tyler, Joe, and Brad. They had played together for four years! And they all loved Coach Dave—he was one of the best coaches in the league. Juan was not even sure if he wanted to play at all. He just knew it would not be any fun.

At the first practice, Juan walked slowly to the field. He saw one guy pitching and one hitting. The guy hitting struck out. "Great!" thought Juan. "I will be on a team with no hitters!" Juan continued on to the field. He saw some guys playing catch. One guy missed an easy ball. "Perfect!" thought Juan. "I will also have to teach them how to catch!"

Juan thought about calling it quits when he suddenly realized that Eric, a friend from school, was on the team. Eric was a great pitcher! "Well, maybe I will stay for a bit," Juan said to himself.

Juan started looking around some more. He recognized two other kids he had watched when he had been on the other team. One was a fast runner, and one never missed a pop fly. "Hey! This team might be okay after all!" thought Juan.

Eric was excited to see Juan. "Hey, Juan! I'm glad you are on our team. We are going to have a great team. Do you know who our coach is?"

Juan was sure the coach would not be as good as Coach Dave, but Eric was excited. "So, who is the coach, Eric?" Juan asked, somewhat indifferently.

"It's Home Run Harvey!" Eric replied excitedly.

"Home Run Harvey!" exclaimed Juan. "The one and only Home Run Harvey from the university team?"

"That is right," said Eric. "His little brother is on our team, and he wants to coach." Juan could not believe how lucky he was to get on Home Run Harvey's team!

"So who is his brother?" Juan asked.

"Tim is over there," said Eric, pointing to the guy who had not caught what Juan had called an "easy ball."

Juan felt badly for thinking negatively about Tim's missed catch. Everyone misses a ball now and then. Juan could not wait to tell his friends about his new team and coach!

Scholastic Professional Books

1. Check how Juan felt in each situation.

	positive	negative
He could not play baseball with his friends.		
He sees a player on his new team strike out.		
He sees his friend, Eric.		
He learns Home Run Harvey is the coach.		

   He could not play baseball with his friends.

   He sees a player on his new team strike out.

   He sees his friend, Eric.

   He learns Home Run Harvey is the coach.

2. Why was Juan angry that he could not play on his old team? _____

   _____

3. Underline when Juan first started feeling more positive about the new team.

   when he saw a player who was a fast runner

   when he saw a player who never missed a pop fly

   when he saw Eric

4. Why do you think Juan felt badly about what he thought when he saw Tim miss

   a catch? _____

5. Circle the words that describe Juan at the end of the story.

   angry   scared   excited   pessimistic   remorseful   timid

6. Circle the main idea of the story.

   Juan's mom made a terrible mistake, and now Juan had to suffer.

   What Juan thought was going to be a negative experience soon looked
   like it could be a positive one.

   Juan is going to get awesome coaching from a very talented ball player.

7. What kind of season do you think Juan's team will have?_____

   _____

   _____

**Choose three characters from a book. On another piece of paper, write two different
words to describe each character.**

Such Choices

 Making predictions *is using information from a story to determine what will happen next.*

Hurray! Spring break is here! Tommy's mom and dad are also on vaction from work all week. They want to plan all kinds of fun things to do, like biking, hiking, fishing, swimming, and tennis. They are hoping for some warm, enjoyable weather. However, they just cannot decide which day to do each activity. So, they decided to check the weather forecast in the newspaper before making some final plans.

THE FIVE-DAY FORECAST

Monday	Tuesday	Wednesday	Thursday	Friday
a beauty with no clouds; high of 82	partly cloudy with a 40% chance of afternoon thunderstorms; high of 80	lingering showers until noon; then clearing and cooler with a high of 70	partly sunny with a high of 60	partly cloudy with a high of 65

1. Tommy and his dad want to spend one whole day fishing. On which day(s) might they not want to go fishing? _____

2. What day would be the best day for swimming? _____

Scholastic Professional Books

3. What other activities could Tommy and his family do on Tuesday and Wednesday?

_____

_____

4. On what days do you think the family might wear jeans and jackets? _____

_____

5. Do you think Tommy and his family are pleased with the forecast? Why or why not?

_____

_____

6. To do the kinds of activities Tommy and his family want to do, which forecast do you think they would like to see every day of spring break? Why?

_____

_____

7. Write the word from the forecast that means "staying." _____

8. Circle the words that describe Tommy's family.

   incompetent   athletic   energetic   listless

9. Circle the things Tommy and his family might want to take with them if they go swimming on Monday.

   jacket   goggles   sunglasses

   cooler with drinks   rain umbrella   sunscreen

10. Write a paragraph about what Tuesday might be like for Tommy.

_____

_____

_____

_____

_____

 Read the weather forecast in the newspaper. Choose four different cities in the country. On another piece of paper, make a list of the activities you could do in each city, based on the forecast. What other information did you use to make your list?

Scholastic Professional Books

A New Start

Every story has certain **story elements**. *These elements include the characters, the setting, the problem, and the solution.*

In the late 1500s, brave men and women and their children sailed from Europe across the Atlantic Ocean to America, looking for a better way of life. These people wanted better jobs than they had in their homelands, and many wanted the freedom to choose their own religion. Still others wanted the opportunity to be able to buy land.

This period of time in America is known as the colonial period. It lasted about 170 years. During this time, many colonists worked very hard creating a new nation. The first colony, Jamestown, was established in 1607. Between 1607 and 1733, 13 permanent colonies were established on the east coast of America. These colonies started to grow and prosper as more and more people from other countries began to immigrate. As the population of the colonies grew, trade and manufacturing developed quickly, especially in towns that had good harbors.

Despite the growth and the many successes of the colonies, the colonists also faced their fair share of problems. One very big problem was the friction between the colonies and Britain. The colonists wanted very much to control themselves and have more say in making decisions that affected them. However, the British Parliament would not allow it. This angered the colonists, so they often ignored British laws.

As Britain imposed more and more taxes on the colonists, the colonists grew angrier and angrier. Acts passed by Parliament, such as the Sugar Act and the Stamp Act, forced the colonists to take action against Britain.

In 1774, delegates from all the colonies except Georgia met to decide how to gain some independence from Britain. Their attempts failed. They met again in 1775. The delegates helped organize an army and a navy to fight the British soldiers. The colonists wanted freedom from Britain. They outlined this freedom on July 4, 1776, in the Declaration of Independence.

Name _____

List each story element.

main characters: _____

setting: _____

problem: _____

solution: _____

Use words from the story to complete the puzzle.

Across

1. Britain _____ many taxes on the colonists, which greatly angered them.

7. People from other countries, looking for better jobs or religious freedom, would _____ to America.

8. The colonies decided they wanted to gain _____ from Britain.

Down

2. Thirteen _____ colonies were established in America between 1607 and 1733.

3. _____ from almost all of the colonies met to discuss how to gain independence from Britain.

4. The colonists tried to organize an army and a navy to fight the British _____ .

5. The men, women, and children who left their countries to come to America were very _____ .

6. There was _____ between the American colonies and Britain.

9. As people from other countries moved to America, the colonies started to grow and _____.

On another piece of paper, list the story elements from your favorite movie.

A "Peachy" Beach Day

 *The **cause** is what makes something happen.*
*The **effect** is what happens as a result of the cause.*

The day was beautiful! Janie and Jake's mom decided to take them to the beach. She even told them that since they had finshed their chores without complaining, they could each bring a friend. Janie and Jake were excited! They loved the beach.

Janie decided to ask Hayley to go since Hayley had just had her over to play last week. Jake asked his friend Charlie— they went everywhere together. Once both friends had arrived, it was time to load up the van. The kids packed some beach toys they might want—shovels, buckets, beach balls, and flippers. Mom packed a cooler with sandwiches and drinks, towels, sunscreen, and a chair for herself.

On the way to the beach, Jake and Charlie groaned. They had forgotten their boogie boards. Oh well! At least they had buckets and shovels they could use to build a huge sandcastle. Jake and Charlie loved to see how big they could make a sandcastle. They even liked to add roads and moats and lots of other details.

Once they reached the beach, everyone helped unload and set up. Then Mom put sunscreen on everyone. It was going to be a hot one—91° with no clouds! Everyone even put on hats.

Right away, the kids started playing. Jake and Charlie started working on their sandcastle, and Janie and Hayley went looking for shells. What a great day!

1. **By each cause, write the letter of the effect.**

   Cause:

   ____ **It was a beautiful, hot day.**

   ____ **They forgot their boogie boards.**

   ____ **Jake and Charlie go everywhere together.**

   Effect:

   A. **Jake asked Charlie to go to the beach.**

   B. **Mom put sunscreen on all the kids.**

   C. **Jake and Charlie were disappointed.**

2. Write *C* for cause or *E* for effect for each pair of sentences.

    a. ____ Mom decided to take the kids to the beach.

       ____ The day was beautiful.

    b. ____ They forgot their boogie boards.

       ____ Jake and Charlie would be building sandcastles instead of
           boogie boarding.

    c. ____ Janie and Jake each got to take a friend to the beach.

       ____ The children finished their chores without complaining.

    d. ____ Janie asked Hayley to go with her to the beach.

       ____ Hayley had just had Janie over to play.

3. Circle the main idea of the first paragraph.

    Janie and Jake loved to go to the beach.

    Janie and Jake finished their chores without complaining.

    Since it was a beautiful day, Janie and Jake's mom was taking them to
    the beach.

4. Janie and Jake each asked a friend to go to the beach for a different reason. Write each child's reason on the correct sandcastle.

Janie   Jake

5. What might Hayley or Charlie have thought on the way home from the beach?

_____

_____

Simon had to miss baseball practice last night. On another piece of paper, write three possible causes for this effect.

Scholastic Professional Books

Planet Particulars

To make an **inference** *is to figure out what is happening in a story from clues the author provides.*

There are nine planets that travel around the sun. They are much smaller than the sun and stars which are shining balls of hot gases. The sun and stars produce their own heat and light. The planets do not produce heat or light. They get almost all of their heat and light from the sun. Each planet has features which make it unique.

1. It takes _____ about 248 years to orbit the sun. It is the smallest planet and is located next to Neptune.

2. The largest planet, _____, is the fifth planet from the sun. It is about 1,000 times bigger than Earth. Saturn is next to this planet.

3. _____ rotates while lying on its side. It takes about 84 years to orbit the sun. It is the seventh planet from the sun.

4. _____ 's surface temperature is about 370° F below zero! Brrrrr! It is the eighth planet from the sun. It is located between Pluto and Uranus.

5. We live on _____, the third planet from the sun. It takes this planet 365 days to orbit the sun. It is often called the "living planet."

6. Many rings surround _____. It takes 10,759 days to orbit the sun. It is located between Uranus and Jupiter.

7. _____ is the closest planet to the sun. It is next to Venus, the second planet from the sun. This planet only takes 88 days to orbit the sun.

8. _____ is often called the "red planet." It lies between Earth and Jupiter, the largest planet. This planet has the largest volcano in the solar system— much higher than Mount Everest!

9. _____ was called the "mystery planet" for a long time because it is covered by thick clouds. It is the second planet from the sun.

Guess the State

Spencer, Jack, Grant, and Kara are new in Mrs. Steen's fourth-grade class. Each of these students came from one of the following states: Pennsylvania, Arizona, Washington, and Massachusetts. They are taking turns giving the class clues about the state from which they moved. The other children are trying to guess the state from the clues.

Use the following clues to help you determine which state was the home of each new student. Write each new student's name on the correct state outline below. Label the state in which all the students now live.

1. Spencer is not from the Keystone State.
2. Grant is not from the south or the east.
3. Kara is not from the south or the west.
4. Jack is not from the south or the west.
5. Grant and Spencer are both from states that border another country.
6. Jack and Kara lived the closest to each other before they moved.
7. Grant used to be able to visit the Space Needle.
8. Many of Spencer's old friends speak Spanish very well.
9. Kara used to live in "the birthplace of the United States."
10. Jack used to vacation on Cape Cod. He also loved strolling along the Freedom Trail.
11. All four children love their new state. It is located in the northeastern corner of the United States. It is the largest New England state. Its nickname is the Pine Tree State. Canada forms its northern boundary.

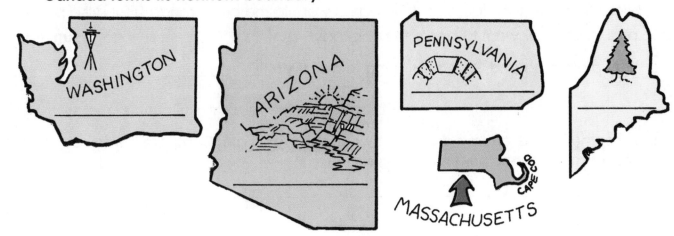

Off to the City

Maura and her grandmother are going into the city today to run some errands and do some shopping. Maura loves spending time with her grandmother. The two of them always have so much to talk about. Maura loves to hear about all the funny things her grandmother did when she was Maura's age. They did some really interesting things way back then when there were no TV's. For example, Maura's grandmother used to play jacks. She and her best friend, Sue, were the best jacks players in their school.

At 10:00 A.M. sharp, Grandma pulled in the driveway to pick up Maura. She honked the horn as she always did on their big shopping days. This was the signal that they had a busy day ahead and could not waste any time.

Maura ran out to the car, dressed in the new jeans and top Grandma bought her on their last trip. Maura knew that Grandma loved to see Maura wearing the clothes she had bought her.

As expected, Grandma told Maura some more funny things she did when she was Maura's age. Today, she told Maura how she and Sue were so hungry for candy one day in July that they decided to put on a performance and charge admission. The two girls dressed up like clowns. Grandma said people laughed so hard that the two girls were able to buy all kinds of fun treats that day. Maura made a note to herself to definitely try that some day.

Before they knew it, Maura and Grandma were in the city. Grandma found a parking spot, and away they went to begin their big day!

1. **Why are Maura and Grandma going to the city?** _____

   _____

2. **List something Grandma did for fun when she was a girl. Compare it with something Maura might spend her time doing for fun.**

   _____

   _____

Scholastic Professional Books

Help Maura and Grandma find their way around the city. Follow the directions to complete the map.

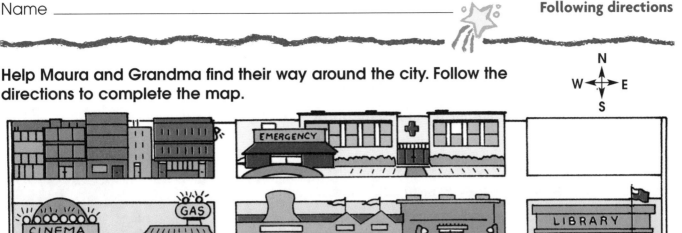
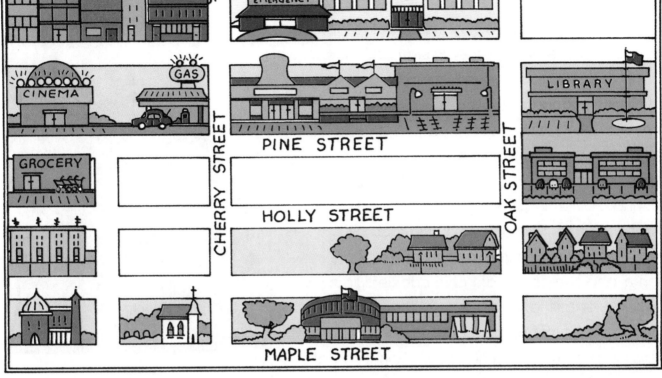

1. Maura wants to go to the mall first. It is just south of the hospital. Cherry Street runs along the western side of the mall. Label the mall.

2. On the southern side of Pine Street and the western side of Oak Street is Grandma's eye doctor. Draw a pair of eye glasses here.

3. There are five houses on Elm Street east of the hospital. Elm Street is south of the hospital. Label Elm Street and draw five houses across from the library.

4. The supermarket is located on the corner of Holly Street and Evergreen Street. Grandma needs some groceries. Label Evergreen Street.

5. There is a great park where Maura wants to play that is located between Maple and Pear streets. Oak Street runs north/south along the western side of the park. Label Pear Street, and draw three trees in the park.

6. The fire station is located on the western side of Cherry Street, north of Holly Street. Draw and label it.

7. The police station is located to the south of the fire department. Draw and label it.

 Draw a map that shows how to get from your house to your favorite fast-food restaurant.

Food for Fitness

 Classifying *means putting things into categories with other similar things.*

Katie knows that it is very important to eat right and to exercise in order to stay healthy. That is why she gets up every morning and has **oatmeal**, a **banana**, and a glass of **milk** for breakfast. Then Katie goes to play kickball.

Katie, Jimmy, Toni, and Anna always organize a two-on-two game of kickball. After playing all morning, the foursome usually sits down for lunch. Katie knows Toni's lunch by heart— **chicken nuggets**, **carrots** and dip, an **apple**, and two **chocolate chip cookies**. Jimmy's lunch varies a little. Some days it is **ham** on **wheat bread**, **grapes**, **yogurt**, and a **candy bar**. Other days his mom will make him come home to eat

a good, hot meal of **peas** and **corn**, **rice**, a **hamburger**, **strawberries**, and homemade **ice cream**. Usually on those days, Jimmy has eaten **doughnuts** for breakfast.

The only meat Anna eats is fish, so she often has **fish sticks**, crunchy **broccoli**, a **pear**, **cheese** and **crackers** and occasionally a piece of her mom's delicious **chocolate cake**. Katie always wants a bite of the cake. Sometimes Anna shares, and sometimes she does not.

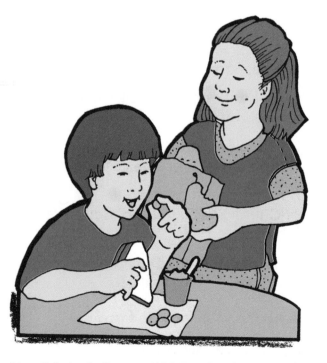

To finish off her day of trying to eat healthy, Katie usually goes home to one of her dad's magnificent meals. Tonight they are having **pork chops**, **pasta**, **cauliflower** with cheese sauce, and her choice of turtle **cheesecake** or a **vanilla milk shake**. Although Katie and her friends eat some sweets, they try not to eat a lot of them, and they exercise each day.

Scholastic Professional Books

Write each bolded word from the story in the chart under the correct category.

Dairy	Vegetables	Grains	Fruits	Meat & Fish	Fats/Sweets

1. What does Katie do to stay healthy? _____

2. Circle the foods Anna would NOT eat.

   hamburger   broccoli   apple   chicken   cheese   ribs   salmon

3. List four foods Katie might have had for a healthy lunch. _____

   _____

4. Write *C* for Cause and *E* for Effect

   ___ Jimmy goes home to eat a good, hot meal.

   ___ Jimmy has probably eaten doughnuts for breakfast.

5. Write *K* for Katie, *J* for Jimmy, *T* for Toni, or *A* for Anna.

   ____ chocolate chip cookies   ____ fish sticks

   ____ candy bar   ____ chicken nuggets

   ____ banana   ____ ham

   ____ pear   ____ corn

   ____ carrots   ____ oatmeal

On another piece of paper, list all the foods you eat in one day. Classify the foods.

Flower Fun

 *To **draw conclusions** is to use the information in a story to make a logical assumption.*

Aaaaaahhhhh! It was that time of year again—time to plant flowers. Christina and her dad were trying to decide what kind of flowers to plant this year. Her dad showed her an ad in the morning paper. He wanted Christina to check it out so she could help him determine what they should buy. The two always like to surprise Christina's mom with beautiful flowers before her "big day" in May. Christina was surprised to see Flower Power was having a sale. She knew they had better hurry to the store.

> FLOWER POWER SALE
> Beautiful flowers of all kinds
> — annuals and perennials—
> are all on sale — 25% OFF!
> All pots and hanging baskets
> are on sale, too
> Buy one, get one FREE!
> Reg. $3.99 to $49.99
> Hurry! Sale ends Tuesday!
> Flower Power
> 2418 Harbor Ave.

1. What time of year is it? _____

2. Circle the day in May on which Christina and her dad want her mother to enjoy beautiful flowers.

   Father's Day   Earth Day   Mother's Day   Easter

3. Circle why Christina and her dad will probably go to Flower Power today.

   because they are having a sale

   because they want to plant today

   because the two always plant flowers together

4. Why was Christina surprised that Flower Power was having a sale? _____

   _____

5. Why might Christina and her dad want to buy new pots or hanging baskets? _____

   _____

6. Why does the ad say to hurry? _____

   _____

Scholastic Professional Books

On the Move

Sam and Danny cannot believe that they have to move away from Florida. Florida is so awesome! They can play outside all day long—every day. It is almost always warm and sunny, and all of their friends live there. What will they do without Brendan, Bailey, John, Alexis, and Brian? They will never have such great friends again. Never!

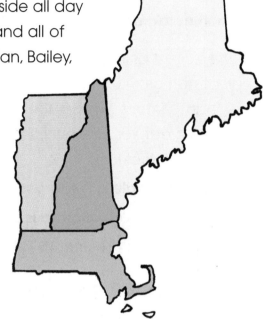

However, Sam and Danny are very excited for their dad. He has a great new job. The only problem is that the job is in New Hampshire. Danny was not even sure where this state was located. After learning that it is way up north near Canada, both boys did get a little excited about playing in the snow. Danny has always wanted to learn to ski, and Sam thinks playing ice hockey sounds like fun.

Sam and Danny also like the location of New Hampshire. It is between Maine and Vermont and not far from Boston, Massachusetts. Quebec, Canada, borders this state on the north. Neither of the boys has ever visited this part of the country, so they are now looking forward to exploring a new area. If only their friends could come with them! Their parents have promised that they can visit their old friends over spring break and even go to Disney World. The boys think that moving to New Hampshire will not be so bad after all.

1. **How do Sam and Danny feel about Florida?** _____

   _____

2. **Circle how Sam and Danny feel about leaving their friends.**

   They are sad.

   They do not know what they will do without their good friends.

   They know they will make a lot of new friends.

3. **Circle how the boys feel about moving to New Hampshire.**

   They think it sounds like a fun, interesting part of the country.

   They are excited about visiting their old friends on spring break.

   They are disappointed that it is next to Vermont.

4. **On the map above, label New Hampshire and the country and states that border it.**

The Wonderful Whale

 A **summary** *tells the most important parts of a story.*

For each paragraph, circle the sentence that tells the most important part.

1.   The largest animal that has ever lived is the blue whale. It can grow up to 300 feet long and weigh more than 100 tons. Whales, for the most part, are enormous creatures. However, some kinds only grow to be 10 to 15 feet long.

The blue whale is the largest animal.

Most whales are enormous creatures.

Some whales are only 10 to 15 feet long.

2.   Whales look a lot like fish. However, whales differ from fish in many ways. For example, the tail fin of a fish is up and down; the tail fin of a whale is sideways. Fish breathe through gills. Whales have lungs and must come to the surface from time to time to breathe. Whales can hold their breath for a very long time. The sperm whale can hold its breath for about an hour.

Whales and fish do not share similar breathing patterns.

Whales can hold their breath for about an hour.

Whales might look a lot like fish, but the two are very different.

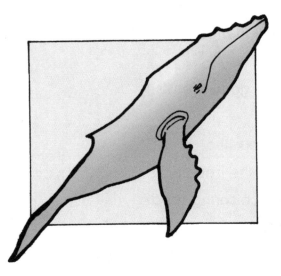

3.   Baleen whales have no teeth. Toothed whales have teeth. Baleen whales have hundreds of thin plates in their mouth. They use these plates to strain out food from the water. Their diet consists of tiny plants and animals. Toothed whales eat such foods as other fish, cuttlefish, and squid.

Whales can be divided into two groups— baleen and toothed.

Baleen whales have plates in their mouths; toothed whales do not.

Toothed whales use their teeth to chew their food.

Scholastic Professional Books

4. Whales have a layer of fat called blubber. Blubber keeps them warm. Whales can live off their blubber for a long time if food is scarce. Blubber also helps whales float, as it is lighter than water.

    Layers of fat are called blubber.

    Blubber is very important to whales and has many purposes.

    Blubber is what makes whales float.

5. Write the main idea of each paragraph to complete a summary about whales.

    _____

    _____

    _____

    _____

    _____

6. Fill in the whale and the fish with the following descriptions. Write what the two have in common in the shared space. Write the descriptions that are specific to each on the spaces that don't overlap.

    can hold breath for long time   people love to watch

    gills   tail fin sideways

    live in ponds   tail fin up and down

    live in oceans   lungs

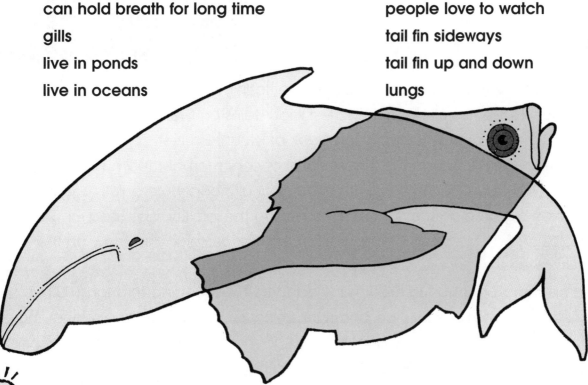

  Read information about another animal. On another piece of paper, write a summary of the information.

Climbing Blindly

 A **fact** is information that can be proven.
(Example: Asia is a continent.)

An **opinion** is information that tells what someone thinks.
(Example: Asia is the most interesting continent in the world.)

Mount Everest is the highest mountain in the world. This mountain is located in Asia. Asia is home to all five of the world's highest mountains. Mount Everest's peak is five and one-half miles above sea level. That is very high!

Many climbers have tried to climb to the top of Mount Everest's approximately 29,141-foot peak. The first people to reach the peak were Sir Edmund Hillary and Tenzing Norgay. Since then, about 900 people have survived the climb to Mount Everest's top.

One of the successful climbers is Erik Weihenmayer. Like all who try to climb this huge mountain, Erik faced strong winds, snow, and avalanches. However, what really made Erik's climb unbelievable is the fact that he is blind. After losing his vision at age 13, Erik began climbing at age 16. He has climbed the tallest mountains on five continents. Erik became the first blind person to reach the peak of Mount Everest.

At the age of 32, Erik began his climb as part of a 19-member team. His team wore bells that he could follow during his climb, and fellow climbers were quick to warn him of such things as a big drop on the right or a boulder to the left. Erik also used long climbing poles and an ice ax to feel his way across the ice, rock, and snow on the mountain.

During his climb, Erik encountered many dangers. He struggled through 100 m.p.h. winds and sliding masses of snow, ice, and rock. Because the air became thinner the higher Erik climbed, he wore an oxygen mask, as do many who climb high mountains. This helped him breathe as he climbed higher and higher. It took Erik about two-and-a half months to reach the top of this incredible mountain.

Scholastic Professional Books

1. Write *F* for fact or *O* for opinion.

   ___ Erik is very courageous.

   ___ The bells made Erik's climb a lot easier.

   ___ Erik is blind.

   ___ All climbers should use climbing poles and ice axes.

   ___ Mount Everest is the world's tallest mountain.

   ___ Erik's oxygen mask helped him breathe.

   ___ Erik used tools to help him climb.

   ___ Erik is proud of his achievement.

2. List three interesting facts from the story. _____

   _____

   _____

3. Write your opinion of Erik's accomplishment. _____

   _____

   _____

4. Circle words that describe Erik.

   brave   foolish   cautious   strong   daring   athletic

5. What are some climbing tools many climbers use? _____

   _____

6. Do you think bells are a good idea for all teams of climbers to use? Why or

   why not? _____

   _____

   _____

7. Why do you think Erik attempted this dangerous climb? _____

   _____

   _____

 Read about another adventurous person. On another piece of paper, write three facts and three opinions about this person.

Don't Worry, Be Happy

*Understanding an author's purpose when writing will make appreciating literature easier for the reader. Authors have a purpose when writing such as to **inform** (give readers facts), to **persuade** (convince readers to do or believe something), or to **entertain** (tell an interesting story).*

If I were a bird, I'd fly up high,
Above the clouds, up in the sky.
I'd float and sing and soar and play,
Without any worries to ruin my day.

If I were a dolphin, I'd splash in the sea,
And dive and flip—what fun for me!
I'd play with friends under the sea so blue.
There'd be no chores or homework to do.

If I were a bear, I'd sleep all day,
And then wake up at night to play.
I'd fish and run and jump and climb,
With no one around to ruin my good time.

If I were a dog, during the day I'd rest,
So when my master came home, I'd be at my best—
Ready to run or play ball or catch,
Ready to jump, roll over, or fetch.

But I'm not a dog or a bird or a bear.
I'm not a dolphin who can swim everywhere.
I'm just a kid who wants to have fun,
But I know I can't till my work's all done!

Scholastic Professional Books

1. Circle why you think the author wrote this poem.

   to persuade   to inform   to entertain

2. Circle what you think the author is trying to tell you.

   The author wants to fly or swim or play all day.

   Working is not what the author would choose to do.

   The author wants to be an animal.

3. Circle why you think the author thinks about being something else.

   The author wants to escape from worries and work and be free like animals.

   The author wants a pet.

   The author would love to be an animal.

4. List three things the author wants to leave behind. _____

   _____

5. Write the following words on the matching animal. Some words will be used more than once.

fly	play ball	splash	jump	climb	float	sing
sleep	run	play	flip	roll over	dive	fetch
soar	rest	fish	catch			

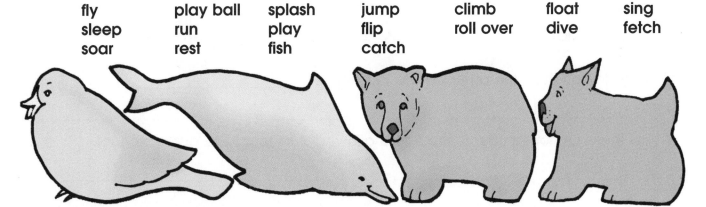

6. Write *F* for Fact or ○ for Opinion.

   ___ The author would like to escape worries and work like a bird or a dolphin.

   ___ The author is unhappy as a human and wants to be an animal.

   ___ The author knows work needs to be finished before playing.

   ___ The author just wants to have fun.

   ___ The author feels sorry for all kids who have to do work.

 Find three articles in a newspaper or magazine that are written for different purposes. Share the articles with a friend.

Improve Learning by Skating

I believe that all students should be able to roller blade during school. Roller blading would allow students to get around the school more quickly. This would leave more class time, and thus, students would learn more. It would also get the students outside quicker, so they could enjoy a longer recess. Because everyone would be moving quickly in the hallways, there would be no time for talking or messing around. The teachers would really like that!

Roller blading is a very good form of exercise. Just think of how physically fit every student would be! Being physically fit often leads to better health. Consequently, students would be absent less and would be learning more.

Finally, roller blading is fun. More learning, better physical fitness, and fun, I believe, are the keys to a successful school.

1. **Circle the author's purpose for writing this passage.**

   to persuade   **to inform**   **to entertain**

2. **Why do you think the author wrote this article?** _____

   _____

3. **List three reasons students should be allowed to roller blade during school.**

   _____

   _____

   _____

4. **List three reasons students should not be allowed to roller blade during school.**

   _____

   _____

   _____

On another piece of paper, write an article about a change you would like to see take place. Read the article to a friend.

Scholastic Professional Books

Scholastic Success With

TESTS:
READING

Reading Comprehension

Read each story. Then fill in the circle that best completes each sentence or answers each question.

SAMPLE

Many people like to glide along the sidewalk on roller skates. They owe a vote of thanks to Joseph Merlin of Belgium. He invented a kind of roller skate back in 1760. His skates **provided** a pretty bumpy ride, however.

1. What is the best title for this story?
○ **A.** "Inventors"
○ **B.** "Famous Inventions"
○ **C.** "Belgium"
○ **D.** "Early Roller Skates"

2. In this story, the word **provided** means
○ **A.** scraped.
○ **B.** invented.
○ **C.** gave
○ **D.** took

A.   Boston Post Road is the oldest road in the United States. It is more than 300 years old! Colonists made the road in the 1670s, more than 100 years before American Revolution. They needed a way to carry mail and messages between two growing cities—Boston and New York. The road followed old Native American trails.

1. What is the best title for this story?
○ **A.** "Building Roads"
○ **B.** "U.S. Mail"
○ **C.** "Two Colonial Cities"
○ **D.** "America's First Road"

2. You can guess that
○ **A.** Boston Post Road is still around.
○ **B.** Boston is a small city.
○ **C.** Boston Post Road is short.
○ **D.** New York is older than Boston.

3. You would probably find this story in a book about
○ **A.** fairy tales.
○ **B.** current events.
○ **C.** how to build roads.
○ **D.** American history.

B. In 1271, Marco Polo left Italy and set out for China. He was just 17 years old! Polo's trip took three and a half years. In China, he discovered a black stone that burned and gave heat. It was coal. Polo also learned about paper-making and the compass. When he got home, he wrote a book about his **journey**.

I. Marco Polo traveled to
   ○ **A.** Greece.
   ○ **B.** the United States.
   ○ **C.** China.
   ○ **D.** Africa.

2. In this story, the word **journey** means
   ○ **A.** trip.
   ○ **B.** findings.
   ○ **C.** sailboat.
   ○ **D.** country.

3. Which of these is an *opinion* about Marco Polo?
   ○ **A.** He lived in the 1200s.
   ○ **B.** He traveled to China
   ○ **C.** He was the greatest explorer of all time.
   ○ **D.** He wrote a book.

C. When you're hungry, or even just thinking about food, you often hear your stomach growl. Sometimes, your stomach also growls when you're nervous or excited. What you are actually hearing is your stomach muscles pushing air around inside your stomach.

   Your stomach also makes noises right after you eat. That's because your stomach muscles move around to mix the food you're eaten with special juices. When they do this, they also move around the air that you swallowed with your food. This causes your stomach to growl, though not as loudly as when your stomach is empty.

I. This story is mainly about
   ○ **A.** how you digest food.
   ○ **B.** muscles of the human body.
   ○ **C.** why your stomach growls.
   ○ **D.** why people get hungry.

2. You can guess that your stomach growls the loudest when you
   ○ **A.** are eating.
   ○ **B.** are at school.
   ○ **C.** yell loudly.
   ○ **D.** need food.

3. Which of the following statements is an *opinion*?
   ○ **A.** Stomach noises are gross.
   ○ **B.** Your stomach growls when its muscles push air around in your stomach.
   ○ **C.** Your stomach can growl when it's full.
   ○ **D.** Sometimes your stomach growls when you're nervous.

4. Your stomach growls because
   ○ **A.** you have eaten too much.
   ○ **B.** there is air in your stomach.
   ○ **C.** you feel sick to your stomach.
   ○ **D.** you are tired.

D. More than 40 fish produce electricity. The most dangerous is the electric eel, a long slimy fish that lives in South America. This snakelike fish gives off electric signals to "see" in the dark water where it lives. These signals bounce off underwater objects and help the eel find fish and frogs to eat.

Once the electric eel **locates** its prey, it fills the water with an electric shock. The organs that produce electricity are in the eel's tail. The shock stuns or kills any small animals in the area around the eel. The electric charge is so strong it could also stun a person or knock over a full-grown horse!

1. The electric eel looks like a
○ **A.** snake.
○ **B.** fish.
○ **C.** turtle.
○ **D.** bird.

2. The author wrote this story to
○ **A.** tell about different kinds of eels.
○ **B.** tell about electric eels.
○ **C.** ask people to protect fish.
○ **D.** explain electricity.

3. In this story, the word **locates** means
○ **A.** swims.
○ **B.** eats.
○ **C.** slides.
○ **D.** finds.

E. Popcorn is one of the oldest American snack foods. By the time European explorers arrived here in the 1400s, Native Americans were already growing about 700 types of corn. They used popcorn for both food and decoration. Some tribes used it in their headdresses and necklaces.

These early popcorn lovers couldn't plug in the electric popper or zap the popcorn in the microwave. Instead, they popped the kernels in clay pots over an open fire. Some kinds of popcorn were even popped right on the cob.

English colonists got a taste of popcorn at the first Thanksgiving feast in 1621. A Native American named Quadequina brought a deerskin bag filled with popcorn to the dinner. It was a hit!

1. What is the best title for this story?
○ **A.** "The History of Popcorn"
○ **B.** "Native Americans"
○ **C.** "The First Thanksgiving"
○ **D.** "Snack Foods"

2. Which happened first?
○ **A.** Colonists ate popcorn.
○ **B.** Electric-poppers were invented.
○ **C.** Movie theaters served popcorn.
○ **D.** Native Americans grew corn.

3. Popcorn has been used for
○ **A.** sewing.
○ **B.** making paint.
○ **C.** heating homes.
○ **D.** making jewelry.

4. This story would probably go on to talk about
○ **A.** how microwaves work.
○ **B.** the popularity of popcorn today.
○ **C.** Native American customs.
○ **D.** snacks of the world.

Vocabulary

Synonyms

Read the underlined word in each phrase. Mark the word below it that has the same (or close to the same) meaning.

Sample:

damage the building
- ○ **A.** hurt
- ○ **B.** deck
- ○ **C.** anger
- ○ **D.** command

1. argue about it
   - ○ **A.** laugh
   - ○ **B.** pickle
   - ○ **C.** fight
   - ○ **D.** whisper

2. gradually cook
   - ○ **A.** boil
   - ○ **B.** slowly
   - ○ **C.** hot
   - ○ **D.** quickly

3. a rose's scent
   - ○ **A.** red
   - ○ **B.** smell
   - ○ **C.** stem
   - ○ **D.** color

4. annoy her
   - ○ **A.** help
   - ○ **B.** necklace
   - ○ **C.** bother
   - ○ **D.** talk

5. wicked character
   - ○ **A.** sweet
   - ○ **B.** boy
   - ○ **C.** helpful
   - ○ **D.** mean

6. unkind words
   - ○ **A.** friendly
   - ○ **B.** mean
   - ○ **C.** happy
   - ○ **D.** shy

7. wee child
   - ○ **A.** small
   - ○ **B.** large
   - ○ **C.** happy
   - ○ **D.** shy

Antonyms

Read the underlined word in each phrase. Mark the word below it that means the opposite or nearly the opposite.

Sample:

silent evening
- ○ **A.** quiet
- ○ **B.** patient
- ○ **C.** noisy
- ○ **B.** perfect

1. worthless watch
   - ○ **A.** leather
   - ○ **B.** ticking
   - ○ **C.** valuable
   - ○ **D.** cart

2. afternoon stroll
   - ○ **A.** walk
   - ○ **B.** sun
   - ○ **C.** pond
   - ○ **D.** run

3. antique chest
   - ○ **A.** brown
   - ○ **B.** old
   - ○ **C.** case
   - ○ **D.** new

4. cheap shoes
   - ○ **A.** blue
   - ○ **B.** strings
   - ○ **C.** expensive
   - ○ **D.** free

5. exit the building
   - ○ **A.** enter
   - ○ **B.** door
   - ○ **C.** roof
   - ○ **D.** leave

6. vast ocean
   - ○ **A.** large
   - ○ **B.** tiny
   - ○ **C.** deep
   - ○ **D.** shallow

7. valuable earrings
   - ○ **A.** worthless
   - ○ **B.** expensive
   - ○ **C.** diamond
   - ○ **D.** pendant

Scholastic Professional Books

Reading Comprehension

Read each story. Then fill in the circle that best completes each sentence or answers each question.

SAMPLE

> Many people get nosebleeds. That's because the lining inside the nose is very **sensitive**. Dry air or sneezing can irritate it. If one of the small blood vessels in the lining should break, the blood starts to flow!

1. What is the best title for this story?
  ○ **A.** "Eyes, Ears, Nose, and Throat"
  ○ **B.** "How the Nose Works"
  ○ **C.** "The Sense of Smell"
  ○ **D.** "Why You Get Bloody Noses"

2. In this story, the word **sensitive** means
  ○ **A.** pinkish-red.
  ○ **B.** often bloody.
  ○ **C.** easily hurt.
  ○ **D.** very tough.

A. Labor Day is a special day for many Americans. They get to take the day off! The holiday honors everyone who works in America—even kids!

The first Labor Day was celebrated in 1882. A carpenter named Peter McGuire decided that workers should have a special day to honor them. So he planned a parade for all of the workers in his hometown of New York City. Ten thousand people marched proudly through the streets. That day, they enjoyed music, picnics, and fireworks.

In 1894, President Grover Cleveland made Labor Day a national holiday. It is always the first Monday in September.

1. What is the best title for this story?
  ○ **A.** "My Favorite Labor Day"
  ○ **B.** "Hooray for Parades!"
  ○ **C.** "The History of Labor Day"
  ○ **D.** "Holidays Around the World"

2. Labor Day became a national holiday
  ○ **A.** in 1882.
  ○ **B.** in 1994.
  ○ **C.** last September.
  ○ **D.** in 1894.

3. Which is an *opinion* about Labor Day?
  ○ **A.** It always takes place on a Monday.
  ○ **B.** It is a great holiday.
  ○ **C.** It was started by Peter McGuire.
  ○ **D.** Its purpose is to honor workers.

B.   If one of your classmates made fun of you in the schoolyard, or cheated at a game you were playing together, what would you do? Many people would get angry. Some might even start yelling, pushing, or punching.

At 75th Street School in Los Angeles, California, kids in every grade learn how to solve problems without fighting. The school has a team of students called conflict managers who are specially trained.

How do students become conflict managers? First, they must be in grades 4 or 5. Then, teachers and other students must choose them. In the playground, these conflict managers keep an eye out for arguments. They help solve problems when students disagree.

1.   This article is mainly about
- ○ **A.** why kids argue.
- ○ **B.** schools in California.
- ○ **C.** one solution to playground fighting.
- ○ **D.** violence in the community.

2.   The conflict managers are
- ○ **A.** college students.
- ○ **B.** teachers at 75th Street School.
- ○ **C.** in 1st or 2nd grade.
- ○ **D.** in 4th or 5th grade.

3.   The story would probably go on to talk about
- ○ **A.** popular playground games.
- ○ **B.** how conflict managers handle arguments.
- ○ **C.** how to do first aid outdoors.
- ○ **D.** downtown Los Angeles.

C.   In honor of Fire Safety Week, here are some fire-safety tips for you to follow:
- Never play with matches or lighters.
- Ask your parents to make sure your home has smoke detectors and a fire extinguisher.
- Make a plan for escaping from your home in case of fire. Learn two ways out of every room. Pick a spot outside where your family will meet. Practice!
- If there is a fire in your home, get out and stay out! Use a neighbor's phone to call for help.
- Find a **route** out of the building that is free from smoke and flames. If you have to go through a smoky area to escape, crawl on your hands and knees. The air near the floor will be cooler and less smoky.
- If your clothes catch fire, do not run. Drop to the ground, and roll back and forth to put out the flames.

1.   The purpose of this article is to
- ○ **A.** explain why fires start.
- ○ **B.** teach fire safety.
- ○ **C.** describe what a fire is like.
- ○ **D.** show how fire can be used safely.

2.   In this story, the word **route** means
- ○ **A.** path.
- ○ **B.** place.
- ○ **C.** door.
- ○ **D.** air.

3.   To escape a smoky area, you should
- ○ **A.** run.
- ○ **B.** scream.
- ○ **C.** crawl.
- ○ **D.** roll back and forth on the ground.

4.   Which is a *fact* about fire safety?
- ○ **A.** You should have fire drills often.
- ○ **B.** In case of fire, save your toys first.
- ○ **C.** In a fire, the air is cooler near the floor.
- ○ **D.** Children should never use matches.

Scholastic Professional Books

D. Once upon a time, a man lived in a gloomy basement, where he worked all day long. Even so, he was happy because he sang as he worked.

Above the poor man lived a rich man, who worried all day long about his money. This made him miserable. Being in a bad mood, he really hated to hear the poor man singing.

He wanted the poor man to feel bad, like he did. He thought if the poor man felt bad, he might stop singing. He thought if the poor man had money, he too might worry. So the rich man gave the poor man a big sack of money.

The poor man was happier than ever—until he realized that someone might steal the money from him. So he decided to hide it. But no place seemed safe enough. There was nothing he could do—except worry.

The poor man worried until he grew thin and pale. He no longer felt like singing.

One day, he gave the money back to the rich man. "I can live without this money," he said. "But I cannot live without my song."

I. This story tells why
○ **A.** a poor man had no money.
○ **B.** money made a poor man unhappy.
○ **C.** a rich man loved his money
○ **D.** money made a poor man sing.

2. The rich man gave the poor man money
○ **A.** to make him happy.
○ **B.** to make him sing more.
○ **C.** to make him worry.
○ **D.** to make him move away.

3. Which happened last?
○ **A.** The rich man worried all day long.
○ **B.** The poor man gave back the money.
○ **C.** The poor man stopped singing.
○ **D.** The rich man gave the poor man a big sack of money.

E. Once the howl of the wolf was heard all over the United States' wilderness. But by 1900, only a few thousand wolves roamed free in the U.S. In 1973, the government put wolves on the endangered-species list.

Today, animal activists are working to bring back the wolf. As an experiment, 31 wild wolves from Canada were released in Yellowstone National Park. Nine wolf pups were born there. Now, animal activists want to repeat this success story in New York, Maine, New Mexico, and Arizona.

But, some farmers and ranchers worry that this meat eater will hunt their **livestock**. In New York, dairy farmers worry that wolves will attack their dairy cows. In New Mexico, ranchers worry about wolf attacks on their cattle and sheep.

I. What is the main idea of this story?
○ **A.** The wolf program in Yellowstone was a big success.
○ **B.** Although wolves are endangered, not everyone wants to help them.
○ **C.** Wolves are meat-eaters.
○ **D.** Ranchers and farmer dislike wolves.

2. In this story, the word **livestock** means
○ **A.** farmers.   ○ **B.** barns.
○ **C.** farm animals.   ○ **D.** grass.

3. From this article, you could guess that wolves
○ **A.** are dangerous to people.
○ **B.** like sheep better than cows.
○ **C.** are happier in Canada.
○ **D.** might roam into ranches or farms.

Vocabulary

Synonyms

Read the underlined word in each phrase. Mark the word below it that has the same (or close to the same) meaning.

Sample:

mend the fence
- ○ **A.** break
- ○ **C.** fix
- ○ **B.** banana
- ○ **D.** climb

I. rapidly stir
- ○ **A.** shake
- ○ **C.** mix
- ○ **B.** quickly
- ○ **D.** slowly

2. the student's task
- ○ **A.** smart
- ○ **C.** school
- ○ **B.** job
- ○ **D.** book

3. tore paper
- ○ **A.** glued
- ○ **C.** ripped
- ○ **B.** sheet
- ○ **D.** wrote

4. an imaginary friend
- ○ **A.** best
- ○ **C.** real
- ○ **B.** kind
- ○ **D.** make-believe

5. a log cabin
- ○ **A.** wood
- ○ **C.** brown
- ○ **B.** house
- ○ **D.** room

6. loud wail
- ○ **A.** song
- ○ **C.** bang
- ○ **B.** siren
- ○ **D.** cry

7. tilt sideways
- ○ **A.** hoe
- ○ **C.** straighten
- ○ **B.** lean
- ○ **D.** tile

Antonyms

Read the underlined word in each phrase. Mark the word below it that means the opposite or nearly the opposite.

Sample:

useless tool
- ○ **A.** metal
- ○ **C.** helpful
- ○ **B.** sharp
- ○ **B.** hammer

I. loud chuckle
- ○ **A.** laugh
- ○ **C.** radio
- ○ **B.** car
- ○ **D.** sob

2. feel ashamed
- ○ **A.** embarrassed
- ○ **C.** sick
- ○ **B.** happy
- ○ **D.** proud

3. silent classroom
- ○ **A.** noisy
- ○ **C.** warm
- ○ **B.** teacher
- ○ **D.** quiet

4. beneath the roof
- ○ **A.** under
- ○ **C.** above
- ○ **B.** raise
- ○ **D.** below

5. a sudden shriek
- ○ **A.** scream
- ○ **C.** whisper
- ○ **B.** reply
- ○ **D.** noise

6. a great triumph
- ○ **A.** success
- ○ **C.** failure
- ○ **B.** trial
- ○ **D.** finish

7. widen the road
- ○ **A.** narrow
- ○ **C.** curve
- ○ **B.** pave
- ○ **D.** straighten

Scholastic Professional Books

Reading Comprehension

Read each story. Then fill in the circle that best completes each sentence or answers each question.

SAMPLE

Being bitten by a bedbug stinks in more ways than one. It hurts and the bug gives off a bad odor. These critters, each about the size of a grain of rice, **nourish** themselves on human blood. Their odor prevents other bugs from feasting on bedbugs!

1. What is the best title for this story?
○ **A.** "Why Bedbugs Live in Beds"
○ **B.** "How Bedbugs Live"
○ **C.** "Bugs that Eat Rice"
○ **D.** "Bedbugs Stink"

2. In this story, the word **nourish** means
○ **A.** feed.
○ **B.** clean.
○ **C.** hungry.
○ **D.** stink.

A. A club called the Graffiti Grapplers won't stand for a mess—especially not in their hometown of San Antonio, Texas. The group of teachers and kids paint over graffiti and sweep up litter in their community.

Since the club was founded in 1993, the Grapplers have won many awards. One year, they won $32,500! The club members use the money they receive for projects such as planting trees and flowers around San Antonio.

"These kids have good hearts," Grappler and teacher Linda Pruski said. "They are seeing the positive effect they can have on the community."

1. What is the best title for this story?
○ **A.** "The History of San Antonio"
○ **B.** "A Club for Kids Who Care"
○ **C.** "The Growing Problem of Graffiti"
○ **D.** "How to Win Big Money"

2. The Graffiti Grapplers club was founded
○ **A.** in 1990.
○ **B.** by teachers and business people.
○ **C.** by graffiti artists.
○ **D.** in Texas.

3. Which of the following is an *opinion* about the Graffiti Grapplers?
○ **A.** Its members are teachers and kids.
○ **B.** It is based in San Antonio, Texas.
○ **C.** It is one of the best clubs in San Antonio.
○ **D.** Its members clean up litter and graffiti.

B. Once upon a time, most people thought the world was flat. Eventually, new discoveries proved them wrong. Scientists have always thought that all planets moved in nearly circular orbits. Now, they believe that idea may be wrong, too.

Why? Just a few years ago, astronomers discovered a planet outside of our solar system that moves around its sun in a very flattened, egg-shaped or oblong path.

The newly discovered planet is 17 times larger than Earth. It was spotted in a constellation called Cygnus, located 600 trillion miles, or about 70 light-years, from Earth. Now scientists are researching to find out what makes this planet move in such a wacky way.

I. The purpose of this article is to
○ **A.** explain why Earth may be flat after all.
○ **B.** show that new discoveries can lead to new ideas.
○ **C.** show that scientists are always right.
○ **D.** discuss how humans could visit Cygnus.

2. In this story, the word oblong means
○ **A.** orbit   ○ **C.** shaped like a circle
○ **B.** egg-shaped   ○ **D.** discovery

3. The newly discovered planet was spotted
○ **A.** in our solar system.
○ **B.** herbivores are small animals.
○ **C.** moving around Earth.
○ **D.** in the constellation Cygnus.

C. Animals can't speak in words, but they have many other ways to "talk" to each other. Here's a look at how several different creatures communicate in the wild.

- Giant otters speak in a unique language of whistles, whines, squeals, and snorts. Each sound means a different thing. For instance, one type of snort warns other otters of danger, such as a nearby human hunter.
- Red howler monkeys communicate by howling. Their howls can be heard up to three miles away. In fact, these monkeys are the world's noisiest land animals.
- Wolves curl their lips above their teeth and snarl at other wolves to show who's in charge, and to warn other wolves to back off. Wolves will also howl to signal danger.
- The elephant seal uses its amazing inflatable nose and its nostrils as a giant microphone.

I. This article is mainly about
○ **A.** why red howler monkeys are so loud.
○ **B.** animals that use their noses to communicate.
○ **C.** ways different animals communicate.
○ **D.** how giant otters stay safe from hunters.

2. According to the article, elephant seals communicate by
○ **A.** inflating their noses.
○ **B.** whistling.
○ **C.** snarling.
○ **D.** wagging their tails.

3. The story would probably go on to talk about
○ **A.** what red howler monkeys eat.
○ **B.** how other animals communicate.
○ **C.** where giant otters live.
○ **D.** how wolves talk to giant otters.

4. Which is a *fact* about animal communication?
○ **A.** The elephant seal's inflatable nose is really strange.
○ **B.** Listening to red howler monkeys all day would really get on your nerves.
○ **C.** Wolves look scary when they snarl.
○ **D.** Whistles and snorts are part of the giant otter's language.

D. What's wet and covers three fourths of the Earth's surface? It's the water that makes up the Earth's four oceans. These oceans are the Pacific, the Atlantic, the Indian, and the Arctic. The Pacific Ocean is the largest and deepest. The Arctic Ocean is the smallest and shallowest.

Oceans are the **source** of many different things people need. Ocean water contains salt, a basic cooking need. Some ocean plants, like seaweed, are used for medicine and food. Ocean fishing provides many people with work and food.

Oceans can also be fun places to visit. People who visit the ocean might swim in the waves, hunt for shells, and play in the sand.

On a map, the Earth's four oceans may look just like giant pools of water. But they are so much more than that.

1. Which ocean is the deepest?
- ○ **A.** the Pacific
- ○ **C.** the Indian
- ○ **B.** the Atlantic
- ○ **D.** the Arctic

2. What is one thing people need that they can get from the ocean?
- ○ **A.** ice
- ○ **C.** sand
- ○ **B.** salt
- ○ **D.** waves

3. How much of the Earth's surface do oceans cover?
- ○ **A.** one third
- ○ **C.** two thirds
- ○ **B.** one half
- ○ **D.** three fourths

4. In this story, the word **source** means
- ○ **A.** store.
- ○ **C.** place to get.
- ○ **B.** salty.
- ○ **D.** place to put.

E. Ghosts and ghouls have raised more than $100 million to help poor children around the world. How? By trick-or-treating!

They were trick-or-treating for UNICEF. UNICEF is the United Nation's Children's Fund.

Founded in 1946, UNICEF has helped children in more than 140 poor or war-torn countries get food, shelter, and medicine. Every year it adopts a new slogan, such as "Increase the Peace!"

A group of kids from Philadelphia founded the trick-or-treat for UNICEF program in 1950. They raised $17. Ever since, kids dressed in their Halloween best have followed suit—and, as the program has grown, the amount of money kids raise has grown far beyond $17 annually. In fact, in a recent year, kids helped raise $2.1 million. This year, they could raise even more!

1. What is the main idea of this story?
- ○ **A.** Halloween is one of kids' favorite holidays.
- ○ **B.** Trick-or-treat for UNICEF is a successful program to raise money for poor children.
- ○ **C.** Trick-or-treat for UNICEF was founded in 1950.
- ○ **D.** Trick-or-treat for UNICEF is no longer a popular program

2. Which happened last?
- ○ **A.** UNICEF was founded.
- ○ **B.** Kids began trick-or-treating for UNICEF.
- ○ **C.** Kids helped raise $2.1 million for UNICEF.
- ○ **D.** A group of kids from Philadelphia raised $17.

3. From this article, you could guess that
- ○ **A.** large numbers of children participate in trick-or-treat for UNICEF.
- ○ **B.** kids from Philadelphia are nicer than most other kids.
- ○ **C.** the trick-or-treat for UNICEF program made more money in the 1950s than it does now.
- ○ **D.** kids get more candy when they trick-or-treat for UNICEF.

Vocabulary

Synonyms

Read the underlined word in each phrase. Mark the word below it that has the same (or close to the same) meaning.

Sample:

argue loudly
- ○ **A.** agree
- ○ **C.** toaster
- ○ **B.** fight
- ○ **D.** shout

1. current event
- ○ **A.** funny
- ○ **C.** recent
- ○ **B.** article
- ○ **D.** old

2. sharp fang
- ○ **A.** tooth
- ○ **C.** mouth
- ○ **B.** knife
- ○ **D.** eat

3. solid foundation
- ○ **A.** rock
- ○ **C.** breeze
- ○ **B.** base
- ○ **D.** ice

4. eerie sound
- ○ **A.** loud
- ○ **C.** monster
- ○ **B.** spooky
- ○ **D.** whisper

5. stroll downtown
- ○ **A.** appear
- ○ **C.** store
- ○ **B.** drive
- ○ **D.** walk

6. false statement
- ○ **A.** loud
- ○ **C.** sworn
- ○ **B.** whispered
- ○ **D.** untrue

7. blend in
- ○ **A.** fill
- ○ **C.** throw
- ○ **B.** mix
- ○ **D.** push

Antonyms

Read the underlined word in each phrase. Mark the word below it that means the opposite or nearly the opposite.

Sample:

latch the door
- ○ **A.** unlock
- ○ **C.** lock
- ○ **B.** slam
- ○ **D.** knob

1. sturdy table
- ○ **A.** strong
- ○ **C.** fragile
- ○ **B.** dining
- ○ **D.** chair

2. descend the staircase
- ○ **A.** go down
- ○ **C.** hide
- ○ **B.** sweep
- ○ **D.** climb up

3. nasty person
- ○ **A.** pleasant
- ○ **C.** wise
- ○ **B.** mean
- ○ **D.** human

4. widen the path
- ○ **A.** enlarge
- ○ **C.** hike
- ○ **B.** trail
- ○ **D.** narrow

5. hero's bravery
- ○ **A.** courage
- ○ **C.** wealth
- ○ **B.** cowardice
- ○ **D.** win

6. assist others
- ○ **A.** help
- ○ **C.** ignore
- ○ **B.** talk to
- ○ **D.** follow

7. brief recess
- ○ **A.** fun
- ○ **C.** short
- ○ **B.** boring
- ○ **D.** long

Reading Comprehension

Read each story. Then fill in the circle that best completes each sentence or answers each question.

SAMPLE

In 1998, Tom Whittaker made history. He became the first disabled person to climb Mount Everest. Ten years earlier, Tom had been in a car accident. He was badly **injured**. He lost both his right foot and his kneecap. Still, Tom wasn't going to let anything keep him from his goal. He was going to climb the world's tallest mountain.

1. In this passage, the word **injured** means
○ **A.** ignored.
○ **B.** annoyed.
○ **C.** shaken.
○ **D.** hurt.

2. This story is mainly about
○ **A.** how people avoid knee injuries.
○ **B.** why Mount Everest is too dangerous to climb.
○ **C.** a disabled person who climbed Mount Everest.
○ **D.** some very serious car accidents.

A. For most of us, headaches aren't a big deal. We get them now and then. They cause a little pain, then they go away. For about one in 10 people, however, headaches are more serious. They get extremely strong headaches called migraines.

Migraine headaches are more than just annoying. They can last for several hours, or even several days. Sometimes, people with migraines have so much pain that they have to stay in bed. They may not be able to do everyday activities. Often, they miss school or work. The problem is larger than you might think. Migraine headaches result in more than one million lost school days every year.

No one knows exactly what causes migraines. In different people, different things can set one off. With some people, eating certain foods can **trigger** a migraine. With others, it may be loud noises or blinking lights.

1. Compared to ordinary headaches, migraines are much
○ **A.** less serious.
○ **B.** less painful.
○ **C.** more painful.
○ **D.** more common.

2. In this story, the word **trigger** means
○ **A.** stop.
○ **B.** cause.
○ **C.** help.
○ **D.** slow down.

B. Wilt Chamberlain was once basketball's greatest superstar. He played in the 1960s and 1970s. The big seven-foot center was a dazzling scorer. During his career, he had many excellent games. One game, however, stands out above the rest. That was the night he scored 100 points.

Why was the 100-point game so amazing? On most nights, it's not easy for a team to score that many points, let alone a player. Yet on March 2, 1962, Wilt did it all by himself. Wilt's team was the Philadelphia 76ers. The 76ers were playing against the New York Knicks. From the very beginning of the game, the 76ers gave the ball to Wilt. Almost every time they did so, Wilt managed to score. By halftime, Wilt had 41 points. After three quarters, he had 79 points. The fans went crazy as the game came to an end. Wilt had scored a record 100 points. This was the first time that it happened. It's never happened again.

I. What is the best title for this story?
○ **A.** "Wilt's 100-Point Game"
○ **B.** "The Philadelphia 76ers"
○ **C.** "How to Play Basketball"
○ **D.** "Isn't This Amazing?"

2. Which of these is an *opinion*?
○ **A.** Wilt played in the 1960s and 1970s.
○ **B.** Wilt was playing for the 76ers.
○ **C.** The 76ers were playing against New York.
○ **D.** Wilt was basketball's greatest superstar.

3. How many points did Wilt have at halftime?
○ **A.** 41
○ **B.** 79
○ **C.** 100
○ **D.** 141

C. In the summer of 1997, a disaster struck Indonesia. The disaster was a series of fires that sent huge clouds of smoke rising into the air. The fires spread across a huge area. Thousands of acres were destroyed by flame. But it wasn't the flames that caused the most serious problems. It was the smoke. The smoke was so thick that it made people sick, even people hundreds of miles away.

The smoke swept over Indonesia. Then it spread to other countries. In Singapore and Malaysia, cities were choked by a thick layer of hazy smog. Millions of people suffered from the air pollution.

The thick smoke also caused accidents. Drivers could barely see the roads through their windshields. One airplane crashed in the haze. Two ships ran into each other in the sea. In November, rains came and put out the raging fires. By that time, tremendous damage had been done.

I. Where did the fires begin?
○ **A.** Malaysia.
○ **B.** Singapore.
○ **C.** Indonesia.
○ **D.** Indonesia and Singapore.

2. The two ships ran into each other because of
○ **A.** heavy rain.
○ **B.** thick smoke.
○ **C.** high waves.
○ **D.** hot flames.

3. The article's main purpose is to
○ **A.** explain how to put out forest fires.
○ **B.** tell you about a disaster in Indonesia.
○ **C.** persuade you not to start fires.
○ **D.** amuse you with a story about accidents.

Scholastic Professional Books

D. All week long, I looked forward to finishing my book. The book was called *The Secret of the Hidden Cave*. It was a mystery, my favorite kind. Because I was busy with homework, I knew I wouldn't get the opportunity to finish it until Friday. Anyway, thinking about the story gave me something to look forward to. It was the most exciting book I had ever **encountered**.

When Friday came, I sat down on the couch and began to read. Each new page was better than the one before. What would the explorers find at the bottom of the cave? This question was driving me crazy! Finally, I got to the next-to-last page. I was about to learn the secret! When I turned the page, I was shocked. The last page was missing!

"It's not fair," I yelled. Then I heard a giggle. Looking into the next room, I saw my little sister. She was running away with something in her hand.

1. What is the best title for this story?
○ **A.** "The Mystery of the Missing Page"
○ **B.** "Why I Read Books"
○ **C.** "Too Much Homework"
○ **D.** "The Story of Famous Explorers"

2. In this story, the word **encountered** means
○ **A.** borrowed.   ○ **C.** finished.
○ **B.** returned.   ○ **D.** came across.

3. What can you guess from this story?
○ **A.** Mystery books are always missing a page.
○ **B.** The explorers found a skeleton in the cave.
○ **C.** The explorers didn't find anything in the cave.
○ **D.** The reader's sister tore out the last page.

E. August, 1999, was a sad month for the Russian space program. After 13½ years, it finally abandoned the space station *Mir*. The *Mir* had been in space since 1986. For years, it was the pride of the Russian program. Lately, however, the space station had been the scene of many accidents. Three occurred within a single year. First, a fire broke out on board. The crew of the *Mir* almost had to leave the space station. Then, a cargo ship crashed into the side of the space station. The crash caused major damage to the *Mir*'s solar panels. Finally, a computer breakdown nearly caused disaster.

In the end, none of these accidents caused the shutdown. The *Mir* was left behind because it was simply too old. The equipment was getting creaky. If astronauts stayed there, they would probably be risking their lives. The *Mir* had lasted far longer than expected. When it was built, the space station was supposed to last only five years.

1. Which of these is an *opinion*?
○ **A.** A cargo ship crashed into the space station.
○ **B.** The *Mir* had been in space since 1986.
○ **C.** August, 1999, was a sad month for the Russian space program.
○ **D.** A fire broke out on board.

2. What is the best title for this story?
○ **A.** "Lost in Space"
○ **B.** "A Safe Journey"
○ **C.** "The End of the *Mir*"
○ **D.** "All About Russia's Space Program"

3. The *Mir* closed down because
○ **A.** It was more than five years old.
○ **B.** The equipment was too old to be safe.
○ **C.** A computer broke down.
○ **D.** The astronaut's had been in space since 1986.

Vocabulary

Synonyms

Read the underlined word in each phrase. Mark the word below it that has the same (or close to the same) meaning.

Sample:

take a <u>stroll</u>
- ○ **A.** look
- ○ **B.** number
- ○ **C.** board
- ○ **D.** walk

1. <u>squirming</u> around
   - ○ **A.** standing
   - ○ **B.** running
   - ○ **C.** laughing
   - ○ **D.** wriggling

2. nonstop <u>wailing</u>
   - ○ **A.** crying
   - ○ **B.** speaking
   - ○ **C.** talking
   - ○ **D.** joking

3. a surprising <u>triumph</u>
   - ○ **A.** solution
   - ○ **B.** victory
   - ○ **C.** friend
   - ○ **D.** day

4. <u>tattered</u> clothing
   - ○ **A.** colorful
   - ○ **B.** new
   - ○ **C.** worn-out
   - ○ **D.** clean

5. <u>waterfront</u> location
   - ○ **A.** central
   - ○ **B.** mountainous
   - ○ **C.** island
   - ○ **D.** shore

6. <u>sole</u> survivor
   - ○ **A.** first
   - ○ **B.** only
   - ○ **C.** last
   - ○ **D.** oldest

7. <u>tilt</u> your head
   - ○ **A.** lean
   - ○ **B.** nod
   - ○ **C.** shake
   - ○ **D.** lay

Antonyms

Read the underlined word in each phrase. Mark the word below it that means the opposite or nearly the opposite.

Sample:

<u>nervous</u> feeling
- ○ **A.** calm
- ○ **B.** frightened
- ○ **C.** angry
- ○ **D.** funny

1. <u>tighten</u> the hold
   - ○ **A.** return
   - ○ **B.** remove
   - ○ **C.** slow down
   - ○ **D.** loosen

2. <u>valuable</u> idea
   - ○ **A.** useful
   - ○ **B.** super
   - ○ **C.** worthless
   - ○ **D.** certain

3. possible <u>solution</u>
   - ○ **A.** problem
   - ○ **B.** surprise
   - ○ **C.** activity
   - ○ **D.** idea

4. <u>unfamiliar</u> faces
   - ○ **A.** pleasant
   - ○ **B.** known
   - ○ **C.** beautiful
   - ○ **D.** strange

5. <u>unfortunate</u> event
   - ○ **A.** important
   - ○ **B.** early
   - ○ **C.** late
   - ○ **D.** lucky

6. <u>tighten</u> your grip
   - ○ **A.** brighten
   - ○ **B.** loosen
   - ○ **C.** increase
   - ○ **D.** maintain

7. <u>spare</u> part
   - ○ **A.** needed
   - ○ **B.** extra
   - ○ **C.** loose
   - ○ **D.** costly

Reading Comprehension

Read each story. Then fill in the circle that best completes each sentence or answers each question.

SAMPLE

Some kids in Japan may not have to feed the fish in their aquariums anymore. That's because they may choose to buy robotic fish instead. Robotic fish are little fish robots powered by light. The light causes the fish to move around inside the aquarium. A special design keeps the fish from bumping into the aquarium's walls.

1. A good title for this story would be
   ○ **A.** "New Aquariums."
   ○ **B.** "Robotic Fish."
   ○ **C.** "Pets in Japan."
   ○ **D.** "The Power of Light."

2. What causes the robotic fish to move?
   ○ **A.** light
   ○ **B.** fish food
   ○ **C.** robots
   ○ **D.** water

A. Squeezed into a ship called the *Amistad*, the 53 slaves aboard could barely breathe. Each day, the crew gave them sips of water and scraps of food. The slaves were beaten and chained.

They had been kidnapped from Africa. On July 4, 1839, they broke free. They killed the captain and took control of *Amistad* off Cuba's coast, making the ship a famous symbol of freedom.

The *Amistad* story is famous for the rebellion and for what followed. After breaking free, the slaves tried to sail the ship back to their native Sierra Leone, in West Africa. The U.S. Navy captured the ship off the coast of Long Island and charged the slaves with murder.

In 1841, the U.S. Supreme Court ruled that the Africans had been illegally kidnapped. The Court allowed them to return to Africa.

1. What did the *Amistad* become a symbol of?
   ○ **A.** slavery
   ○ **B.** Africa
   ○ **C.** the Supreme Court
   ○ **D.** freedom

2. What happened after the U.S. Navy captured the ship?
   ○ **A.** The slaves were charged with murder.
   ○ **B.** The slaves were chained and beaten.
   ○ **C.** The slaves killed the ship's captain.
   ○ **D.** The slaves tried to sail to Sierra Leone.

3. The best title for this story is
   ○ **A.** "A History of Slavery."
   ○ **B.** "The Supreme Court."
   ○ **C.** "The Story of the *Amistad*."
   ○ **D.** "U.S. Navy Rescues."

B. Now that the Summer Olympics are over, it's time to test your Australia awareness. Known as the "Land Down Under," Australia may be the world's most beautiful country. It's certainly the only country in the world that's both an island and a continent.

Want more Australia facts? It's about the size of the continental United States. Nineteen million people live there. Some of these people are Aborigines. Aborigines were Australia's first settlers, like Native Americans here in the U.S.

Australia is also home to some **unique** and interesting animals. Koala bears are one example. These picky eaters will only eat leaves from eucalyptus trees. They never drink water. Another famous Australian animal is the kangaroo. There are more kangaroos than people in Australia. A newborn kangaroo lives in its mother's pouch for as long as six months.

I. Which of these is an *opinion*?
- ○ **A.** Australia may be the world's most beautiful country.
- ○ **B.** Australia is about the size of the continental United States.
- ○ **C.** Some Australians are Aborigines.
- ○ **D.** There are more kangaroos than people in Australia.

2. Koala bears are picky eaters because
- ○ **A.** they never drink water.
- ○ **B.** they live in Australia.
- ○ **C.** they only eat kangaroos.
- ○ **D.** they only eat eucalyptus leaves.

3. In this story, the word **unique** means
- ○ **A.** large.
- ○ **B.** small.
- ○ **C.** one-of-a-kind.
- ○ **D.** popular.

C. Have you heard the buzz about bees? It's possible that the common honeybee can help scientists **detect** deadly land mines, or underground bombs.

Land mines kill more than 20,000 people each year. Soldiers bury the mines during wars, but the mines stay even after the wars have ended. People can't tell where land mines are until they explode.

Scientists are hoping that honeybees can help to find buried land mines and save people's lives.

How will it work? Honeybees' fuzzy bodies collect particles from the air, including particles from land mines. Scientists will use special sensors to check the bees for land mine particles. If they find some, the scientists can track the bees back to the mines and destroy them.

I. In this story, the word **detect** means
- ○ **A.** kill.
- ○ **B.** find.
- ○ **C.** collect.
- ○ **D.** bury.

2. According to the story, honeybees will
- ○ **A.** lead scientists to special sensors.
- ○ **B.** help lead scientists to land mines.
- ○ **C.** explode land mines.
- ○ **D.** sting the soldiers who bury land mines.

3. Which is the best summary of this article?
- ○ **A.** Land mines are dangerous weapons that kill people.
- ○ **B.** No one can find land mines after soldiers bury them.
- ○ **C.** Honeybees have fuzzy bodies that collect particles from the air.
- ○ **D.** Honeybees may be able to help scientists detect land mines.

Scholastic Professional Books

D. When Buddy Koerner eats an orange or a banana at school, he doesn't throw the peels into the trash. Buddy and his class have found a better use for fruit peels, limp lettuce, and soggy bread crusts. With the help of a few hundred worms, the class turns food scraps into a nourishing snack for planet Earth.

Each week, Buddy's class dumps food scraps into a special bin in their classroom. Red worms live inside the bin. They eat the scraps and make castings, or worm poop. The castings form compost, which looks like dark soil. Compost is rich in nutrients to help plants and lawns grow better.

Farmers have been making compost for at least 2,000 years. Today, more and more people are learning to compost in homes and schools. This kind of recycling can really help the planet.

1. Castings are
○ **A.** food scraps.
○ **B.** worms.
○ **C.** worm poop.
○ **D.** soil.

2. Buddy and his classmates make compost from
○ **A.** worms.
○ **B.** food scraps.
○ **C.** soil.
○ **D.** plants.

3. This story probably goes on to talk about
○ **A.** other kinds of worms.
○ **B.** other kinds of recycling.
○ **C.** what Buddy has for lunch every day.
○ **D.** the life cycle of worms.

E. Exercise helps to keep people healthy. But not everyone wants to play basketball or run marathons. Fortunately, there are plenty of other ways to get exercise. One good way is hiking.

What is hiking? Hiking really just means taking a long walk. Often, hiking involves going up or down a hill. Most people do it in the countryside, but you can also do it in town. And hiking doesn't really require any special equipment. All you need is a comfortable pair of shoes, a nutritious snack, and some water.

The shoes are very important. Uncomfortable hiking shoes can make walking painful. They can cause blisters or worse. It shouldn't hurt to hike, so wear sturdy, comfortable shoes.

The snack and water are also important. Hiking uses up the body's energy and fluids. A snack and some water can replace what you've lost. That means you'll be able to go up that one last hill.

1. If you hike in uncomfortable shoes you could
○ **A.** run out of energy.
○ **B.** get blisters.
○ **C.** fall down.
○ **D.** need more water.

2. What is the best title for this story?
○ **A.** "All Kinds of Exercise"
○ **B.** "A Guide to Hiking"
○ **C.** "The Importance of Shoes"
○ **D.** "Nutritious Snacks"

3. Which of these is not true about hiking?
○ **A.** It's like walking.
○ **B.** You can do it in the country.
○ **C.** You use a lot of special equipment.
○ **D.** It's important to take water on a hike.

Vocabulary

Synonyms

Read the underlined word in each phrase. Mark the word below it that has the same (or close to the same) meaning.

Sample:

weary legs
- ○ **A.** tired
- ○ **B.** long
- ○ **C.** active
- ○ **D.** jumpy

I. unexpected defeat
- ○ **A.** game
- ○ **B.** number
- ○ **C.** loss
- ○ **D.** win

2. soaring through the air
- ○ **A.** falling
- ○ **B.** flying
- ○ **C.** walking
- ○ **D.** blowing

3. family tradition
- ○ **A.** party
- ○ **B.** gathering
- ○ **C.** friend
- ○ **D.** custom

4. fierce animal
- ○ **A.** huge
- ○ **B.** mean
- ○ **C.** tiny
- ○ **D.** hungry

5. weekly chore
- ○ **A.** meal
- ○ **B.** meeting
- ○ **C.** party
- ○ **D.** job

6. feeling uneasy
- ○ **A.** unfit
- ○ **B.** difficult
- ○ **C.** disappointed
- ○ **D.** uncomfortable

7. wring the wet clothes
- ○ **A.** hang
- ○ **B.** wash
- ○ **C.** squeeze
- ○ **D.** dry

Antonyms

Read the underlined word in each phrase. Mark the word below it that means the opposite or nearly the opposite.

Sample:

talk rapidly
- ○ **A.** quickly
- ○ **B.** slowly
- ○ **C.** funnily
- ○ **D.** normally

I. sure thing
- ○ **A.** tiring
- ○ **B.** uncertain
- ○ **C.** new
- ○ **D.** old

2. airplane takeoff
- ○ **A.** wheel
- ○ **B.** landing
- ○ **C.** ticket
- ○ **D.** flight

3. sloppy work
- ○ **A.** neat
- ○ **B.** good
- ○ **C.** hard
- ○ **D.** easy

4. back to reality
- ○ **A.** life
- ○ **B.** fantasy
- ○ **C.** school
- ○ **D.** work

5. thorough search
- ○ **A.** incomplete
- ○ **B.** neat
- ○ **C.** incorrect
- ○ **D.** successful

6. unseen problems
- ○ **A.** unknown
- ○ **B.** hard
- ○ **C.** serious
- ○ **D.** visible

7. valuable gift
- ○ **A.** expensive
- ○ **B.** birthday
- ○ **C.** useless
- ○ **D.** good

Reading Comprehension

Read each story. Then fill in the circle that best completes each sentence or answers each question.

SAMPLE

Do you think you own the world's tiniest dog? *The Guinness Book of World Records* is the place to check! For 40 years, the *Guinness Book* has been **resolving** arguments about the biggest, the smallest, the fastest, and the strangest things in the world. Want to find out who blew the biggest bubble-gum bubble? Now you know where to look.

1. In this passage, the word **resolving** means
   ○ **A.** starting.
   ○ **B.** settling.
   ○ **C.** causing.
   ○ **D.** recording.

2. What is the best title for this passage?
   ○ **A.** "The World's Smallest Dog"
   ○ **B.** "Arguing for 40 Years"
   ○ **C.** "How to Blow a Giant Bubble"
   ○ **D.** "The Book With All the Records"

A. One winter day, a young girl named Jenny was walking her dog named Hero. Jenny took Hero's tennis ball and threw it. "Rats!" she thought as the ball rolled onto the frozen pond. Hero ran out after it in a flash. "Hero!" Jenny screamed, running after her dog.

After about three large steps, the ice cracked under Jenny's feet and she fell into the pond. Hero ran to Jenny, but he fell in the water too. Jenny kept slipping as she tried to climb out. Meanwhile, Hero lifted his body up and slammed it down on the ice like a hammer until he made a path to the shore. That day Hero was a real hero.

1. What is the best title for this story?
   ○ **A.** "Hero Saves the Day "
   ○ **B.** "Recognizing Thin Ice"
   ○ **C.** "Favorite Pets"
   ○ **D.** "They Used to Play Fetch"

2. What can you guess from this story?
   ○ **A.** Hero hates the water.
   ○ **B.** Jenny can't swim.
   ○ **C.** Hero is a smart dog.
   ○ **D.** Jenny plays Little League baseball.

3. Why did Jenny go out on the ice?
   ○ **A.** to save Hero
   ○ **B.** to slide around on it
   ○ **C.** to see how strong it was
   ○ **D.** to play with Hero

B. It happened in 1947. For the first time, an African-American was stepping onto the field to play in a major-league baseball game. Jackie Robinson was playing for the Brooklyn Dodgers, the only team with enough courage to let this great athlete play. That day, baseball's color barrier was broken forever.

Despite the racism he met both on and off the field, Jackie was named Rookie of the Year and led the league in stolen bases. Two years later, he won the National League's Most Valuable Player (MVP) award. Robinson made it to the Baseball Hall of Fame in 1962.

Jackie changed baseball, but he also changed the way people thought. Civil rights leader Martin Luther King Jr. said, "Without Jackie Robinson, I could never have done what I did."

I. In 1947, Jackie Robinson
○ **A.** made the Baseball Hall of Fame.
○ **B.** was honored by Martin Luther King.
○ **C.** became the first African-American to play in the major leagues.
○ **D.** won the MVP award.

2. You can guess from this story that Robinson is most famous for
○ **A.** breaking baseball's color barrier.
○ **B.** leading the league in stolen bases.
○ **C.** playing for the Brooklyn Dodgers.
○ **D.** being named Rookie of the Year.

3. When did Robinson win the MVP award?
○ **A.** the year he joined the Dodgers
○ **B.** the year after he joined the Dodgers
○ **C.** two years after he joined the Dodgers
○ **D.** the year he made it to the Baseball Hall of Fame

C. Almost everyone likes bread. But not everyone knows how easy it is to make it. All you need are yeast, flour, and water.

First, mix a package of yeast with two cups of warm water. Let the mixture stand until bubbles form. Then start adding four cups of flour, a half a cup at a time. When the dough gets too thick to stir, scrape it onto a floured board and knead it. To knead, turn the dough in a circle and fold and punch it. Knead it for ten minutes as you add one more cup of flour. The dough is ready when it feels soft and smooth, not sticky.

After kneading, put the dough in a buttered bowl and cover it with a dish towel. Leave it there for an hour or more to rise. It should double in size. Then, knead it for another minute or so, and shape it into a loaf. Let it rise again for 45 minutes. Pop it in the oven to bake for 45 minutes in a 375-degree oven. When it's done, let it cool for ten minutes before slicing.

I. After the dough has doubled in size, you
○ **A.** knead it for ten minutes.
○ **B.** mix the yeast with two cups of water.
○ **C.** add flour a half a cup at a time.
○ **D.** knead it and shape it into a loaf.

2. The purpose of this article is to
○ **A.** teach you how to make bread.
○ **B.** tell you a funny cooking story.
○ **C.** persuade you to cook more.
○ **D.** make you like bread.

3. From this article, you can conclude that
○ **A.** bread requires many ingredients.
○ **B.** the author doesn't like bread.
○ **C.** making bread takes several hours.
○ **D.** dough is difficult to knead.

Scholastic Professional Books

D. Put away those surfboards! Even the best surfer wouldn't want to ride a tsunami. The name tsunami comes from the Japanese language. It's the scientific term for a seismic sea wave, a giant wave caused by an undersea earthquake.

Scientists believe tsunamis occur when an earthquake lifts or tilts the ocean floor. The quake creates very long waves that speed across the sea. Tsunamis travel at up to 500 miles an hour. The waves grow in height as they reach the shore. Some monster-sized tsunamis can tower 60 feet or more above the ocean's surface.

Tsunamis are sometimes called tidal waves, but that name is misleading. High and low tides never cause tsunamis, only earthquakes or volcanic eruptions do. But by any name, tsunamis can be very dangerous. Hawaii has been hit by over 40 tsunamis!

I. What can cause a tsunami?
- ○ **A.** high and low tides
- ○ **B.** seismic sea waves
- ○ **C.** undersea earthquakes
- ○ **D.** scientific experiments

2. Which of these is an *opinion*?
- ○ **A.** Hawaii has been hit by over 40 tsunamis.
- ○ **B.** The best surfer wouldn't want to ride a tsunami.
- ○ **C.** Tsunamis grow in height as they reach the shore.
- ○ **D.** Tsunamis travel at up to 500 miles per hour.

3. This article would probably go on to talk about
- ○ **A.** destruction caused by tsunamis.
- ○ **B.** destruction caused by earthquakes.
- ○ **C.** surfers who like to ride tsunamis.
- ○ **D.** what causes high and low tides.

E. At 7:52 a.m. on May 20, 1927, Charles Lindbergh sat in the cockpit of his plane, the *Spirit of St. Louis*. The 25-year-old American was trying to fly nonstop across the Atlantic Ocean, from New York to Paris. The distance was 3,600 miles. No one had ever done this. If he made it, air travel would never be the same.

After taking off, Lindbergh had to find his way to Paris without the radar, radios, and computer equipment planes use today. Instead, he had a compass, maps, and the stars to help him find his way. Getting lost would be dangerous. He could easily run out of fuel before reaching land.

Finally, over 33 hours after he began his trip, Lindbergh landed in Paris. As he did, 25,000 people cheered. Lindbergh became an instant hero with a new nickname: the Lone Eagle.

I. How was Lindbergh's plane different from planes today?
- ○ **A.** It didn't have a name.
- ○ **B.** It had to take off and land on water.
- ○ **C.** It didn't have computer equipment.
- ○ **D.** It needed two people to fly it.

2. What is the best title for this story?
- ○ **A.** "The Next Plane to Paris"
- ○ **B.** "Pilots and Their Planes"
- ○ **C.** "A Trip Across the Atlantic"
- ○ **D.** "Lindbergh's Famous Flight"

3. Which of these is an *opinion*?
- ○ **A.** Lindbergh's plane was named the *Spirit of St. Louis*.
- ○ **B.** Lindbergh was the greatest pilot ever.
- ○ **C.** Lindbergh's trip took over 33 hours.
- ○ **D.** When he landed in Paris, 25,000 people cheered.

Scholastic Professional Books

Vocabulary

Synonyms

Read the underlined word in each phrase. Mark the word below it that has the same (or close to the same) meaning.

Sample:

abandon the ship
- ○ **A.** leave
- ○ **B.** sail
- ○ **C.** board
- ○ **D.** hide

1. narrow corridor
   - ○ **A.** road
   - ○ **B.** minded
   - ○ **C.** door
   - ○ **D.** hallway

2. riding solo
   - ○ **A.** quickly
   - ○ **B.** alone
   - ○ **C.** carefully
   - ○ **D.** fast

3. unique flavor
   - ○ **A.** sweet
   - ○ **B.** first-rate
   - ○ **C.** one-of-a-kind
   - ○ **D.** ordinary

4. soothe the pain
   - ○ **A.** ignore
   - ○ **B.** relieve
   - ○ **C.** feel
   - ○ **D.** worsen

5. unravel the mystery
   - ○ **A.** solve
   - ○ **B.** enjoy
   - ○ **C.** forget
   - ○ **D.** notice

6. possess a book
   - ○ **A.** own
   - ○ **B.** lend
   - ○ **C.** carry
   - ○ **D.** read

7. stale ideas
   - ○ **A.** fresh
   - ○ **B.** original
   - ○ **C.** bad
   - ○ **D.** old

Antonyms

Read the underlined word in each phrase. Mark the word below it that means the opposite or nearly the opposite.

Sample:

gush out of the tap
- ○ **A.** spill
- ○ **B.** trickle
- ○ **C.** topple
- ○ **D.** flow

1. confident character
   - ○ **A.** funny
   - ○ **B.** unsure
   - ○ **C.** smug
   - ○ **D.** pesky

2. gritty texture
   - ○ **A.** smooth
   - ○ **B.** stubby
   - ○ **C.** tasty
   - ○ **D.** bumpy

3. expand your horizons
   - ○ **A.** visit
   - ○ **B.** shrink
   - ○ **C.** color
   - ○ **D.** widen

4. an agreement between friends
   - ○ **A.** apology
   - ○ **B.** formula
   - ○ **C.** contract
   - ○ **D.** dispute

5. coastal highway
   - ○ **A.** interstate
   - ○ **B.** inland
   - ○ **C.** frontier
   - ○ **D.** circular

6. solemn occasion
   - ○ **A.** frequent
   - ○ **B.** rare
   - ○ **C.** sorry
   - ○ **D.** cheerful

7. elated look
   - ○ **A.** happy
   - ○ **B.** unsure
   - ○ **C.** sad
   - ○ **D.** pleased

Name _____

Reading Comprehension

Read each story. Then fill in the circle that best completes each sentence or answers each question.

SAMPLE

Since 1886, the Statue of Liberty has stood on Liberty Island in New York Bay. The beautiful statue was given to the United States by the people of France. With its torch raised high, the statue has welcomed immigrants from all over the world. It has become a **symbol** of American freedom.

I. What is the best title for this story?
  ○ **A.** "Immigrant Land"
  ○ **B.** "An American Symbol"
  ○ **C.** "Liberty Island"
  ○ **D.** "How a Statue Is Made"

2. In this story, the word **symbol** means
  ○ **A.** sculpture.
  ○ **B.** celebration.
  ○ **C.** sign.
  ○ **D.** warning.

A. Adobe is a Spanish word meaning "sun-dried brick." Adobe bricks are made by mixing sand, water, and small amounts of straw or grass. The mixture is then shaped into bricks, dried, and baked in the sun for about two weeks. Since sand is widely available in many deserts, desert dwellers have used adobe to make their homes for thousands of years.

I. The main idea of this story is that
  ○ **A.** adobe bricks are difficult
       to make.
  ○ **B.** deserts are hot.
  ○ **C.** people in deserts often build
       with adobe.
  ○ **D.** adobe is a Spanish word.

2. You would probably find this story in a book about
  ○ **A.** weather.
  ○ **B.** the sun.
  ○ **C.** building materials.
  ○ **D.** cactuses.

3. Which of these is an *opinion*?
  ○ **A.** Adobe is made from sand.
  ○ **B.** Adobe homes are beautiful
  ○ **C.** Adobe is a Spanish word.
  ○ **D.** Adobe is used in building.

B. Today, when you send a letter to a friend, it can get there in seconds—by electronic mail. However, centuries ago, sending a letter took much longer. About 2,400 years ago, a Persian king named Cyrus the Great **introduced** the first postal system. Messengers on horseback raced from station to station delivering letters. It took weeks or even months to receive a message from far away!

1. In this story, the word **introduced** means
○ **A.** met.
○ **B.** mailed.
○ **C.** used.
○ **D.** started.

2. The story would probably go on to talk about
○ **A.** other famous kings.
○ **B.** horses throughout history.
○ **C.** advances in sending mail.
○ **D.** the cost of stamps.

C. Scientists have been studying volcanoes for many years. They want to find ways to predict when volcanoes will erupt. Such knowledge could help protect people from a volcano's sudden burst of hot lava and ash. Although scientists can't say exactly when a volcano will erupt, they know that a slight change in the shape of the earth is one warning sign. Another is that some volcanoes emit a gas called sulfur dioxide before they erupt.

1. This story is mainly about
○ **A.** becoming a scientist.
○ **B.** natural disasters.
○ **C.** the dangers of volcanoes.
○ **D.** predicting volcanic eruptions.

2. You can guess that
○ **A.** scientists can predict all volcanic eruptions.
○ **B.** studying volcanoes is important.
○ **C.** volcanoes usually erupt in summer.
○ **D.** all volcanoes are tall.

D. As American pioneers headed west in the late 1700s and early 1800s, they used Conestoga wagons. These wagons were named for the valley in Pennsylvania where they were first built. Teams of four to six horses were used to **draw** the wagons. When it was hot or stormy, pioneers put canvas roofs on their wagons. When the pioneers came to rivers, they removed the vehicles' wide wheels, turning the wagons into boats!

1. Conestoga wagons were first made
○ **A.** in the West.
○ **B.** on the prairies.
○ **C.** in Pennsylvania.
○ **D.** in the 1800s.

2. In this story, the word **draw** means
○ **A.** run.
○ **B.** float.
○ **C.** paint.
○ **D.** pull.

3. Pioneers removed wagon wheels because
○ **A.** they had to cross rivers.
○ **B.** the wheels were broken.
○ **C.** the weather was stormy.
○ **D.** they wanted to sell them.

E. Have you ever used an encyclopedia? These reference books contain articles about many subjects. The articles are arranged in alphabetical order. To research a subject, follow these steps:

1. Find the encyclopedia index. It is usually in a separate volume. Use the index to find key words related to the subject you are researching.

2. Record from the index the names of articles related to your subject. Jot down the volume and page numbers so you can find the articles.

3. Using your list of articles, find the correct encyclopedia volumes. Then turn to the page on which each article begins.

4. Read each article. Write down the important information you want to remember.

5. Look at the end of the article for cross references. These references will send you to other articles related to your subject.

1. What is the best title for this story?
   ○ **A.** "Using an Encyclopedia"
   ○ **B.** "Taking Notes"
   ○ **C.** "Finding Cross References"
   ○ **D.** "Locating Subjects"

2. You can find cross references
   ○ **A.** in the front of each volume.
   ○ **B.** at the end of an article.
   ○ **C.** in your notes.
   ○ **D.** at the start of an article.

3. You can guess that encyclopedias
   ○ **A.** are useful research tools.
   ○ **B.** are just like dictionaries.
   ○ **C.** are difficult to use.
   ○ **D.** have very short articles.

4. What should you do right after you find the correct volume?
   ○ **A.** Find the index.
   ○ **B.** Take notes.
   ○ **C.** Look for cross references.
   ○ **D.** Find the article.

F.   Dear Editor,
   I am a fourth-grade student here in West Elmville. I am writing to respond to last week's article about school lunches. In the article, school officials said they planned to add more vegetables to the school lunch menu. That's a great idea. However, I would like to make a **recommendation**. Instead of adding more mushy canned veggies, our school cafeterias should have salad bars. A fresh salad is tasty and full of vitamins. And with a salad bar, kids can choose the veggies they like best.
                    Sincerely,
                    A Salad Fan

1. In this letter, the word **recommendation** means
   ○ **A.** meal.
   ○ **B.** suggestion.
   ○ **C.** vote.
   ○ **D.** addition.

2. You would probably see this letter
   ○ **A.** in a local newspaper.
   ○ **B.** on a school principal's desk.
   ○ **C.** in your mailbox.
   ○ **D.** in a book about nutrition.

3. The author wrote this letter to
   ○ **A.** get a job in a cafeteria.
   ○ **B.** share his or her opinion.
   ○ **C.** entertain readers.
   ○ **D.** tell how to grow fresh vegetables.

Vocabulary

Synonyms

Read the underlined word in each phrase. Mark the word below it that has the same (or close to the same) meaning.

Sample:

massive creature
- ○ **A.** huge
- ○ **B.** quiet
- ○ **C.** hungry
- ○ **D.** ugly

1. link together
- ○ **A.** key
- ○ **B.** connect
- ○ **C.** blast
- ○ **D.** walk

2. important mission
- ○ **A.** secret
- ○ **B.** day
- ○ **C.** task
- ○ **D.** title

3. humorous story
- ○ **A.** long
- ○ **B.** funny
- ○ **C.** short
- ○ **D.** sad

4. purchase goods
- ○ **A.** clean
- ○ **B.** paint
- ○ **C.** sell
- ○ **D.** buy

5. heavy parcel
- ○ **A.** weight
- ○ **B.** rain
- ○ **C.** light
- ○ **D.** package

6. cautious driver
- ○ **A.** fast
- ○ **B.** careful
- ○ **C.** unsafe
- ○ **D.** taxi

7. conceal a smile
- ○ **A.** hide
- ○ **B.** draw
- ○ **C.** reveal
- ○ **D.** force

Multiple Meanings

Read each set of sentences. Mark the word that makes sense in both sentences.

Sample:

The doctor said her _____ had a stomach flu.
Be _____ while others at the table finish eating.
- ○ **A.** son
- ○ **B.** staff
- ○ **C.** patient
- ○ **D.** kind

1. Wheat and corn are both examples of _____.
I found a few _____ of sand in my shoe.
- ○ **A.** plants
- ○ **B.** grains
- ○ **C.** foods
- ○ **D.** pieces

2. He works the early _____ at the library.
Mary had to _____ her chair to get a better view.
- ○ **A.** job
- ○ **B.** turn
- ○ **C.** move
- ○ **D.** shift

3. The family bought a _____ of farmland.
Did you enjoy that book's exciting _____?
- ○ **A.** piece
- ○ **B.** plot
- ○ **C.** mile
- ○ **D.** hero

4. The baby can't walk, but she _____ along the floor.
The scary movie gave me the _____.
- ○ **A.** creeps
- ○ **B.** moves
- ○ **C.** slithers
- ○ **D.** crawls

Reading Comprehension

Read each story. Then fill in the circle that best completes each sentence or answers each question.

SAMPLE

American girls are shooting pucks and scoring goals all over the U.S. They are skating their way into a sport once thought to be just for boys. Since 1992, the number of American girls playing in organized ice-hockey leagues has **increased** from 5,500 to more than 20,000.

1. What is the main idea of this story?
○ **A.** Ice hockey is a dangerous sport.
○ **B.** Many girls play ice hockey now.
○ **C.** Only boys should play hockey.
○ **D.** Only girls should play hockey.

2. In this story, the word **increased** means
○ **A.** gone up.
○ **B.** skated.
○ **C.** fallen.
○ **D.** gone down.

A. The next time you pick up a bag of potato chips, read the label. You might notice a new ingredient—Olestra. Olestra was invented as a **substitute** for ingredients that are high in fat, such as butter or oil. But unlike butter and oil, Olestra doesn't add fat or calories to foods. That's because Olestra is not a food. It just passes through the body, without being digested.

Some people say that snacks containing Olestra taste as delicious as the real things. But Olestra can cause stomach cramps and other side effects. "I would rather see kids eat healthy snacks rather than potato chips," says diet expert Jodie Shield. "That's a better goal than choosing Olestra chips over regular high-fat chips."

1. What is the best title for this story?
○ **A.** "Everyone Loves Potato Chips"
○ **B.** "Olestra Tastes Great"
○ **C.** "Olestra May Not Be the Answer"
○ **D.** "How to Improve Your Diet"

2. In this story, the word **substitute** means
○ **A.** greasy.   ○ **C.** addition.
○ **B.** replacement.   ○ **D.** subtraction.

3. Which is an *opinion* about Olestra?
○ **A.** It tastes delicious.
○ **B.** It isn't digested by the body.
○ **C.** It can be used in snack foods.
○ **D.** It may cause stomach cramps.

4. Olestra can be used to make foods
○ **A.** taste better.
○ **B.** saltier.
○ **C.** lower in fat.
○ **D.** lower in cost.

B. The state of Connecticut used to have one official hero—a man named Nathan Hale. But in 1993, a fourth-grade class from New Canaan Country School decided that their state should have a female hero too. So the students began researching important women in Connecticut's history. They chose Prudence Crandall, a teacher who had let black students attend her school—even though it was against the law—back in 1832. Eventually, Crandall went to jail for her efforts. After the students chose Crandall, they asked lawmakers to introduce a bill recognizing her as a hero. That bill was made a law in 1995.

I. Prudence Crandall was a teacher in
○ **A.** 1993.   ○ **C.** 1832.
○ **B.** 1995.   ○ **D.** 1997.

2. Which happened last?
○ **A.** Crandall became a state hero.
○ **B.** Crandall went to jail.
○ **C.** The students chose Crandall.
○ **D.** Crandall let black students go to her school.

3. From this story, you can guess that
○ **A.** the fourth-graders went to jail.
○ **B.** Nathan Hale is no longer a hero.
○ **C.** only men can be heroes.
○ **D.** women probably aren't recognized as heroes as often as they could be.

C.   November 20, 1997
Dear Principal,
        I think the students at our school should wear uniforms. Many schools already have them. Uniforms will help our families save money, since we would have to **purchase** only one or two uniforms for the whole year. Uniforms could also give us more pride in our school. And best of all, if we all wore uniforms, kids wouldn't tease each other about their clothes.
        I know some students think uniforms are ugly and uncomfortable. But maybe we can pick a uniform that everyone likes. I think this is a terrific idea for our school.

                Sincerely,
                Justin Jones

I. This letter was written by
○ **A.** a father.
○ **B.** a mother.
○ **C.** a teacher.
○ **D.** a student.

2. In this letter, the word **purchase** means
○ **A.** wear.   ○ **C.** buy.
○ **B.** see.   ○ **D.** sell.

3. Which of these is a *fact* about uniforms?
○ **A.** They are uncomfortable.
○ **B.** Some schools already have them.
○ **C.** They are ugly.
○ **D.** They aren't too expensive.

4. Justin wrote this letter to
○ **A.** ask for new clothes.
○ **B.** apologize to the principal.
○ **C.** suggest that students wear uniforms.
○ **D.** thank the principal.

5. Some students don't want to wear uniforms because they think
○ **A.** uniforms are expensive.
○ **B.** school pride is silly.
○ **C.** the principal is mean.
○ **D.** uniforms can be ugly and uncomfortable.

D. Zoom! Each spring, dozens of cars race from New York City to Washington, D.C.—without using a single drop of gas! These cars run on electricity.

Most cars run on gasoline. When cars burn this fuel, they pollute the air with smelly exhaust. Electric cars run on batteries. Since they don't burn fuel, they produce much less pollution.

Events, like this 310-mile race, give electric carmakers a chance to show off their **vehicles**. They hope to convince people that electric cars are the wave of the future. But so far, electric cars can travel only about 40 miles on one charge of electricity. A gasoline-powered car could probably go about 200 miles on one tank of gas. That means electric cars require five times as many pit stops—and that may be the reason that these cars haven't caught on yet.

I. What is the main idea of this article?
  ○ **A.** Gasoline is an expensive fuel.
  ○ **B.** Electric-car races are exciting.
  ○ **C.** Everyone wants an electric car.
  ○ **D.** The electric car is a clean, if slow, way to travel.

2. In this article, the word **vehicles** means
  ○ **A.** cars.   ○ **C.** speed.
  ○ **B.** gasoline.   ○ **D.** tires.

3. Cars produce smelly exhaust when they
  ○ **A.** recharge.   ○ **C.** burn gasoline.
  ○ **B.** speed.   ○ **D.** use batteries.

4. The next paragraph might talk about
  ○ **A.** monster trucks.
  ○ **B.** other ways to cut down on car pollution.
  ○ **C.** other uses of electricity.
  ○ **D.** famous race-car drivers.

E. Many years ago in Greece, there lived a king named Midas. He wished for the power to turn things to gold simply by touching them. Since Midas was a good king, a god named Dionysus granted his wish. Shouting with joy, Midas ran through his palace, touching everything. And everything he owned became gold. He was rich beyond his wildest dreams.

At dinner time, King Midas reached for some bread, and the bread turned to gold. He reached for some water, and his lips turned the water to gold. King Midas realized he would soon die of hunger or thirst. Weeping gold tears, he went to the god Dionysus and begged the god to remove the golden touch.

"You have been greedy and foolish," scolded Dionysus. But he took pity on Midas, and sent the king to a special river to wash his hands. Midas did so, and the golden touch was washed away.

I. This story is mainly about
  ○ **A.** how Midas got to be very rich.
  ○ **B.** how Midas learned a lesson about being greedy.
  ○ **C.** how Dionysus played a mean trick.
  ○ **D.** how to cook gold food.

2. Midas got rid of the golden touch by
  ○ **A.** eating bread and water.
  ○ **B.** washing his hands in a fountain.
  ○ **C.** sleeping in a special bed.
  ○ **D.** washing his hands in a special river.

3. This story teaches that
  ○ **A.** all wishes are foolish.
  ○ **B.** some things are more important than gold.
  ○ **C.** some rivers are cleaner than others.
  ○ **D.** Greek gods should feel sorry for kings who love gold.

Vocabulary

Synonyms

Read the underlined word in each phrase. Mark the word below it that has the same (or close to the same) meaning.

Sample:

injure your foot
- ○ **A.** hurt
- ○ **B.** kill
- ○ **C.** toe
- ○ **D.** tickle

I. holler loudly
- ○ **A.** noisy
- ○ **B.** whisper
- ○ **C.** shout
- ○ **D.** laugh

2. take a ferry
- ○ **A.** car
- ○ **B.** boat
- ○ **C.** grab
- ○ **D.** taxi

3. faithful dog
- ○ **A.** brown
- ○ **B.** furry
- ○ **C.** collar
- ○ **D.** loyal

4. bewildered student
- ○ **A.** smart
- ○ **B.** book
- ○ **C.** confused
- ○ **D.** teacher

5. solid foundation
- ○ **A.** base
- ○ **B.** rock
- ○ **C.** roof
- ○ **D.** hard

6. essential equipment
- ○ **A.** necessary
- ○ **B.** expensive
- ○ **C.** cheap
- ○ **D.** sturdy

7. rigid material
- ○ **A.** stiff
- ○ **B.** red
- ○ **C.** natural
- ○ **D.** soft

Antonyms

Read the underlined word in each phrase. Mark the word below it that means the opposite or nearly the opposite.

Sample:

felt sorrow
- ○ **A.** silly
- ○ **B.** joy
- ○ **C.** saw
- ○ **D.** sadness

I. brief message
- ○ **A.** short
- ○ **B.** long
- ○ **C.** note
- ○ **D.** funny

2. the nearest exit
- ○ **A.** entrance
- ○ **B.** slow
- ○ **C.** door
- ○ **D.** leave

3. a harmless spider
- ○ **A.** safe
- ○ **B.** ugly
- ○ **C.** hairy
- ○ **D.** poisonous

4. a harsh sound
- ○ **A.** gentle
- ○ **B.** scream
- ○ **C.** noise
- ○ **D.** alarm

5. visit frequently
- ○ **A.** often
- ○ **B.** travel
- ○ **C.** rarely
- ○ **D.** gladly

6. efficient worker
- ○ **A.** busy
- ○ **B.** hard
- ○ **C.** wasteful
- ○ **D.** careful

7. defiant attitude
- ○ **A.** unhappy
- ○ **B.** respectful
- ○ **C.** confused
- ○ **D.** poor

Scholastic Professional Books

Reading Comprehension

Read each story. Then fill in the circle that best completes each sentence or answers each question.

SAMPLE

More hurricanes happen in September than in any other month. Why? In the late summer and early fall, ocean water is warm after a summer in the sun. The warm, **moist** air rises off the surface of the ocean and forms thunderstorms. The thunderstorms can spin into powerful hurricanes.

1. What is the best title for this story?
○ **A.** "Why Hurricanes Are So Powerful"
○ **B.** "Why Hurricanes Often Happen in September"
○ **C.** "Why the Ocean Is Warm in September"
○ **D.** "Why Late Summer and Early Fall Are Great Seasons"

2. In this story, the word **moist** means
○ **A.** makes.
○ **B.** wet.
○ **C.** stops.
○ **D.** hides.

A. Kids at Dupuy Elementary school in Birmingham, Alabama, study more than reading, writing, and math. They also take classes in manners! They practice when to say "please" and "thank you" and learn the polite way to pass food at the lunch table.

They also learn to eat with a fork, not fingers; to say "hello" and not "yo" when they answer the phone; to shake hands when meeting someone—especially a grown-up; not to interrupt when others are speaking; and to say "excuse me" instead of pushing.

1. This story is mostly about
○ **A.** how to pass food at the lunch table.
○ **B.** a school's classes in manners.
○ **C.** why Alabama students are so polite.
○ **D.** how one school teaches reading, writing, and math.

2. At Dupuy Elementary school, kids learn the polite way to
○ **A.** study math.
○ **B.** interrupt when others are speaking.
○ **C.** pass food at the lunch table.
○ **D.** pass food on the school bus.

3. Which of the following statements is an *opinion*?
○ **A.** More schools should teach classes in manners.
○ **B.** Dupuy Elementary school teaches classes in manners.
○ **C.** Many schools don't teach classes in manners.
○ **D.** Dupuy's classes teach kids to shake hands when meeting someone.

Scholastic Professional Books

B. When people think about wildlife, they often think about fields and forests. But many wild animals live in cities. One creature often found in city skies is the peregrine falcon.

In the wilderness, peregrine falcons make their homes on steep, rocky cliffs. In cities, these birds nest on skyscrapers. Peregrine falcons like to be high in the sky so they can spot their favorite food—pigeons. Then the falcons swoop down and snatch their **prey** right out of the sky!

So if you live in a city and you see something whiz by faster than 200 miles per hour, it may not be a jet plane. It may be a peregrine falcon—the fastest flying animal alive!

1. In this story, the word **prey** means an animal that
○ **A.** can fly.   ○ **B.** is hunted.
○ **C.** has wings.   ○ **D.** lives in cities.

2. A peregrine falcon can fly faster than
○ **A.** 2,000 miles per hour.
○ **B.** a jet plane.
○ **C.** a few other flying animals.
○ **D.** 200 miles per hour.

3. From this story, you can guess that
○ **A.** peregrine falcons eat nothing but pigeons.
○ **B.** peregrine falcons build huge nests.
○ **C.** peregrine falcons live both in cities and in the wilderness.
○ **D.** peregrine falcons live only in cities.

C. If you're a kid under 18, and you live in New Orleans, Louisiana, you can't be out on the street on a school night after 8 p.m. If you are under 16 and you want to visit the country's largest mall—the Mall of America in Bloomington, Minnesota—on a Friday or Saturday night, you have to be with your mom or dad, or another grown-up.

Rules like these are called curfews. They prevent people from traveling freely, usually after dark. In many places, curfews are a cause of debate. Many people think curfews are a good way to **reduce** crimes committed by young people. They say curfews make communities safer. But other people say curfews are unfair because they punish all kids for the behavior of a few troublemakers.

1. In this story, the word **reduce** means
○ **A.** make more.
○ **B.** stop totally.
○ **C.** make fewer.
○ **D.** spread.

2. In New Orleans, kids under 18 can't be out on the streets after 8 p.m.
○ **A.** on any night.
○ **B.** on school nights.
○ **C.** on Fridays and Saturdays.
○ **D.** near the mall.

3. The story tells
○ **A.** why the Mall of America is a safe place to visit.
○ **B.** why most people want curfews in their communities.
○ **C.** why most people think curfews are unfair.
○ **D.** why people disagree about curfews.

4. Which of these is a *fact* about curfews?
○ **A.** They are unfair to kids.
○ **B.** They prevent people from traveling freely.
○ **C.** They always make communities safer.
○ **D.** The city of New Orleans is lucky to have one.

Scholastic Professional Books

D. If you saw Stan Herd at work, you'd probably think that he looked like an ordinary farmer. And most of the **materials** he works with—like seeds, soil, and a tractor—are just ordinary farm items. But in one very big way, Stan has little in common with other farmers. Stan Herd doesn't just plant crops, he's a crop artist! Stan plants and shapes crops into pictures so huge you need to view them from an airplane.

Many of Stan's pictures are modeled after famous works of art. For example, he once planted 20 acres of crops in the shape of Vincent van Gogh's painting "Sunflowers." Naturally, Stan used real sunflowers

Stan does most of his work on his farm in Kansas. But recently, he traveled to New York City to plant a landscape along the East River. No need for an airplane in the city—you can see Stan's work from nearby skyscrapers!

I. What is the main idea of this story?
○ **A.** Stan Herd is a better artist than Vincent van Gogh.
○ **B.** Stan Herd uses some very strange materials on his farm.
○ **C.** Stan Herd's art is so big, you must view it from an airplane.
○ **D.** Stan Herd is not just a farmer, he's a crop artist.

2. In this story, the word **materials** means
○ **A.** tools.   ○ **C.** fabrics.
○ **B.** crops.   ○ **D.** tractor.

3. In this story, where did Stan Herd plant a landscape?
○ **A.** along the East River in Kansas.
○ **B.** on top of a skyscraper in New York City
○ **C.** along the East River in New York City
○ **D.** near the Kansas River

E. One day the sun and the wind had an argument. The wind claimed that he was stronger than the sun. "Wrong," replied the sun. "I am stronger than you."

As they were disputing, a woman came down the road, wearing a heavy woolen coat.

"Here's how we can decide who is stronger," shouted the wind. "See that woman. Let's see which of us can remove her coat."

"Good idea," the sun replied. "You go first." So the wind started to blow. He blew and blew, as hard as he could. Trees swayed almost to the ground, but the woman only wrapped her coat more tightly around her.

Now the sun began to shine. She shone down on the woman, until the woman grew warm and unbuttoned her coat. The sun kept on shining. Soon, the woman removed her coat and laid it over her arm.

"Alas, you win," said the wind to the sun. "Your gentleness has succeeded where my rudeness failed."

I. This story is mainly about
○ **A.** solar power.
○ **B.** how the wind beat the sun in a contest.
○ **C.** how the wind learned a lesson from the sun.
○ **D.** why we don't wear coats when it's warm out.

2. The woman removed her coat because
○ **A.** the wind was blowing it off.
○ **B.** she became too warm in the sun.
○ **C.** she wanted the wind to lose the contest.
○ **D.** she didn't like the coat.

3. This story teaches that
○ **A.** you shouldn't wear a coat in warm weather.
○ **B.** the wind shouldn't blow so hard.
○ **C.** bullies often get their way.
○ **D.** kindness may get you further than rudeness.

Vocabulary

Synonyms

Read the underlined word in each phrase. Mark the word below it that has the same (or close to the same) meaning.

Sample:

annoy your brother
- ○ **A.** help
- ○ **B.** bother
- ○ **C.** sister
- ○ **D.** please

1. summer drought
   - ○ **A.** dry spell
   - ○ **B.** rainy season
   - ○ **C.** winter
   - ○ **D.** sunshine

2. brief lesson
   - ○ **A.** long
   - ○ **B.** tennis
   - ○ **C.** teacher
   - ○ **D.** short

3. strong ability
   - ○ **A.** smell
   - ○ **B.** muscle
   - ○ **C.** skill
   - ○ **D.** weakness

4. hastily finished
   - ○ **A.** quickly
   - ○ **B.** completed
   - ○ **C.** purple
   - ○ **D.** slowly

5. soar through the sky
   - ○ **A.** run
   - ○ **B.** fly
   - ○ **C.** float
   - ○ **D.** cloud

6. became hysterical
   - ○ **A.** emotional
   - ○ **B.** calm
   - ○ **C.** tired
   - ○ **D.** energetic

7. elevate the temperature
   - ○ **A.** read
   - ○ **B.** criticize
   - ○ **C.** describe
   - ○ **D.** raise

Antonyms

Read the underlined word in each phrase. Mark the word below it that means the opposite or nearly the opposite.

Sample:

grandmother's kindness
- ○ **A.** age
- ○ **B.** grandchild
- ○ **C.** meanness
- ○ **D.** happiness

1. fortunate event
   - ○ **A.** unlucky
   - ○ **B.** lucky
   - ○ **C.** happening
   - ○ **D.** exciting

2. student's failure
   - ○ **A.** books
   - ○ **B.** teacher
   - ○ **C.** problem
   - ○ **D.** success

3. friendly youngster
   - ○ **A.** adult
   - ○ **B.** puppy
   - ○ **C.** child
   - ○ **D.** rude

4. amuse the child
   - ○ **A.** bore
   - ○ **B.** scare
   - ○ **C.** watch
   - ○ **D.** entertain

5. fled the disaster
   - ○ **A.** ran to
   - ○ **B.** caused
   - ○ **C.** ran from
   - ○ **D.** tragedy

6. an earned privilege
   - ○ **A.** punishment
   - ○ **B.** paycheck
   - ○ **C.** treat
   - ○ **D.** position

7. the courage to persist
   - ○ **A.** speak
   - ○ **B.** act
   - ○ **C.** continue
   - ○ **D.** quit

Reading Comprehension

Read each story. Then fill in the circle that best completes each sentence or answers each question.

SAMPLE

For centuries, humans have lived in cities. People came to cities to trade goods, to find jobs, and to be near other people. Today, however, experts are asking if cities are still **necessary**. E-mail and the Internet have changed the way people live. They can work from their homes, even if their homes are far from any town. They can shop over the Internet. They can even use the Internet to talk with friends.

1. In this passage, the word **necessary** means
○ **A.** growing.
○ **B.** fun.
○ **C.** needed.
○ **D.** uncertain.

2. This story is mainly about
○ **A.** how to work in a city.
○ **B.** how people talk with friends.
○ **C.** whether or not people still need cities.
○ **D.** what is was like to live in old cities

A. Are you tired of plain-old apples and oranges? Add some spice to your diet by trying tropical fruit! If you look around the supermarket, you'll find flavorful items to give your lunch a whole new twist. Here are some possibilities:

Try a mango. You may already be familiar with mango-flavored food, like candy or ice cream. There's nothing quite like a real mango, however. A fresh ripe mango has sweet orange meat. It's the perfect snack in summer.

There's also the star fruit. Shaped like its name, the star fruit is a special crunchy treat.

The pomelo is another idea. Pomelos are like large grapefruits, but sweeter and drier. Since they don't have too much juice, they're a great fruit to eat when you don't want to get your hands sticky.

If none of these interest you, here are some more **suggestions**: papayas, kumquats, cherimoyas, lychees, or mangosteens.

1. Compared to pomelos, grapefruits are
○ **A.** crunchier.
○ **B.** less sweet.
○ **C.** less juicy.
○ **D.** larger.

2. In this story, the word **suggestions** means
○ **A.** answers.
○ **B.** flavors.
○ **C.** ideas.
○ **D.** vegetables.

Scholastic Professional Books

B. This was a big year for zoos! Many of them opened new attractions.

The San Diego Zoo is famous. Now there's a new reason to visit. It's called Ituri Forest. The forest is modeled after an African river basin. Visitors can watch swimming hippos, otters, and buffalo.

In Philadelphia, the zookeepers built a new home for the gorillas. The gorillas have to share their house. Eleven kinds of animals live there.

The Dallas Zoo was very busy. For starters, they opened the Endangered Tiger area. Tigers roam through an actual rain forest. It's the best place to see big cats. They also have a new hospital. It's 20 times bigger than the old one. It has lots of space to help sick animals.

1. What is the best title for this story?
○ **A.** "Zoos Get Better"
○ **B.** "See the Swimming Hippos"
○ **C.** "Tigers in the Zoo"
○ **D.** "The Dallas Zoo Hospital"

2. Which of these is an *opinion*?
○ **A.** Visitors can watch swimming hippos.
○ **B.** It's 20 times bigger than the old one.
○ **C.** It's the best place to see big cats.
○ **D.** The Dallas Zoo opened an Endangered Tiger area.

3. Where can a visitor see tigers roam?
○ **A.** The Philadelphia Zoo
○ **B.** The Dallas Zoo
○ **C.** The San Diego Zoo
○ **D.** Ituri Forest

C. Is there life on other planets? Some scientists think so. They don't expect to find human-like creatures or little green men. If life exists, it's probably tiny bacteria. Discoveries here on Earth have shaped this thinking.

For a long time, scientists thought other planets were too cold for life. Now they've changed their minds. It's because of studies done near the South Pole, one of the coldest places on Earth. They've found bacteria that live in the ice. The bacteria survive in tiny pockets of water.

If there's life near the South Pole, there may be life on cold planets. Mars is one possibility. Europa, a moon of Jupiter, is another. Europa is covered with ice. Beneath the ice, there may be an ocean. Scientists say that this water may support life.

1. Which is the best summary of this article?
○ **A.** Scientists have been studying the South Pole.
○ **B.** Life is found on Mars and Europa.
○ **C.** Scientists think there may be life on other planets.
○ **D.** Europa, an icy moon, may be covered in water.

2. Scientists used to believe that
○ **A.** cold planets could not support life.
○ **B.** little green men lived on other planets.
○ **C.** life could be found on Europa.
○ **D.** life could be found on Mars.

3. Scientists changed their mind about life on other planets because
○ **A.** Mars and Europa are not very cold.
○ **B.** of voyages to other planets.
○ **C.** of studies done here on Earth.
○ **D.** Jupiter's moon is covered in ice.

Scholastic Professional Books

D. "Take your rain gear," Sarah's mom said as Sarah ran out the door to catch her ride. "Don't need it," Sarah yelled back. "It's a beautiful day."

In fact, it was a little bit cloudy, but the sun was out. The nature walk was only supposed to take two hours. Sarah was sure that the weather wouldn't change that quickly. As Sarah and her troop walked through the woods, the sky **became** dark and gray. As they marched up the hill toward Skinner's Lake, the wind howled. "I'm glad I brought my poncho," said Shawn. "You never know around here; the weather can change in a second."

Sarah glared at him. "What do you know? It's a beautiful day, Shawn."

"I agree," he replied. "A beautiful day for a thunderstorm."

I. How does Sarah seem to feel toward Shawn?
○ **A.** friendly   ○ **C.** worried about
○ **B.** annoyed   ○ **D.** sorry for

2. In this story, the word **became** means
○ **A.** grew.   ○ **C.** sounded.
○ **B.** felt.   ○ **D.** was no longer.

3. This story probably goes on to talk about
○ **A.** what Sarah and Shawn ate for lunch.
○ **B.** other nature hikes the troop had taken.
○ **C.** different kinds of insects found in the forest.
○ **D.** whether or not it rained.

E. People in the United States love their ice cream. The average American eats about 47 pints each year. That's almost two hundred scoops of the frozen stuff! There's no doubt about it. We're the biggest ice cream eaters in the world! Who's next? Believe it or not, New Zealand. New Zealanders **consume** about 40 pints a year. Australians are in third place at 32 pints each.

You might think that Canadians would be big ice cream eaters. After all, Canada is right next to the United States. The average Canadian, however, only eats 27 pints. Maybe it's just too cold in Canada to eat that much ice cream.

The top-selling flavor is vanilla. Some call it boring, but people seem to eat it up. Believe it or not, chocolate is only the fifth favorite flavor. It trails fruit flavors, nut flavors, and candy-mix flavors in popularity.

I. Which of these is an *opinion*?
○ **A.** New Zealanders eat 40 pints a year.
○ **B.** Canadians eat 27 pints a year.
○ **C.** It's too cold to eat ice cream in Canada.
○ **D.** The top-selling flavor is vanilla.

2. What is the best title for this story?
○ **A.** "Ice Cream Facts and Figures"
○ **B.** "Chocolate Ice Cream"
○ **C.** "New Zealand Takes Second Place in Ice Cream Race"
○ **D.** "How Much Is a Pint?"

3. After the United States and New Zealand, which country eats the most ice cream?
○ **A.** Canada
○ **B.** Australia
○ **C.** France
○ **D.** Sweden

4. In this story, the word **consume** means
○ **A.** melt.   ○ **C.** make.
○ **B.** eat.   ○ **D.** borrow.

Vocabulary

Synonyms

Read the underlined word in each phrase. Mark the word below it that has the same (or close to the same) meaning.

Sample:

weary legs
- ○ **A.** tired
- ○ **B.** long
- ○ **C.** active
- ○ **D.** jumpy

I. unexpected victory
- ○ **A.** game
- ○ **B.** number
- ○ **C.** loss
- ○ **D.** win

2. soaring through the air
- ○ **A.** falling
- ○ **B.** flying
- ○ **C.** walking
- ○ **D.** blowing

3. family tradition
- ○ **A.** party
- ○ **B.** gathering
- ○ **C.** friend
- ○ **D.** custom

4. giant animal
- ○ **A.** fierce
- ○ **B.** huge
- ○ **C.** tiny
- ○ **D.** hungry

5. early sunset
- ○ **A.** meltdown
- ○ **B.** suntan
- ○ **C.** sunrise
- ○ **D.** sundown

6. a vague idea
- ○ **A.** bad
- ○ **B.** unclear
- ○ **C.** near
- ○ **D.** great

7. an outlandish outfit
- ○ **A.** outgrown
- ○ **B.** handsome
- ○ **C.** silly
- ○ **D.** common

Antonyms

Read the underlined word in each phrase. Mark the word below it that means the opposite or nearly the opposite.

Sample:

walking steadily
- ○ **A.** unevenly
- ○ **B.** quickly
- ○ **C.** slowly
- ○ **D.** normally

I. sure thing
- ○ **A.** tiring
- ○ **B.** uncertain
- ○ **C.** new
- ○ **D.** old

2. airplane takeoff
- ○ **A.** wheel
- ○ **B.** landing
- ○ **C.** ticket
- ○ **D.** flight

3. pleased to meet you
- ○ **A.** lucky
- ○ **B.** surprised
- ○ **C.** happy
- ○ **D.** unhappy

4. wicked ways
- ○ **A.** good
- ○ **B.** smart
- ○ **C.** stout
- ○ **D.** awful

5. thorough search
- ○ **A.** incomplete
- ○ **B.** neat
- ○ **C.** incorrect
- ○ **D.** successful

6. renew the friendship
- ○ **A.** end
- ○ **B.** begin
- ○ **C.** enjoy
- ○ **D.** abuse

7. decline the offer
- ○ **A.** ignore
- ○ **B.** accept
- ○ **C.** debate
- ○ **D.** consider

Scholastic Professional Books

Reading Comprehension

Read each story. Then fill in the circle that best completes each sentence or answers each question.

SAMPLE

Are you letting too much water go down the drain in your house? We all know that it's important not to waste water. But most of us use a lot more water than we think. Try these two simple ways to cut your water **consumption.** First, try taking a shower instead of a bath. Showers use a lot less water. You should also turn off the tap while you brush your teeth. Turn it on again to rinse.

1. A good title for this story would be
  ○ **A.** "How to Brush Your Teeth."
  ○ **B.** "Saving Water."
  ○ **C.** "Shower Power."
  ○ **D.** "The World of Water."

2. In this story the word **consumption** means
  ○ **A.** running.   ○ **B.** bill.
  ○ **C.** action.   ○ **D.** use.

A.　Something is happening to kids in the United States today. They are getting more and more out of shape. Why? Today's kids exercise less.

　　Many of them don't spend enough time playing sports and games outside. Instead, they sit inside watching TV or using the computer. This can be bad for their health. It's important to exercise. Exercise helps keep your body running smoothly.

　　Besides, exercise is fun. Playing a sport with other people is much more exciting than watching a TV show alone. So get off that couch and go outside. Join a soccer game or play hide-and-seek. Your body will thank you!

1. According to the story, why are today's kids out of shape?
  ○ **A.** They don't exercise enough.
  ○ **B.** They don't watch enough TV.
  ○ **C.** They play too many sports.
  ○ **D.** They don't eat well.

2. The purpose of this story is to
  ○ **A.** inform you that computers are bad.
  ○ **B.** entertain you with fun and games.
  ○ **C.** inform you that kids today are in good shape.
  ○ **D.** persuade you that it's important to exercise.

3. Which of these is an *opinion*?
  ○ **A.** Many kids today are out of shape.
  ○ **B.** Not exercising can be bad for your health.
  ○ **C.** Exercise is fun.
  ○ **D.** Exercise is good for you.

B. STELLA: I wish I knew what to do for that art project about my neighborhood.

TYRONE: I'm making a collage. I'm going to put in pictures of my neighbors and their homes.

STELLA: That's a great idea. But I don't have any neighbors. In fact, I don't really have a neighborhood. That's why I'm having such a hard time.

TYRONE: How can you not have neighbors or a neighborhood?

STELLA: I live out in the country.

TYRONE: Do you have wild animals where you live?

STELLA: Some. We have raccoons and deer.

TYRONE: Well then, those are your neighbors.

I. Why doesn't Stella think she has neighbors?
○ **A.** She lives alone.
○ **B.** She lives in the country.
○ **C.** She lives with too many animals.
○ **D.** She doesn't live near Tyrone.

2. According to the play, which of the following is probably true?
○ **A.** Tyrone lives in the city.
○ **B.** Tyrone lives in the country.
○ **C.** Stella and Tyrone are neighbors.
○ **D.** Stella and Tyrone go to different schools.

3. What How are Stella and Tyrone different?
○ **A.** One lives in the country and the other doesn't.
○ **B.** One has an art project and the other doesn't.
○ **C.** One is a raccoon and the other is a deer.
○ **D.** One hates animals and the other one loves them.

4. What is Tyrone making?
○ **A.** a painting
○ **B.** a photograph
○ **C.** a painting
○ **D.** a collage

C. Do you think a supermarket is only for shopping? Well, think again. In fact, it's a good place to practice your reading skills. Try reading food labels. They're full of information. A label can tell you a lot about what you're eating.

For instance, a label will tell you the ingredients, or what's in the food. The ingredients are listed from greatest to least amounts. Is sugar first or second on the ingredient list? That means the food has a lot of it.

Labels can also tell you how many calories a serving of food has. But be sure to also look at the serving size. A serving of your favorite cookies may have 100 calories. But the serving size may only be one cookie. If you eat four, you're eating 400 calories!

I. If a food has a lot of sugar, where will it be listed on the ingredient list?
○ **A.** at the beginning
○ **B.** at the end
○ **C.** in the middle
○ **D.** nowhere

2. Why is it important to know a food's serving size?
○ **A.** to know how much it costs
○ **B.** to know how much to serve others
○ **C.** to know how many calories are in what you eat.
○ **D.** to know what the food's main ingredients are.

3. This story will probably go on to talk about
○ **A.** more foods that are 100 calories a serving.
○ **B.** popular food ingredients.
○ **C.** people's favorite cookies.
○ **D.** other information available on food labels.

4. What can labels tell you about a food?
○ **A.** the size of a serving
○ **B.** the number of calories in a serving
○ **C.** the ingredients in a food
○ **D.** all of the above

Scholastic Professional Books

D. You're eating pizza at the mall. A friend starts to choke. She is coughing and gasping for air. She can't speak. Would you know what to do?

Carlos Barbosa Jr. did. He performed a lifesaving action called the Heimlich maneuver when he was only 7 years old. He did it after his dad began to choke on some baby carrots.

"I got behind my father and gave his stomach two squeezes," Carlos said. "The carrot popped out of his mouth and flew across the room."

Dr. Henry Heimlich, an Ohio surgeon, developed the Heimlich maneuver 25 years ago. It **dislodges** food that gets stuck in the throat and blocks breathing and speaking. Pressing the stomach forces air out of the lungs. This creates an artificial cough. The rush of air from the cough pushes out the food.

I. What is the Heimlich maneuver?
   ○ **A.** a lifesaving action
   ○ **B.** a way of eating
   ○ **C.** a deathly action
   ○ **D.** a way of choking

2. What happened after Carlos squeezed his dad's stomach?
   ○ **A.** His dad began to choke.
   ○ **B.** His dad began to laugh.
   ○ **C.** Pizza popped out of his dad's mouth.
   ○ **D.** A carrot popped out of his dad's mouth.

3. In this story the word **dislodges** means
   ○ **A.** removes.   ○ **C.** squeezes
   ○ **B.** chokes..   ○ **D.** clogs.

4. From this story you can conclude that
   ○ **A.** people choke all the time.
   ○ **B.** Carlos's dad shouldn't eat carrots.
   ○ **C.** the Heimlich maneuver saves lives.
   ○ **D.** it's dangerous to eat pizza.

E. The movie audience holds its breath. A kid is splashing around in the warm ocean. Suddenly, a shark's fin breaks the surface. It's heading for the unsuspecting swimmer. The background music rises. And then? The kid escapes. And the audience leaves the movie the same way it came in, believing that sharks are evil, people-eating creatures.

The truth is that sharks are neither our enemies nor our friends. Sharks live in every part of the world's oceans, from warm, shallow waters to the darkest depths. They are not evil. But they are fierce **predators.**

In fact, one of the most amazing sights in nature is to watch a shark hunt its prey. First, the shark cruises slowly. When it has its target in sight, it explodes into action. It charges and attacks. Yikes! No wonder sharks have the reputation they do.

But whatever people think of sharks, they must learn to live with these marine creatures.

I. What happens first when a shark hunts?
   ○ **A.** It cruises slowly.
   ○ **B.** It explodes into action.
   ○ **C.** It charges.
   ○ **D.** It attacks.

2. What is the best title for this story?
   ○ **A.** "Scary Scary Sharks"
   ○ **B.** "The Truth About Sharks"
   ○ **C.** "Where Sharks Live"
   ○ **D.** "Good Shark Movies"

3. Which of these is <u>not</u> true about sharks?
   ○ **A.** They live in every part of the ocean.
   ○ **B.** They are good hunters.
   ○ **C.** They are evil.
   ○ **D.** They have fins.

4. In this story, the word **predators** means
   ○ **A.** hunters.   ○ **C.** swimmers.
   ○ **B.** monsters.   ○ **D.** divers.

Vocabulary

Synonyms

Read the underlined word in each phrase. Mark the word below it that has the same (or close to the same) meaning.

Sample:

adore her
- A. help
- B. harm
- C. love
- D. hate

1. herd of cattle
   - A. sheep
   - B. goats
   - C. horses
   - D. cows

2. gang of people
   - A. group
   - B. party
   - C. crowd
   - D. lack

3. with all his might
   - A. will
   - B. money
   - C. strength
   - D. desire

4. squeal with joy
   - A. cry
   - B. squeak
   - C. fill
   - D. dance

5. boundless energy
   - A. unlimited
   - B. violent
   - C. bright
   - D. silly

6. wool and cotton blend
   - A. fabric
   - B. material
   - C. mix
   - D. layer

7. resemble him
   - A. look like
   - B. resent
   - C. hate
   - D. watch

Antonyms

Read the underlined word in each phrase. Mark the word below it that means the opposite or nearly the opposite.

Sample:

swift runner
- A. slow
- B. fast
- C. front
- D. small

1. weak arms
   - A. thin
   - B. fat
   - C. strong
   - D. soft

2. busy highway
   - A. active
   - B. quiet
   - C. large
   - D. major

3. lean and hungry
   - A. good
   - B. thin
   - C. bad
   - D. fat

4. flunk the test
   - A. fail
   - B. take
   - C. miss
   - D. pass

5. very ordinary
   - A. different
   - B. nice
   - C. orderly
   - D. famous

6. adore her
   - A. love
   - B. hate
   - C. like
   - D. dislike

7. wintry day
   - A. cold
   - B. warm
   - C. long
   - D. tiring

Name _____

Reading Comprehension

Read each story. Then fill in the circle that best completes each sentence or answers each question.

SAMPLE

Do you know how to stay safe? The No. 1 safety tip is: Never talk to stangers. When you go out, stick to the safest routes. It's also a good idea to tell a parent or another trusted adult where you'll be. If you're home alone, keep all the doors and windows locked.

I. The No. 1 safety tip is
○ **A.** keep doors and windows locked.
○ **B.** stick to the safest routes.
○ **C.** tell you parents where you'll be.
○ **D.** never talk to strangers.

2. From this story, you can conclude that talking to strangers is
○ **A.** dangerous.
○ **B.** interesting.
○ **C.** fun.
○ **D.** safe.

A. The marine toad looks—and acts—like a creature right out of a horror movie. This fat amphibian from South America weighs three pounds and makes a sound like a chugging tractor. When threatened, it oozes poison.

Now, marine toads are terrorizing Florida. They've moved out of the wilds and into the suburbs, where they eat almost anything—small birds, garbage, garden vegetables. They've even developed a taste for pet food!

So how did this monster from South America get to the Sunshine State? In the 1930s, insects were eating the local sugarcane crop. Marine toads were brought to Florida to gobble up the pests. Now the toads have become pests themselves.

I. Why were marine toads brought to Florida?
○ **A.** to be pets
○ **B.** to eat garbage
○ **C.** to be food for pets
○ **D.** to eat insects

2. What is the best title for this story?
○ **A.** "Insects Damage Crops"
○ **B.** "Horror Movies Are a Scream!"
○ **C.** "How to Grow Sugarcane"
○ **D.** "Toad Solution Becomes a Problem"

3. The next paragraph might talk about
○ **A.** other types of toads.
○ **B.** pets in other countries.
○ **C.** how to solve the marine toad problem.
○ **D.** other crops grown in Florida.

Scholastic Professional Books

B. Who's the biggest athlete in the world? If you're talking size, there's no contest. It's American-born sumo wrestler Salevaa Atisanoe, known in Japan as Konishiki. He tips the scales at 580 pounds.

Sumo wrestling is the national sport of Japan. Thousands of fans attend sumo matches each week. And wrestlers such as Konishiki are treated like movie stars.

What happens at a sumo match? Two sumo wrestlers face each other. There is a lot of pushing and shoving. One wrestler wins when he forces his opponent out of the 15-foot ring, or knocks him to the ground. Each match lasts 20 seconds.

I. What happens first during a sumo match?
- ○ **A.** They push and shove each other.
- ○ **B.** They face each other.
- ○ **C.** One forces the other out of the ring.
- ○ **D.** One knocks the other to the ground.

2. Which is a *fact*?
- ○ **A.** Konishiki is the best sumo wrestler.
- ○ **B.** Sumo wrestling is a fun sport.
- ○ **C.** Sumo wrestlers should be treated better than movie stars.
- ○ **D.** Sumo matches last 20 seconds.

3. Salevaa Atisanoe is also known as
- ○ **A.** Amercia.
- ○ **B.** Konishiki
- ○ **C.** Japan.
- ○ **D.** Sumo.

C. Yellowstone National Park contains some of the most beautiful land in the United States. It has more than 2 million acres of glorious geysers, deep canyons, and vast forests. No wonder it's a top vacation spot.

But many conservationists fear that Yellowstone is becoming a victim of its own success. Increasing numbers of visitors are overcrowding campgrounds and straining park resources. Last year, more than 3 million people packed into the park.

Yellowstone Park may have its problems, but it is also full of success stories—especially for endangered animals like the gray wolf. Thanks to scientists who set up a wolf-breeding program in 1995, gray wolves are roaming free in Yellowstone for the first time in more than 50 years. Wildlife protection laws have also allowed grizzly bears and bison to bounce back from low numbers in recent years.

I. Which of these is an *opinion* about Yellowstone?
- ○ **A.** It has geysers, canyons, and forests.
- ○ **B.** It contains some of the most beautiful land in the United States.
- ○ **C.** Last year, more than 3 million people packed into the park.
- ○ **D.** Gray wolves are roaming free there.

2. How is Yellowstone different now than it was 10 years ago?
- ○ **A.** It has fewer visitors and forests.
- ○ **B.** It's smaller than it was.
- ○ **C.** It has fewer bison and grizzly bears.
- ○ **D.** It has more visitors and gray wolves.

3. The main idea of this story is that
- ○ **A.** Yellowstone Park has both problems and successes.
- ○ **B.** Yellowstone is a top vacation spot.
- ○ **C.** Yellowstone Park contains more than 2 million acres.
- ○ **D.** Gray wolves are endangered.

D. It's important to eat a balanced diet. That means plenty of fresh fruit, vegetables, and grains, but less fat and sugar. A **nutritious** diet helps you feel your best. Then you'll be able to do your best in school and in sports. So say good-bye to fatty cheeseburgers and salty french fries! Say hello to pasta with tomato sauce. What's for dessert? How about some fresh fruit topped with yogurt?

You don't have to change your whole diet overnight. A good way to begin is to try substituting one healthful food for one less healthful food each day. Have your cheeseburger with salad instead of with french fries. The next day, try having oatmeal and fruit for breakfast instead of a sugary cereal. You may be surprised one day to find that you have come to like healthful food as much as the junk food you like now!

I. The main purpose of this story is to
- ○ **A.** scare.
- ○ **B.** persuade.
- ○ **C.** sell food.
- ○ **D.** amuse.

2. In this story, the word **nutritious** means
- ○ **A.** high-fat.
- ○ **B.** unhealthful.
- ○ **C.** sugary.
- ○ **D.** healthful.

3. A good way to begin changing your diet is
- ○ **A.** to eat only candy bars.
- ○ **B.** to eat only healthful food.
- ○ **C.** to eat one healthful food instead of a less healthful food each day.
- ○ **D.** to eat salad at every meal.

4. You can conclude from this story that
- ○ **A.** high-fat foods are less healthful than lower-fat foods.
- ○ **B.** everyone likes bananas.
- ○ **C.** candy bars taste better than apples.
- ○ **D.** you should never eat foods you like.

E. Jim came over for lunch wearing a blue suit with a short brown tie and a green plaid shirt. I couldn't believe this was going to be my new stepfather. It couldn't be true that my beautiful mother would marry someone who dressed like a clown. I hated him.

Lunch was terrible. Mother kept trying to start a conversation, but neither Jim nor I would say much. Finally, I offered to bring in the dessert just to get away from the clown.

I didn't mean to do it. I guess the plate slipped. But one minute I was handing Jim his blackberry pie, and the next, dark purple berries were oozing all over his shirt and tie.

I was **mortified**. My cheeks turned bright red. Jim looked startled at first, but then he began to laugh. I started laughing too. Maybe this guy was all right, after all. Then I glanced at my mother. She looked happier than I had seen her in a long time.

I. In this story the word **mortified** means
- ○ **A.** happy.
- ○ **B.** angry.
- ○ **C.** bored.
- ○ **D.** embarrassed.

2. The narrator thinks Jim's clothes look
- ○ **A.** nice.
- ○ **B.** expensive.
- ○ **C.** ridiculous.
- ○ **D.** old and worn.

3. From the story, you might guess that
- ○ **A.** Jim didn't seem likeable at first.
- ○ **B.** the narrator liked Jim from the start.
- ○ **C.** Jim had no sense of humor.
- ○ **D.** Jim didn't like blackberry pie.

4. What is the best title for this story?
- ○ **A.** "I Love Pie"
- ○ **B.** "My New Stepfather"
- ○ **C.** "The World's Best Lunch"
- ○ **D.** "Mothers Shouldn't Marry"

Vocabulary

In each of the following paragraphs, a word is missing. First, read the paragraph. Then find the missing word in the list of words beneath the paragraph. Fill in the circle next to the word that is missing.

Sample:

Jerome's dad belongs to the neighborhood safety association. Last night, it was his turn to _____ the block. He walked up and down all night, keeping everyone safe.

○ **A.** sweep   ○ **C.** patrol
○ **B.** leave   ○ **D.** study

I. When airplanes were first _____ they were small and relatively slow. However, today's jets can go very fast. Some go faster than the speed of sound!

○ **A.** improved   ○ **C.** searched
○ **B.** repaired   ○ **D.** invented

2. One thing that hasn't changed is the seriousness of a pilot's job. A pilot should never be _____. Doing careless or dangerous things risks lives.

○ **A.** reckless   ○ **C.** energetic
○ **B.** accurate   ○ **D.** strict

3. Passengers are certainly more comfortable than they used to be. Old jet planes were very noisy. People used to wear earplugs to keep out the _____.

○ **A.** filth   ○ **C.** din
○ **B.** music   ○ **D.** moisture

4. Airports have changed too. Passengers used to walk onto the runway when getting on and off the plane. Now, upon _____, the plane parks at a gate that leads right inside the airport.

○ **A.** transportation   ○ **C.** publication
○ **B.** landscape   ○ **D.** arrival

5. Many people would say that having chocolate cake for _____ is a great treat. They can't think of a better way to end dinner.

○ **A.** lunch   ○ **C.** dessert
○ **B.** delightful   ○ **D.** menu

6. It's rare that these people will leave even a _____ of chocolate cake on their plates. They want to eat every bite.

○ **A.** morsel   ○ **C.** mortal
○ **B.** meager   ○ **D.** variety

7. For them, a delicious chocolate cake is absolute _____. Nothing could make it better.

○ **A.** elegant   ○ **C.** keen
○ **B.** perfection   ○ **D.** perilous

8. Chocolate is native to the Americas. Its delightfully _____ smell has been making people's mouths water for a long time.

○ **A.** fragile   ○ **C.** plentiful
○ **B.** fragrant   ○ **D.** vivid

9. Today, a chocolate _____ can produce many different products. A chocolate factory might make candy bars, cocoa powder, chocolate-chip cookies, and lots of other delicious treats.

○ **A.** gourmet   ○ **C.** manufacturer
○ **B.** compound   ○ **D.** provision

Scholastic Professional Books

Reading Comprehension

Read each story. Then fill in the circle that best completes
each sentence or answers each question.

SAMPLE

Have you ever seen someone on the beach with a sunburn? A sunburn can be quite
painful. If the burn is really bad, the skin might blister and peel. Sunburn is caused by the
sun's powerful ultraviolet (UV) rays. Wearing sunscreen can **shield** your skin from those
damaging rays.

1. What is the main idea of this story?
○ **A.** Ultraviolet rays cause sunburn.
○ **B.** Sunburn can cause fever.
○ **C.** Sunscreen makes skin peel.
○ **D.** The sun is strong at the beach.

2. In this story, the word **shield** means
○ **A.** burn.
○ **B.** lift.
○ **C.** protect.
○ **D.** open.

A. For thousands of years, the Inuit people
have lived in what is now the northwest part
of Canada. For the last 150 years, the
Canadian government has ruled the land.
Recently, the government has agreed to let the
Inuit **govern** part of Canada's Northwest
Territory.

Since April 1, 1999, the Canadian map
has included the land of Nunavut, which
means "our land" in Inuktitut, the Inuit
language. The Inuit want control of this land
because it is the land of their ancestors. They
plan to set up their own government.

1. In this story, the word **govern** means
○ **A.** build.
○ **B.** rule.
○ **C.** map.
○ **D.** live.

2. The Inuit language is called
○ **A.** Canadian.   ○ **C.** Nunavut.
○ **B.** Inuktitut.   ○ **D.** Inuit.

3. You can guess from the story that
○ **A.** Canada's government once took
over Inuit land.
○ **B.** Canada's government is unfair.
○ **C.** the Inuit cannot speak English.
○ **D.** many Canadian people will soon be
homeless.

4. Which would come first on a time line?
○ **A.** The Inuit make a deal with
Canada's government.
○ **B.** The Canadian government begins
ruling the Inuit's land.
○ **C.** The Inuit settle in Canada.
○ **D.** Nunavut appears on a map.

Scholastic Professional Books

B. Animals depend on plants and other animals for food. The relationship among these animals and plants is called a food chain. The food chain keeps nature in balance. Here's how it works:

1. Producers: Plants and other organisms that provide food for animals make up the first link in a food chain.

2. Herbivores: These are animals that eat only plants. Called "prey," they are hunted by meat eaters.

3. Carnivores: These meat eaters feed on herbivores. They are also called "predators." When they die, their remains fertilize the ground and help plants grow.

I. What is the best title for this story?
○ **A.** "Plant-Eating Animals"
○ **B.** "Understanding the Food Chain"
○ **C.** "Predators"
○ **D.** "Plants That Need Animals"

2. Animals that eat meat are called
○ **A.** herbivores.　　○ **C.** prey.
○ **B.** producers.　　○ **D.** carnivores.

3. You can guess from this story that
○ **A.** herbivores are hungrier than carnivores.
○ **B.** herbivores are small animals.
○ **C.** carnivores eat lots of vegetables.
○ **D.** each link in the food chain is important.

C. In Greek mythology, Zeus and Hera were the leaders of the Greek gods. They were husband and wife, and Hera sometimes became angry with Zeus when he spent too much time away from home.

Sometimes, Zeus went to the mountains to play with the forest creatures who lived there. Hera always chased after him because she thought Zeus was wasting time. But every time, a charming creature named Echo chatted with Hera and distracted her until Zeus had escaped.

When Hera figured out that Echo had been tricking her, she was **furious**. "Your talk has made a fool of me!" she screamed. "From now on you will have nothing to say, except what others say to you first!"

From that day on, poor Echo could only repeat the last words of what others said.

I. This story is mostly about
○ **A.** Greek gods.　　○ **C.** Greece.
○ **B.** forests.　　　○ **D.** tricks.

2. You can guess from this story that
○ **A.** Zeus was tall and handsome.
○ **B.** Echo had a loud voice.
○ **C.** Hera was very gentle.
○ **D.** Echo lived in the forest.

3. In this story, the word **furious** means
○ **A.** angry.　　　○ **C.** happy.
○ **B.** foolish.　　 ○ **D.** tricky.

4. Zeus and Hera were
○ **A.** soldiers.　　○ **C.** forest creatures.
○ **B.** married.　　 ○ **D.** human.

5. This story is an example of a
○ **A.** myth.　　　○ **C.** news article.
○ **B.** poem.　　　○ **D.** fairy tale.

Scholastic Professional Books

D. When you play a sport, do you feel that you must win—or else? The Youth Sports Institute in Michigan surveyed 26,000 boys and girls on this topic, and found that many feel pushed to be the best.

Where does the pressure come from? Some kids put pressure on themselves, but many say that parents and coaches are also to blame. They say these adults care only about the final score—not whether kids tried hard or had a good time.

I. What is the main idea of this article?
   ○ **A.** Fewer kids should play baseball.
   ○ **B.** Youth sports are always fun.
   ○ **C.** Many kids feel a lot of pressure to win at sports.
   ○ **D.** Parents should be banned from going to kids' games

2. Which of these statements is a *fact*?
   ○ **A.** Sports pressure is the worst part of kids' sports.
   ○ **B.** The Youth Sports Institute surveyed 26,000 kids.
   ○ **C.** Winning is important.
   ○ **D.** Coaches should not be allowed to pressure players.

3. The author wrote this article to
   ○ **A.** tell why baseball is good exercise.
   ○ **B.** tell kids to quit playing sports.
   ○ **C.** tell about the history of youth sports.
   ○ **D.** tell about a problem in youth sports.

4. The article probably goes on to talk about
   ○ **A.** solving the problem of sports pressure.
   ○ **B.** baseball training camps for kids.
   ○ **C.** ways for teams to win more games.
   ○ **D.** youth football programs.

E. In 1844, young Elizabeth Blackwell dreamed of becoming a doctor. There was just one problem: No medical school in the U.S. would accept a woman as a student. Blackwell convinced several doctors to teach her privately. Then, in 1847, she was accepted by a small college in New York. She graduated at the top of her class.

Blackwell traveled to Paris, France, where she studied at a hospital. Even after losing her sight in one eye, Blackwell did not give up her work as a doctor. In the 1850s, she returned to the U.S. and **established** a hospital for women and children. Today, we remember Elizabeth Blackwell as the trailblazer who opened the field of medicine for women in America.

I. In this story, the word **established** means
   ○ **A.** set up.   ○ **C.** named.
   ○ **B.** cured.   ○ **D.** lost.

2. What is the best title for this story?
   ○ **A.** "Elizabeth Blackwell: Opening College Doors"
   ○ **B.** "Elizabeth Blackwell: First Woman Doctor"
   ○ **C.** "The Autobiography of Elizabeth Blackwell"
   ○ **D.** "Famous Doctors in History"

3. Which of these is an *opinion*?
   ○ **A.** Blackwell lost sight in one eye.
   ○ **B.** Blackwell became a doctor.
   ○ **C.** Blackwell lived in the 1800s.
   ○ **D.** Blackwell was very brave.

4. You can guess from this story that Elizabeth Blackwell
   ○ **A.** got good grades in college.
   ○ **B.** had French parents.
   ○ **C.** eventually became totally blind.
   ○ **D.** died in 1860.

Name _____

Vocabulary

In each of the following paragraphs, a word is missing. First, read the paragraph. Then find the missing word in the list of words beneath the paragraph. Fill in the circle next to the word that is missing.

Sample:

The car suddenly stopped in the middle of the road. It had run out of ____. The driver had forgotten to fill up the gas tank.

- ○ **A.** miles
- ○ **B.** fuel
- ○ **C.** water
- ○ **D.** popcorn

The driver was late for his soccer game. That was too bad, because he was the best ____ on his team. His teammates counted on him to stop the other team from scoring.

- ○ **A.** coach
- ○ **B.** goalie
- ○ **C.** gardener
- ○ **D.** catcher

1. Some really large animals live on the plains of Africa. You might think the biggest ones would be the mightiest hunters, but that's not the case at all. Some of the world's biggest animals eat nothing but leaves, grasses, and shrubs. Instead of hunting other animals, these huge creatures ____ on plant life to survive.

- ○ **A.** dwell
- ○ **B.** sit
- ○ **C.** grow
- ○ **D.** graze

2. The largest plant eater of all is the African elephant. In fact, the African elephant is the largest land ____ in the entire world! An adult elephant can weigh as much as 12,000 pounds. And a baby elephant is not exactly tiny: It can weigh up to 250 pounds at birth!

- ○ **A.** shark
- ○ **B.** soil
- ○ **C.** mammal
- ○ **D.** farmer

3. Another very large African plant eater is the white rhinoceros. It is second in size only to the elephant. The adult white rhino can weigh up to 5,000 pounds, or two-and-a-half ____.

- ○ **A.** dollars
- ○ **B.** tons
- ○ **C.** ounces
- ○ **D.** feet

4. The black rhino is a ____ of the white rhino. Although the two are kin, the black rhino doesn't get nearly as large. At 3,000 pounds, though, the adult black rhino is still pretty big. Both rhinos are very good at using their horns to break off tree branches for dinner.

- ○ **A.** relative
- ○ **B.** neighbor
- ○ **C.** friend
- ○ **D.** killer

5. A somewhat smaller African plant eater is the hippopotamus. At 700 pounds, the adult hippo seems almost ____ compared with an elephant or a rhino—but you'd still feel pretty small standing next to one! A hippo has teeth about 20 inches long. They are excellent tools for munching coarse plants.

- ○ **A.** giant
- ○ **B.** desperate
- ○ **C.** dainty
- ○ **D.** loyal

6. The hippo's teeth also come in handy for fighting off crocodiles. That's important, because hippos spend lots of time in rivers, where crocs live. Hippos have sensitive skin that can easily get too dry. They hang out in the river to keep their skin ____.

- ○ **A.** nasty
- ○ **B.** moist
- ○ **C.** brown
- ○ **D.** clean

Reading Comprehension

Read each story. Then fill in the circle that best completes each sentence or answers each question.

SAMPLE

During a 1992 storm, a ship lost thousands of plastic turtles, frogs, and ducks in the Pacific Ocean. Since then, the toys have drifted thousands of miles. Some have shown up in the ocean off of Alaska. The toys' trip helps scientists study how wind affects drifting objects.

1. A good title for this story would be
 ○ **A.** "Drifting Toys."
 ○ **B.** "The Great State of Alaska."
 ○ **C.** "The Big Storm."
 ○ **D.** "Turtles in the Sea."

2. Scientists study the toys to find out about
 ○ **A.** how turtles swim.
 ○ **B.** how wind affects drifting objects.
 ○ **C.** how far it is from Russia to Alaska.
 ○ **D.** how ducks find food.

A. Ten-year-old Caitlin Gionfriddo makes money in a funny way. She chews Gummi Worms, tastes peanut butter, and chomps on chocolate.

Caitlin has more than a big appetite. The fifth-grader from Cincinnati, Ohio, helps companies dream up new flavors, names, and colors for their products.

"When kids design things, it's what kids want, not what adults want," says Caitlin.

To understand what kids want, companies need to think like kids. So they hire them. For instance, when Curad was looking for a new kid bandage design, they went straight to the experts. They asked 25 kids what they wanted to put on their cuts and bruises. The kids came up with ideas for fun bandages. Then a cartoonist sketched the ideas. The winner? Tattoo bandages.

1. Why did Curad hire 25 kids?
 ○ **A.** They wanted them to taste Gummi Bears.
 ○ **B.** They wanted them to taste chocolate.
 ○ **C.** They wanted them to help design a new bandage.
 ○ **D.** They wanted them to help design a new toy.

2. The main purpose of this story is to
 ○ **A.** inform you about why companies hire kids.
 ○ **B.** persuade you to eat more peanut butter.
 ○ **C.** amuse you with details about Caitlin's life.
 ○ **D.** explain how bandages are designed.

3. You can conclude from this story that
 ○ **A.** Companies don't care what kids think.
 ○ **B.** Caitlin really hates what she does.
 ○ **C.** Companies are out of touch with today's kids.
 ○ **D.** Products designed for kids are important to companies.

B. Tiny ocean **creatures** with horse-shaped heads may seem like characters from a fairy tale. But sea horses are real. And, they're in real danger.

The World Conservation Union, a group that protects nature, has said that sea horses are in danger of becoming extinct. That means that soon there may be no more sea horses left in the world's oceans.

Sea horses are curly-tailed fish. They are usually no more than a few inches long. Though small, they're in big demand. Some people collect the odd-looking fish. Others eat them. They're also used in Chinese cures for skin diseases and other illnesses.

Fishermen from Florida to the Philippines support their families by selling sea horses. But overfishing causes the loss of at least 20 million sea horses each year. If something isn't done, the only horses on the planet will be the ones left on dry land.

I. What is the best title for this story?
○ **A.** "All Kinds of Horses"
○ **B.** "Disappearing Sea Horses"
○ **C.** "What To Do with Sea Horses"
○ **D.** "Fishing Around the World"

2. In this story, the word **creatures** means
○ **A.** animals.
○ **B.** plants.
○ **C.** boats.
○ **D.** waves.

3. Why are sea horses disappearing?
○ **A.** They are being eaten by other fish.
○ **B.** They are being overfished.
○ **C.** They are too small to survive in the ocean.
○ **D.** They are suffering from a disease.

C. Students in the city of Houston, Texas, are climbing the walls. They're not bored. They're working out!

These days, sports like rock climbing are hot in gym class. Hundreds of physical education programs across the country now offer students all sorts of sports. In-line skating, aerobics, mountain biking, and hiking top the list.

According to the experts, kids ages 4 to 12 should exercise for 60 minutes or more each day. But kids won't exercise if they don't enjoy it. So physical education teachers have found new ways to make exercise fun. For some kids, this means harder and more exciting sports, like rock climbing. For others, it means making activities less competitive. One teacher replaced her school's 1-mile run with a 12-minute run. That way, everyone finishes at the same time. Even slow runners can enjoy themselves.

I. According to the story, how long should kids exercise each day?
○ **A.** 12 minutes
○ **B.** 4 minutes
○ **C.** 60 minutes
○ **D.** 30 minutes

2. What is the best title for this story?
○ **A.** "Gym Is Great"
○ **B.** "A New Kind of Gym Class"
○ **C.** "Dodge Ball"
○ **D.** "Rainy Day Activities"

3. From this story, you can guess that
○ **A.** it's important to exercise.
○ **B.** it's important to be good at sports.
○ **C.** gym classes are boring.
○ **D.** most schools don't have gym classes.

D. Stop. Extreme danger. Access strictly **prohibited**. These warnings greet scientist Tim Dixon as he goes to work each day. Dixon works on El Popocatépetl (Poh-poh-kah-tep-eh-tuhl). El Popo, as it's known, is one of the most dangerous volcanoes in the world.

Dixon is putting special equipment on the Mexican volcano. He hopes the equipment will help scientists predict future eruptions. He has already discovered how surprising El Popo can be. "We were up there when, without warning, there was a large blast," he says. "We felt the shock waves hit us. Then, we saw red-hot pieces of rock falling down." But Dixon was fortunate. The eruption was small. It only lasted a few minutes. He wasn't hurt.

El Popo's last big eruption was 1,200 years ago. It killed many people. Dixon and other scientists want to make sure it doesn't happen again. They hope that before the next big eruption, there will be time to warn people.

1. What happened after Dixon felt shock waves on El Popo?
- ○ **A.** Red-hot pieces of rock fell down.
- ○ **B.** Many people were killed.
- ○ **C.** There was a large blast.
- ○ **D.** Dixon's equipment was ruined.

2. In this story, the word **prohibited** means
- ○ **A.** special
- ○ **B.** expensive
- ○ **C.** not watched
- ○ **D.** not allowed

3. Why is Dixon putting special equipment on El Popo?
- ○ **A.** He wants to keep it from erupting.
- ○ **B.** He wants to collect some red-hot rocks.
- ○ **C.** He wants to make it erupt more often.
- ○ **D.** He wants to predict future eruptions.

E. How does getting lowered into the ground by your ankles sound? That's what one worker had to do to reach three ancient mummies in Argentina. It was worth it, though. The mummies were in "near-perfect" condition. Now scientists want to use them to learn about the past.

The mummies are the remains of three kids who died 500 years ago. They were buried under dirt and rock on top of a volcano. There are two girls and a boy. It's hard to tell the exact age of a mummy, but scientists know that the kids were between 8 and 15 years old when they died. No one is certain how they died.

Scientists hope the mummies will help them learn more about the Inca civilization. The Inca were an ancient South American people. They had a huge empire that lasted over 100 years. The mummies may reveal new information about the Inca.

1. Which of these is an *opinion*?
- ○ **A.** There are two girls and a boy.
- ○ **B.** It was worth it, though.
- ○ **C.** No one is certain how they died.
- ○ **D.** The Inca were an ancient South American people.

2. Which is the best title for this story?
- ○ **A.** "The Ancient Inca"
- ○ **B.** "Three New Mummies"
- ○ **C.** "How Mummies Are Made"
- ○ **D.** "Volcanoes in Argentina"

3. According to the story, why are the mummies important?
- ○ **A.** They are in "near-perfect" condition.
- ○ **B.** They are very young.
- ○ **C.** Scientists don't know how they died.
- ○ **D.** Scientists can use them to learn more about the Inca.

Vocabulary

Synonyms

Read the underlined word in each phrase.
Mark the word below it that has the same
(or close to the same) meaning.

Sample:

tilt the picture
- ○ **A.** straighten
- ○ **B.** turn
- ○ **C.** hang
- ○ **D.** frame

I. building site
- ○ **A.** place
- ○ **B.** time
- ○ **C.** event
- ○ **D.** window

2. stout person
- ○ **A.** skinny
- ○ **B.** heavy
- ○ **C.** loud
- ○ **D.** small

3. big victory
- ○ **A.** loss
- ○ **B.** win
- ○ **C.** smile
- ○ **D.** frown

4. uncover the truth
- ○ **A.** hide
- ○ **B.** find out
- ○ **C.** cover up
- ○ **D.** change

5. solemn face
- ○ **A.** smiling
- ○ **B.** happy
- ○ **C.** unhappy
- ○ **D.** serious

6. shield your face
- ○ **A.** protect
- ○ **B.** hide
- ○ **C.** wipe
- ○ **D.** hurt

7. startled expression
- ○ **A.** puzzled
- ○ **B.** surprised
- ○ **C.** unhappy
- ○ **D.** bothered

Antonyms

Read the underlined word in each phrase.
Mark the word below it that means the
opposite or nearly the opposite.

Sample:

unkind words
- ○ **A.** mean
- ○ **B.** nice
- ○ **C.** angry
- ○ **D.** funny

I. bright room
- ○ **A.** dim
- ○ **B.** loud
- ○ **C.** large
- ○ **D.** airy

2. thorough cleaning
- ○ **A.** detailed
- ○ **B.** careful
- ○ **C.** careless
- ○ **D.** yearly

3. tremendous force
- ○ **A.** great
- ○ **B.** very little
- ○ **C.** scary
- ○ **D.** unbelievable

4. unfriendly people
- ○ **A.** mean
- ○ **B.** kind
- ○ **C.** strange
- ○ **D.** unfamiliar

5. terrible time
- ○ **A.** happy
- ○ **B.** great
- ○ **C.** boring
- ○ **D.** surprising

6. ancient treasure
- ○ **A.** sunken
- ○ **B.** gold
- ○ **C.** new
- ○ **D.** expensive

7. graceful dancer
- ○ **A.** clumsy
- ○ **B.** ballet
- ○ **C.** light
- ○ **D.** young

Reading Comprehension

Read each story. Then fill in the circle that best completes each sentence or answers each question.

SAMPLE

The Canadian province of Manitoba has a rather snaky reputation. That's because thousands and thousands of red-sided garter snakes gather there every winter. Most snakes can't live as far north as Manitoba. The winters are just too cold. But red-sided garter snakes have a way of keeping warm. Every year they slither into an area in central Manitoba. There they pack themselves into underground dens. One den might hold more than 20,000 snakes!

I. What is the best title for this story?
○ **A.** "All About Manitoba"
○ **B.** "All About Snakes"
○ **C.** "Winter in the Far North"
○ **D.** "Red-Sided Garter Snakes"

2. Why can't most snakes live in the far north?
○ **A.** The winters are too cold.
○ **B.** There aren't enough underground dens.
○ **C.** The red-sided garters attack other snakes.
○ **D.** They are not allowed into Manitoba.

A. On May 13, 1607, colonists from England landed their boats on an island that is now part of Virginia. They built a settlement there. They called it Fort James—and later Jamestown—in honor of the king of England.

Life in Jamestown was difficult. The settlers suffered from disease and hunger. The winters were very cold. **Disputes** with neighboring settlements made life in Jamestown dangerous. Many people died. But the survivors did not give up. When their fort burned down, they rebuilt it and made it larger. The colonists stayed in Jamestown for almost 100 years.

I. What happened first?
○ **A.** The colonists built Fort James.
○ **B.** The colonists died from disease and hunger.
○ **C.** The colonists rebuilt Fort James after it burned down.
○ **D.** The colonists landed on an island.

2. In this story, the word **disputes** means
○ **A.** ceremonies.   ○ **C.** illnesses.
○ **B.** fights.   ○ **D.** discussions.

3. What is the main idea of this story?
○ **A.** Life in Jamestown was difficult.
○ **B.** The colonists rebuilt the fort that burned down.
○ **C.** Winters in Jamestown were very cold.
○ **D.** The settlers died from disease and hunger.

Scholastic Professional Books

B. Everyone knows that salads are delicious and good for you. But making a salad can seem tricky to some people. How do you make a good salad? Just follow these tips:

- Always dry your lettuce or spinach after washing it. Salad dressing won't stick to wet leaves.
- Just lettuce and tomatoes make an okay salad. But why not perk it up with some other vegetables? Try carrots, cucumbers, or mushrooms.
- Try adding a can of beans to your salad. They're tasty, and they make the salad even more nutritious.
- Go easy on the salad dressing. It should complement the taste of the vegetables, not **conceal** it.

I. What is one reason it's good to add beans to salad?
○ **A.** Salad dressing sticks to them.
○ **B.** Salad isn't tasty without them.
○ **C.** They make salad more nutritious.
○ **D.** They hide the taste of salad dressing.

2. In this story, the word **conceal** means
○ **A.** hide.
○ **B.** reveal.
○ **C.** control.
○ **D.** close.

3. What is the best title for this story?
○ **A.** "Salad-Making Tips"
○ **B.** "How to Wash Lettuce"
○ **C.** "How to Make Salad Dressing"
○ **D.** "Why Salad Is Good for You"

C. Imagine the most famous person you know of. Michael Jordan. Britney Spears. Prince William. Now think of this: Not one of them is as famous as Helen Keller was in her day.

When she was a baby, Helen Keller became blind and deaf because of an illness. Helen's family didn't think she would ever learn to communicate well. But they didn't count on Helen's teacher, Annie Sullivan. Annie taught Helen to speak and to communicate through sign language. She also taught Helen to read and write Braille, an alphabet system used by blind people. Annie made the world open up for Helen.

Word of Helen's learning spread quickly. She became famous, and people all over the country wanted to meet her. Helen went on to graduate from college, travel the world, and write 13 books. When she died, at the age of 87, she had become one of America's great heroes.

I. Why did Helen Keller become so famous?
○ **A.** She was a famous author.
○ **B.** She was Annie Sullivan's student.
○ **C.** She did not let disabilities stop her from achieving her goals.
○ **D.** She met famous people and traveled the world.

2. What would Helen's life have been like without Annie Sullivan?
○ **A.** She may not ever have been able to communicate.
○ **B.** She would have been famous anyway.
○ **C.** Her parents would have taught her to read and write.
○ **D.** She would have grown up like any other kid.

3. Which of these is the best comparison for how Annie Sullivan changed Helen's life?
○ **A.** a car crashing
○ **B.** a bubble bursting
○ **C.** a rock falling
○ **D.** a flower opening

D. Mariel didn't see the new girl coming toward her on the sidewalk until it was too late. She bumped right into the girl, sending books flying everywhere.

"Oh excuse me!" she cried. "I'm so sorry. I didn't see you!"

The new girl smiled. "That's okay. I didn't see you either. I'm Shamala. What's your name?"

"I'm Mariel. Where did your family move here from?"

"We came from Chicago. But before that we lived in Houston. And before that we lived in Santa Ana. And I was born in India, so I guess we lived there too, but I was too young to remember."

"Wow, you've lived in a lot of places. I've lived here in the same house all my life. You're really lucky."

Shamala laughed. "That's funny. I was just thinking that you're the lucky one!"

I. Why did Mariel bump into Shamala?
  ○ **A.** She didn't like Shamala.
  ○ **B.** Shamala was new.
  ○ **C.** She didn't see Shamala coming.
  ○ **D.** Shamala had lived in a lot of places.

2. How are Mariel and Shamala alike?
  ○ **A.** They are both new in the neighborhood.
  ○ **B.** They have both lived in a lot of places.
  ○ **C.** They are both unfriendly.
  ○ **D.** They both envy the other one's life.

3. What is most likely to happen next in this story?
  ○ **A.** Mariel and Shamala never see each other again.
  ○ **B.** Mariel and Shamala become friends.
  ○ **C.** Mariel's family moves.
  ○ **D.** Mariel and Shamala become enemies.

E. The year is 1912. The day is April 10. The *Titanic* sets sail from England. The enormous ship is three football fields long. Eleven stories high, it is the largest moving object ever built. The ship has elegant restaurants, a swimming pool, and indoor gardens. Some of the world's richest people stroll through its fine rooms. No one seeing it at this moment would guess that tragedy lies ahead.

It is the ship's first voyage. This floating palace is bound for New York City. The crew intends to set a record getting there. The *Titanic* is the most powerful ship on the sea, brags its builder. There is nothing to fear. Let other ships' crews worry about iceberg warnings. Other ships aren't the *Titanic*. The *Titanic* is **unsinkable**.

Sadly, pride goes before the fall. Around midnight on April 14, 1912, a massive iceberg rips open the mighty ship's steel hull. Tons of water gush in. For the *Titanic*, the end has come.

I. In this story the word **unsinkable** means
  ○ **A.** luxurious.   ○ **B.** large.
  ○ **C.** heavy.   ○ **D.** buoyant.

2. The *Titanic* was
  ○ **A.** made of stone, just like a palace.
  ○ **B.** filled with luxuries such as swimming pools and gardens.
  ○ **C.** a large restaurant that had been fitted to float.
  ○ **D.** just like every other ship of the time.

3. Which adjective best describes the *Titanic's* builder?
  ○ **A.** excited
  ○ **B.** modest
  ○ **C.** proud
  ○ **D.** deceitful

4. What is the purpose of this story?
  ○ **A.** to entertain you with details of the *Titanic* tragedy
  ○ **B.** to scare you into avoiding big ships
  ○ **C.** to help you picture what the *Titanic* was like
  ○ **D.** to persuade you that the *Titanic's* builder was cruel.

Scholastic Professional Books

Vocabulary

In each of the following sentences, a word is missing. First, read the sentence. Then find the missing word in the list of words beneath the sentence. Fill in the circle next to the word that is missing.

Sample:

It was getting late, so they _____ their pace.
- ○ **A.** ambled
- ○ **B.** measured
- ○ **C.** quickened
- ○ **D.** slowed

1. He was _____ around new people and didn't talk much.
- ○ **A.** bold
- ○ **B.** timid
- ○ **C.** angry
- ○ **D.** antsy

2. If this _____ weather continues, we will need to turn up the heat.
- ○ **A.** balmy
- ○ **B.** pleasant
- ○ **C.** frigid
- ○ **D.** sweltering

3. It is good to be _____ of others, no matter how different they are.
- ○ **A.** tolerant
- ○ **B.** critical
- ○ **C.** suspicious
- ○ **D.** wary

4. The mystery of who took his lunch continued to _____ him.
- ○ **A.** surprise
- ○ **B.** delight
- ○ **C.** baffle
- ○ **D.** excite

5. Their _____ was about whose turn it was to clean up after dinner.
- ○ **A.** dispute
- ○ **B.** occasion
- ○ **C.** assignment
- ○ **D.** encounter

6. "Follow that car!" the woman shouted _____.
- ○ **A.** quietly
- ○ **B.** frantically
- ○ **C.** contentedly
- ○ **D.** blissfully

7. She was _____ in her decision and never regretted it.
- ○ **A.** wavering
- ○ **B.** steadfast
- ○ **C.** discouraged
- ○ **D.** disappointed

8. The beautiful painting was _____ by a large black mark on it.
- ○ **A.** created
- ○ **B.** attacked
- ○ **C.** helped
- ○ **D.** marred

9. He was always _____, shaking hands and thanking everyone.
- ○ **A.** tragic
- ○ **B.** cordial
- ○ **C.** tasteful
- ○ **D.** remote

10. Despite being dropped three times, the television made it upstairs _____.
- ○ **A.** shattered
- ○ **B.** happily
- ○ **C.** roundly
- ○ **D.** intact

11. My friend's _____ the way I draw realistic-looking animals.
- ○ **A.** admire
- ○ **B.** pity
- ○ **C.** ignore
- ○ **D.** scorn

12. She was _____ about moving to a new town where she knew nobody.
- ○ **A.** thrilled
- ○ **B.** jealous
- ○ **C.** anxious
- ○ **D.** mean

13. He loves to write so much that we _____ he will be a writer when he grows up.
- ○ **A.** explain
- ○ **B.** predict
- ○ **C.** regret
- ○ **D.** ignore

Scholastic Professional Books

Scholastic Success With

GRAMMAR

Types of Sentences

A. What kind of sentence is each of the following? Write *declarative, interrogative, exclamatory,* or *imperative* on the line.

> **RETEACHING:** A **declarative sentence** makes a statement. An **interrogative sentence** asks a question. An **exclamatory sentence** shows strong feeling. An **imperative sentence** states a command.

1. Merlin carried the baby to safety. _____

2. Why did traitors poison the town's wells? _____

3. Go back and fetch the missing sword. _____

4. Slip the sword into the groove, and pull it out. _____

5. The king was England's bravest ruler! _____

6. Who will follow Selene? _____

B. Identify which groups of words are incomplete sentences and which are complete sentences. Write *incomplete* or *complete* on the line.

1. Sarah at the edge of the square. _____

2. The knights fought so bravely! _____

3. How did Kay treat her dog? _____

4. The sword out of the stone. _____

5. Natalie was trained to be a pilot. _____

C. Correct the incomplete sentences in part B. Add an action word to each one. Then rewrite the complete sentence on the line.

1. _____

2. _____

Types of Sentences

A. Add the correct end punctuation mark
to each sentence. Then write *declarative,*
interrogative, exclamatory, or *imperative*
to tell what kind of sentence it is.

> **RETEACHING:** A **declarative sentence**
> makes a statement. An **interrogative**
> **sentence** asks a question. An **exclamato-**
> **ry sentence** shows strong feeling. An
> **imperative sentence** states a command.

1. How do turtles protect themselves_ _____

2. What heavy, hot suits of steel they wore_ _____

3. Pretend that you are an acrobat or juggler_ _____

4. The students sang songs, told stories, and recited poems_ _____

B. Use one of the words below to complete each sentence.
Then identify each sentence by writing *declarative, interrogative,*
exclamatory, or *imperative.*

     pass   **won**   **listened**   **play**

1. The audience _____ to the bagpipes. _____

2. What kind of games did pioneers like

   to _____? _____

3. Please _____ me the pepper. _____

4. I've _____ three chess games in a row! _____

C. Write an example of a declarative, interrogative, exclamatory, and
imperative sentence. Be sure to use the correct end punctuation.

1. Declarative: _____

2. Interrogative: _____

3. Exclamatory: _____

4. Imperative: _____

Scholastic Professional Books

Types of Sentences

Decide if there is an error in the underlined part of each sentence. Fill in the bubble next to the correct answer.

1. <u>you do like</u> to see movies about knights and castles?

   ⓐ You do like
   ⓑ Do you like
   ⓒ correct as is

2. Please hand me that mystery book about <u>the Middle Ages?</u>

   ⓐ the Middle Ages!
   ⓑ the Middle Ages.
   ⓒ correct as is

3. Grandfather described life in the early part <u>of the century.</u>

   ⓐ of the century?
   ⓑ of the century!
   ⓒ correct as is

4. Why don't you write about <u>your life!</u>

   ⓐ your life?
   ⓑ your life.
   ⓒ correct as is

5. <u>Begin by describing</u> your very first memory.

   ⓐ begin by describing
   ⓑ By describing
   ⓒ correct as is

6. I had such fun swimming <u>in the ocean?</u>

   ⓐ in the ocean
   ⓑ in the ocean!
   ⓒ correct as is

7. What do you remember about your first day <u>in school?</u>

   ⓐ in school!
   ⓑ in school.
   ⓒ correct as is

8. <u>another story</u> about our relatives in Mexico.

   ⓐ Tell me another story
   ⓑ Another story
   ⓒ correct as is

9. The fish looked so colorful swimming in <u>the Caribbean Sea</u>

   ⓐ the Caribbean Sea!
   ⓑ the Caribbean Sea?
   ⓒ correct as is

10. He told us about <u>his trip?</u>

   ⓐ his trip
   ⓑ his trip.
   ⓒ correct as is

Simple and Complete Subjects and Predicates

A. Draw a line between the complete subject and the complete predicate. Underline the complete subject once and the simple subject twice.

> **RETEACHING:** The **simple subject** is the main noun or pronoun that tells whom or what the sentence is about. The **complete subject** is the simple subject and all of the words that go with it. The **simple predicate** is the verb that tells what the subject does or is. The **complete predicate** is the verb and all the words that tell what the subject does or is.

1. A small family lived on a faraway planet.

2. The family's two children played near the space launch.

3. The little girl dreamed about life on Earth.

4. Huge spaceships landed daily on the planet.

5. The spaceship mechanics repaired huge cargo ships.

6. Twinkling stars appeared in the black sky.

B. Draw a line between the complete subject and the complete predicate. Underline the complete predicate once and the simple predicate twice.

1. The planet's inhabitants lived in underground homes.

2. A special machine manufactures air inside the family's home.

3. The athletic girl jumped high into the air.

4. Many toys and games cluttered the children's playroom.

5. The children's father described weather on Earth.

C. Circle the complete subject in each sentence. Underline the complete predicate.

1. The underground home contained large, comfortable rooms.

2. The playful child rolled his clay into a ball.

Simple and Complete Subjects and Predicates

A. Read each sentence. Circle the complete subject. Underline the simple subject.

1. My whole family had a picnic on Saturday.

2. The warm, sunny day was perfect for an outing in the park.

3. My cousin Fred brought his guitar and harmonica.

4. Everyone sang favorite folk songs.

5. The people in the park applauded us.

> **RETEACHING:** The **simple subject** is the main noun or pronoun that tells whom or what the sentence is about. The **complete subject** is the simple subject and all of the words that go with it. The **simple predicate** is the verb that tells what the subject does or is. The **complete predicate** is the verb and all the words that tell what the subject does or is.

B. Read each sentence. Circle the complete predicate. Underline the simple predicate.

1. We watched the space shuttle on TV this morning.

2. The huge spaceship rocketed into space at 6:00 A.M.

3. During the flight, the six astronauts released a satellite into space.

4. The space shuttle *Columbia* circled Earth for three days.

5. The spacecraft landed smoothly on Monday at noon.

C. Write three sentences. Circle the complete subject and underline the complete predicate in each sentence.

1. _____

2. _____

3. _____

Simple and Complete Subjects and Predicates

What part of each sentence is underlined? Fill in the bubble next to the correct answer.

1. My cousin lives on a big ranch in Montana.
   - ⓐ simple subject
   - ⓑ complete subject
   - ⓒ simple predicate

2. Her family raises cattle on the ranch.
   - ⓐ complete subject
   - ⓑ simple predicate
   - ⓒ complete predicate

3. Rosa's job is feeding the chickens before school.
   - ⓐ simple subject
   - ⓑ complete subject
   - ⓒ simple predicate

4. Her brother John feeds the horses.
   - ⓐ complete subject
   - ⓑ simple predicate
   - ⓒ complete predicate

5. My cousin Rosa rides her horse across the range.
   - ⓐ simple subject
   - ⓑ complete subject
   - ⓒ complete predicate

6. John spreads fresh hay in the pasture.
   - ⓐ simple subject
   - ⓑ simple predicate
   - ⓒ complete predicate

7. Their nearest neighbors often go into town with them.
   - ⓐ simple subject
   - ⓑ complete subject
   - ⓒ simple predicate

8. The dinner bell rings at 6:30 every evening.
   - ⓐ simple subject
   - ⓑ complete subject
   - ⓒ simple predicate

9. The whole family sits on the porch and reads about space.
   - ⓐ simple subject
   - ⓑ complete subject
   - ⓒ complete predicate

10. Rosa searches the Internet for sites about animals.
    - ⓐ complete subject
    - ⓑ simple predicate
    - ⓒ complete predicate

Compound Subjects and Predicates

> **RETEACHING:** A **compound subject** is two or more subjects in the same sentence, usually joined by a connecting word such as *and* or *or*. A **compound predicate** is two or more verbs in the same sentence, usually joined by a connecting word such as *and* or *or*.

A. **Underline the compound subject in each sentence.**

1. Pig One, Pig Two, and Pig Three wrote Goldilocks a letter.

2. The bears, rabbits, and pigs attended a party.

3. Carrots, beets, and squash grow in the garden.

4. Later this month Teddy and Osito will visit Baby Bear.

5. My brothers and sisters really enjoyed the housewarming.

B. **Circle the compound predicate in each sentence.**

1. Peter's mother cleaned and peeled the crispy carrots.

2. The guests laughed and giggled at June's funny jokes.

3. The sly wolves waited and watched for the passing animals.

4. Goldilocks weeds and waters her garden every day.

5. The author writes and edits her amusing fairy tales.

C. **Write the compound subject or compound predicate that completes each sentence. Then write *CS* for compound subject or *CP* for compound predicate.**

authors and illustrators   buys and reads

1. My friend _____ all of that author's books. _____

2. Many _____ visit our school. _____

Compound Subjects and Predicates

> **RETEACHING:** A compound **subject** is two or more subjects in the same sentence, usually joined by a connecting word such as *and* or *or*. A **compound predicate** is two or more verbs in the same sentence, usually joined by a connecting word such as *and* or *or*.

A. Underline the simple subject in each sentence. Then rewrite the two sentences as one sentence with a compound subject.

1. The teacher visited the ocean. Her students visited the ocean.

   _____

2. Seagulls flew overhead. Pelicans flew overhead.

   _____

3. Seashells littered the sand. Seaweed littered the sand.

   _____

4. Carlos ran on the beach. Tanya ran on the beach.

   _____

B. Circle the simple predicate in each sentence. Then rewrite the two sentences as one sentence with a compound predicate.

1. The artist paints sea life. The artist draws sea life.

   _____

2. I collect driftwood. I decorate driftwood.

   _____

3. Seals swim near the pier. Seals dive near the pier.

   _____

Compound Subjects and Predicates

A. Fill in the bubble next to the compound subject.

1. The deer and bison grazed in the high mountain meadow.
   - ⓐ deer and bison
   - ⓑ grazed in
   - ⓒ high mountain meadow

2. Last weekend Rosa and Kay camped by the lake.
   - ⓐ Last weekend
   - ⓑ Rosa and Kay
   - ⓒ camped by

3. On Friday Alice and I saw a movie about gray wolves.
   - ⓐ Alice and I
   - ⓑ saw a movie
   - ⓒ about gray wolves

4. Last year students and teachers created a wildlife mural.
   - ⓐ Last year
   - ⓑ wildlife mural
   - ⓒ students and teachers

5. My friends and I were hiking in the White Mountains.
   - ⓐ were hiking
   - ⓑ friends and I
   - ⓒ the White Mountains

B. Fill in the bubble next to the compound predicate.

1. All night long the chilly wind moaned and howled.
   - ⓐ All night long
   - ⓑ chilly wind
   - ⓒ moaned and howled

2. Joan picked and peeled the apples in the morning.
   - ⓐ picked and peeled
   - ⓑ the apples
   - ⓒ in the morning

3. Last night Ed and Cody washed and dried the dishes.
   - ⓐ Last night
   - ⓑ Ed and Cody
   - ⓒ washed and dried

4. Many students wrote and revised their book reports.
   - ⓐ Many students
   - ⓑ wrote and revised
   - ⓒ their book reports

5. The famous sculptor cut and polished the cold, gray granite.
   - ⓐ famous sculptor
   - ⓑ cut and polished
   - ⓒ cold, gray granite

Compound Sentences

A. Read each sentence. Decide if it is a simple sentence or a compound sentence. Write *simple* or *compound* on the line.

> **RETEACHING:** A **compound sentence** joins two simple sentences with a comma and a **coordinating conjunction**. *And, but,* and *or* are commonly used coordinating conjunctions.

1. Dad had been horseback riding before.   _____

2. Lizzie felt a little nervous on a horse, but he would never admit it.   _____

3. He discovered that riding was a lot of fun, and he couldn't wait to tell his friends about it.   _____

4. There don't seem to be many bears in the national park this year.   _____

5. Suddenly Mom pointed out the car window toward some trees.   _____

6. We all looked out the window, but the bears turned out to be people in brown coats.   _____

B. Underline the simple sentences that make up each compound sentence.

1. Connor had seen many parks in his life, but he never had seen a park like this one.

2. Dad brought a pair of binoculars, and Nate used them to look for animals.

3. He saw his first live bear, and the hair stood up on his arms.

4. It was an exciting moment, but it only lasted a second.

5. The bear was no bear at all, and Felicia was embarrassed.

6. He hadn't seen a bear, but he kept looking.

Compound Sentences

A. Read each sentence. Underline the simple sentences that make up the compound sentence. Circle the coordinating conjunction in each sentence.

> **RETEACHING:** A **compound sentence** joins two simple sentences with a comma and a **coordinating conjunction**. *And, but,* and *or* are commonly used coordinating conjunctions.

1. One day we were in the park, and we saw two ducks swimming by.

2. We watched the ducks for a while, but they disappeared into the tall grass.

3. The ducks might have gone to a nest, or they could have swum to the shore.

4. We walked along the grassy bank, but we could not find them anywhere.

5. We sat down on the dock, and out came the ducks again.

6. One adult duck led six ducklings around the pond, and the other adult followed behind the babies.

B. Read each compound sentence. Choose the coordinating conjunction that makes sense and write it on the line.

1. The ducklings are brown, _____ the adult ducks are white. (but, or)

2. The ducklings were playing, _____ they were learning, too. (but, or)

3. The ducklings ate a lot, _____ they grew quickly. (but, and)

4. We brought bread with us, _____ we fed the ducks. (and, but)

5. Maybe they knew us, _____ maybe they just liked the food we fed them. (and, or)

C. Write a compound sentence. Underline the simple sentences, and circle the coordinating conjunction you used.

_____

_____

Compound Sentences

A. Fill in the bubble that tells whether the sentence is a simple sentence or a compound sentence.

1. There are nine planets in our solar system, but there is only one sun.
   - ⓐ simple
   - ⓑ compound

2. The sun is a star, and a star is a giant ball of burning gases.
   - ⓐ simple
   - ⓑ compound

3. A moon is a satellite that moves around a planet.
   - ⓐ simple
   - ⓑ compound

4. Earth has only one moon, but the planet Mars has two moons.
   - ⓐ simple
   - ⓑ compound

5. The word *orbit* means "to travel around something."
   - ⓐ simple
   - ⓑ compound

B. Is the underlined part correct? Fill in the bubble next to the right answer.

1. The sun is <u>a star, but It is not</u> the biggest star.
   - ⓐ a star, but it is not
   - ⓑ a star but, it is not
   - ⓒ correct as is

2. Some stars are bigger than <u>the sun and, some stars</u> are smaller.
   - ⓐ the sun and some stars
   - ⓑ the sun, and some stars
   - ⓒ correct as is

3. Other stars seem smaller than <u>the sun, they are</u> just farther away.
   - ⓐ the sun, but they are
   - ⓑ the sun, They are
   - ⓒ correct as is

4. Do hot stars give off <u>blue light or do they</u> give off red light?
   - ⓐ blue light or, do they
   - ⓑ blue light, or do they
   - ⓒ correct as is

5. Our sun is not the <u>hottest star, but it</u> is not the coolest star either.
   - ⓐ hottest star but it
   - ⓑ hottest star but, it
   - ⓒ correct as is

Scholastic Professional Books

Common and Proper Nouns

A. Circle the common nouns in each sentence.

> **RETEACHING:** A **common noun** names a person, place, thing, or idea. A **proper noun** names a specific person, place, thing, or idea. A proper noun begins with a capital letter.

1. The farmer lives in the green house down the road.

2. The farmer grows wheat, soybeans, and corn.

3. The fields are plowed before he plants the crop.

4. Crops are planted in rows so that they can be watered easily.

5. As the plants grow, the farmer removes weeds and looks for bugs.

B. Underline the proper nouns in each sentence.

1. John Vasquez grows soybeans and alfalfa on a 30-acre farm near Tulsa, Oklahoma.

2. The Vasquez Farm is next to the Rising J Horse Ranch.

3. Mr. Vasquez and his daughter Sally sell alfalfa to the owner of the ranch.

4. Sometimes Joker, a quarter horse, knocks down the fence to get the alfalfa.

5. Every October people come to the Vasquez Farm for the annual Harvest Celebration.

C. Rewrite each sentence. Replace each underlined common noun with a proper noun.

1. We walked down the street to the park.

_____

2. My aunt lives in the city.

_____

Common and Proper Nouns

> **RETEACHING:** A **common noun** names a person, place, thing, or idea. A **proper noun** names a specific person, place, thing, or idea. A proper noun begins with a capital letter.

A. Circle the common nouns in each sentence. Underline the proper nouns.

1. The *Atlanta Constitution* published a story about celebrations.

2. *Three Dogs on a Summer Night* is a movie about poodles.

3. We like to sing "She'll Be Comin' 'Round the Mountain" at the campfire.

4. Last August my friend John went to Germany with his grandparents.

5. My family always goes to the beach for Memorial Day.

B. Complete the chart below by writing each common and proper noun in the correct column. Then add three common nouns and three proper nouns to the chart.

newspaper	The Sun News
city	Cobblestone
day	book
magazine	month
Chicago	July
park	Tuesday
Young Arthur	
Yellowstone National Park	

Common Nouns	Proper Nouns
newspaper	*The Sun News*

Common and Proper Nouns

**Read each sentence. Are the nouns underlined written correctly?
Fill in the bubble next to the right answer.**

1. I go to <u>abraham lincoln school</u>.

   ⓐ abraham lincoln School
   ⓑ Abraham Lincoln School
   ⓒ correct as is

2. I brought <u>a peanut butter sandwich</u>.

   ⓐ a Peanut Butter sandwich
   ⓑ a peanut butter Sandwich
   ⓒ correct as is

3. I sang <u>row, row, row your boat</u> today.

   ⓐ Row, Row, Row Your Boat today.
   ⓑ "Row, Row, Row Your Boat" today.
   ⓒ correct as is

4. My school is located on the <u>corner of Maple Avenue and Elm Street</u>.

   ⓐ Corner of Maple Avenue and Elm Street
   ⓑ corner of Maple avenue and Elm street
   ⓒ correct as is

5. I wrote a book report on *<u>cherokee summer</u>* for reading class.

   ⓐ *Cherokee Summer*
   ⓑ *Cherokee summer*
   ⓒ correct as is

6. <u>My best friend John</u> sits in the third row.

   ⓐ My Best Friend John
   ⓑ My best Friend John
   ⓒ correct as is

7. My <u>spanish class begins at noon</u>.

   ⓐ Spanish class begins at Noon
   ⓑ Spanish class begins at noon
   ⓒ correct as is

8. That painting <u>is called "Sunflowers."</u>

   ⓐ is Called sunflowers.
   ⓑ is called <u>Sunflowers</u>.
   ⓒ correct as is

9. I wrote <u>about washington, d.c.</u>

   ⓐ about Washington, D.C.
   ⓑ about Washington, d.c.
   ⓒ correct as is

10. Later I'll go to <u>austin's better books</u>.

    ⓐ Austin's Better Books
    ⓑ austin's Better Books
    ⓒ correct as is

Singular and Plural Nouns

> **RETEACHING:** A **singular noun** names one person, place, thing, or idea.
> A **plural noun** names more than one person, place, thing, or idea. Add –s to form the plural of most nouns. Some plural nouns are irregular, and their spellings need to be memorized.

A. Underline the singular nouns in each sentence.

1. I opened the door and found the shoes, cap, and bat I needed for the game.

2. I headed down to the fields with my bat on my shoulder.

3. My friends were standing by the fence near the dugout.

4. We were playing on the same team.

5. That day I hit two grounders, a foul, and a homer.

B. Underline the plural nouns in each sentence.

1. My uncles taught me to stand with my feet closer together.

2. The first time I hit a home run, I danced on each of the bases.

3. In the third game, all the players hit the ball.

4. My brothers, sisters, and cousins came to every game.

5. Four teams were in the playoffs, but our team won the championship.

C. Circle the singular nouns in each sentence. Underline the plural nouns.

1. The teams and players received awards when the season ended.

2. In the games to come, I will try to be a better hitter, catcher, and teammate.

3. My mother and father were the proudest parents at the assembly.

4. They gave me a new glove for my achievements.

Scholastic Professional Books

Singular and Plural Nouns

A. Circle the singular nouns in each sentence.
Underline the plural nouns in each sentence.

1. My homework last night was to write a story about friends.

2. At home I thought about the people who are my friends.

3. My three dogs, one cat, and four birds are also my pals.

4. I wrote about adventures with my pets and my buddies.

5. My teacher liked my story so much that he read it to his classes.

B. Write each noun in the box in the correct column on the chart. Remember that some nouns keep the same form in the singular and plural.

chair	mice
mouse	chairs
teeth	tooth
sheep	men
foot	feet
man	

	Singular Nouns	Plural Nouns
1.	_____	_____
2.	_____	_____
3.	_____	_____
4.	_____	_____
5.	_____	_____
6.	_____	_____

C. Write two sentences. Use one singular noun and one plural noun from the chart in each sentence.

1. _____

2. _____

Singular and Plural Nouns

Decide if the underlined part of the sentence has an error.
Fill in the bubble next to the correct answer.

1. I read seven <u>chapter in my book</u> last night.
   - ⓐ chapter in my books
   - ⓑ chapters in my book
   - ⓒ correct as is

2. In chapter one, <u>a father and a son</u> went to the mountains.
   - ⓐ a fathers and a son
   - ⓑ a father and a sons
   - ⓒ correct as is

3. They built their campsite under some <u>trees near a creeks</u>.
   - ⓐ tree near a creeks
   - ⓑ trees near a creek
   - ⓒ correct as is

4. The first night the father saw <u>a bear eating nut</u>.
   - ⓐ a bear eating nuts
   - ⓑ a bears eating nuts
   - ⓒ correct as is

5. Two <u>bear cubs</u> were in the bushes hiding.
   - ⓐ bear cub
   - ⓑ bears cub
   - ⓒ correct as is

6. The <u>bear cubs' mother</u> helped them find berries to eat.
   - ⓐ bear cub's mother
   - ⓑ bear cubs mother
   - ⓒ correct as is

7. In the morning, there were four <u>deers and a sheep</u> nearby.
   - ⓐ deers and a sheeps
   - ⓑ deer and a sheep
   - ⓒ correct as is

8. The <u>son's teeths</u> were red after eating berries.
   - ⓐ son's teeth
   - ⓑ son's tooths
   - ⓒ correct as is

9. A bird flew <u>by Dads head</u> and into the tent.
   - ⓐ by Dad's head
   - ⓑ by Dads' head
   - ⓒ correct as is

10. It took almost an hour to get that <u>bird out of the tent's</u>.
    - ⓐ birds out of the tents
    - ⓑ bird out of the tent
    - ⓒ correct as is

Subject and Object Pronouns

A. Read the sentences. Circle the subject pronoun in the second sentence that replaces the underlined word or words.

> **RETEACHING:** A **subject pronoun**—*I, you, he, she, it, we,* or *they*—can replace the subject of a sentence. An **object pronoun**—*me, you, him, her, it, us,* or *them*—can replace a noun that is the object of an action verb or that follows a preposition.

1. The fourth graders read a book about the rain forest.

   They read a book about the rain forest.

2. Then Ada wrote a poem about a huge Kapok tree.

   Then she wrote a poem about a huge Kapok tree.

3. Juan, Jill, and I painted a mural of rain forest mammals.

   We painted a mural of rain forest mammals.

B. Read the sentences. Draw two lines under the object pronoun in the second sentence that replaces the underlined word or words.

1. Mr. Patel's class sent a fan letter to the author.

   Mr. Patel's class sent a letter to her.

2. Ms. Torres, a rain forest expert, visited the fourth graders last week.

   Ms. Torres, a rain forest expert, visited them last week.

3. She said, "You can find information in the library.

   She said, "You can find it in the library."

C. Circle the subject pronoun and underline the object pronoun in each sentence.

1. I saw you at the library yesterday.

2. You can call me tonight about our class project.

3. Will he make an informative poster for us?

Subject and Object Pronouns

A. Choose the pronoun in parentheses ( ) that completes each sentence, and write it on the line. Then identify the kind of pronoun in the sentence by writing *S* for *subject* or *O* for *object*.

1. _____ took a boat trip through the Everglades. (We, Us)   _____

2. The boat's captain gave _____ a special tour. (we, us)   _____

3. The captain said, " _____ will love the wildlife here!" (You, Us)   _____

4. _____ brought an instant camera in my backpack. (I, Me)   _____

5. I used _____ to photograph birds, turtles, and alligators. (he, it)   _____

6. My sister Kit carried paper and pencils with _____. (she, her)   _____

7. Kit used _____ to sketch scenes of the Everglades. (they, them)   _____

8. _____ is an excellent artist. (She, Her)   _____

B. Rewrite each sentence. Replace the underlined words with the correct subject or object pronoun.

1. <u>Our grandparents</u> sent a postcard to <u>my sister, my brother, and me</u>.

   _____

2. The <u>postcard</u> was addressed to <u>my older brother</u>.

   _____

C. Write two sentences. In the first, use a subject pronoun. In the second, use an object pronoun.

1. _____

2. _____

Subject and Object Pronouns

A. Fill in the bubble next to the pronoun that can replace the underlined words.

1. <u>Carlos and Sue</u> have a very popular pet-care service.
   - (a) They
   - (b) Them
   - (c) He

2. Many people hire <u>Carlos and Sue</u> to feed their cats.
   - (a) her
   - (b) they
   - (c) them

3. Carlos asked <u>Jenna and me</u> to help out for a day.
   - (a) we
   - (b) us
   - (c) me

4. <u>Jenna and I</u> were delighted to help.
   - (a) We
   - (b) Us
   - (c) They

5. I agreed to meet <u>Sue</u> at the Chan's house this afternoon.
   - (a) she
   - (b) her
   - (c) them

B. Fill in the bubble next to the pronoun that correctly completes each sentence.

1. Dot, Ed, and _____ visited the Air and Space Museum recently.
   - (a) I
   - (b) me
   - (c) us

2. Fortunately, _____ knew his way around the huge exhibition hall.
   - (a) her
   - (b) he
   - (c) him

3. _____ really wanted to see the biplanes.
   - (a) She
   - (b) Them
   - (c) Her

4. Then Ed told Dot and _____ about the Wright Brothers' flight.
   - (a) I
   - (b) me
   - (c) she

5. I persuaded Dot and _____ to visit the museum again soon.
   - (a) he
   - (b) him
   - (c) we

Name _____ **Practice**

Possessive Pronouns

A. Underline the possessive pronoun in each sentence.

> **RETEACHING:** A **possessive pronoun** is a pronoun that shows ownership or belonging.

1. I miss my best friend, Carlos, because he is spending the summer in Seattle, Washington.

2. He is staying with his favorite cousins, Blanca and Eduardo, during July and August.

3. The cousins have been showing Carlos around their city.

4. When I opened my e-mail this morning, I read about the ferry ride they took across Puget Sound.

5. Blanca also showed Carlos her favorite beach for clam digging.

6. Eduardo said, "Carlos, this will be your best vacation ever!"

7. Then Blanca added, "Our next stop will be the Space Needle."

B. Write the possessive pronoun from the box that completes each sentence. Use the underlined word or words to help you.

my	her	his	their	our

1. _____ grandparents sent me a long letter in Spanish.

2. They said that _____ goal was to help me learn the language.

3. Grandmother included the words to _____ favorite Spanish song.

4. Grandfather wrote a list of _____ special tips for learning a language.

5. During _____ next visit, we will try to speak as much Spanish as possible.

6. I know that _____ speaking ability will improve with this kind of help.

Scholastic Professional Books

Possessive Pronouns

A. **Write the possessive pronoun in parentheses ( )**
that correctly completes each sentence.

> **RETEACHING:** A **possessive pronoun** is a pronoun that shows ownership or belonging.

1. The sports magazine and newspaper are _____. (my, mine)

2. Where is _____ atlas of the United States? (your, yours)

3. Which of the mysteries on the shelf is _____? (your, yours)

4. These new dictionaries will soon be _____. (our, ours)

5. Where is _____ copy of *Charlotte's Web*? (her, hers)

B. **Write the possessive pronoun that completes each sentence.**

1. My brother and I really enjoy visiting _____ neighborhood library.

2. Every year Ms. Lee, the librarian, displays _____ choices for the year's best reading.

3. Then all the library users vote for _____ favorite books, too.

4. For _____ favorite, I chose a photo biography about Babe Ruth.

5. Luke said that _____ first choice was Jerry Spinelli's new novel.

6. _____ friends Sue and Ed told me that they voted for the same book.

7. I asked them, "What is _____ reason for choosing this book?"

8. They replied, "It's because _____ taste in books is the best."

C. **Write three sentences about something you treasure.**
Use a possessive pronoun in each sentence.

1. _____

2. _____

3. _____

Possessive Pronouns

Look at the underlined words in each sentence. Fill in the bubble next to the possessive pronoun that refers back to the underlined word or words.

1. <u>I</u> love baseball, and _____ hobby is collecting baseball cards.

    ⓐ his   ⓒ your
    ⓑ our   ⓓ my

2. Many <u>baseball-card collectors</u> buy _____ cards from special dealers.

    ⓐ your   ⓒ their
    ⓑ his   ⓓ her

3. A <u>classmate named Ralph</u> keeps _____ cards in an album.

    ⓐ my   ⓒ our
    ⓑ his   ⓓ your

4. <u>Sue</u> treasures that rare Jackie Robinson card of _____.

    ⓐ ours   ⓒ hers
    ⓑ mine   ⓓ his

5. On Saturday <u>Mom and I</u> packed _____ lunch and ate it at the ballpark.

    ⓐ his   ⓒ your
    ⓑ their   ⓓ our

6. Once <u>all the players</u> signed _____ names on a baseball for me.

    ⓐ his   ⓒ my
    ⓑ their   ⓓ her

7. "<u>I</u> exclaimed, "This signed baseball is _____ greatest treasure!"

    ⓐ theirs   ⓒ ours
    ⓑ my   ⓓ yours

8. Grandfather asked <u>me</u> whether this new baseball cap was _____.

    ⓐ her   ⓒ you
    ⓑ your   ⓓ mine

9. When the players scored, <u>people in the audience</u> waved _____ baseball caps.

    ⓐ his   ⓒ their
    ⓑ my   ⓓ her

10. I just read a book about <u>Roberto Clemente</u> and _____ amazing career.

    ⓐ his   ⓒ their
    ⓑ my   ⓓ your

Action Verbs

A. Underline the action verb in each sentence, and then write it on the line.

> **RETEACHING:** An **action verb** is a word that shows action. Some action verbs, such as *jump*, name actions you can see. Others, such as *think*, name actions you can't see.

1. Judy Hindley wrote a book about the history of string. _____

2. An illustrator painted funny pictures about string. _____

3. Long ago people twisted vines into long, strong ropes. _____

4. People still weave long, thin fibers into cloth. _____

5. My sister knits sweaters from thick wool yarn. _____

6. We stretched the rope hammock from tree to tree. _____

7. I always tie a ribbon around a birthday package. _____

8. We learned about different kinds of knots. _____

9. He made a belt from three different colors of string. _____

10. We wished for another book by Judy Hindley. _____

B. Underline the action verb that is more vivid.

1. The rabbit quickly (moved, hopped) across the lawn.

2. I (pounded, touched) the nail with my hammer.

3. The thirsty dog (drank, slurped) the water noisily.

4. I (made, sewed) a quilt from scraps of fabric.

C. Write two sentences about how someone did something. Include a vivid action verb in each sentence.

1. _____

2. _____

Action Verbs

A. Circle the action verb in each sentence.

1. People use string in many different ways.

2. Fran and I tie the packages with string.

3. We imagine people from earlier times.

4. These people invented rope, string, and cord.

5. The lively, happy tone of this story amazes me.

B. For each sentence, underline the action verb in parentheses that creates a more vivid picture.

6. We (sit, lounge) on the big chairs near the pool.

7. The horses (go, gallop) across the field.

8. Minna and Max (gulp, eat) their sandwiches in a hurry.

9. The workers (drag, move) the heavy load across the yard.

10. Rosa and I (put, staple) the parts together.

 Use each of these action verbs in a sentence: follow, shout, rush, slip, pound. Write your sentences on another sheet of paper.

Scholastic Professional Books

Action Verbs

A. Fill in the bubble next to the action verb in each sentence.

1. The space shuttle circled the Earth twenty times.
   - (a) space
   - (b) circled
   - (c) twenty

2. Yesterday morning my class watched the newscast on TV.
   - (a) morning
   - (b) class
   - (c) watched

3. I think about space exploration all the time.
   - (a) think
   - (b) exploration
   - (c) time

4. Before a mission, astronauts train for months.
   - (a) mission
   - (b) train
   - (c) months

5. She read a biography about the first woman in space.
   - (a) read
   - (b) about
   - (c) space

B. For each sentence, fill in the bubble next to the more vivid action verb.

1. At the beach, we _____ for pieces of driftwood.
   - (a) looked
   - (b) hunted

2. We _____ into the foamy waves.
   - (a) walked
   - (b) plunged

3. Several artists _____ a huge castle out of sand.
   - (a) sculpted
   - (b) made

4. I _____ my beach towel under a large umbrella.
   - (a) put
   - (b) spread

5. The wild horses _____ along the sandy seashore.
   - (a) galloped
   - (b) ran

Verb Tenses

A. Write *present* if the underlined word is a present tense verb, *past* if the underlined word is a past tense verb, and *future* if it is future tense.

> **RETEACHING: Present tense verbs** show action that is happening now or on a regular basis. Present tense verbs agree in number with who or what is doing the action. **Past tense verbs** show action that took place in the past. Most past tense verbs end in *-ed*. **Future tense verbs** show action that will happen in the future. The future tense is formed with the verb *will*.

1. The story of sneakers <u>started</u> with the development of rubber. _____

2. People in Central and South America <u>melted</u> gum from trees. _____

3. On Friday she <u>will celebrate</u> her tenth birthday. _____

4. Rubber <u>protected</u> the wearer's feet. _____

5. Gum <u>acts</u> as an eraser. _____

6. Everyone <u>will carry</u> a small backpack. _____

7. Unfortunately, pure rubber <u>cracks</u> in cold weather. _____

8. Charles Goodyear <u>believed</u> in a solution. _____

9. We <u>will visit</u> two museums. _____

10. Goodyear <u>licenses</u> the process to shoe companies. _____

11. The shoe companies <u>manufactured</u> shoes with rubber soles. _____

B. Look at the sentences with present tense verbs in part A. Then rewrite each one with the past tense form of the verb.

1. _____

2. _____

3. _____

Scholastic Professional Books

Verb Tenses

A. Underline each subject. Decide whether it is singular or plural. Then circle the present tense verb that correctly completes the sentence, and write it on the line.

1. Anna _____ dark-purple sneakers.   wear   wears

2. The sneakers _____ a squeaky sound on the floor.   make   makes

3. The girl _____ her sister how to tie her sneakers. teach   teaches

4. Tight sneakers _____ your feet.   hurt   hurts

5. Loose sneakers _____ blisters.   cause   causes

6. Joe _____ his new sneakers under his bed.   place   places

7. Rachel _____ new sneakers before the race.   buy   buys

8. The students _____ comfortable sneakers.   want   wants

B. Look at the present tense verbs in the box. Decide whether they agree in number with a singular or a plural subject. Then write each word in the correct column on the chart. An example is given.

lace	laces
design	designs
reach	reaches
erase	erases

Present-Tense Verbs	
With Most Singular Subjects and *he, she, it*	**With Plural Subjects and *I, we,* and *you***
laces	lace
_____	_____
_____	_____
_____	_____

Verb Tenses

A. Look at the underlined verb or verbs. Fill in the bubble next to the correct tense.

1. Tomorrow we <u>will march</u> in the Independence Day parade.

   ⓐ past
   ⓑ present
   ⓒ future

2. Last week my sister and I <u>sewed</u> our old-fashioned costumes.

   ⓐ past
   ⓑ present
   ⓒ future

3. Many townspeople <u>will dress</u> as Western pioneers.

   ⓐ past
   ⓑ present
   ⓒ future

4. Everyone <u>participates</u> in the celebration.

   ⓐ past
   ⓑ present
   ⓒ future

5. <u>Will</u> local cowhands <u>ride</u> their horses?

   ⓐ past
   ⓑ present
   ⓒ future

B. Decide if the underlined verbs are correct. Fill in the bubble next to the right answer.

1. The parade <u>will began</u> at 10:00 tomorrow morning.

   ⓐ will begin
   ⓑ will begins
   ⓒ correct as is

2. The marching bands <u>will arrive</u> in town this afternoon.

   ⓐ will arrives
   ⓑ will arrived
   ⓒ correct as is

3. One parade float <u>will shows</u> an old-time newspaper office.

   ⓐ will showed
   ⓑ will show
   ⓒ correct as is

4. When <u>will</u> the square dancers <u>performed</u>?

   ⓐ will perform
   ⓑ will performs
   ⓒ correct as is

5. Later we <u>will celebrate</u> with a picnic.

   ⓐ will celebrates
   ⓑ will celebrated
   ⓒ correct as is

Main and Helping Verbs

A. Read each sentence. Underline the helping verb once and the main verb twice.

> **RETEACHING: Main verbs** show the main action in a sentence. **Helping verbs** help the main verb show tense. Helping verbs, such as *am, is, are, was, were, has, have, had,* or *will,* work with main verbs to tell when an action occurs.

1. What will happen to the doughnuts?

2. Uncle Ulysses has equipped the lunchroom with labor-saving devices.

3. Homer was polishing the metal trimmings.

4. Uncle Ulysses had tinkered with the inside workings.

5. The Ladies' Club was gathering.

6. Homer will handle everything.

7. Mr. Gabby was talking to Homer about his job.

8. A chauffeur had helped a woman out of a black car.

9. Now she is wearing an apron.

10. She will need some nutmeg.

B. In each sentence, circle the main verb and underline the helping verb. Then identify when the action occurs by writing *past, present,* or *future.*

1. The lady had asked for baking powder.   _____

2. The rings of batter will drop into the hot fat.   _____

3. Homer is learning about the doughnut machine.   _____

4. People will enjoy the doughnuts later.   _____

5. Everyone has eaten Homer's doughnuts.   _____

6. We are taking doughnuts for friends.   _____

Main and Helping Verbs

A. Read each incomplete sentence. Underline the main verb. Then circle the helping verb that correctly completes the sentence, and write it on the line.

> **RETEACHING: Main verbs** show the main action in a sentence. **Helping verbs** help the main verb show tense. Helping verbs, such as *am, is, are, was, were, has, have, had,* or *will,* work with main verbs to tell when an action occurs.

1. Justin _____ cooking seafood stew. (will, was)

2. He _____ added spices and lemon juice. (had, is)

3. Sally and Mick _____ prepared stew before. (will, have)

4. Justin _____ tasting the broth. (is, had)

5. "I _____ add a little more pepper," Justin says. (will, has)

6. His friends _____ just arrived for dinner. (are, have)

B. Underline the main verbs, and write the helping verbs on the lines.

1. On Saturday Betty will bake rye bread.   _____

2. Henry has pickled some fresh cucumbers.   _____

3. Gertrude is picking raspberries and blackberries.   _____

4. Alison had planted an herb garden.   _____

5. Marie and Harry have tossed the salad.   _____

6. They are planning another picnic.   _____

C. Write sentences using the main and helping verbs below.

1. will meet _____

2. had arrived _____

3. is listening _____

Scholastic Professional Books

Main and Helping Verbs

**Decide if the underlined verbs in each sentence are correct.
Then fill in the bubble next to the correct answer.**

1. Today Francesca <u>will traveled</u> to Peru by plane.

   - ⓐ is traveling
   - ⓑ am traveling
   - ⓒ correct as is

2. She <u>is photograph</u> the stone ruins of Machu Picchu next week.

   - ⓐ will photograph
   - ⓑ had photographed
   - ⓒ correct as is

3. An American explorer <u>had discovered</u> the ancient Incan city in 1911.

   - ⓐ has discovered
   - ⓑ is discovering
   - ⓒ correct as is

4. Since then, many people <u>will visited</u> the ruins of the city.

   - ⓐ have visited
   - ⓑ have visiting
   - ⓒ correct as is

5. Yesterday Francesca's brothers <u>had looking</u> at pictures of Machu Picchu.

   - ⓐ have looking
   - ⓑ were looking
   - ⓒ correct as is

6. They <u>were wondering</u> about the Incan civilization.

   - ⓐ had wondering
   - ⓑ has wonder
   - ⓒ correct as is

7. Centuries ago the Inca <u>had creating</u> a great empire.

   - ⓐ have creating
   - ⓑ had created
   - ⓒ correct as is

8. What <u>had happening</u> to them?

   - ⓐ has happening
   - ⓑ had happened
   - ⓒ correct as is

9. The Spanish explorers <u>will conquered</u> the Inca in 1532.

   - ⓐ had conquered
   - ⓑ are conquered
   - ⓒ correct as is

10. Francesca <u>will discover</u> Incan culture in present-day Peru.

    - ⓐ has discovering
    - ⓑ was discover
    - ⓒ correct as is

Linking Verbs

A. Underline the linking verb in each sentence, and circle the words it links.

> **RETEACHING:** A **linking verb** links the subject of a sentence to other words in the sentence. A linking verb does not show action. It tells what the subject is, was, or will be.

1. I am an enthusiastic reader.

2. My favorite books are nonfiction.

3. This bookstore is the best one in town.

4. The nonfiction books here are always interesting.

5. The store's owner is very knowledgeable.

6. His name is Terry Baldes.

7. Mr. Baldes was once an inventor and a scientist.

8. The bookstore's windows were very attractive last month.

9. Last Saturday's main event was an appearance by my favorite author.

10. My friends are big admirers of Mr. Baldes.

B. Write the linking verb in each sentence on the line.

1. An important invention is the telephone.   _____

2. The telephone's inventor was Alexander Graham Bell.   _____

3. At one time, most telephones were black.   _____

4. Today cellular phones are very popular.   _____

5. Cell phones and beepers were uncommon ten years ago.   _____

C. Write two sentences. Include a linking verb in each one.

1. _____

2. _____

Linking Verbs

A. Underline the correct linking verb in ( ).
Write *S* if the subject is singular and *P* if
it is plural.

1. The natural history museum (was, were) very busy last weekend. _____

2. Many visitors (was, were) tourists. _____

3. The new displays of rocks and gems (is, are) very popular. _____

4. One amazing rock (is, are) bright blue. _____

5. My favorite gems (was, were) the purple amethysts. _____

6. The gold nuggets (is, are) bright yellow. _____

7. The museum's first floor (is, are) full of Native American artifacts. _____

8. The carved wooden canoes (is, are) enormous. _____

9. The Tlingit woodcarvers (was, were) true artists. _____

10. This canoe (was, were) hand painted over a hundred years ago. _____

11. I (am, is) a big supporter of the museum. _____

B. Complete each sentence. Write *is* or *are* on the line.

1. The apatasaurus skeleton _____ gigantic.

2. These saber-tooth tigers _____ very impressive.

3. The exhibit cards _____ most informative.

4. The tiny dinosaur _____ really cute.

C. Write a sentence with a singular subject and a sentence with a
plural subject. Include a linking verb in each sentence.

1. _____

2. _____

Linking Verbs

**Read each incomplete sentence below. Then fill in the bubble
next to the linking verb that correctly completes the sentence.**

1. Denver, Colorado, _____ a large city.
   - ⓐ were
   - ⓑ are
   - ⓒ is

2. This growing metropolis _____ a
   mile high.
   - ⓐ are
   - ⓑ is
   - ⓒ were

3. Gold prospectors _____ the city's
   founders in 1858.
   - ⓐ is
   - ⓑ was
   - ⓒ were

4. From 1860 to 1945, Denver _____ a
   mining and agricultural community.
   - ⓐ were
   - ⓑ was
   - ⓒ will be

5. Today many local residents _____
   government workers.
   - ⓐ are
   - ⓑ is
   - ⓒ was

6. Now the automobile _____ the
   quickest way to travel.
   - ⓐ were
   - ⓑ is
   - ⓒ are

7. In earlier times, horses and buggies
   _____ popular modes of
   transportation.
   - ⓐ were
   - ⓑ is
   - ⓒ was

8. I _____ a student in a Denver
   public school.
   - ⓐ were
   - ⓑ am
   - ⓒ is

9. Last year my school's sports teams
   _____ very successful.
   - ⓐ was
   - ⓑ were
   - ⓒ is

10. I _____ a spectator at the local games.
    - ⓐ was
    - ⓑ were
    - ⓒ is

Irregular Verbs

A. **Underline the irregular verb in each sentence.**

> **RETEACHING:** An **irregular verb** does not form the past tense by adding *-ed*.

1. This morning Mom bought a red and a green toothbrush.

2. Pat made a tuna sandwich in the kitchen.

3. Mom quickly came into the dining room.

4. Deever rode her bicycle over to Pat's house.

5. Deever shook her head in great amusement.

6. They heard a great deal of noise in the kitchen.

7. Deever took a close look at the bright red toothbrush.

8. Pat carefully thought about the green and red toothbrushes.

9. Deever broke the silence with a sly laugh.

B. **Circle the irregular past tense verb in parentheses ( ). Then write it on the line to complete the sentence.**

1. We _____ a funny story about two toothbrushes. (hear, heard)

2. Pat _____ his decision after fifteen long minutes. (made, make)

3. Mom finally _____ E.J. an orange toothbrush. (buy, bought)

4. E.J. _____ into a song with a big smile on his face. (broke, break)

5. We all _____ to the nearest supermarket on our bikes. (ride, rode)

6. Deever _____ to the store with us. (came, come)

7. E.J. _____ with laughter at Pat's joke. (shook, shake)

Irregular Verbs

A. Underline the helping verb and the irregular past participle in each sentence.

> **RETEACHING:** An **irregular verb** does not form the past tense by adding *-ed*. The past participle is the form of the verb used with *has, have, had,* or *will have.*

1. We have chosen a fantastic day for our school picnic.

2. Mr. Torres has brought all the food and beverages in his van.

3. We have eaten all of the carrots on the table.

4. Ms. Chang has hidden the prizes for the treasure hunt.

5. By noon our teacher had taken over forty photographs.

6. All the fourth graders have gone on a short walk to the lake.

7. They had heard about the great paddleboats there.

8. Some of my friends have ridden in the boats.

9. The school has bought new sports equipment for our afternoon game.

B. Circle the irregular past participle in parentheses ( ). Then write it on the line to complete the sentence.

1. By May I had _____ about an amazing automobile. (hear, heard)

2. Test drivers have _____ it on experimental runs. (taken, took)

3. My friend's family has _____ to Utah to see it. (went, gone)

4. My friend has _____ in the automobile, too. (ridden, rode)

5. I have _____ this car as a research topic. (chose, chosen)

6. My mom has _____ photos of the car, too. (bought, buy)

7. I have also _____ home articles and books about the car. (bring, brought)

Scholastic Professional Books

Irregular Verbs

A. Complete each sentence. Fill in the bubble next to the irregular past-tense verb.

1. Last week, we _____ the news about our baseball team's victory.
   - ⓐ hear
   - ⓑ heard
   - ⓒ hears

2. Yesterday morning, Mom and I _____ the bus downtown.
   - ⓐ rode
   - ⓑ rides
   - ⓒ ride

3. Then we _____ in line for an hour.
   - ⓐ stand
   - ⓑ stands
   - ⓒ stood

4. We finally _____ four tickets to the first game in the playoffs.
   - ⓐ bought
   - ⓑ buys
   - ⓒ buying

5. Then we _____ lunch to celebrate.
   - ⓐ eat
   - ⓑ ate
   - ⓒ eats

B. Complete each sentence. Fill in the bubble next to the correct helping verb and past participle.

1. That old adobe house _____ on top of the mesa for a century.
   - ⓐ has stood
   - ⓑ has stand
   - ⓒ has stands

2. We _____ up there many times.
   - ⓐ have rode
   - ⓑ have ride
   - ⓒ have ridden

3. Our great-grandfather _____ pictures of the house long ago.
   - ⓐ had drawn
   - ⓑ had draw
   - ⓒ had drew

4. We _____ the sketches for many years.
   - ⓐ have keep
   - ⓑ have kept
   - ⓒ have keeps

5. Fortunately, my family _____ very good care of the drawings.
   - ⓐ has took
   - ⓑ has take
   - ⓒ has taken

Adjectives

A. **In the following sentences, circle the adjectives that tell what kind. Underline the adjectives that tell how many.**

> **RETEACHING:** An **adjective** is a word that tells more about a person, place, or thing.

1. We watched many colorful creatures swim through the dark water.

2. A few tilefish were building small burrows.

3. Suddenly one strange and unusual fish swam by us.

4. Eugenie swam over to the mysterious fish.

5. It looked like a jawfish with a big head and four dark patches on its back.

6. Was this rare fish a new species?

7. We put the tiny fish in a large bucket of cold seawater.

8. Eugenie has made several amazing discoveries.

B. **Complete each sentence with an adjective that tells what kind or how many.**

1. The _____ fish was named after David.

2. The fish had a _____ head.

3. The fish lived in a _____ burrow at the bottom of the ocean.

4. The tiny fish turned out to be a _____ species.

5. David took _____ photographs that appeared in magazines.

C. **Write two sentences. Use adjectives that tell what kind and how many in each sentence.**

1. _____

2. _____

Adjectives

A. Write an adjective to complete each sentence.

> **RETEACHING:** An **adjective** is a word that tells more about a person, place, or thing.

1. The _____ dog ate most of the cat's food.

2. The _____ cat found a nearly empty bowl.

3. The cat ate what remained of her _____ meal.

4. The cat pushed the _____ dish over to where a _____ girl was sitting.

5. The girl refilled the dish with _____ food.

B. Read each sentence. Circle the adjective that describes each underlined noun.

1. The gray <u>cat</u> saw the shaggy <u>dog</u> sitting in the dark <u>corner</u>.

2. The cat saw some <u>cat food</u> on the dog's droopy <u>mouth</u>.

3. The cat slipped out of the little <u>kitchen</u> and went into the quiet <u>backyard</u>.

4. She started digging in the soft <u>dirt</u> under a shady <u>tree</u>.

5. The dog looked out the enormous <u>window</u> and saw the cat with a large <u>bone</u>.

C. Write two sentences that tell what happened next. Use vivid adjectives in your writing.

1. _____

_____

2. _____

_____

Adjectives

Fill in the bubble next to the word in each sentence that is an adjective.

1. I had an important decision to make this morning.
   - ⓐ important
   - ⓑ decision
   - ⓒ morning

2. I wanted to buy an appropriate pet for my sister.
   - ⓐ wanted
   - ⓑ buy
   - ⓒ appropriate

3. First, I looked at a striped lizard.
   - ⓐ First
   - ⓑ striped
   - ⓒ lizard

4. Then, I considered getting two hamsters.
   - ⓐ considered
   - ⓑ two
   - ⓒ hamsters

5. The white hamster was named George.
   - ⓐ white
   - ⓑ hamster
   - ⓒ George

6. I admired the noisy parrot.
   - ⓐ I
   - ⓑ noisy
   - ⓒ parrot

7. I watched a gigantic turtle on a rock.
   - ⓐ gigantic
   - ⓑ turtle
   - ⓒ rock

8. Several gerbils ran on a wheel.
   - ⓐ Several
   - ⓑ gerbils
   - ⓒ wheel

9. I finally decided to get a saltwater aquarium.
   - ⓐ decided
   - ⓑ saltwater
   - ⓒ aquarium

10. I'm sure my family will enjoy the colorful fish.
    - ⓐ sure
    - ⓑ family
    - ⓒ colorful

Scholastic Professional Books

Adjectives That Compare

A. In each sentence, underline the adjective that compares.

> **RETEACHING: Comparative adjectives** compare two things by adding –er to the adjective or by using the word *more*. **Superlative adjectives** compare three or more things by adding –est or by using the word *most*.

1. Anna is older than her brother Caleb.

2. That was the loudest thunderstorm of the entire summer.

3. Seal is the biggest cat that I have ever seen.

4. Papa is quieter than Sarah.

5. The roof of the barn is higher than the top of the haystack.

6. The kitten's fur was softer than lamb's wool.

7. Sarah pointed to the brightest star in the sky.

8. What is the saddest moment in the story?

B. Underline the adjective in parentheses ( ) that completes each sentence correctly. On the line write *two* or *more than two* to show how many things are being compared.

1. On the (hotter, hottest) day in July, we went swimming. _____

2. Today is (warmer, warmest) than last Tuesday. _____

3. Is winter (colder, coldest) on the prairie or by the sea? _____

4. This is the (taller, tallest) tree in the entire state. _____

5. Sarah's hair is (longer, longest) than Maggie's. _____

6. Of the three dogs, Nick was the (friendlier, friendliest). _____

7. Caleb's horse is (younger, youngest) than Anna's pony. _____

8. The new foal is the (livelier, liveliest) animal on the farm. _____

Adjectives That Compare

Choose the adjective that completes each sentence and write it on the line.

funnier   funniest

1. The _____ book I've ever read is about a family of mice.

2. The book is much _____ than the movie.

busier   busiest

3. The book department is _____ than the shoe department.

4. The _____ bookstore in the city is on King Street.

more exciting   most exciting

5. Hiking in the woods is _____ than watching TV.

6. This is the _____ ride at the amusement park.

more challenging   most challenging

7. Is a game of checkers _____ than a game of chess?

8. I think that soccer is the _____ of all the field games.

more tiring   most tiring

9. We found that swimming was _____ than walking.

10. Of all the afternoon's activities, tennis was the _____.

more delicious   most delicious

11. The strawberries are _____ than the green grapes.

12. This is the _____ apple that I have ever eaten.

Adjectives That Compare

Fill in the bubble next to the correct comparative or superlative adjective.

1. I believe that a dog is much _____ than a cat.
   - ⓐ friendlier
   - ⓑ friendliest

2. My poodle is the _____ dog of all the dogs in the dog-training class.
   - ⓐ more intelligent
   - ⓑ most intelligent

3. The gazelle is the _____ animal in the animal park.
   - ⓐ more graceful
   - ⓑ most graceful

4. The movie about turtles is _____ than the book about frogs.
   - ⓐ more fascinating
   - ⓑ most fascinating

5. The diamondback rattler is _____ than a bull snake.
   - ⓐ more dangerous
   - ⓑ most dangerous

6. I think that the jaguar is the _____ of all the big cats.
   - ⓐ more beautiful
   - ⓑ most beautiful

7. Did you know that a cheetah is _____ than a lion?
   - ⓐ swifter
   - ⓑ swiftest

8. Your parrot is _____ than my cockatoo.
   - ⓐ noisier
   - ⓑ noisiest

9. This chimpanzee is _____ than that gorilla.
   - ⓐ more playful
   - ⓑ most playful

10. That polar bear is the _____ mammal I've ever seen.
    - ⓐ larger
    - ⓑ largest

Prepositions

A. Read each sentence. Underline each group of words that begins with a preposition, and circle the preposition. Some sentences have more than one prepositional phrase.

> **RETEACHING: Prepositions** show the relationship between a noun or pronoun and another word or group of words in a sentence such as *in, on, of, for,* or *at.* Groups of words introduced by a preposition are called **prepositional phrases.**

1. The boy cut out pictures of mountains, rivers, and lakes.

2. He enjoyed pasting them on the walls of his room.

3. His father responded to the scenes in the pictures.

4. He decided that he would take his son on a camping trip.

5. They carried supplies in a backpack and knapsack.

6. The boy drank a hot drink from his father's mug.

7. That afternoon they hiked in the mountains for hours.

8. They were disappointed when they found many campers at the Lost Lake.

9. The boy and his father continued on their journey.

10. Finally, they stopped at a quiet place for the night.

11. The boy and his father ate and slept in a tent.

12. The tent kept them safe from the wind and rain.

13. Will this trip make the boy feel closer to his father?

14. What else will they see on their camping trip?

B. Complete each sentence with a prepositional phrase.

1. Let's go to the store _____

2. I just received a letter _____

3. Eduardo found his missing sneaker _____

4. Tanya always plays soccer _____

Prepositions

A. Circle the preposition in each sentence.

1. Herb often goes hiking in the Rocky Mountains.

2. He always carries a water jug and a compass with him.

3. Today he saw wild columbines growing on the mountainsides.

4. Then he passed a doe and her fawn searching for food.

5. The deer stood very still and stared at him.

6. Then the two creatures disappeared into the woods.

B. Complete each sentence with a prepositional phrase. You may wish to use some of the prepositions from part A or the prepositions *from, over, under, to,* **or** *by.*

1. Each summer Suzanne goes camping _____

2. Usually they camp _____

3. They pitch their small, green tent _____

4. Her mother cooks _____

5. Suzanne sometimes hears ravens cawing _____

6. Once she saw a black bear running very quickly _____

C. Use the prepositions *of, with,* **and** *at* **in three sentences of your own.**

1. _____

2. _____

3. _____

Prepositions

Fill in the bubble next to the word from the sentence that is a preposition.

1. Last summer the Camachos took a trip to three national parks.
   - ⓐ to
   - ⓑ trip
   - ⓒ Last

2. The family was from San Antonio, Texas.
   - ⓐ family
   - ⓑ was
   - ⓒ from

3. The family left their home on a Saturday morning.
   - ⓐ family
   - ⓑ on
   - ⓒ left

4. First they headed for Carlsbad Caverns, New Mexico.
   - ⓐ for
   - ⓑ First
   - ⓒ Caverns

5. Rita saw bats fly over her head.
   - ⓐ saw
   - ⓑ bats
   - ⓒ over

6. Next the family visited cliff dwellings left by the Anasazi people.
   - ⓐ Next
   - ⓑ cliff
   - ⓒ by

7. Then they camped at Arches National Park.
   - ⓐ at
   - ⓑ they
   - ⓒ Then

8. Edwin sat under a sandstone formation called Delicate Arch.
   - ⓐ sat
   - ⓑ under
   - ⓒ called

9. Rita and Edwin took photographs of their favorite sites.
   - ⓐ took
   - ⓑ their
   - ⓒ of

10. They talked with their friends the next week.
    - ⓐ talked
    - ⓑ with
    - ⓒ their

Scholastic Professional Books

Subject-Verb Agreement

A. Underline the subject once and the verb twice. Write *present* if the verb is in the present tense and *past* if the verb is in the past tense.

> **RETEACHING: Subjects** and **verbs** in a sentence must agree in number. Add *–s* or *–es* to present tense verbs used with *he, she, it,* or a singular noun. Do not add *–s* or *–es* to present tense verbs used with *I, you, we, they,* or a plural noun.

1. Tucker lives in a drain pipe. _____

2. It opens into a pocket. _____

3. Tucker collected stuffing for the pocket. _____

4. The mouse filled the pocket with paper and cloth. _____

5. Tucker sits at the opening of the drain pipe. _____

6. He watches the people in the subway station. _____

7. The young boy worked at his father's newsstand. _____

8. They sell papers there on weekdays. _____

B. Underline the subject once and the verb twice. Then write *singular* if the subject and verb are singular and *plural* if the subject and verb are plural.

1. The nighttime crowd passes by quickly. _____

2. Trains run less often at that time. _____

3. Papa waits for business. _____

4. The station feels quiet and lonely. _____

5. People rush home at the end of the day. _____

6. Mama and Papa make very little money. _____

Subject-Verb Agreement

A. Underline the subject. Then circle the verb in parentheses ( ) that agrees with the subject.

> **RETEACHING: Subjects** and **verbs** in a sentence must agree in number. Add *–s* or *–es* to present tense verbs used with *he, she, it,* or a singular noun. Do not add *–s* or *–es* to present tense verbs used with *I, you, we, they,* or a plural noun.

1. Crickets _____ a musical sound. (make, makes)

2. Actually, only the males _____ sounds. (produce, produces)

3. I _____ for the sound of crickets on a summer night. (listen, listens)

4. You _____ them in places outside the city. (hear, hears)

5. Mario _____ a cricket in the subway station. (find, finds)

6. His mother _____ the cricket a "bug." (call, calls)

B. Underline the subject and verb in each sentence. Then rewrite each sentence in the present tense. Be sure your subjects and verbs agree.

1. Mario wanted the cricket for a pet.

   _____

2. He wished for a pet of his own.

   _____

3. Crickets seemed like unusual pets to his mother.

   _____

4. Maybe insects scared her!

   _____

Subject-Verb Agreement

A. Fill in the bubble next to the verb that agrees with the subject of the sentence.

1. Chester _____ tall buildings for the first time.
   - ⓐ see
   - ⓑ sees

2. The city _____ him.
   - ⓐ surprise
   - ⓑ surprises

3. The stars _____ Chester's attention.
   - ⓐ catch
   - ⓑ catches

4. Maybe he _____ for his home in Connecticut.
   - ⓐ wish
   - ⓑ wishes

5. One star _____ familiar to Chester.
   - ⓐ is
   - ⓑ are

B. Is the underlined verb correct? Fill in the bubble next to the right answer.

1. Now the animals <u>crouch</u> against the cement.
   - ⓐ crouches
   - ⓑ crouched
   - ⓒ correct as is

2. At this moment, their eyes <u>is</u> on the sky.
   - ⓐ are
   - ⓑ were
   - ⓒ correct as is

3. The sky <u>looks</u> so beautiful right now.
   - ⓐ look
   - ⓑ looked
   - ⓒ correct as is

4. Last night the cricket <u>view</u> Times Square for the first time.
   - ⓐ views
   - ⓑ viewed
   - ⓒ correct as is

5. One week ago, Chester <u>experiences</u> a much different world.
   - ⓐ experience
   - ⓑ experienced
   - ⓒ correct as is

Punctuating Dialogue

A. **Underline the exact words of the speaker. Circle the quotation marks.**

1. Eva exclaimed, "I really like tall tales!"

2. "Davy Crockett is my favorite character," said Juan.

3. I asked, "Who likes Sally Ann Thunder Ann Whirlwind?"

B. **Add the missing quotation marks to each sentence.**

1. __I am a big fan of hers,__ replied Shavon.

2. I added, __Sally can even sing a wolf to sleep.__

3. __How did Sally tame King Bear?__ asked our teacher.

4. __Sally really ought to be in the movies,__ said Don.

C. **Write the missing punctuation marks in each sentence.**

1. __What kind of person is Sally __ __ asked Davy Crockett__

2. The schoolmarm replied__ __Sally is a special friend__ __

3. __She can laugh the bark off a pine tree__ __ added Lucy__

4. The preacher said__ __She can dance a rock to pieces__ __

5. __I'm very impressed__ __ exclaimed Davy__

D. **Write two sentences of dialogue between Davy Crockett and Sally.**

1. _____

2. _____

Scholastic Professional Books

Punctuating Dialogue

A. Add the missing commas to the sentences.

1. "Well__ we are having a canned-food drive
   next week."

2. "Oh__ Ed__ can you bring some containers to school?"

3. "Yes__ I have several at home, Jody."

4. "Thank you__ Mr. Poole, for all your suggestions."

B. Add the missing quotation marks and/or commas to each sentence.

1. __ Kim, your posters for the talent contest are terrific!__ I exclaimed.

2. She replied, __ Thank you, Doug, for your kind words.__

3. Our teacher asked, __ Meg__ will you play your guitar or sing?__

4. "Oh__ I plan to do both,__ said Meg.

5. __ Will you perform your juggling act this year Roberto?__ Jay asked.

6. __ No__ I want to do a comedy routine,__ he replied.

C. Add the missing punctuation to each sentence.

1. __ Kit__ which act did you like best__ __ asked Mina__

2. He replied__ __ Oh__ I enjoyed the singing pumpkins and the tap
   dancing elephants__ __

3. __ Well__ I liked the guitar player__ __ said Mina__

D. Write two more sentences of dialogue about a school talent show.

1. _____

2. _____

Punctuating Dialogue

Decide if there is an error in the underlined part of each sentence.
Fill in the bubble next to the correct answer.

1. "Rosa, tell me one of your <u>favorite jokes</u>" said Ken.
   - ⓐ favorite jokes."
   - ⓑ favorite jokes,"
   - ⓒ correct as is

2. "What do <u>sharks eat?</u> she asked.
   - ⓐ sharks eat?"
   - ⓑ sharks eat"
   - ⓒ correct as is

3. Ken replied <u>"tell</u> me. I don't know.
   - ⓐ Ken replied. "Tell
   - ⓑ Ken replied, "Tell
   - ⓒ correct as is

4. "They eat peanut butter and jellyfish <u>sandwiches," replied</u> Rosa.
   - ⓐ sandwiches" replied
   - ⓑ sandwiches." replied
   - ⓒ correct as is

5. <u>Oh, that</u> was funny!" exclaimed Ken.
   - ⓐ "Oh, that
   - ⓑ Oh that
   - ⓒ correct as is

6. <u>Rosa? tell</u> me another one," he said.
   - ⓐ "Rosa tell
   - ⓑ "Rosa, tell
   - ⓒ correct as is

7. "What years do frogs <u>like best</u> asked Rosa smugly.
   - ⓐ like best?"
   - ⓑ like best,"
   - ⓒ correct as is

8. "Frogs like Hoppy New <u>Years,"</u> <u>laughed</u> Ken.
   - ⓐ Years" laughed
   - ⓑ Years, laughed
   - ⓒ correct as is

9. <u>"No frogs</u> like leap years," insisted Rosa.
   - ⓐ "No, frogs
   - ⓑ No frogs
   - ⓒ correct as is

10. "Ken <u>said. "my</u> joke is funnier."
    - ⓐ said "My
    - ⓑ said, "My
    - ⓒ correct as is

Scholastic Professional Books

Adverbs

A. Underline the verb. Then circle the adverb that tells when.

> **RETEACHING:** An **adverb** is a word that describes a verb, an adjective, or another adverb. Some adverbs tell when or where something happens.

1. Later, newsboys shouted the weekend forecast.

2. That night, a huge snowstorm hit New York City.

3. It got very cold soon.

4. A train tried to plow through the snow earlier.

5. Then the train went off the track.

B. Underline the verb. Then circle the adverb that tells where.

1. Snow fell everywhere.

2. Drifts of snow piled up.

3. People were trapped inside.

4. Some people tunneled out from their homes.

5. People there traveled by sled.

C. Underline the adverb in each sentence. Write *when* if the adverb tells when or *where* if it tells where.

1. People had never seen a storm so bad.   _____

2. Pipes burst underground.   _____

3. The water inside had frozen.   _____

4. Soon people started to freeze, too.   _____

Adverbs

A. Underline the verb once. Then circle the adverb that describes the verb and tells how.

> **RETEACHING:** An **adverb** describes a verb, an adjective, or another adverb. Some adverbs tell how. Many adverbs that tell how end in *-ly*.

1. Grandma talked happily to the frolicking sea lions.

2. The sea birds squawked sharply as they dived.

3. Andy greeted the girl and Grandma warmly.

4. He guided them expertly through the Galápagos Islands.

5. Grandma wrote about the islands regularly in her diary.

6. The girl recorded the trip faithfully in her diary.

7. She responded personally to everything she saw.

8. Andy and the girl looked eagerly at the creatures on the shore.

9. Grandma and the girl jumped quickly off the boat.

10. They snorkeled easily with their breathing tubes and fins.

11. The girl saw sea creatures clearly through her face mask.

12. She gazed intently at the yellow-tailed surgeonfish.

13. Swiftly the sea lions surrounded Grandma and the girl.

14. The sea lion pups chased and nipped one another playfully.

B. Complete each sentence with an action verb and an adverb that describes it and tells how.

1. The big male sea lion _____

2. The girl and her grandmother _____

Adverbs

A. Fill in the bubble next to the adverb that tells how.

1. Carolina and Gabriella dove rapidly under a big wave.

   ⓐ rapidly
   ⓑ under
   ⓒ big

2. Then a wave crashed loudly against the shore.

   ⓐ crashed
   ⓑ loudly
   ⓒ against

3. Both Carolina and Gabriella were very strong swimmers.

   ⓐ Both
   ⓑ very
   ⓒ strong

4. At the beach, the tide was somewhat low.

   ⓐ At
   ⓑ low
   ⓒ somewhat

5. Carolina quickly spotted a group of bottle-nose dolphins.

   ⓐ quickly
   ⓑ spotted
   ⓒ bottle-nose

B. Fill in the bubble next to the word that is <u>not</u> an adverb.

1. Gabriella and Carolina swam very slowly toward the playful mammals.

   ⓐ very
   ⓑ slowly
   ⓒ playful

2. "They are so curious!" Carolina exclaimed excitedly.

   ⓐ so
   ⓑ curious
   ⓒ excitedly

3. One baby dolphin came very close.

   ⓐ One
   ⓑ very
   ⓒ close

4. The mother dolphin nudged Carolina so gently.

   ⓐ nudged
   ⓑ so
   ⓒ gently

5. Then swiftly and mysteriously, the dolphins disappeared.

   ⓐ swiftly
   ⓑ disappeared
   ⓒ mysteriously

Scholastic Success With

WRITING

Sassy Sentences

 A **sentence** is a group of words that expresses a complete thought. When you write a sentence, you put your thoughts into words. If the sentence is complete, the meaning is clear. It contains a subject (the naming part) and a predicate (an action or state of being part).

These are sentences.
Sally sells seashells at the seashore.
Betty Botter bought a bit of better butter.

These are not sentences.
Peck of pickled peppers.
Flying up a flue.

Make complete sentences by adding words to each group of words. Try to create tongue twisters like the sentences above.

1. _____ flips fine flapjacks.

2. Sixty slippery seals _____.

3. _____ fed Ted _____.

4. Ruby Rugby's baby brother _____.

5. _____ managing an imaginary magazine.

6. Sam's sandwich shop _____.

7. _____ back blue balloons.

8. _____ pink peacock pompously _____.

9. Pete's pop Pete _____.

10. _____ sawed Mr. Saw's _____.

11. A flea and a fly _____.

12. _____ black-backed bumblebee.

 Create your own tongue twisters to share with friends. Make sure each one expresses a complete thought.

Link It Together

 A sentence needs two parts, a subject and a predicate,
to express a complete thought.
The **subject part** tells whom or what the sentence is about.
The **predicate part** tells what the subject is or does.

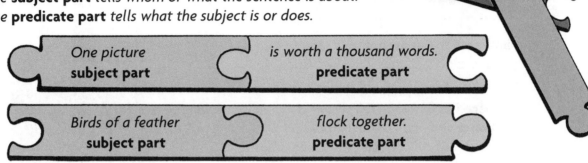

One picture	is worth a thousand words.
subject part	**predicate part**

Birds of a feather	flock together.
subject part	**predicate part**

A. Read the subject and predicate parts from some other famous sayings.
Write *S* next to each subject part. Write *P* next to each predicate part.

_____ half a loaf   _____ must go on

_____ one good turn   _____ gathers no moss

_____ spoils the whole barrel   _____ has a silver lining

_____ the show   _____ makes waste

_____ every cloud   _____ one rotten apple

_____ deserves another   _____ a rolling stone

_____ catches the worm   _____ is better than none

_____ the early bird   _____ haste

B. Now combine the subject and predicate parts to create these famous sayings.

1. _____

2. _____

3. _____

4. _____

5. _____

6. _____

7. _____

8. _____

 **Make up some sayings of your own. Then circle the subject part and underline the predicate
part of each sentence.**

That's Groovy!

 There are four kinds of sentences. Each one does something different.

A **declarative sentence** *tells something.*
It is a **statement** *and ends with a period.*
> **My grandparents grew up during the 1960s.**

An **interrogative sentence** *asks something.*
It is a **question** *and ends with a question mark.*
> **Do you know who the hippies were?**

An **imperative sentence** *tells someone to do something.*
It is a **command** *and ends with a period.*
> **Check out this photo of my grandmother.**

An **exclamatory sentence** *shows strong feeling.*
It is an **exclamation** *and ends with an exclamation mark.*
> **Now that's one strange-looking outfit she has on!**

Read the following sentences. Identify what kind of sentence each one is. Write *S* for statement, *Q* for question, *C* for command, and *E* for exclamation.

_____ **1.** Grandma says there was a fashion revolution in the 1960s.

_____ **2.** What an amazing time it must have been!

_____ **3.** Here's a photo of my grandfather in his teens.

_____ **4.** How do you like those sideburns and the long hair?

_____ **5.** Take a look at what he's wearing.

_____ **6.** I don't believe those bellbottoms and sandals!

_____ **7.** Please tell me he's not wearing beads.

_____ **8.** I'm glad these fashions are no longer in style!

_____ **9.** Have you ever seen anything so funny?

_____ **10.** Try not to laugh too hard.

_____ **11.** One day our grandchildren may laugh at us.

_____ **12.** What's so funny about what we're wearing?

Now, look at other "photos" from the sixties and write a statement (S), a question (Q), a command (C), and an exclamation (E) about each one. Make sure to begin and end your sentences correctly.

S _____

Q _____

C _____

E _____

S _____

Q _____

C _____

E _____

S _____

Q _____

C _____

E _____

Invite someone to listen as you expressively read aloud the sentences that you wrote, showing what kind of sentences they are by the way that you read them.

A Whale of a Fish

When you write, the words and phrases in your sentences must be in an order that makes sense. Compare the sentences in each pair. Which ones make more sense?

An enormous fish what the whale shark is!
What an enormous fish the whale shark is!

The largest fish in the world the whale shark is.
The whale shark is the largest fish in the world.

Use each group of words to write a sentence that makes sense.

1. of 60 feet?   that the whale shark   Did you know   to a length   can grow

_____

2. two school buses   end to end!   That's about   parked   as long as

_____

3. are not a threat   These huge creatures   like some other sharks are.   to humans

_____

4. to look for   float near the surface   plankton and tiny fish.   Whale sharks

_____

5. it must be   alongside a whale shark.   Imagine   to swim   how amazing

_____

Now rewrite the following sentences so that the words and phrases are in an order that makes better sense.

6. An estimated 20,000 known species of fish there are in the world.

_____

7. Of all these species the smallest is the dwarf pygmy goby?

_____

8. When it is fully grown is less than a half-inch long this species of goby!

_____

9. In the massive Indian Ocean makes its home this tiny fish.

_____

Number Sentences

Words such as who, what, where, why, when, *and* how, *and helping verbs such as* is, are, was, were, do, did, *and* can *at the beginning of sentences, signal interrogative sentences, or questions.*

What *is an odd number?*
Do *you know what an even number is?*
Is *2 an odd number or an even number?*

Change each statement below into a question. Remember to begin and end each sentence correctly.

1. Numbers that cannot be divided evenly by 2 are called odd numbers.

_____

2. All even numbers can be divided evenly by 2.

_____

3. Zero is considered an even number.

_____

4. Numbers that have 0, 2, 4, 6, or 8 in the ones place are even numbers.

_____

5. Odd numbers end in 1, 3, 5, 7, or 9.

_____

6. The number 317,592 is an even number because it ends in 2.

_____

7. The sum is always an even number when you add two even numbers.

_____

8. The sum of two odd numbers is also an even number.

_____

9. The same rule applies if you subtract an odd number from an odd number.

_____

10. You can figure out all the rules for working with odd and even numbers.

_____

Proofing Pays

Capitalization and end punctuation help show where one sentence ends and the next one begins. Whenever you write, proofread to make sure each sentence begins with a capital letter and ends correctly. Here's an example of how to mark the letters that should be capitalized.

have you ever heard of a Goliath birdeater? it is
the world's largest spider. this giant tarantula can grow
to 11 inches in length and weigh about 6 ounces. now that's
a big spider! although it is called a birdeater, it usually
eats small reptiles and insects. these spiders are
mostly found in rain forests .

Read the passage below. It is about another amazing animal, but it is not so easy to read because the writer forgot to add end punctuation and to use capital letters at the beginning of sentences. Proofread the passage. Mark the letters that should be capitals with the capital letter symbol. Put the correct punctuation marks at the ends of sentences. Then reread the passage.

think about the fastest car you've ever seen in the Indianapolis 500 race

that's about how fast a peregrine falcon dives it actually reaches speeds up to

175 miles an hour how incredibly fast they are peregrine falcons are also very

powerful birds did you know that they can catch and kill their prey in the air

using their sharp claws what's really amazing is that peregrine falcons live in

both the country and in the city keep on the lookout if you're ever in New York

City believe it or not, it is home to a very large population of falcons

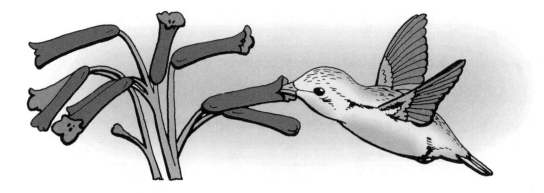

What do you know about the bee hummingbird, atlas moth, or capybara? Choose one, do some research, and write several sentences about it on a piece of paper. Then proofread your writing. Does every sentence begin and end correctly? Are all the words spelled correctly?

Spout Some Specifics

 To be a good writer, it is important to know what you are writing about, to be specific, and to include details. All this helps to create a picture for your readers and will make your writing more interesting and informative. Compare the two phrases below. Which one is more specific, interesting, and informative? Which one creates a more vivid picture?

a vehicle or *an old, rusty, dilapidated pick-up truck with flat tires and a shattered windshield*

For each general word or phrase, write a more specific word. Then add details to describe each specific word.

	Specific Word	Details
1. a body of water		
2. a piece of furniture		
3. an article of clothing		
4. a child's toy		
5. a noise or sound		
6. a tool		
7. a group of people		
8. a reptile		
9. garden plants		
10. a kind of fruit		
11. a kind of vegetable		
12. a drink		
13. footwear		
14. musical instrument		
15. a holiday		

 Look at yourself in the mirror. Then write on a piece of paper as many words and phrases as you can to describe yourself so that someone who does not know you would get a clear, vivid picture of what you look like.

Make It Interesting

 A sentence can be very simple. This sentence tells who did what.

The crew worked.

As you write and revise your writing, add details about people, places, or things, or about where, when, and what happens. This will make your writing more interesting. Here's how the sentence above was revised several times. Each sentence gives a little more information.

The construction crew worked.
The construction crew worked quickly.
The construction crew worked quickly to clear the rubble.
The construction crew worked quickly to clear the rubble at the building site.
The construction crew worked quickly yesterday to clear the rubble at the building site.

Rewrite each sentence four times. Add new details each time to tell more about whom or what, how, where, and when.

The children played.

1. _____

_____

2. _____

_____

3. _____

_____

4. _____

_____

A package arrived.

1. _____

_____

2. _____

_____

3. _____

_____

4. _____

_____

 Rewrite the following sentence several times on a piece of paper. Remove a detail each time until you are left with a very simple sentence.

The excited team cheered wildly after winning the championship basketball game.

Order the Combination

Have you ever noticed how short sentences can make your writing sound choppy? When two sentences have different subjects and the same predicate, you can use the conjunction and *to combine them into one sentence with a compound subject.*

My friends ordered a pepperoni pizza. I ordered a pepperoni pizza.
My friends and I ordered a pepperoni pizza.

When two sentences have the same subject and different predicates, you can use and *to combine them into one sentence with a compound predicate.*

My mom ordered. She had pasta instead.
My mom ordered and had pasta instead.

When two sentences have the same subject and predicate and different objects, you can combine them into one sentence with a compound object using and.

My dad wanted anchovies on his pizza. He also wanted onions.
My dad wanted anchovies and onions on his pizza.

Fill in the missing subject, object, or predicate in each set of shorter sentences. Then combine the sentences by making compound subjects, objects, or predicates using *and*.

1. _____ are sweet and juicy.

   _____ are sweet and juicy.

   _____

2. I _____ about the history of basketball for homework.

   I _____ about the history of basketball for homework.

   _____

3. _____ is so much fun!

   _____ is also so much fun! (Change *is* to *are*.)

   _____

4. I like _____ more than broccoli or cauliflower.

   I like _____ more than broccoli or cauliflower.

   _____

5. I'd like to have _____ for breakfast.

   I'd also like to have _____ for breakfast.

   _____

A New Challenge

When you write, you may want to show how the ideas in two simple sentences are related. You can combine the two sentences by using a comma and the conjunctions and, but, *or* or *to show the connection.* And *shows a link between the ideas,* but *shows a contrast, and* or *shows a choice. The new sentence is called a* **compound sentence**.

My sister wants to join a football team. My parents aren't so happy about it.
My sister wants to join a football team, but **my parents aren't so happy about it.**

Annie is determined. Her friends think she'd make a great place kicker.
Annie is determined, and **her friends think she'd make a great place kicker.**

Should Annie play football? Should she try something else?
Should Annie play football, or **should she try something else?**

Combine each pair of sentences. Use *and, but,* or *or* to show the connection between the ideas and make a compound sentence.

1. My sister Annie has always participated in sports. Many say she's a natural athlete.

_____

_____

2. Soccer, basketball, and softball are fun. She wanted a new challenge.

_____

_____

3. My sister talked to my brother and me. We were honest with her.

_____

_____

4. I told Annie to go for it. My brother told her to stick with soccer or basketball.

_____

_____

5. Will Dad convince her to try skiing? Will he suggest ice skating?

_____

_____

Continue the story about Annie's choice on another piece of paper. Include some compound sentences to tell what happens. Make sure your sentences begin and end correctly. Remember to check for spelling errors.

Scholastic Professional Books

Hot Subjects

 If two sentences share the same subject, information about the subject can be written as a phrase after the subject in the new sentence. Be sure to use commas to set apart the phrase from the rest of the sentence.

Sentence 1: **The Gateway Arch is America's tallest human-made monument.**

Sentence 2: **The monument rises 630 feet above the ground.**

Combined: **The Gateway Arch, America's tallest human-made monument, rises 630 feet above the ground.**

Read the sentences. Combine the ideas in each pair into one sentence by including information in a phrase after the subject in the sentence.

1. **The Caspian Sea is the world's largest lake.**
The lake covers an area about the same size as Montana.

_____

2. **The Komodo dragon is a member of the monitor family.**
It can grow to a length of 10 feet.

_____

3. **Our closest star is the sun.**
It is estimated to be more than 27,000,000°F.

_____

4. **Ronald W. Reagan was our nation's 40th president.**
He worked as a Hollywood actor for almost 30 years.

_____

5. **Georgia is the state that grows the most peanuts.**
It harvests over 1.3 billion pounds each year.

_____

6. **Hank Aaron is major league baseball's all-time home-run hitter.**
He broke Babe Ruth's record in 1974.

_____

Sentence Building

When you write about something, try to include interesting details. Sometimes you can take the important details from several related sentences and add them to the main sentence.

Kyle and Jim had a great plan.
They're my brothers.
The plan was for a tree house.

Now here's a sentence that combines all the important details.
My brothers Kyle and Jim had a great plan for a tree house.

Read each group of sentences. Take the important details from the two related sentences and add them to the main sentence to make one sentence.

1. My brothers built a tree house. They built it in the old oak tree. It's in our backyard.

_____

2. Jim made a ladder for the tree house. He made it out of rope. It is sturdy.

_____

3. Kyle bought paint. The paint was brown. He bought a gallon.

_____

4. Kyle and Jim finished painting. They painted the walls. It took an hour.

_____

5. Jim painted a sign. He painted "no trespassing." The sign is on the tree house door.

_____

6. A squirrel leaped into their tree house. It leaped from a branch. It was curious.

_____

7. The visitor startled my brothers. It was unexpected. My brothers were unsuspecting.

_____

8. The squirrel leaped out of the tree house. It was frightened. It was in a big hurry.

_____

 Write three short sentences on a piece of paper about a funny experience. Then try to combine them into one sentence. Which sounds better, one sentence with lots of details or two or three shorter sentences each with one detail? Why?

Scholastic Professional Books

Applause for the Clause

Sometimes you can use words such as when, because, while, *and* before *to combine two sentences with related ideas into one sentence with a main clause and a dependent clause. A* **clause** *is a group of words with a subject and a predicate. A* **dependent clause** *cannot stand alone. An* **independent clause** *can stand alone.*

> **Lee woke up late today. He realized he hadn't set the alarm last night.**
> <u>**When Lee woke up late today,**</u> <u>**he realized he hadn't set his alarm last night.**</u>
>   ↑   ↑
>
> *This is a dependent clause.*   *This is an independent clause.*

When the dependent clause comes before the main clause as in the above sentence, add a comma after the dependent clause. If the dependent clause follows the main clause, you do not need a comma. Here's an example.

> **Lee was upset. He was going to be late for school.**
> **Lee was upset** because **he was going to be late for school.**

Use the word inside the parenteses to combine each pair of sentences into one.

1. I waited for my parents to get home. I watched a movie. **(while)**

_____

2. My brother was in his room. He had homework to do. **(because)**

_____

3. The movie was over. The power went out. **(before)**

_____

4. This happens all the time. I wasn't concerned. **(since)**

_____

5. I didn't mind the dark at first. I heard a scratching sound. **(until)**

_____

6. I found my flashlight. I started to look around. **(when)**

_____

7. I was checking the living room. I caught Alex trying to hide. **(when)**

_____

Triple the Fun

When you write, you may want to list three or more items or ideas in a series in a single sentence. Be sure to use a comma after each item in a series except after the last item.

Max dressed quickly, ate breakfast, and raced out the door.
Luis, Jamie, Leroy, and Sam met Max at the baseball field.
They were hopeful, excited, and nervous about their first game.

Answer each question below in a complete sentence. Use commas where they are needed. Make sure each sentence begins and ends correctly. Remember to check your spelling.

1. What are the titles of three books you've read recently or would like to read? Remember to underline the title of each book.

_____

2. What are four of the planets in our solar system closer to the sun than Pluto?

_____

3. What are three green, leafy vegetables?

_____

4. What countries would you like to visit? Include at least three in your answer.

_____

5. What months fall between January and July?

_____

6. What three things have you done today to help out at home?

_____

7. What states or bodies of water border your state?

_____

8. What activities do you and your friends enjoy in the summer?

_____

9. Who are some of the most important people in your life?

_____

Make up some questions like the ones above and challenge someone you know to answer them on a piece of paper. Correct the sentences.

Scholastic Professional Books

Comma Capers

 You know that you must use commas in a series of three or more items.
Max, Sam, and Alex ordered burgers, fries, and milkshakes for lunch.

Here are some additional rules you need to know about commas.
Use commas

— *to set off the name of the person or group you are addressing.*
Here's your order, boys.

— *after words like* yes, no, *and* well.
Well, what do you want to do now?

— *before a conjunction that joins two sentences.*
The boys finished lunch, and then they went to a movie.

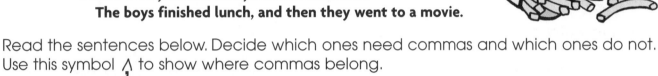

Read the sentences below. Decide which ones need commas and which ones do not.
Use this symbol ⋏ to show where commas belong.

1. I'd like a bike a pair of in-line skates and a snowboard for my birthday.

2. Well my friend you can't always have what you want when you want it.

3. No but I can always hope!

4. My friends and I skate all year long and snowboard during the winter.

5. I used to like skateboarding but now I prefer snowboarding and in-line skating.

6. What sports games or hobbies do you enjoy most Jody?

7. I learned to ski last year and now I'm taking ice-skating lessons.

8. Skiing ice skating and skateboarding are all fun things to do.

Review the four rules above for using commas. Then write an original sentence for each
rule. Begin and end each sentence correctly. Remember to check your spelling.

9. _____

10. _____

11. _____

12. _____

 **Writers use commas for other reasons. As you read a newspaper, an article in your favorite
magazine, a letter, or a book, look for examples of commas in sentences and jot them down
on a piece of paper. Then see if you can figure out the rules.**

Show Time

Sometimes a writer can change the order of the words in a sentence to
make it more interesting.

The telephone rang just as the girls were about to leave.
Just as the girls were about to leave, the phone rang.

Gina decided to answer it in spite of the time.
In spite of the time, Gina decided to answer it.

Do not forget to add a comma when you begin a sentence with a clause
or a phrase that cannot stand alone as in the second and last sentences.

Rewrite each sentence by changing the order of the words.

1. Marta watched for the bus while Gina answered the phone.

_____

2. The caller hung up just as Gina said, "Hello."

_____

3. The girls were going to miss the one o'clock show unless they hurried.

_____

4. The bus had already come and gone by the time they got to the corner.

_____

5. The next bus to town finally showed up after the girls had waited a half hour.

_____

6. The girls decided to catch the four o'clock show since they missed the earlier show.

_____

7. They wouldn't have to stand in line later since Gina bought the tickets first.

_____

8. Gina and Marta were at the theater by three o'clock even though it was early.

_____

9. They bought a tub of popcorn and drinks once they were inside.

_____

Scholastic Professional Books

Keeps On Going

 *Writers sometimes make the mistake of running together two or more sentences without telling how the ideas are related. This kind of sentence is called a **run-on sentence**.*

Kansas holds the record for having the largest ball of twine in the United States can you believe it weighs over 17,000 pounds in fact, the giant ball is 40 feet in circumference, 11 feet tall, and made up of more than 1,100 miles of twine!

To fix a run-on sentence, identify each complete thought or idea and break it into shorter sentences.

Kansas holds the record for having the largest ball of twine in the United States. Can you believe it weighs over 17,000 pounds? In fact, the giant ball is 40 feet in circumference, 11 feet tall, and made up of more than 1,100 miles of twine!

Rewrite each run-on sentence correctly. Remember to begin and end each sentence correctly.

1. Did you know that the United States is the top meat-eating country in the world each person consumes about 260 pounds of meat each year beef is the most commonly eaten meat.

_____

_____

_____

2. Have you ever noticed that Abraham Lincoln faces right on a penny he is the only president on a U.S. coin who does Sacagawea faces right on the new dollar coin, but she was not a president?

_____

_____

_____

3. It would be fantastic to have a robot to do all my chores, help do my homework, and play games I really think the day will come unfortunately, it won't come soon enough for me.

_____

_____

_____

A Long School Year

Have you ever accidentally left out words when you write? Whenever you write, it is always a good idea to proofread for words that may be missing. Here is an example of what to do when you want to add a missing word as you proofread.

    e-mail
I got an ∧ **from my friend last night.**

  met
We ∧ **last summer when my family was in Japan.**

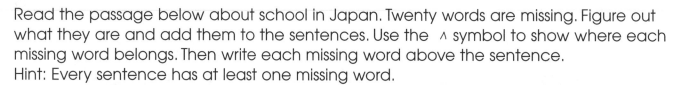

Read the passage below about school in Japan. Twenty words are missing. Figure out what they are and add them to the sentences. Use the ∧ symbol to show where each missing word belongs. Then write each missing word above the sentence.
Hint: Every sentence has at least one missing word.

  How would like to go to school on Saturdays? If you lived in the of Japan,

that's just where you'd be each Saturday morning. I have a who lives in Japan.

Yuichi explained that attend classes five and one-half a week. The day is on

Saturday. I was also surprised to that the Japanese school is one of the longest

in the world–over 240 days. It begins in the of April. While we have over two

months off each, students in Japan get their in late July and August. School

then again in fall and ends in March. The people of believe that a good is very

important. Children are required to attend school from the age of six to the of

fifteen. They have elementary and middle just like we do. Then most go on to

school for another three years. Yuichi says that students work very because the

standards are so high. He and some of his friends even extra classes after

school. They all want to get into a good someday.

Write several sentences about something that interests you on a piece of paper. Rewrite the sentences on another piece of paper, this time leaving out a key word in each one. Challenge someone you know to add the missing words. Then compare the two sets of sentences.

Parts of a Paragraph

*A **paragraph** is a group of sentences that tells about one main idea. The **topic sentence** tells the main idea and is usually the first sentence. **Supporting sentences** tell more about the main idea. The **closing sentence** of a paragraph often retells the main idea in a different way. Here are the parts for one paragraph.*

Paragraph Title: **Starting Over**

Topic Sentence: **Today started off badly and only got worse.**

Supporting Sentences: 1. **Everyone in my family woke up late this morning.**

2. **I had only 15 minutes to get ready and catch the bus.**

3. **I dressed as fast as I could, grabbed an apple and my backpack, and raced to get to the bus stop on time.**

4. **Fortunately, I just made it.**

5. **Unfortunately, the bus was pulling away when several kids pointed out that I had on two different shoes.**

Closing Sentence: **At that moment, I wanted to start the day over.**

When you write a paragraph, remember these rules:

- **Indent** *the first line to let readers know that you are beginning a paragraph.*
- **Capitalize** *the first word of each sentence.*
- **Punctuate** *each sentence correctly (? ! . ,).*

Use all the information above to write the paragraph. Be sure to follow the rules.

_____
paragraph title

_____

_____

_____

_____

_____

_____

_____

What's the Topic?

 Every paragraph has a topic sentence that tells the main idea of the paragraph, or what it is about. It usually answers several of these questions:

Who? What? Where? When? Why? How?

Here are some examples.

> **The doe and her fawn faced many dangers in the forest.**
> **We were amazed by our guest's rude behavior.**
> **Baking bread from scratch is really not so difficult, or so I thought.**
> **Getting up in the morning is the hardest thing to do.**

Did these topic sentences grab your attention? A good topic sentence should.

Here are some topics. Write a topic sentence for each one.

1. convincing someone to try octopus soup

_____

2. an important person in your life

_____

3. an embarrassing moment

_____

4. the importance of Independence Day

_____

5. lunchtime at the school cafeteria

_____

Now list some topics of your own. Then write a topic sentence for each one.

_____
Topic #1

_____   _____
Topic #2   **Topic #3**

_____
Topic sentence #1

_____
Topic sentence #2

_____
Topic sentence #3

Topic Talk

 Most paragraphs begin with a topic sentence, but it can appear elsewhere in a paragraph. Sometimes a topic sentence is located at the end of a paragraph or even in the middle.

A boiling mass of clouds was almost overhead. A bolt of lightning streaked across the darkened sky. Thunder boomed, and it began to rain and hail. <u>We had to find a safe place quickly!</u> There wasn't a moment to spare because early summer storms sometimes turn into tornadoes.

Read the paragraph again. This time try the topic sentence elsewhere in the paragraph.

Read each paragraph. Notice that each one is missing a topic sentence. Think about the supporting sentences. What main idea do you think they support? Write a topic sentence to tell the main idea of each paragraph. Remember that a topic sentence is not always the first sentence of a paragraph.

1. **The days are growing longer. The winter snows are melting as the temperatures rise. Colorful crocuses are popping up here and there. Robins have begun to return north, and creatures are beginning to come out of their winter burrows. _____**

_____

2. _____

It was fun and easy. Students, parents, and teachers began saving the box tops from all Healthful Foods products. After we collected 100,000 box tops, we mailed them to Healthful Foods headquarters. We earned 10 cents for each box top for a total of $10,000. Our school will use the money to buy computers.

3. **The last weekend in June is quickly approaching. You know what that means.**

_____

This year the festivities will begin at 10:00 A.M. at Twin Lakes Picnic Grove, pavilion 12. As always, there will be music, dancing, lots of great food, games, and some new surprises! We look forward to seeing you.

A Lot of Details

 When you are ready to write a topic sentence, think about the main topic or idea of the paragraph you will be writing and the details you plan to include. Then jot down several possible sentences and choose the best one. Remember that a topic sentence can answer several questions: Who? What? Where? When? Why? How?

Tony Hawk
- *skateboarder*
- *in his thirties*
- *turned professional at age 14*
- *has won more skateboarding contests than anyone*
- *made history at Summer X Games in 1999—landed a "900"*
   (a complete somersault done 2 ¹/₂ times in midair)

Possible topic sentences: **There is no other skateboarder like Tony Hawk.**
Tony Hawk is an extraordinary skateboarder.
Tony Hawk is the "old man" of skateboarding.

Here are some topics with details. Write two topic sentences for each one on the lines below.

1. **Pet Rocks**	2. **Komodo Dragon**	3. **A Great Dessert**
— fad in the 1970s — idea came from Gary Dahl, a salesman — sold rocks as pets — came with a manual — manual had tips on how to teach a pet rock tricks	— member of monitor family — grows to 10 feet and weighs 300 pounds — meat eater — dangerous to humans — largest lizard in the world — long neck and tail, strong legs — found on Komodo Island	— slice a banana — add vanilla ice cream — sprinkle on some walnuts — cover with lots of hot fudge sauce — top with mounds of whipped cream and a cherry

1. _____

_____

2. _____

_____

3. _____

_____

Remember that the supporting
sentences you write support or tell
more about the main idea in your
topic sentence. Read the
paragraph below. Draw one line
under the <u>topic sentence</u>. Draw
two lines under the <u>supporting
sentences</u>. Check (√) the closing
sentence.

Tony Hawk

Tony Hawk is an extraordinary skateboarder. He turned professional when he
was only 14 years old. Now in his thirties, Tony has won more skateboarding
contests than anyone else has. He even made history in 1999 by landing a trick
called the "900" at the Summer X Games. Tony Hawk may just be the greatest
skateboarder in the world.

Now, review the topics on page 200. Choose one. Then review the details listed about
the topic in the box. Next, use the information to write at least three supporting
sentences to support the topic sentence you wrote. Include a closing sentence and a
title. Write the paragraph below.

_____

_____

_____

_____

_____

_____

_____

**Make a list of topics you would like to write about. Choose one. Then list on a piece of paper
details you know about the topic. Do some research if necessary. Then write a topic sentence
and several supporting sentences.**

Drizzle With Details

 A good paragraph needs supporting sentences that tell more about the main idea of the topic sentence. Supporting sentences are sometimes called detail sentences. Every detail sentence in a paragraph must relate to the main idea. In the following paragraph, the one supporting sentence that does not relate to the main idea has been underlined.

My first day of softball practice was a total disaster! Not only was I ten minutes late, but I also forgot my glove. Then during batting practice, I missed the ball every time I took a swing. <u>I definitely have improved on my catching skills.</u> To make matters even worse, I tripped in the outfield and twisted my ankle. I was definitely not off to a very good start.

Read the following paragraph. Underline the topic sentence. Then cross out any supporting sentences that do not relate to the main idea.

Yesterday our science class went on a field trip to a pond. Next month we're going to the ocean. That will be fun. We've been studying the pond as an ecosystem in class. Our teacher wanted us to observe firsthand all the different habitats in and around the pond. She had us keep a checklist of the different kinds of plants and animals in each pond habitat. One of the boys accidentally fell in. He was really embarrassed. Along the water's edge I saw several kinds of plants partly underwater, two salamanders, snails, and water bugs. I observed many different habitats.

Scholastic Professional Books

Name _____

Read the title and topic sentence for each of the following paragraph plans. Then write four supporting sentences that relate to and support each one.

1. Paragraph Title: Uniforms--To Wear or Not to Wear?
   Topic Sentence: Our school should require all students to wear uniforms.

   Supporting Sentences:

   1. _____

   2. _____

   3. _____

   4. _____

2. Paragraph Title: An Adventure in Dreamland
   Topic Sentence: Last night I had the most incredible dream.

   Supporting Sentences:

   1. _____

   2. _____

   3. _____

   4. _____

3. Paragraph Title: A Sad Day
   Topic Sentence: I will always remember how sad I was that day.

   Supporting Sentences:

   1. _____

   2. _____

   3. _____

   4. _____

 Choose one of the titles and topic sentences above. On a piece of paper, write a paragraph using the supporting sentences you wrote above. Include more supporting sentences that relate to the topic sentence if you want. Then add a closing sentence. Remember to indent, begin and end sentences correctly, punctuate correctly, and check your spelling.

A Musical Lesson

*There are many kinds of paragraphs. When you write a **comparison paragraph**, you compare by telling how things are similar and contrast by telling how things are different. You can use a Venn diagram to help organize your ideas. Here is an example.*

Trumpet   **Both**   **Violin**

• brass

• has a mouthpiece

• has three valves

• are played in orchestras

• musical instruments

• take practice

• wood

• four strings

• played with a bow

Complete the paragraph using details to compare and contrast the trumpet and violin. Remember to capitalize and punctuate correctly.

Trumpet Versus Violin

The trumpet and violin are both musical instruments that are _____

_____. However, there are some

important differences. The trumpet _____

_____

_____

_____

On the other hand, the violin _____

_____

_____

_____

Both instruments_____

_____

 Make a list on a piece of paper of things to compare and contrast such as a house and an apartment building, ice skating and skateboarding, or spinach and broccoli. Choose one pair. Make and complete a Venn diagram like the one above. Then write a paragraph to tell how they are similar and different.

Scholastic Professional Books

Is That a Fact?

 *What is the difference between a fact and an opinion? A **fact** can be checked or proven. An opinion is what someone believes or feels about something. An **opinion** cannot be proven.*

Fact → **Cocoa beans are used to make chocolate.**

Opinion → **Chocolate pudding is better than chocolate ice cream.**

Read each sentence. Write *F* next to each fact. Write *O* next to each opinion.

_____ **1.** Everyone in the world thinks chocolate makes the best candy.

_____ **2.** In Switzerland, the average person eats about 22 pounds of chocolate in a year.

_____ **3.** That means the Swiss eat about 160 million pounds of chocolate annually.

_____ **4.** I think Americans eat more chocolate than that.

_____ **5.** People also use chocolate to make drinks and to flavor recipes.

_____ **6.** There's nothing better than a chocolate donut with chocolate glaze.

Look at the pictures. Then write two facts and two opinions about each snack food. Use clue words such as *think, best, believe, like,* and *dislike* to signal an opinion.

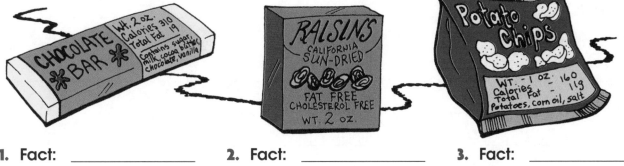

1. Fact: _____

_____

_____

Opinion: _____

_____

_____

2. Fact: _____

_____

_____

Opinion: _____

_____

_____

3. Fact: _____

_____

_____

Opinion: _____

_____

_____

 As you listen to a conversation among your friends about an issue that is important to them, try to identify the facts and opinions you hear and write them down on a piece of paper. Then ask, "Can this statement be proven?" If the answer is yes, then it is a fact. If not, then it is an opinion. Circle any clue words or phrases that signal opinions.

I'm Convinced!

 *In a **persuasive paragraph,** you give an opinion about something and try to convince readers to think or feel the way you do. A convincing persuasive paragraph includes*

— **a topic sentence that clearly states your opinion.**
— **reasons that support your opinion.**
— **facts to back up your opinion.**
— **a strong closing sentence that summarizes your opinion.**

Pretend you are a world famous chef who prepares dishes that include edible insects—insects that you can eat. You want to persuade people to include insects in their diet. Here is a topic sentence for a persuasive paragraph.

Everyone should try cooking with insects.

Here are some reasons and facts.
• Many insects like mealworms, crickets, and weevils are edible.
• People in many cultures around the world eat insects.
• Many insects are low in fat and rich in vitamins.
• Lots of tasty recipes include insects.
• Insects are really quite delicious.

Now put it all together. Write a persuasive paragraph that includes a title and a strong closing sentence. Remember the rules for writing a paragraph.

Paragraph Title: _____

Topic Sentence: _____

_____

Reasons/Facts: _____

_____

_____

_____

_____

_____

_____

Closing Sentence: _____

_____

Scholastic Professional Books

Step by Step

*When you write an **expository paragraph**, you give facts and information, explain ideas, or give directions. An expository paragraph can also include opinions. Here are some topic ideas for an expository paragraph.*

Explain how to play the flute.
Tell why you do not like brussels sprouts.
Give facts about yourself.

Explain how to bathe a dog.
Tell what skills you need to skateboard.
Give the facts about your favorite band.

Here is an example of an expository paragraph. It explains how to fry an egg.

Frying an egg is not all that difficult. After melting a little bit of butter in a frying pan, just crack the eggshell along the rim of the pan and let the egg drop into the pan. Do it gently so the yolk does not break. Let the egg fry over a low heat for about a minute or so. That is all it takes.

Complete the following topics for expository paragraphs with your own ideas.

Explain how to

_____

_____

_____

Give facts about

_____

_____

_____

Tell why

_____

_____

_____

Use the form below to develop one of your ideas for an expository paragraph.

Paragraph Title: _____

Topic Sentence: _____

_____

Details/Facts/Steps: _____

_____

_____

_____

_____

Closing Sentence: _____

_____

Now, use the plan above to write a paragraph on a piece of paper. If you are giving directions for doing or making something, include words such as *first, next, after that,* and *finally* to make the steps clear for your readers.

A Sentence Relationship

 You can write sentences about cause and effect relationships. A **cause** *is the reason something happens. An* **effect** *is the result of the cause, or what actually happens. Words such as* so, because, *and* since *are used in cause and effect sentences.*

effect   *cause*

School was cancelled today because **the storm dumped two feet of snow.**

cause   *effect*

The snow and wind knocked out power lines, so **many homes were without electricity.**

cause   *effect*

Since **there was no school today, I went back to bed and slept another hour.**

Add a cause to each of the following sentences about the day that school was cancelled because of snow.

1. Many shops, stores, and offices were closed _____

_____

2. My friends and I love snow days _____

_____

3. It took several minutes to open the back door _____

_____

4. Our snow blower would not start _____

_____

Add an effect to each of the following sentences.

5. I shoveled snow for two hours, _____

_____

6. My sister could not find her boots, _____

_____

7. Since our street was finally plowed by noon, _____

_____

8. By late afternoon it began snowing again, _____

_____

Scholastic Professional Books

What a Mess!

 You can write a paragraph using a cause and effect relationship. One way to begin is to state a cause. Then you write about the effects that happen as a result of that cause.

The piercing sound of the smoke alarm reminded Max that he had forgotten to check the pot of stew heating up on the stove. The stew had boiled over, the bottom of the pot was scorched, and smoke was filling the kitchen. Dinner was obviously ruined, and Max was in big trouble. What a mess!

Answer each question about the paragraph above.

1. What is the cause? _____

_____

2. What were the effects? List them. _____

_____

_____

Read the first sentence of the following paragraph. It states a cause. What might happen as a result? Continue the paragraph. Write what you think the effects will be.

I walked into my room just as Sebastian, our very inquisitive cat, managed to

tip over the goldfish bowl that had been on my desk. _____

_____

_____

_____

_____

_____

 Brainstorm a list of causes on a piece of paper. Here are some to get you started:

eating too many cookies   staying up too late   not studying for a test

Then list some possible effects. Develop your ideas into a paragraph.

A Vivid Picture

 A **descriptive paragraph** creates a vivid image or picture for readers. By choosing just the right adjectives, you can reveal how something looks, sounds, smells, tastes, and feels. Compare the sentences from two different paragraphs. Which one creates a more vivid picture?

The pizza with sausage and onions tasted so good.

The smooth, sweet sauce and bubbly mozzarella topped with bite-sized chunks of extra hot sausage and thin slivers of sweet onion on a perfectly baked, thin crust delighted my taste buds.

Cut out a picture of something interesting and paste it in the box. Then brainstorm a list adjectives and descriptive phrases to tell about it.

_____ _____

_____ _____

_____ _____

_____ _____

_____ _____

_____ _____

Now, write a paragraph about the picture. Begin your paragraph with a topic sentence that will grab readers. Add supporting sentences that include the adjectives and descriptive phrases listed to create a vivid picture.

_____

_____

_____

_____

_____

 Here is a set of adjectives: bumpy, dusty, narrow, steep, curvy, unpaved, well-worn. Think about what they might describe. Then, on a piece of paper use the words to write a descriptive paragraph that paints a picture.

Numerous, Spectacular Words

When you write, do you sometimes overuse descriptive words like good, bad, nice, *or* wonderful? *Overused words can make your writing boring.*

> *The weather was* **good** *for our first camping trip. (fair)*
> *A ranger gave us some really* **good** *tips about the park. (useful)*
> *Mom thought the campsite near the stream was* **good**. *(lovely)*
> *My older brother is a* **good** *fly fisherman. (skilled)*
> *He said his equipment is too* **good** *for me to use, though! (valuable)*

Now reread the sentences. This time use the words in parentheses in place of the word good. *You can use a thesaurus to help find words. A thesaurus is a reference book that gives synonyms and antonyms for words.*

Identify eight frequently overused descriptive words in the passage below and list them in the answer spaces. Next, use a thesaurus to write three synonyms for each word, or write three synonyms you know. Then revise the passage. Use editing symbols to cross out the overused words and add the more effective synonyms to replace them.

Our family has a dog named Scooter. He's normally very good until it's time
to bathe him. That's when our nice, little terrier turns into a big, furry monster.
Scooter isn't really bad. He's just hard to handle when he doesn't want to do
something. I think he's afraid of water. You should see how sad he looks once we
manage to get him into the tub.

1. _____ _____

2. _____ _____

3. _____ _____

4. _____ _____

5. _____ _____

6. _____ _____

7. _____ _____

8. _____ _____

Reread a composition you have recently written. Look for overused words and then use a thesaurus to find other words that you could use instead to make your writing more interesting.

Action Alert

 When you write, think about the verbs that you choose to express action in your sentences. Are they as exact as they can be? Do they tell your readers exactly what you want to say?

The child **broke** the plastic toy.
The child **smashed** the plastic toy.
The child **cracked** the plastic toy.

Each verb creates a different picture of what happened.

Read each sentence. Underline the verb. Then rewrite each sentence using a more exact verb. You may want to use a thesaurus.

1. Three young hikers went up the steep hill.

_____

2. A lone runner ran around the track.

_____

3. The wind blew through the treetops.

_____

4. The janitor cleaned the scuff marks off the floor.

_____

5. The audience laughed at the hilarious scene.

_____

6. The diners ate the delicious meal.

_____

7. The young tourists liked the castle most of all.

_____

8. The children slept for about an hour.

_____

9. The biologist looked at the unusual specimen.

_____

 Here are some commonly used verbs: make, tell, say, speak, ride. On a piece of paper, list as many exact verbs as you can think of for each one. Use a thesaurus for additional words. Then write several sentences using the exact words on your list.

Scholastic Professional Books

Colorful Clues

You can compare two things that are not alike in order to give your readers a clearer and more colorful picture. When you use like *or* as *to make a comparison, it is called a* **simile**.

Max is as slow as molasses when he doesn't want to do something.
My sister leaped over the puddles like a frog to avoid getting her shoes wet.
The angry man erupted like a volcano.

When you make a comparison without like *or* as*, it is called a* **metaphor**.
You compare things directly, saying the subject is something else.

The disturbed anthill was a whirlwind of activity.
The oak trees, silent sentries around the cabin, stood guard.
Jenny and I were all ears as we listened to the latest gossip.

Finish the metaphors and similes.

1. Crowds of commuters piled into the subway cars like _____

_____

2. Chirping crickets on warm summer night are _____

_____

3. After rolling in the mud, our dog looked like _____

4. Happiness is _____

5. Just learning to walk, the toddler was as wobbly as _____

_____

6. After scoring the winning point, I felt as _____

_____

7. Having a tooth filled is about as much fun as _____

_____

8. A summer thunderstorm is _____

_____

9. _____ is _____

10. _____ is like _____

Name _____

Adding Spice

Sometimes you can spice up your writing by giving human characteristics and qualities to non-human things such as animals and objects. This is called **personification**.

The sagging roof groaned under the weight of all the snow.
The falling leaves danced in the wind.

You can also use **hyperbole**, or deliberate exaggeration, to make a point clearer or to add drama to your writing.

The lost hiker is so hungry he could eat a bear.
Yesterday was so hot, we could have fried eggs on the sidewalk.

Personify the animal or object in each sentence by giving it human qualities.

1. The rusted hinges on the old wooden door _____

_____

2. As several birds began feasting on the farmer's corn, the scarecrow _____

_____

3. A gentle summer breeze _____

_____

4. Just as I walked past the statue of Ben Franklin, it _____

_____

Complete each sentence with an example of a hyperbole.

5. The salsa was so spicy hot _____

_____

6. The pumpkin grew so large _____

_____

7. If we placed all the books in the library end to end, they _____

_____

8. My room was so cold last night that by morning _____

_____

Listen for examples of hyperbole in the conversations that you hear throughout the day. Jot them down in a notebook. Then make up some of your own.

Scholastic Professional Books

Daily Notes

When you keep a journal, you can record the facts and details about events that happen in your life and your feelings or opinions about them. Your journal entries can be a valuable resource when you are looking for writing ideas.

3/9 We had to take Fuzzer to his new home today. Our new landlord said he could not stay with us at our apartment anymore. I know Fuzzer will be much happier at the farm where he can run and play, but I still felt so sad. I tried not to cry, but I could not help it. Fuzzer has been part of our family for nine years. We grew up together. I will miss him very much!

3/15 I had to go to my sister's dance recital at the Palace Theater last night. She performed in three numbers. At first I didn't want to go because I thought it would be boring, but it wasn't. I actually felt really proud of my sister! She was fantastic. I guess I really should tell her.

3/19 Today, the entire fourth grade went on a field trip to the state capital. It was incredible! We met a state senator. She showed us around the capitol building. We even got to listen to the senators discuss a new law. Later, we toured the governor's mansion. Boy, is that a big house!

Think about the events that have happened in your life over the last several days. Did anything of special importance happen at home, on the way to or from school, or in your community, the country, or the world? Record the facts, details, and your feelings or opinions about two events on the journal page below. Write the date for each entry.

_____/_____/_____

_____

_____

_____

_____/_____/_____

_____

_____

_____

Story Time

 *A story has **characters**, a **setting** (where and when the story takes place), and a **plot** (the events that happen in a story). The main story character often faces a problem which is introduced at the **beginning** of a story, developed in the **middle**, and solved at the **end**.*

Develop your own story about the picture. First, answer the questions.

1. **What or who is the story about?** _____

_____

_____

_____

2. **Where and when does it take place?** _____

_____

_____

_____

3. **How will the story begin?** _____

_____

_____

_____

_____

4. **What happens in the middle?** _____

_____

_____

5. **How will the story end?** _____

_____

_____

Use your answers to write a story on another sheet of paper. Include a title. Be sure to tell the events in the order they happen. Remember the rules for writing a paragraph.

 Compile magazine pictures that spark story ideas. From time to time choose one of the pictures and make up an oral story about it. If you have an audiocassette recorder, tape your story and save it. Use it to write a story at another time.

Scholastic Professional Books

What Did You Say?

 Some stories may include dialogue, or the exact words of story characters. Dialogue lets readers know something about the characters, plot, setting, and problem or conflict in a story. Use quotation marks around a speaker's exact words and commas to set off quotations. Remember to put periods, question marks, exclamation points, and commas inside the quotation marks.

"Get away from my bowl!" yelled Little Miss Muffet when she saw the approaching spider.

"Please don't get so excited," replied the startled spider. "I just wanted a little taste. I've never tried curds and whey before."

Use your imagination to complete the dialogue between the fairy tale or nursery rhyme characters. Include quotation marks and commas where they belong and the correct end punctuation.

1. When Baby Bear saw the strange girl asleep in his bed, he asked his parents, _____

   _____

   His mother replied, _____

2. Humpty Dumpty was sitting on the wall when he suddenly fell off. On the way down

   he shouted, _____

   Two of the king's men approached. One whispered nervously to the other, _____

   _____

3. When Jack realized he was about to fall down the hill with a pail of water, he yelled,

   _____

   _____cried Jill,

   as she went tumbling down the hill after Jack.

4. The wolf knocked on the door of the third little pig's house. When there was no

   answer, the wolf bellowed, _____

   Knowing that he and his brother were safe inside his sturdy brick house, the third

   little pig replied, _____

   _____

Let's Get Organized

When you write a report or story, it helps to review your notes and organize them into an outline to show the order in which you want to discuss them.

Chester Greenwood → **subject of the report**

I. **Who was Chester Greenwood?** → **main idea becomes topic sentence**
   A. **born in 1858** → **supporting details become supporting sentences**
   B. **grew up in Farmington, Maine**
   C. **as a child had ear problems in winter**

II. **His first invention–earmuffs**
   A. **needed a way to protect ears from cold**
   B. **1873 at age 15 began testing his ideas**
   C. **idea for fur-covered earflaps worked**
   D. **people saw and also wanted earflaps**
   E. **grandmother helped produce them**

III. **His later accomplishments**
   A. **founded a telephone company**
   B. **manufactured steam heaters**
   C. **over 100 inventions**

Study the outline above. Then answer the questions.

1. **What is the topic of the report?** _____

2. **How many paragraphs will there be?** _____

3. **What is main topic of the first paragraph?** _____

_____

4. **How many details tell about the second main idea?** _____

Use the form on the next page to develop an outline for preparing an interesting and unusual dish that your family enjoys.

Scholastic Professional Books

How to Prepare _____

I. Background about the dish

A. _____

B. _____

C. _____

D. _____

E. _____

II. Ingredients

A. _____

B. _____

C. _____

D. _____

E. _____

III. Equipment

A. _____

B. _____

C. _____

D. _____

E. _____

IV. Steps

A. _____

B. _____

C. _____

D. _____

E. _____

 Share your outline with someone you know.

Read All About It

A **news story** reports just the facts about an event and answers the questions who, what, when, where, why, *and* how. *The most important information is included at the beginning of the article in a paragraph called the* **lead**.

Grass Fires Burn Out of Control   headline

WHERE did it happen? ⟶ GREENSBURG—Grass fires, fueled by wind gusts up to 50 miles per hour, spread into a   **WHY did it happen?**
residential area early Tuesday morning. All   **WHEN did it happen?**
residents had to be evacuated. Within min-
utes over 25 homes were engulfed by flames   **WHO was affected?**
and destroyed. According to officials, no
injuries have been reported.

Planes and helicopters battling the blaze had to be grounded because the heat of the flames was so intense.

Write a news story using the information below. Remember to write about the facts and events in the order they occurred. Follow the model lead above.

Who: Roseville Emergency Rescue Team
When: April 10, 2003; 5 A.M.
Where: Slate Run River
What: team and rescue vehicles sent;
　　　worked for three hours; rescued residents
How: used helicopter and boats
Why: residents along river stranded by flash flood after storm

_____

_____ — _____

_____
_____
_____
_____
_____
_____

Use your imagination to write a news story on a piece of paper for one of the following headlines or one of your own.

Mystery of the Missing Dinosaur Solved   **Students Protest School Lunch Menu**

City High Wins Championship   **First Female Elected President**

CHARTS, TABLES & GRAPHS

The Winning Team

This table displays the win-loss record for five major-league baseball teams in 2000. Use the table to choose the best answer to each question below.

BASEBALL STANDINGS: AMERICAN LEAGUE EAST				
Team	Wins	Losses	Percent	Games Behind
New York Yankees	87	74	.540	—
Boston Red Sox	85	77	.525	$2\frac{1}{2}$
Toronto Blue Jays	83	79	.512	$4\frac{1}{2}$
Baltimore Orioles	74	88	.457	$13\frac{1}{2}$
Tampa Bay Devil Rays	69	92	.429	18

1 Which team had the most wins?
ⓐ Baltimore Orioles   ⓒ New York Yankees
ⓑ Boston Red Sox   ⓓ Toronto Blue Jays

2 How many games did the Boston Red Sox lose?
ⓐ 74   ⓒ 79
ⓑ 77   ⓓ 85

3 Which team had 74 wins and 88 losses?
ⓐ New York Yankees   ⓒ Toronto Blue Jays
ⓑ Boston Red Sox   ⓓ Baltimore Orioles

4 How many games did the Tampa Bay Devil Rays win?
ⓐ 69   ⓒ 83
ⓑ 74   ⓓ 92

5 How many of these teams won more than half of their games?
ⓐ 2   ⓒ 4
ⓑ 3   ⓓ 5

Measuring Up

Mrs. Umberto made this table to use when she buys clothing for her children. Use the table to answer the questions below.

MY CHILDREN'S CLOTHING SIZES			
Child	**Height (inches)**	**Weight (pounds)**	**Size**
Emilio	60	103	14
Teresita	54	75	12
Pablo	52	60	8
Juana	43	51	5

1 How tall is Emilio? _____

2 How much more does Teresita weigh than Juana?

_____

3 Which two children are about the same height?

_____

4 What size clothing does Juana wear?

_____

5 According to this table, how do children's clothing sizes change as children grow taller?

_____

Tori's Sandwich Study

Tori asked her classmates to name their favorite sandwiches. She made a tally chart showing how many kids chose each kind. Use the chart to choose the best answer to each question below.

OUR FAVORITE SANDWICHES	
KIND OF SANDWICH	NUMBER OF KIDS
Ham and cheese	✓✓✓✓
Tuna fish	✓✓✓
Peanut butter and jelly	✓✓✓✓✓
Egg salad	✓✓

1 How many kids named tuna fish as their favorite kind of sandwich?
  ⓐ 2   ⓒ 4
  ⓑ 3   ⓓ 5

2 How many kids named egg salad?
  ⓐ 2   ⓒ 4
  ⓑ 3   ⓓ 5

3 Which kind of sandwich was named by the most kids?
  ⓐ ham and cheese   ⓒ peanut butter and jelly
  ⓑ tuna fish   ⓓ egg salad

4 If each kid named only one favorite sandwich, how many kids in all answered Tori's question?
  ⓐ 4   ⓒ 12
  ⓑ 5   ⓓ 14

Pete's Chores

Pete made this tally chart to show how often he did chores around the house. He recorded his chores for one week. Use the chart to choose the best answer to each question below.

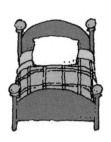

MY WEEKLY RECORD	
CHORE	NUMBER OF TIMES
Making bed	✓✓✓✓✓✓
Taking out trash	✓
Setting table	✓✓✓✓✓
Picking up toys	✓✓✓✓
Feeding cats	✓✓✓

1 Which chore did Pete do most often?
    ⓐ making bed   ⓒ picking up toys
    ⓑ setting table   ⓓ feeding cats

2 How many times did Pete take out the trash?
    ⓐ 5   ⓒ 3
    ⓑ 4   ⓓ 1

3 How many times did Pete set the table?
    ⓐ 4   ⓒ 6
    ⓑ 5   ⓓ 7

4 How many times in all did Pete do chores?
    ⓐ 13   ⓒ 17
    ⓑ 14   ⓓ 20

Name _____

Drew's Newspaper Route

Drew made a pictograph to show how many newspapers he delivers on each street of his newspaper route. Use the graph to choose the best answer to each question below.

MY DAILY DELIVERIES	
Gold Street	🗞🗞🗞🗞🗞🗞🗞
Harold Street	🗞🗞🗞🗞🗞🗞🗞🗞🗞
Lower Road	🗞🗞🗞
Morris Drive	🗞🗞🗞🗞🗞🗞
Burnham Street	🗞🗞🗞🗞🗞🗞🗞🗞

Each 🗞 stands for one newspaper.

1 How many newspapers does Drew deliver on Morris Drive?
  ⓐ 6   ⓒ 8
  ⓑ 7   ⓓ 9

2 On which street does Drew deliver the most newspapers?
  ⓐ Harold Street   ⓒ Morris Drive
  ⓑ Gold Street   ⓓ Lower Road

3 How many more newspapers does Drew deliver on Burnham Street than on Lower Road?
  ⓐ 7   ⓒ 3
  ⓑ 5   ⓓ 1

4 What is the total number of newspapers Drew delivers on his newspaper route?
  ⓐ 38   ⓒ 33
  ⓑ 36   ⓓ 30

Scholastic Professional Books

Cool Inventions

Third graders in the Town School asked all the students to name the most important invention of the last 200 years. This pictograph shows how many students chose each of the inventions listed. Use the graph to answer the questions below.

KIDS' CHOICES	
Automobile	🚶🚶🚶🚶
Computer	🚶🚶🚶🚶🚶🚶🚶
Electric light	🚶🚶🚶
Telephone	🚶🚶🚶🚶
Television	🚶🚶🚶🚶🚶🚶

KEY
🚶 = 5 students

1 Which invention was named by the most students?

_____

2 How many students named television as the most important invention?

_____

3 Which two inventions were named by an equal number of students?

_____

4 How many more students named the computer than the electric light?

_____

The Class Field Trip

Mrs. Smith's class took a field trip to the park, and a park ranger explained how different trees grow to different heights. This bar graph shows the trees' heights. Use the graph to choose the best answer to each question below.

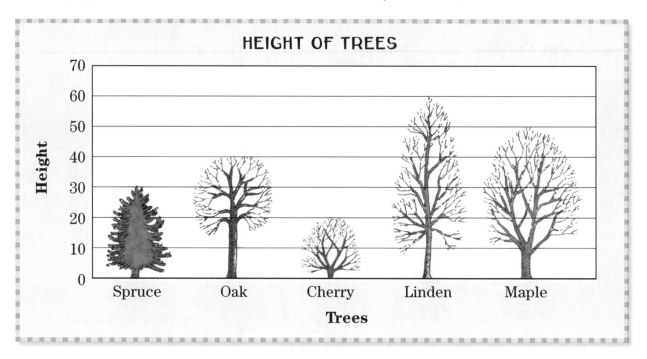

1 Which tree is the shortest?
- (a) cherry
- (b) linden
- (c) maple
- (d) spruce

2 How tall is the oak tree?
- (a) 20 feet
- (b) 30 feet
- (c) 40 feet
- (d) 50 feet

3 Which tree is twice as tall as the spruce?
- (a) maple
- (b) linden
- (c) cherry
- (d) oak

4 How much taller is the maple tree than the cherry tree?
- (a) 40 feet
- (b) 30 feet
- (c) 20 feet
- (d) 10 feet

Hannah and Her Cousins

Hannah's cousins live in five different states. She made this bar graph to show how many cousins live in each state. Use the graph to answer the questions below.

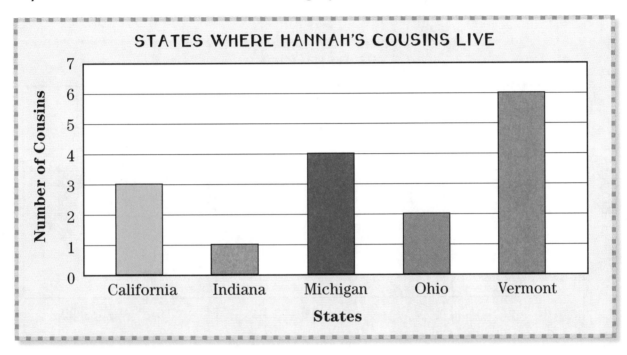

1 How many cousins live in Ohio?

_____

2 The greatest number of Hannah's cousins live in which state?

_____

3 How many more cousins live in Michigan than in California?

_____

4 How many cousins does Hannah have altogether?

_____

Name _____

Soccer Contest

Five friends held a contest to see how far they could kick a soccer ball. The bar graph below shows the results of their contest. Use the graph to choose the best answer to each question.

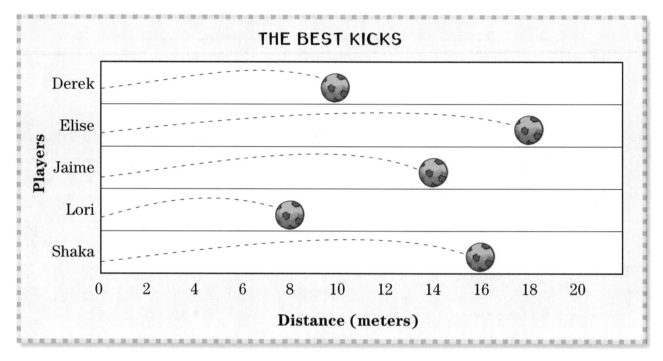

1 Who won the contest?
- **a** Derek
- **c** Lori
- **b** Elise
- **d** Shaka

2 How far did Jaime kick the ball?
- **a** 8 meters
- **c** 12 meters
- **b** 10 meters
- **d** 14 meters

3 Who kicked the ball half as far as Shaka?
- **a** Elise
- **c** Jaime
- **b** Lori
- **d** Derek

4 Compared with Derek, how much farther did Elise kick the ball?
- **a** 12 meters
- **c** 8 meters
- **b** 10 meters
- **d** 6 meters

Scouts' Honors

The Adventure Scouts earn badges by doing special projects. Their scout leader made this bar graph to show how many scouts have earned each type of badge. Use the graph to answer the questions below.

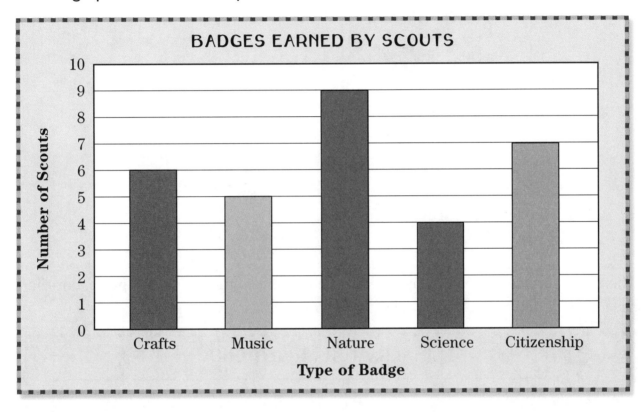

1 How many scouts have earned a music badge? _____

2 How many more scouts have earned citizenship badges than science badges?

_____

3 Which badge has been earned by the most scouts?

_____

4 How many badges have been earned altogether? _____

5 Which type of badge is most difficult to earn? Explain your thinking below.

_____

_____

Zack's Lazy Afternoon

Zack spent an afternoon at Sunrise Pond. He made this tally chart to show how many animals he saw at the pond.

KIND OF ANIMAL		NUMBER
Turtle		✓
Duck		✓✓✓✓✓
Frog		✓✓✓
Beaver		✓✓
Fish		✓✓✓✓✓✓✓

Then Zack started making a bar graph of the animals he saw at the pond, but didn't have time to finish it. Use the tally chart to finish Zack's bar graph.

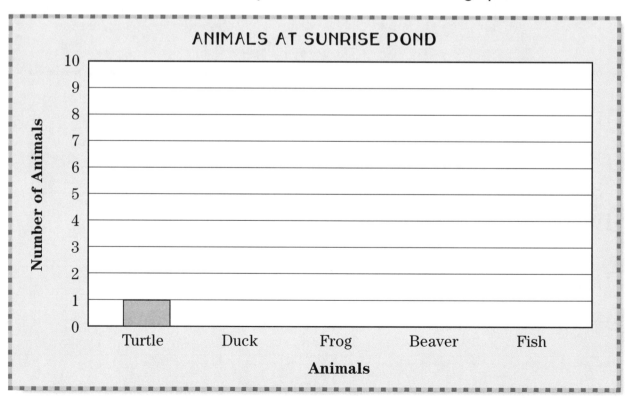

Scholastic Professional Books

The Class Takes a Trip

Mrs. Fieldstone's students live in Boston, Massachusetts. They took a vote to decide where to go for their class trip in May and made a circle graph to help analyze the results. Use the graph to answer the questions.

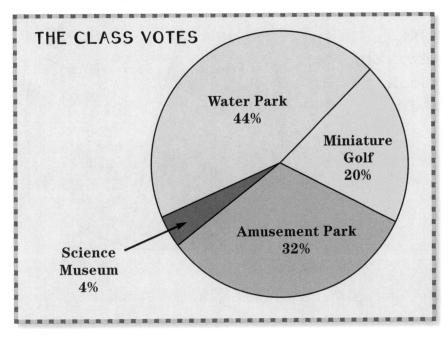

THE CLASS VOTES

Water Park
44%

Miniature
Golf
20%

Amusement Park
32%

Science
Museum
4%

1 Which choice received the fewest votes?

_____

2 If there are 25 students in the class, how many voted for miniature golf?

_____

3 Which two activities together were picked by about $\frac{3}{4}$ of the students?

_____

4 Which activity was chosen by about $\frac{1}{3}$ of the students?

_____

5 How do you think the votes would be different if the class trip took place in February instead of May?

_____

_____

Recycling Efforts

Every week, the town of Galway collects trash for recycling. The circle graph on the right shows what kinds of items are collected. Use the graph to choose the best answer to each question below.

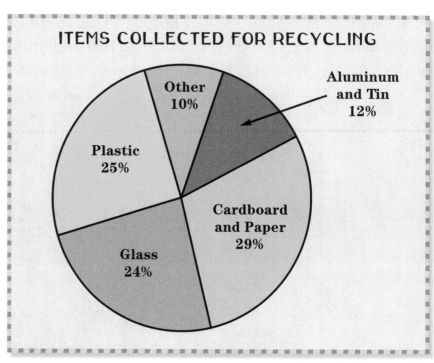

ITEMS COLLECTED FOR RECYCLING

Other 10%
Aluminum and Tin 12%
Plastic 25%
Cardboard and Paper 29%
Glass 24%

1. Cardboard and paper make up what percentage of the recycled items?
   - (a) 12%
   - (b) 24%
   - (c) 25%
   - (d) 29%

2. What fraction shows what part of the recycled items are plastic?
   - (a) $\frac{1}{4}$
   - (b) $\frac{1}{3}$
   - (c) $\frac{1}{2}$
   - (d) $\frac{2}{3}$

3. Of every 100 items recycled, how many are glass?
   - (a) 10
   - (b) 12
   - (c) 15
   - (d) 24

4. What percentage of the recycled items are aluminum and tin?
   - (a) 10%
   - (b) 12%
   - (c) 24%
   - (d) 25%

5. One half of the items in the "Other" category were batteries. If batteries were shown on the graph, what percentage would they represent?
   - (a) 50%
   - (b) 10%
   - (c) 5%
   - (d) 3%

Best-Selling Books

The line graph below shows how many books were sold each day at a school book fair. Use the graph to answer the questions.

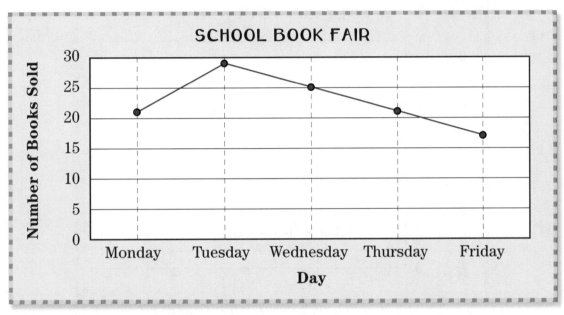

SCHOOL BOOK FAIR

Number of Books Sold

Day

1 How many books were sold on Monday? _____

2 On what day were the same number of books sold as on Monday?

_____

3 How many more books were sold on Tuesday than on Thursday?

_____

4 What was the greatest number of books sold in one day?

_____

5 If the sales trend continued to Saturday, how many books would you expect to sell on Saturday?

_____

Compare the Squares

The line graph below shows the areas of squares of different sizes. Use the graph to answer the questions.

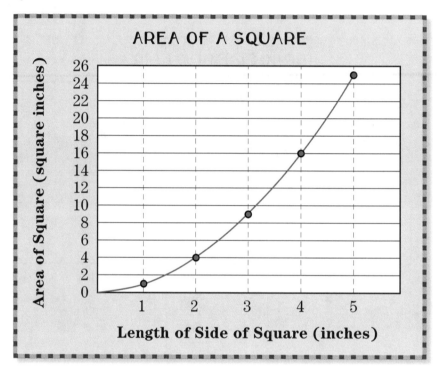

1. What is the area of a square with sides that are 4 inches long?

_____

2. If the area of a square is 25 square inches, how long are its sides?

_____

3. What is the approximate area of a square with 4.5-inch sides?

_____

4. About how long are the sides of a square with an area of 12 square inches?

_____

5. Write one or two sentences describing the trend shown on this line graph.

_____

_____

Adorable Animals

Do you know what a baby goat is called? The chart below provides the names for many baby animals. Use the chart to choose the best answer to each question.

NAMES FOR BABY ANIMALS			
Animal	Name for Baby	Animal	Name for Baby
Bear	Cub	Fox	Kit
Cow	Calf	Goat	Kid
Deer	Fawn	Kangaroo	Joey
Dog	Pup	Sheep	Lamb

1 What is the name for a baby deer?
- (a) cub
- (c) fawn
- (b) calf
- (d) pup

2 What is a baby fox called?
- (a) kit
- (c) cub
- (b) kid
- (d) lamb

3 Which kind of animal has cubs?
- (a) goat
- (c) kangaroo
- (b) sheep
- (d) bear

4 A "joey" is what kind of animal?
- (a) cow
- (c) kangaroo
- (b) fox
- (d) sheep

5 A baby goat is a —
- (a) kid
- (c) pup
- (b) lamb
- (d) calf

Joel's Trip Planner

Joel made a chart for his family to help them plan trips to local parks. Use the chart to answer the questions below.

THINGS TO DO AT LOCAL PARKS	
Blue Summit Park	
Lilac Lake Park	
Mead Canyon Park	
Pinetop Park	
Underwood Park	

KEY

Hiking Trails

Picnic Area

Swimming
Beach

Campground

1 What can visitors do at Underwood Park?

_____

2 How many parks have a picnic area? _____

3 Which parks have a swimming beach?

_____

4 Which park offers the most activities?

_____

5 In which park can you ONLY camp or hike?

_____

Ordering Dinner

The Magic Meal Restaurant has a special children's menu. Use the chart to choose the best answer to each question below.

CHILDREN'S MENU

Sandwiches   *Served with potato chips and a pickle*
Egg Salad $2.50
Ham Salad $3.00
Tuna Fish $2.75
Grilled Cheese $2.50

Dinners   *Served with salad and a dinner roll*
Macaroni and Cheese $3.75
Spaghetti $3.00
Chicken Pot Pie $4.00
Beef Stew $4.00

Drinks
Milk, Chocolate Milk, Lemonade $1.00

Desserts
Dish of Ice Cream or Pudding $1.50

1 How much does a grilled cheese sandwich cost?
  ⓐ $2.50   ⓒ $3.00
  ⓑ $2.75   ⓓ $3.50

2 Which food is served with any dinner on the menu?
  ⓐ ice cream   ⓒ salad
  ⓑ potato chips   ⓓ pudding

3 Which drink is listed on the menu?
  ⓐ milk shake   ⓒ orange juice
  ⓑ lemonade   ⓓ hot chocolate

4 How much does a spaghetti dinner cost?
  ⓐ $4.00   ⓒ $3.00
  ⓑ $3.75   ⓓ $2.50

The Bookworm Club

Use this chart from the Bookworm Club to answer the questions below.

OUR BOOKS OF THE MONTH		
Item Number	Title	Price
1	*Amy Grows Up*	$3.25
2	*Beginner's Luck*	$2.95
3	*Dinosaur Dig*	$4.50
4	*Famous Firsts*	$3.95
5	*Jump Rope Games*	$4.25
6	*Lightning and Thunder*	$2.95
7	*Never Say Never*	$3.50
8	*Queen Mary of Scotland*	$2.95
9	*Science in Your Kitchen*	$3.25
10	*Yellowstone Park*	$4.50

1 What is the title of item number **1** on the book list?

_____

2 How much does the book *Queen Mary of Scotland* cost?

_____

3 What is the item number of the book *Jump Rope Games*?

_____

4 Look at this part of a book order form. Fill in the missing information.

Item Number	Title	Price
3		

Scholastic Professional Books

Niko's Aquarium

Niko wants to set up an aquarium for tropical fish. He is reading a library book about aquariums before he begins this project. Use the table to choose the best answer to each question below.

TROPICAL FISH AQUARIUMS
Contents

Chapter		Page
1	Buying a Tank for Tropical Fish	5
2	Setting up the Aquarium	11
3	Selecting Tropical Fish	21
4	Cleaning the Aquarium	29
5	Feeding Tropical Fish	35
6	Magazines and Websites for Tropical Fish Fans	42

1 Niko wonders which fish get along well in an aquarium. Which chapter should he read to find this information?

    (a) chapter 1   (c) chapter 5

    (b) chapter 3   (d) chapter 6

2 Which of Niko's questions about tropical fish aquariums is probably answered in Chapter 2?

    (a) How much gravel should I put in the bottom of the tank?

    (b) How often should I feed my fish?

    (c) How can I be sure I'm buying healthy fish?

    (d) How much will a five-gallon tank cost?

3 Where should Niko start reading to find out how to clean the sides of his aquarium?

    (a) page 5   (c) page 21

    (b) page 11   (d) page 29

4 Which chapter explains how to find information about tropical fish online?

    (a) chapter 2   (c) chapter 5

    (b) chapter 4   (d) chapter 6

Card Sharks

Do you like to play cards? Use the table to choose the best answer to each question below.

LET'S PLAY CARDS
Contents

Chapter 1   Words Used by Card Players 7

Chapter 2   Games for One Player
  Beehive... 11
  Hit or Miss... 12
  Solitaire 14

Chapter 3   Games for Two Players
  Baby Snap 15
  Gops 17
  Spade Oklahoma 19

Chapter 4   Games for a Group
  Authors 21
  Jacks... 22
  Rolling Stone 24

1 Which chapter has information about games for two players?

   (a) chapter 1   (c) chapter 3
   (b) chapter 2   (d) chapter 4

2 Where should you start reading if you need to find out what a "wild card" is?

   (a) page 7   (c) page 21
   (b) page 12   (d) page 24

3 Which game might be a good one to play with three friends?

   (a) *Beehive*   (c) *Hit or Miss*
   (b) *Jacks*   (d) *Gops*

4 The directions for playing *Spade Oklahoma* begin on which page?

   (a) page 14   (c) page 17
   (b) page 15   (d) page 19

School Birthdays

The table below shows how many students in Grades 3 and 4 at the Rand School were born during each month. Use the table to answer the questions.

BIRTHDAY UPDATE											
Month of Birth	Sep.	Oct.	Nov.	Dec.	Jan.	Feb.	Mar.	Apr.	May	June	July	Aug.
Number of Students	2	1	2	3	2	4	6	9	6	5	4	3
Season	Fall			Winter			Spring			Summer		

1 How many students were born in November?_____

2 What month had the same number of births as February?

_____

3 How many students were born in the fall?

_____

4 During which season were the most students born?

_____

5 In which month would it be most likely to have two students share the same birthday?

_____

Presidential Studies

The table below shows information about recent presidents of the United States. Use the table to choose the best answer to each question.

U.S. PRESIDENTS SINCE 1970			
Number	Name	Birth–Death	Years in Office
37	Richard M. Nixon	1913–1994	1969–1974
38	Gerald R. Ford	1913–	1974–1977
39	Jimmy Carter	1924–	1977–1981
40	Ronald Reagan	1911–	1981–1989
41	George Bush	1924–	1989–1993
42	William J. Clinton	1946–	1993–2001
43	George W. Bush	1946–	2001–

1 Who was the 40th president of the United States?
- (a) Gerald Ford
- (b) Jimmy Carter
- (c) Ronald Reagan
- (d) George Bush

2 In what year was Richard Nixon born?
- (a) 1911
- (b) 1913
- (c) 1924
- (d) 1946

3 Which president spent the shortest time in office?
- (a) Richard Nixon
- (b) George Bush
- (c) Jimmy Carter
- (d) Gerald Ford

4 Who was president in 1992?
- (a) Jimmy Carter
- (b) Ronald Reagan
- (c) George Bush
- (d) Bill Clinton

5 Which number president is George W. Bush?
- (a) 43
- (b) 42
- (c) 41
- (d) 40

Beautiful Bridges

The chart below lists six of the longest suspension bridges in the United States. Use the chart to answer the questions.

SUSPENSION BRIDGES OF THE UNITED STATES			
Year Completed	Bridge	Location	Main Span (feet)
1931	George Washington	New York–New Jersey	3,500
1937	Golden Gate	California	4,200
1950	Tacoma Narrows	Washington	2,800
1957	Mackinac Straits	Michigan	3,800
1964	Verrazano–Narrows	New York	4,260
1968	Delaware Memorial	Delaware	2,150

1 Which bridge has the longest main span?

_____

2 Which bridge was completed in 1957, and where is it located?

_____

3 Where is the Golden Gate Bridge, and when was it completed?

_____

4 How long is the main span of the George Washington Bridge?

_____

5 If the chart listed these bridges from shortest to longest, which two bridges would be listed first?

_____

The Wild Wild West

The chart below provides information about six states in the western United States. Use the chart to answer the questions.

WESTERN STATES				
State	Capital	Date of Statehood	State Bird	State Flower
Colorado	Denver	1876	Lark Bunting	Rocky Mountain Columbine
Idaho	Boise	1890	Mountain Bluebird	Syringa
Nevada	Carson City	1864	Mountain Bluebird	Sagebrush
Oregon	Salem	1859	Western Meadowlark	Oregon Grape
Utah	Salt Lake City	1896	Seagull	Sego Lily
Washington	Olympia	1889	Willow Goldfinch	Western Rhododendron

1 What is the capital of Washington? _____

2 In what year did Idaho become a state? _____

3 Which of these states gained statehood first? _____

4 What is Colorado's state bird? _____

5 Salem is the capital of which state? _____

6 What is Nevada's state flower? _____

7 Which states have the same state bird, and what bird is it?

_____

The Story of Paper

The flow chart below shows how paper is made. Use the chart to answer the questions.

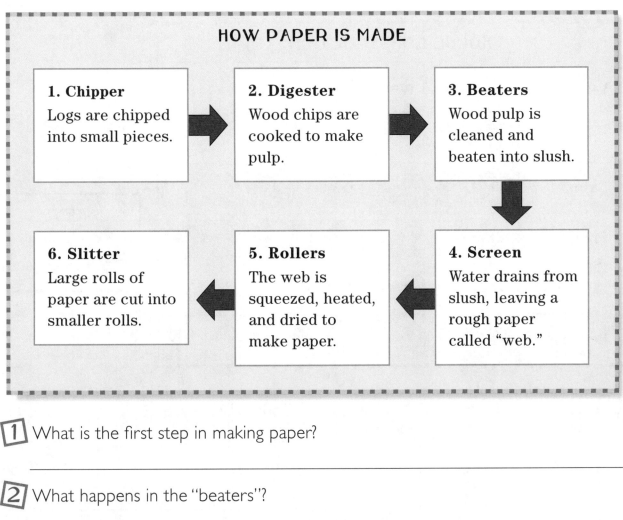

HOW PAPER IS MADE

1. Chipper
Logs are chipped into small pieces.

2. Digester
Wood chips are cooked to make pulp.

3. Beaters
Wood pulp is cleaned and beaten into slush.

4. Screen
Water drains from slush, leaving a rough paper called "web."

5. Rollers
The web is squeezed, heated, and dried to make paper.

6. Slitter
Large rolls of paper are cut into smaller rolls.

1 What is the first step in making paper?

_____

2 What happens in the "beaters"?

_____

3 In which step does slush become rough paper?

_____

4 What tasks are done with the use of heat?

_____

_____

Building Houses

The pictograph below shows the number of new houses built in five different counties last year. Use the graph to answer the questions.

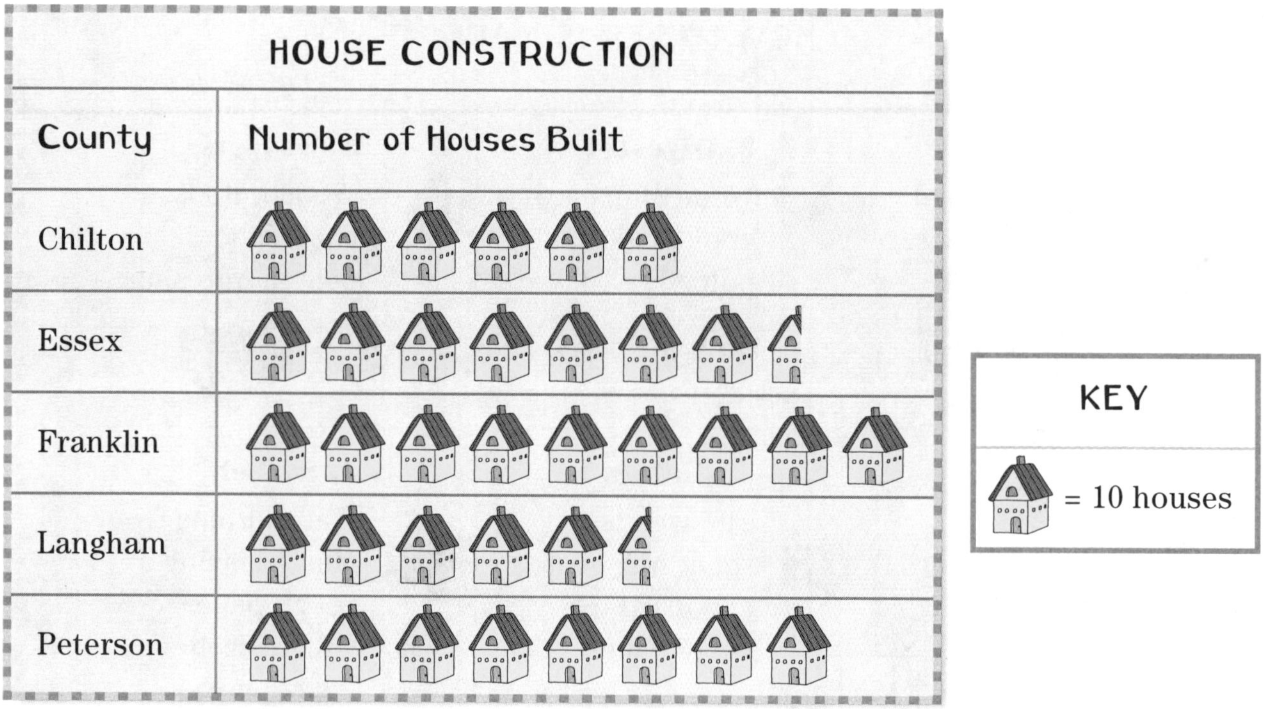

HOUSE CONSTRUCTION	
County	**Number of Houses Built**
Chilton	🏠🏠🏠🏠🏠🏠
Essex	🏠🏠🏠🏠🏠🏠🏠🏠
Franklin	🏠🏠🏠🏠🏠🏠🏠🏠🏠🏠
Langham	🏠🏠🏠🏠🏠🏠
Peterson	🏠🏠🏠🏠🏠🏠🏠🏠

KEY

🏠 = 10 houses

1 How many houses were built in Chilton County last year?

_____

2 In which county were the most houses built?

_____

3 In which county were the fewest houses built?

_____

4 How many more houses were built in Peterson County than in Langham County?

_____

5 A total of 42 houses were built in Winwood County last year. How would this number be shown on the graph? (Draw a picture on the back of this paper.)

How Does Susan's Garden Grow?

Susan made a bar graph showing the heights of the flowers in her garden. Use the graph to choose the best answers to the questions below.

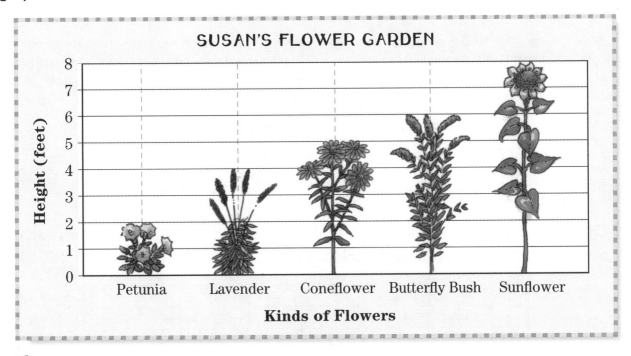

1. How tall is the coneflower?
   - a 3 feet
   - b 4 feet
   - c 5 feet
   - d 6 feet

2. Which plant is tallest?
   - a lavender
   - b coneflower
   - c butterfly bush
   - d sunflower

3. Which plant is 4 feet tall?
   - a petunia
   - b lavender
   - c coneflower
   - d butterfly bush

4. Which plant is three times as tall as the petunia?
   - a lavender
   - b coneflower
   - c butterfly bush
   - d sunflower

5. Which plant is closest in height to the lavender?
   - a petunia
   - b coneflower
   - c butterfly bush
   - d sunflower

Name _____

Alex the Sports Reporter

Alex conducted a survey of his classmates about their favorite team and individual sports. He made these charts to show the results of his survey. Use the charts to make your own bar graphs.

FAVORITE TEAM SPORTS	
Basketball	卌 卌 III
Soccer	卌 卌 II
Hockey	卌 III
Softball	卌 I

FAVORITE INDIVIDUAL SPORTS	
Tennis	卌 卌 III
Running	卌
Golf	卌 I
Swimming	卌 卌 卌

1. On the grid below, make a bar graph to show how many students picked each *team* sport. Be sure to include labels and a title.

2. On the grid below, make a bar graph to show how many students picked each *individual* sport. Be sure to include labels and a title.

Scholastic Professional Books

Name _____

Mindy Minds the Money

Mindy and her Dad made a circle graph to show how the family's money was spent each month. Use the graph to choose the best answer to each question below.

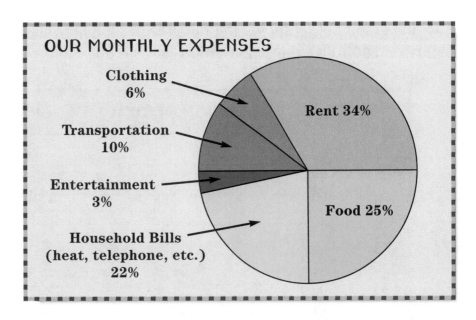

OUR MONTHLY EXPENSES

Clothing 6%
Transportation 10%
Entertainment 3%
Household Bills (heat, telephone, etc.) 22%
Rent 34%
Food 25%

1 Which is the largest cost each month?
- (a) food
- (b) rent
- (c) clothing
- (d) transportation

2 How much of the money spent each month goes to food?
- (a) More than $\frac{1}{2}$
- (b) $\frac{1}{3}$
- (c) Less than $\frac{1}{6}$
- (d) $\frac{1}{4}$

3 The least amount of money is spent on _____.
- (a) household bills
- (b) clothing
- (c) transportation
- (d) entertainment

4 What part of the family's money is spent on clothing each month?
- (a) 3%
- (b) 6%
- (c) 10%
- (d) 22%

5 When Dad takes the bus to work each day, that cost is part of what category?
- (a) transportation
- (b) household bills
- (c) clothing
- (d) entertainment

6 Which cost is probably higher in winter than in summer?
- (a) rent
- (b) transportation
- (c) household bills
- (d) entertainment

Population Growth

The line graph below shows the number of people living in Newtown between 1900 and 2000. Use the graph to answer the questions.

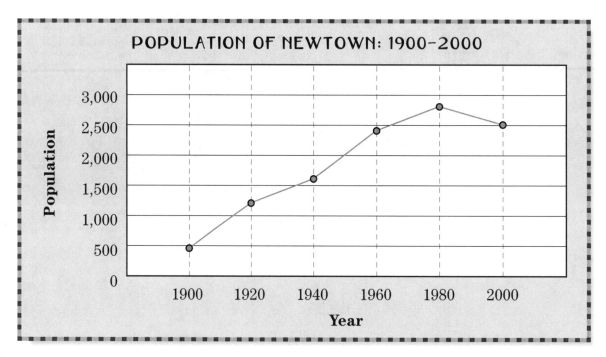

POPULATION OF NEWTOWN: 1900–2000

1. What was the population of Newtown in 1920? _____

2. How much did the population increase from 1920 to 1940?

   _____

3. What was the population in 1960? _____

4. In which 20-year period did the size of the population change the most?

   _____

5. Describe the general changes in Newtown's population from 1900 to 2000.

   _____

   _____

6. If this trend continues, what will the population of Newtown be in 2020?

   _____

A Trip Through Time

The timeline below shows when different ways of telling time were invented. Use the timeline to answer the questions.

TIME MACHINE TIMELINE

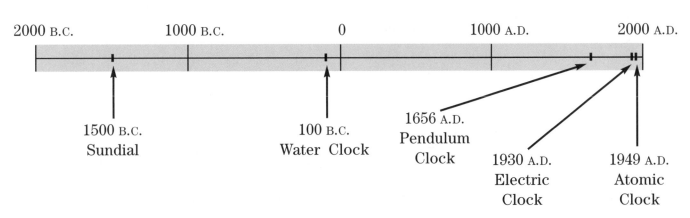

1 When was the sundial invented?
- **a** 1500 B.C.
- **b** 100 B.C.
- **c** 1656 A.D.
- **d** 1930 A.D.

2 Which type of clock was invented first?
- **a** atomic
- **b** pendulum
- **c** water
- **d** electric

3 What type of clock was invented in 1930?
- **a** pendulum
- **b** sundial
- **c** water
- **d** electric

4 This timeline covers about how many years?
- **a** 2000
- **b** 3000
- **c** 4000
- **d** 5000

5 For hundreds of years, people had to wind their clocks every day. When do you think winding became unnecessary? Explain why.

_____

_____

Mimi's Sunny Vacation

Mimi made a table to show when the sun rose and set each Saturday during her summer vacation. Use the table to answer the questions below.

SUNRISE AND SUNSET ON SUMMER SATURDAYS					
Date	Sunrise	Sunset	Date	Sunrise	Sunset
June 23	5:08 AM	8:25 PM	July 28	5:33 AM	8:08 PM
June 30	5:11 AM	8:25 PM	August 4	5:40 AM	8:00 PM
July 7	5:14 AM	8:23 PM	August 11	5:47 AM	7:51 PM
July 14	5:20 AM	8:20 PM	August 18	5:55 AM	7:41 PM
July 21	5:26 AM	8:15 PM	August 25	6:02 AM	7:30 PM

1 What time did the sun rise on July 21?

_____

2 On which date did the sun set at exactly 8:00 PM?

_____

3 Which Saturday had the earliest sunrise?

_____

4 How much earlier did the sun set on August 18 than on August 11?

_____

5 Which Saturday had exactly 15 hours between sunrise and sunset?

_____

6 How do the times of sunrise and sunset change from June 23 to the end of August?

_____

Weather Reporting

Fourth-grade students involved in a nation-wide project recorded the weather conditions each day for a week. Use the table to answer the questions below.

WEATHER DATA: SEPTEMBER 24-30					
Day	High Temperature	Low Temperature	Wind Speed (knots)	Precipitation	Conditions
Sunday	68°F	42°F	0–5	0	Sunny
Monday	69°F	44°F	0–5	0	Sunny
Tuesday	72°F	43°F	5–10	0	Cloudy
Wednesday	70°F	38°F	10–15	0	Partly Cloudy
Thursday	64°F	36°F	25–30	1.2 inches	Rainy
Friday	52°F	30°F	20–25	0.3 inches	Rainy
Saturday	52°F	32°F	10–15	0	Partly Cloudy

1 What were the high and low temperatures on Sunday?

_____

2 Which day was warmest? _____

3 On which days did the temperature go as low as the freezing point of 32°F?

_____

4 What were the weather conditions on Wednesday?

_____

5 In all, how much rain fell during the week? _____

6 Write one or two sentences describing how the weather changed from Sunday to Saturday.

_____

_____

Dining With Dinosaurs

This "Dino" chart provides specific information about different kinds of dinosaurs. Use the chart to choose the best answer to each question below.

DINOSAUR FACTS

Name	What It Means	Size	Weight	Food
Ankylosaurus	Crooked lizard	25 feet	3 tons	plants
Baryonyx	Heavy claw	30 feet	3,300 pounds	fish
Eoraptor	Dawn thief	3 feet	11–16 pounds	meat, insects
Maiasaura	Good mother lizard	30 feet	3 tons	plants
Plateosaurus	Broad lizard	20–26 feet	2,000–4,000 lb.	plants
Seismosaurus	Earthquake lizard	120–150 feet	40 tons	plants
Spinosaurus	Spined lizard	40 feet	4 tons	fish
Velociraptor	Fast thief	6 feet	30 pounds	meat

1 How much did the dinosaur called *Maiasaura* weigh?
    a 30 pounds   **c** 4 tons
    b 3 tons   **d** 40 tons

2 Which dinosaur's name means "broad lizard?"
    a *Ankylosaurus*   **c** *Plateosaurus*
    b *Eoraptor*   **d** *Spinosaurus*

3 How many feet long was the dinosaur called *Velociraptor*?
    a 3 feet   **c** 25 feet
    b 6 feet   **d** 30 feet

4 Which of these dinosaurs ate fish?
    a *Ankylosaurus*   **c** *Velociraptor*
    b *Maiasaura*   **d** *Spinosaurus*

5 Which is the largest, heaviest dinosaur listed in the chart?
    a *Seismosaurus*   **c** *Eoraptor*
    b *Plateosaurus*   **d** *Baryonyx*

Scholastic Professional Books

How Hurricanes Get Their Names

When hurricanes form each year, the National Hurricane Center gives each one a name. The chart below shows some of the names for hurricanes in the Atlantic Ocean in the years 2002, 2003, and 2004. Use the chart to answer the questions.

HURRICANE NAMES: ATLANTIC OCEAN		
2002	2003	2004
Arthur	Ana	Alex
Bertha	Bill	Bonnie
Cristobal	Claudette	Charley
Dolly	Danny	Danielle
Edouard	Erika	Earl
Fay	Fabian	Frances
Gustav	Grace	Gaston
Hanna	Henri	Hermine
Isidore	Isabel	Ivan
Josephine	Juan	Jeanne
Kyle	Kate	Karl

1   What name will be given to the first hurricane in 2003?

_____

2   What name will be given to the fifth hurricane in 2004?

_____

3   What name came after Gustav in 2002?

_____

4   What name beginning with the letter "D" will be used in 2004?

_____

5   From this chart, what can you tell about the "rules" used in naming hurricanes? Explain your idea.

_____

_____

_____

Speedy Animals

The bar graph below shows how fast some animals can run. Use the graph to answer the questions.

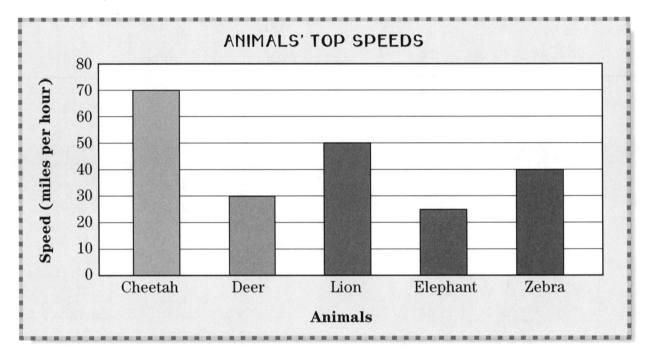

ANIMALS' TOP SPEEDS

Speed (miles per hour)

Animals: Cheetah, Deer, Lion, Elephant, Zebra

1. How fast can a lion run? _____

2. How fast can an elephant run? _____

3. Which animal runs the fastest? _____

4. What is a zebra's top speed? _____

5. List all five animals in order from slowest to fastest.

_____

_____

_____

_____

_____

Scholastic Professional Books

All About Energy

The circle graph below shows the sources of energy used in the United States today. Use the circle graph to choose the best answer to each question.

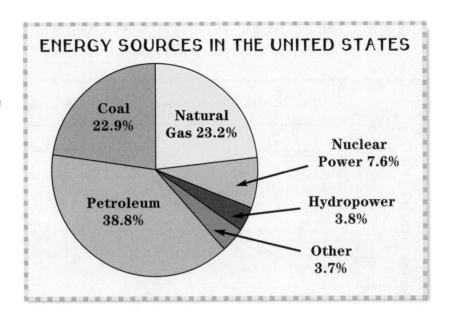

ENERGY SOURCES IN THE UNITED STATES

Coal
22.9%

Natural
Gas 23.2%

Nuclear
Power 7.6%

Petroleum
38.8%

Hydropower
3.8%

Other
3.7%

1 Which energy source provides about 8% of the power in the United States?
- (a) petroleum
- (b) coal
- (c) nuclear power
- (d) hydropower

2 What portion of the energy used in the United States comes from hydropower?
- (a) 38.8%
- (b) 23.2%
- (c) 7.6%
- (d) 3.8%

3 More than one third of the energy used in the United States comes from which source?
- (a) petroleum
- (b) natural gas
- (c) nuclear power
- (d) hydropower

4 About what percentage of energy used in the United States comes from fossil fuels (petroleum, natural gas, and coal)?
- (a) 65%
- (b) 75%
- (c) 85%
- (d) 95%

5 From this graph, you can conclude that the energy in the United States provided by solar power is _____.
- (a) less than 4%
- (b) about 4%
- (c) about 10%
- (d) more than 10%

Cleveland's Weather Update

The line graph below shows the average temperature each month in Cleveland, Ohio. Use the graph to answer the questions.

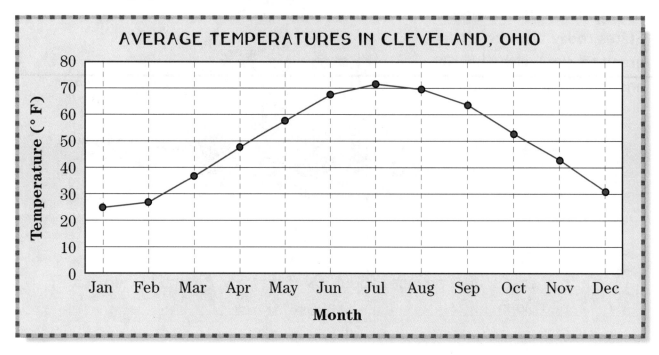

AVERAGE TEMPERATURES IN CLEVELAND, OHIO

1. What is the average temperature in Cleveland in March? _____

2. What is the average temperature in Cleveland in September? _____

3. Which is the warmest month? _____

4. Which is the coldest month? _____

5. What is the difference in average temperature between the warmest month and the coldest? _____

6. Write one or two sentences that describe the changes in temperature during the year.

_____

_____

_____

Scholastic Professional Books

Scholastic Success With

ADDITION, SUBTRACTION, MULTIPLICATION & DIVISION

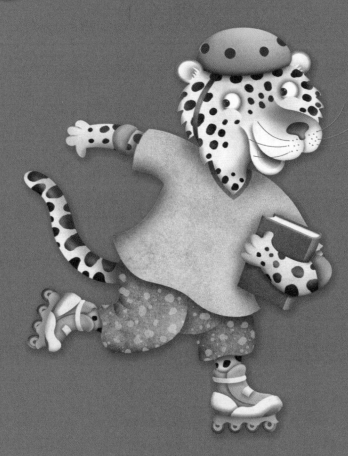

A Sick Riddle

Riddle: What sickness can't you talk about until it's cured?

Find each sum. Then use the Decoder to solve the riddle by filling in the spaces at the bottom of the page.

1 $12 + 7$ = _____

2 $32 + 10$ = _____

3 $50 + 4$ = _____

4 $13 + 22$ = _____

5 $47 + 19$ = _____

6 $97 + 68$ = _____

7 $204 + 41$ = _____

8 $37 + 331$ = _____

9 $670 + 98$ = _____

10 $857 + 466$ = _____

Decoder

66...................	I
57	W
42...................	I
216	M
19	Y
97...................	C
768...................	G
35...................	S
46...................	E
100...................	X
245...................	R
1,257	D
54...................	A
52...................	O
368	L
82...................	P
1,323	T
155...................	Q
165...................	N

____ ____ ____ ____ ____ ____ ____ ____ ____ ____
 8   3   7   1   6   9   5   10   2   4

Blooming Octagon

Solve the problems. ◆ If the answer is between 1 and 300, color the
shape yellow. ◆ If the answer is between 301 and 600, color the shape
blue. ◆ If the answer is between 601 and 1,000, color the shape orange.
◆ Finish by coloring the outer shapes with the colors of your choice.

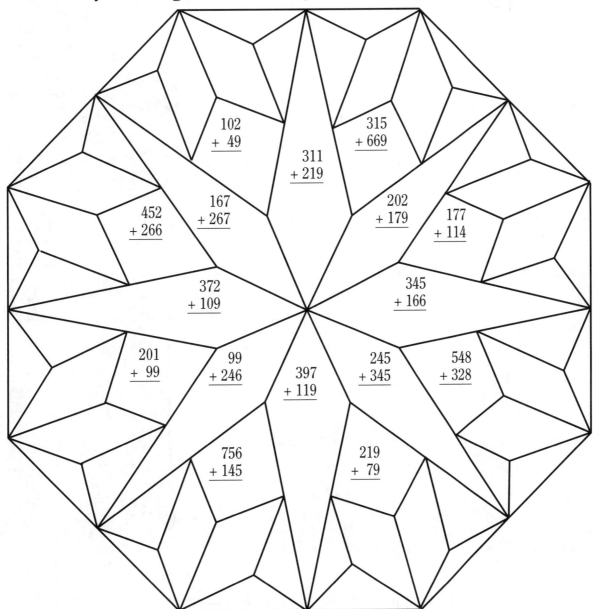

$$102 + 49$$

$$315 + 669$$

$$311 + 219$$

$$452 + 266$$

$$167 + 267$$

$$202 + 179$$

$$177 + 114$$

$$372 + 109$$

$$345 + 166$$

$$201 + 99$$

$$99 + 246$$

$$397 + 119$$

$$245 + 345$$

$$548 + 328$$

$$756 + 145$$

$$219 + 79$$

Taking It Further: Fill in the next three numbers in this pattern.

150, 300, 450, 600, _____, _____, _____.

The Big Cheese

 Always complete the operation inside the parentheses ( ) first. Then complete the rest of the problem.

$$7 + (3 + 6) =$$
$$7 + 9 = 16$$

$$(4 + 4) + 8 =$$
$$8 + 8 = 16$$

Add.

A. $(7 + 2) + 4 = \underline{13}$ $(3 + 4) + 7 = \underline{14}$

B. $(5 + 4) + 9 = \underline{18}$ $9 + (2 + 3) = \underline{14}$

C. $8 + (3 + 5) = \underline{16}$ $6 + (2 + 4) = \underline{12}$

D. $(2 + 6) + (5 + 2) = \underline{15}$ $(5 + 1) + (4 + 4) = \underline{14}$

E. $(3 + 3) + (5 + 4) = \underline{15}$ $(4 + 3) + (6 + 2) = \underline{15}$

F. $(6 + 6) + 3 = \underline{15}$ $4 + (5 + 4) = \underline{13}$

G. $5 + (4 + 8) = \underline{17}$ $(3 + 7) + 7 = \underline{17}$

H. $(2 + 9) + 8 = \underline{19}$ $5 + (5 + 5) = \underline{15}$

I. $(8 + 5) + 4 = \underline{17}$ $(9 + 3) + 2 = \underline{14}$

J. $(8 + 2) + (3 + 2) = \underline{15}$ $(5 + 7) + (4 + 4) = \underline{20}$

K. $(2 + 5) + (5 + 8) = \underline{20}$ $(6 + 5) + (7 + 4) = \underline{22}$

 The director ordered a big piece of cheese for each actor in the movie. He ordered 6 pieces from Charlie's Cheese Shop, 3 pieces from Holes and More, and 7 pieces from Mouse Munchers. Write a number sentence using parentheses to solve the problem.

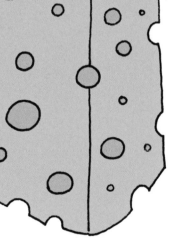

Scholastic Professional Books

A-Mazing Eighteen

 *The answer to an addition problem is called the **sum**.*

Find the path that leads from the mouse to the cheese by following the sums of eighteen. Add.

(5 + 4) + (3 + 6)	(7 + 6) + 5	(5 + 6) + (4 + 2)	(7 + 5) + 7	3 + (7 + 5)
4 + (6 + 6)	3 + (8 + 7)	(5 + 3) + (3 + 4)	(4 + 6) + 5	(5 + 9) + 3
(9 + 2) + 6	(5 + 3) + (6 + 4)	2 + (8 + 8)	8 + (6+ 2)	(4 + 5) + (2 + 5)
5 + (6 + 6)	(6 + 6) + (4 + 6)	(2 + 3) + (9 + 4)	3 + (7 + 5)	(6 + 7) + 6
(7 + 8) + 2	5 + (4 + 6)	7 + (4 + 7)	(5 + 6) + (4 + 3)	(8 + 4) + 6

 Write another number sentence with 18 as the sum. Do not use a number sentence from above.

Name _____

Climbing High

To add multiple-digit numbers without regrouping, follow these steps.
1. Add the ones column.
2. Add the tens column.
3. Add the hundreds column.
4. Continue working through each column in order.

Add.

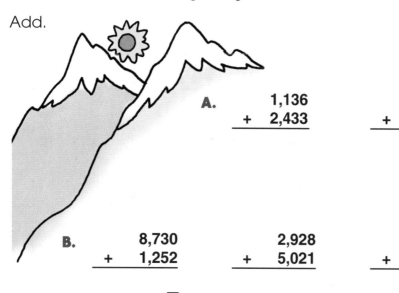

A.
```
    1,136          9,025
  + 2,433        +   851
  _____        _____
```

B.
```
    8,730          2,928          3,650         80,662
  + 1,252        + 5,021        + 4,210       + 11,136
  _____        _____        _____       _____
```

C.
```
   55,100         60,439         81,763         36,034
 + 31,892       + 30,310       +  8,231       + 41,753
 _____       _____       _____       _____
```

D.
```
  321,957        623,421        264,870        592,604        127,094
+ 260,041      + 151,441      + 303,120      + 102,335      + 832,502
_____       _____       _____       _____       _____
```

 Mount Everest is the highest mountain in the world. To find the height of Mount Everest, begin climbing in Row D. Write the underlined numbers in order. Continue writing the numbers in Row C, Row B, and Row A. How many feet did you climb?

Scholastic Professional Books

Reaching New Heights

To add multiple-digit numbers with regrouping, follow these steps.
1. *Add the ones column.*
2. *If the sum is greater than 9, regroup to the tens column.*
3. *Add the tens column.*
4. *If the sum is greater than 9, regroup to the hundreds column.*
5. *Continue working through each column in order.*

Which of these mountains is the tallest? To find out add. The sum with the greatest number in each row shows the height of the mountain in feet. Circle the height for each mountain.

Kilimanjaro

A.
$$7,542 + 8,439$$ $$9,831 + 9,510$$ $$6,905 + 3,492$$ $$4,671 + 4,319$$

Mount Cook

B.
$$5,725 + 6,624$$ $$3,642 + 8,546$$ $$4,863 + 7,066$$ $$5,677 + 5,307$$

Mount McKinley

C.
$$10,375 + 8,615$$ $$12,575 + 4,192$$ $$18,410 + 1,910$$ $$8,754 + 8,217$$

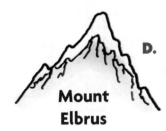

Mount Elbrus

D.
$$13,825 + 3,934$$ $$13,257 + 2,727$$ $$8,251 + 6,236$$ $$9,060 + 9,450$$

Find the total height of the two mountains with the greatest heights.

Wild Birds

 Some addition problems will require regrouping several times. The steps look like this.

1. Add the ones column. Regroup if needed.	2. Add the tens column. Regroup if needed.	3. Add the hundreds column. Regroup if needed.	4. Continue working through each column in order.
1	11	111	111
37,462	37,462	37,462	37,462
+ 22,798	+ 22,798	+ 22,798	+ 22,798
0	60	260	60,260

Add. Then use the code to finish the fun fact below.

bald eagle

Z.	953	B.	295	R.	418	Q.	565	S.	862	X.	478
	+ 418		+ 337		+ 793		+ 957		+ 339		+ 283

falcon

I.	2,428	C.	1,566	Y.	3,737	A.	9,289	Y.	8,754
	+ 6,679		+ 2,487		+ 6,418		+ 4,735		+ 368

vulture

L.	57,854	P.	29,484	E.	36,238	F.	67,139
	+ 45,614		+ 46,592		+ 46,135		+ 25,089

owl

D.	240,669	O.	476,381	R.	882,948
	+ 298,727		+ 175,570		+ 176,524

What do all of these birds have in common?

They are ____ ____ ____ ____ ____   ____ ____
     632   9,107   1,211   539,396   1,201   651,951 92,228

____ ____ ____ ____ .
76,076 1,059,472 82,373 10,155

Name _____

The American Bald Eagle

 To add numbers that require regrouping in more than one column, follow these steps.
1. Add the ones column. Regroup if needed.
2. Add the tens column. Regroup if needed.
4. Add the hundreds column. Regroup if needed.
5. Continue working through each column in order.

Add. Then use the code to finish the fun fact below.

H. 8,754
  + 368

L. 7,789
  + 4,759

I. 8,997
  + 9,978

A. 8,599
  + 8,932

E. 5,476
  + 4,846

O. 9,475
  + 7,725

C. 8,838
  + 9,668

T. 6,867
  + 7,256

M. 9,891
  + 3,699

N. 92,854
  + 37,898

U. 25,748
  + 85,362

Y. 99,977
  + 82,943

R. 57,544
  + 78,587

The bald eagle is found ____ ____ ____
  17,200   130,752   12,548   182,920   17,200   130,752

____ ____ ____   ____ ____ ____ ____ ____
14,123   9,122   10,322   130,752   17,200   136,131   14,123   9,122

____ ____ ____ ____ ____ ____ ____ ____
17,531   13,590   10,322   136,131   18,975   18,506   17,531   130,752

____ ____ ____ ____ ____ ____ ____ ____ ____ .
18,506   17,200   130,752   14,123   18,975   130,752   10,322   130,752   14,123

Name _____

Funny Bone

 Use the same steps to add several addends. Some columns will require regrouping, and some will not.

Add. Then use the code to find the answer to the riddle below.

W.	T.	P.	N.	O.	E.
1,233	6,314	2,305	1,238	3,541	3,525
1,442	3,380	2,404	6,281	309	2,213
+ 5,226	+ 2,606	+ 2,439	+ 5,366	+ 7,845	+ 9,281

H.	R.	S.	!	A.	U.
444	4,327	4,024	5,441	2,653	5,560
7,283	4,331	678	421	3,338	4,202
+ 8,217	+ 1,746	+ 4,505	+ 3,954	+ 2,924	+ 1,541

What is the difference between a man and a running dog?

‾‾‾‾‾‾‾ ‾‾‾‾‾‾‾ ‾‾‾‾‾‾‾
11,695   12,885   15,019

‾‾‾‾‾‾‾ ‾‾‾‾‾‾‾ ‾‾‾‾‾‾‾ ‾‾‾‾‾‾‾ ‾‾‾‾‾‾‾
7,901   15,019   8,915   10,404   9,207

‾‾‾‾‾‾‾ ‾‾‾‾‾‾‾ ‾‾‾‾‾‾‾ ‾‾‾‾‾‾‾ ‾‾‾‾‾‾‾ ‾‾‾‾‾‾‾ ‾‾‾‾‾‾‾ ‾‾‾‾‾‾‾ .
12,300   10,404   11,695   11,303   9,207   15,019   10,404   9,207

‾‾‾‾‾‾‾ ‾‾‾‾‾‾‾ ‾‾‾‾‾‾‾
12,300   15,944   15,019

‾‾‾‾‾‾‾ ‾‾‾‾‾‾‾ ‾‾‾‾‾‾‾ ‾‾‾‾‾‾‾ ‾‾‾‾‾‾‾
11,695   12,300   15,944   15,019   10,404

‾‾‾‾‾‾‾ ‾‾‾‾‾‾‾ ‾‾‾‾‾‾‾ ‾‾‾‾‾‾‾ ‾‾‾‾‾‾‾ ‾‾‾‾‾‾‾
7,148   8,915   12,885   12,300   9,207   9,816

Scholastic Professional Books

Canine Calculations

 The numbers being added together are called **addends**.

Use the sum to help you find the missing numbers of each addend.

A.

```
   1 1
   6, 7 4 □
 + □, 3 8 2
 ──────────
  10, 1 2 3
```

```
   1   1
   9, 4 4 3
 + 9, □ 1 □
 ──────────
  19, 2 6 0
```

```
        1
  □, 5 □ 8
 + 5, 3 6 1
 ──────────
   9, 9 3 9
```

```
  1 1 1
  □, 2 2 7
 + 6, □ 7 3
 ──────────
  9, 2 0 0
```

B.

```
      1
  3, 8 4 1
 +□, 0 6 □
 ─────────
  7, 9 0 5
```

```
        1
  7, 0 □ 4
 + 9, □ 3 8
 ──────────
  16, 4 6 2
```

```
  1
 □, □ 1 0
+ 9, 3 8 5
──────────
 19, 1 9 5
```

```
  1
 □, 4 2 6
+ 7, 9 2 □
──────────
 15, 3 4 9
```

C.

```
    1 1
  1, 7 □ 3
 +   □ 5 8
 ─────────
  1, 9 3 1
```

```
  1 1
  3, □ 5 4
 + 6, 4 □ 4
 ──────────
  10, 1 2 8
```

```
  1 1
 □, 2 8 4
+ 3, □ 2 1
──────────
  8, 1 0 5
```

```
  1   1
  8, 8 6 □
 +□, 3 1 7
 ─────────
  11, 1 8 0
```

D.

```
  1 1 1
  3, □ 4 □
 + 9, 2 □ 5
 ──────────
  13, 2 1 3
```

```
  1   1
 □, 7 □ 9
+ 8, □ 2 □
──────────
 18, 4 8 3
```

```
  1 1 1
  7, 5 5 □
 +□, □ 4 8
 ──────────
  17, 5 0 6
```

```
  1 1 1
  4, □ 9 5
 +□, 6 □ 8
 ──────────
  11, 2 2 3
```

 Wag'n Tail Kennels bought two enormous bags of dog treats. One bag had 38, □ 69 dog treats in it. The other bag had 4 □,510 pieces of dog treats. Altogether the bags had 80,879 treats. On another piece of paper, find the number of dog treats in each bag.

Scholastic Professional Books

Money Fun

 Remember to include a decimal point and a dollar sign in the answer when adding money.

Add. Then use the code to answer the riddle below.

A. $63.54 + 29.29	**G.** $65.35 + 27.18	**U.** $24.12 + 90.48	**O.** $15.79 + 48.08
B. $27.60 + 44.65	**N.** $77.88 + 92.90	**E.** $86.91 + 70.44	**R.** $39.75 + 29.62
M. $103.90 + 64.82	**C.** $291.26 + 473.83	**S.** $485.13 + 494.92	**T.** $630.57 + 39.52
D. $184.64 + 292.43	**Y.** $354.60 + 261.74	**F.** $964.36 + 252.04	**W.** $904.86 + 95.82

Why are birds poor?

___ ___ ___ ___ ___ ___ ___
$72.25 $157.35 $765.09 $92.83 $114.60 $980.05 $157.35

___ ___ ___ ___ ___
$168.72 $63.87 $170.78 $157.35 $616.34
,

___ ___ ___ ___ ___ ___ ___ ___ ___ ___
$477.07 $63.87 $157.35 $980.05 $170.78 $670.09 $92.53 $69.37 $63.87 $1,000.68
!

___ ___ ___ ___ ___ ___ ___
$63.87 $170.78 $670.09 $69.37 $157.35 $157.35 $980.05

Bathtub Brunch

Riddle: What's the best thing to eat in a bathtub?

Find each sum. Then use the Decoder to solve the riddle by filling in the spaces at the bottom of the page.

Decoder

5,429	A
10,493	F
2,133	S
14,983	R
10,439	P
712	U
3,489	K
1,840	M
1,063	E
4,523	W
689	N
2,009	B
8,292	O
3,234	I
7,538	G
1,804	C
4,708	H
6,521	L
8,234	E

❶ $1,004 + 800$ = _____

❷ $512 + 177$ = _____

❸ $364 + 699$ = _____

❹ $1,245 + 888$ = _____

❺ $1,876 + 1,613$ = _____

❻ $2,010 + 6,224$ = _____

❼ $5,470 + 2,068$ = _____

❽ $4,526 + 3,766$ = _____

❾ $1,017 + 4,412$ = _____

❿ $2,588 + 7,851$ = _____

___ ___ ___ ___ ___ ___ ___ ___ ___ ___
4 10 8 2 7 6   1 9 5 3

Food to Go

Figure it out!

1. Woovis the Dog found a $5 bill. Which item can he buy from the menu that will give the least change?

_____

2. Molly Mouse gets Crumbs & Cheese for breakfast. She pays with the $5 bill. With the leftover money, what can Woovis buy to eat?

_____

3. Which item can Woovis buy with the $5 bill that will give the most change?

_____

4. Which two items can Woovis buy with the $5 bill so that he gets about $1 back in change?

_____

5. Woovis ordered two items from the menu and gave the cashier the $5 bill. But the two items cost more than $6.50. Which two items did Woovis order?

_____

SUPER CHALLENGE: Can Woovis use the $5 bill to buy three different items from the menu? Why or why not?

Name _____

A Penny Saved Is a Penny Earned

Write a number sentence for each problem. Solve.

A. Aimee and her 2 sisters are saving to buy a camera. Aimee has $12.89. Each of her sisters has $28.53. How much money do all the girls have combined?

B. Katie has $23.95 in her purse, $17.23 in her bank, and $76.82 in her savings account. What is the total amount of Katie's money?

C. Jonah worked in the yard for 3 days. The first day he earned $7.96. The second day he earned $2.00 more than the first day. The third day he earned $2.00 less than the first day. How much did Jonah earn altogether?

D. Jack has $9.29. He also has 79 dimes and 139 pennies. How much money does he have altogether?

E. Kelsey has 478 coins in her collection. The silver dollars equal $79.00, and the quarters equal $99.75. How much is Kelsey's collection worth in all?

F. Claire bought lemonade for herself and two friends. Each cup costs $1.75. How much did Claire spend in all?

 On another piece of paper, write a word problem with a sum equal to $41.68.

Reach for the Stars

Always complete the operation inside the parentheses ( ) first.
Then complete the rest of the problem.

(18 − 9) − 3 = ____   18 − (9 − 3) = ____
9 − 3 = 6   18 − 6 = 12

Subtract. Then use the code to answer the question below.

N. (16 − 8) − 5 = ____   **T.** (18 − 6) − 2 = ____

B. 17 − (12 − 4) = ____   **L.** 19 − (10 − 6) = ____

U. (23 − 4) − 5 = ____   **E.** (13 − 5) − (10 − 9) = ____

D. (12 − 3) − (16 − 7) = ____   **O.** (14 − 7) − (12 − 6) = ____

L. (17 − 5) − (12 − 8) = ____   **I.** (16 − 8) − (11 − 9) = ____

W. 13 − (11 − 3) = ____   **D.** 17 − (14 − 9) = ____

R. (22 − 6) − 5 = ____   **N.** (21 − 2) − (15 − 9) = ____

I. (21 − 1) − (16 − 12) = ____   **O.** (10 − 3) − (11 − 6) = ____

H. (11 − 3) − 4 = ____

How many stars are in the Milky Way Galaxy?

___ ___ ___   ___ ___ ___ ___ ___ ___ ___   ___ ___ ___ ___ ___ ___ ___
10   5   1   4   14 13   0   11   7   12   9   16   8   15   6   2   3

Scholastic Professional Books

Moon Madness

 *The answer to a subtraction problem is called the **difference**.*

Subtract. Then write the differences in order to answer the fun fact.

How fast does the moon travel in its orbit? m.p.h.

A. 11 – (15 – 9) = ____   14 – (18 – 9) = ____

B. (15 – 7) – (11 – 5) = ____   17 – (14 – 6) = ____

C. 16 – (15 – 8) = ____   18 – (16 – 7) = ____

D. 15 – (15 – 8) = ____   (16 – 8) – (10 – 4) = ____

E. (13 – 9) – (11 – 8) = ____   13 – (14 – 7) = ____

F. 12 – (13 – 6) = ____   17 – (12 – 3) = ____

G. (17 – 9) – (13 – 8) = ____   (15 – 6) – (12 – 5) = ____

H. 18 – (13 – 4) = ____   16 – (17 – 9) = ____

I. 14 – (13 – 5) = ____   15 – (16 – 8) = ____

J. 12 – (18 – 9) = ____   (20 – 7) – (6 – 2) = ____

 On another piece of paper, write subtraction problems with a code to answer this question: What is the diameter of the moon? (2,160 miles) Have a friend solve the problems.

Chess, Anyone?

 To subtract multiple-digit numbers without regrouping, follow these steps.

1. Subtract the ones column.

2. Subtract the tens column.

3. Subtract the hundreds column.

4. Subtract the thousands column.

$$6,48\boxed{9}$$
$$-\ 2,16\boxed{5}$$
$$\boxed{4}$$

$$6,4\boxed{8}9$$
$$-\ 2,1\boxed{6}5$$
$$\boxed{2}4$$

$$6,\boxed{4}89$$
$$-\ 2\boxed{1}65$$
$$\boxed{3}24$$

$$\boxed{6},489$$
$$-\ \boxed{2},165$$
$$\boxed{4},324$$

Subtract.

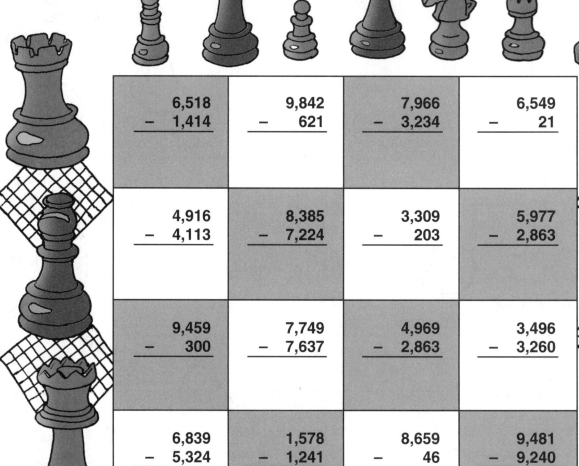

6,518 − 1,414	9,842 − 621	7,966 − 3,234	6,549 − 21
4,916 − 4,113	8,385 − 7,224	3,309 − 203	5,977 − 2,863
9,459 − 300	7,749 − 7,637	4,969 − 2,863	3,496 − 3,260
6,839 − 5,324	1,578 − 1,241	8,659 − 46	9,481 − 9,240

Scholastic Professional Books

Checkmate

 To subtract with regrouping, follow these steps.

1. Subtract the ones column. Regroup if needed.

$$\begin{array}{r} 2\ 11 \\ 4\,\cancel{3}\,\cancel{1} \\ -\ 2\,6\,6 \\ \hline 5 \end{array}$$

2. Subtract the tens column. Regroup if needed.

$$\begin{array}{r} 12 \\ 3\,\cancel{2}\,11 \\ \cancel{4}\,\cancel{3}\,\cancel{1} \\ -\ 2\,6\,6 \\ \hline 6\,5 \end{array}$$

3. Subtract the hundreds column. Regroup if needed.

$$\begin{array}{r} 12 \\ 3\,\cancel{2}\,11 \\ \cancel{4}\,\cancel{3}\,\cancel{1} \\ -\ 2\,6\,6 \\ \hline 1\,6\,5 \end{array}$$

Subtract. Cross out the chess piece with the matching difference. The last piece standing is the winner of the match.

63

464

$$\begin{array}{r} \overset{8}{9}56 \\ -\ 492 \\ \hline 464 \end{array} \qquad \begin{array}{r} 239 \\ -\ 176 \\ \hline 063 \end{array} \qquad \begin{array}{r} \overset{3}{8}42 \\ -\ 426 \\ \hline 416 \end{array}$$

179

$$\begin{array}{r} \overset{0}{1}53 \\ -\ 80 \\ \hline 73 \end{array} \qquad \begin{array}{r} \overset{24}{3}51 \\ -\ 172 \\ \hline 179 \end{array} \qquad \begin{array}{r} \overset{817}{9}83 \\ -\ 284 \\ \hline 699 \end{array}$$

416

$$\begin{array}{r} \overset{4}{5}26 \\ -\ 286 \\ \hline 240 \end{array} \qquad \begin{array}{r} \overset{513}{6}43 \\ -\ 479 \\ \hline 164 \end{array} \qquad \begin{array}{r} \overset{4}{2}58 \\ -\ 139 \\ \hline 119 \end{array}$$

699

73

240

$$\begin{array}{r} \overset{2}{9}32 \\ -\ 426 \\ \hline 506 \end{array} \qquad \begin{array}{r} \overset{74}{8}52 \\ -\ 476 \\ \hline 376 \end{array}$$

164

119

$\boxed{479}$ **is left standing.**

506

479

376

Out of the Park!

 To subtract with regrouping, follow these steps.

1.
```
      5 10
  3,4 6 0
 −   8 7 6
 ─────────
          4
```

2.
```
        15
     3 8 10
  3 , 4 6 0
 −     8 7 6
 ──────────
         8 4
```

3.
```
    13 15
  2 8 8 10
  3 , 4 6 0
 −     8 7 6
 ──────────
        5 8 4
```

4.
```
    13 15
  2 8 8 10
  3 , 4 6 0
 −     8 7 6
 ──────────
      2 , 5 8 4
```

Subtract. Then use the code to solve the riddle below.

E. 4,622 − 1,284	**E.** 5,198 − 469	**H.** 3,469 − 890
T. 6,077 − 1,258	**A.** 9,617 − 759	**R.** 3,804 − 115
H. 8,941 − 1,895	**N.** 952 − 95	**C.** 7,263 − 4,772	**B.** 7,603 − 3,728
E. 9,550 − 4,298	**L.** 6,451 − 868	**S.** 2,850 − 1,976	**I.** 2,972 − 984

In what part of the ballpark do you find the whitest clothes?

____ ____   ____ ____ ____
1,988 857   4,819 2,579 5,252

____ ____ ____ ____ ____ ____ ____ ____ ____ !
3,875 5,583 4,729 8,858 2,491 7,046 3,338 3,689 874

 On another piece of paper, write a subtraction problem that requires regrouping two times. Ask someone at home to solve it.

Scholastic Professional Books

Touchdown!

Subtract. The final score of the game will be written in the footballs at the bottom of the page.

 Colts

 Panthers

7,694 − 1,986	8,049 − 862	9,217 − 972	5,473 − 864
[ ]	[ ]	[ ]	[ ]
− 874	− 1,479	− 1,366	− 1,953
[ ]	[ ]	[ ]	[ ]
− 3,782	− 2,896	− 3,899	− 1,838
[ ]	[ ]	[ ]	[ ]
− 561	− 1,778	− 1,597	− 692
[ ]	[ ]	[ ]	[ ]
− 488	− 1,027	− 1,379	− 117

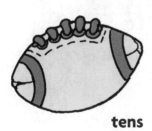  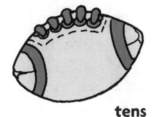 

tens | ones | tens | ones

Who won? _____

 On another piece of paper, write a series of four subtraction problems that have a final difference equal to your age.

A Funny Fixture

Continue regrouping into the ten thousands column if necessary.

Subtract. Then use the code to find the answer to the riddle below.

E. 63,210 − 11,799	**I.** 41,392 − 38,164	**R.** 76,146 − 34,982	**E.** 12,388 − 9,891
P. 54,391 − 23,689	**H.** 68,612 − 59,446	**T.** 97,413 − 89,608	**L.** 32,602 − 19,561
A. 18,546 − 11,798	**G.** 92,475 − 76,097	**S.** 29,816 − 17,909	**!** 78,752 − 69,275

Why did the man climb up the chandelier?

,

9,166	51,411	11,907		6,748

13,041	3,228	16,378	9,166	7,805

11,907	13,041	2,497	51,411	30,702	2,497	41,164	9,477

Name _____

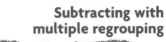

Bright Idea!

 Each part of a subtraction problem has a name:

$$
\begin{array}{r}
3,486 \leftarrow \textbf{minuend} \\
-\ \ 2,371 \leftarrow \textbf{subtrahend} \\
\hline
1,115 \leftarrow \textbf{difference}
\end{array}
$$

Find each missing subtrahend by subtracting the difference from the minuend.

9,416 − 812		32,194 − 5,778
63,417 − 21,759		91,753 − 18,475
8,110 − 3,794		17,942 − 8,786
49,234 − 39,741		23,976 − 18,687

 On another piece of paper, write two subtraction problems with missing subtrahends. Ask a friend to solve the problems.

Scholastic Professional Books

Cross-Number Puzzle

Subtract. Complete the puzzle.

Across

2. 3,016
   − 1,209

6. 246,342
   − 156,129

8. 64,293
   − 28,318

9. 5,249
   − 3,928

10. 36,425
    − 18,929

11. 5,264
    − 3,192

12. 818,462
    − 131,910

14. 3,642
    − 1,813

15. 7,645
    − 1,328

Down

1. 6,429
   − 3,298

3. 9,145
   − 2,189

4. 9,142
   − 1,381

5. 58,142
   − 13,098

7. 76,418
   −39,291

10. 31,642
    − 18,945

13. 814,603
    −148,231

Scholastic Professional Books

Map It Out

 Always write a long subtraction problem vertically before solving it. When subtracting decimals, write each place value column so the decimal points are aligned.

$82.17 - 74.16 =$

$$\begin{array}{r} 82.71 \\ -74.16 \\ \hline \end{array}$$

Write each subtraction problem vertically. Subtract.

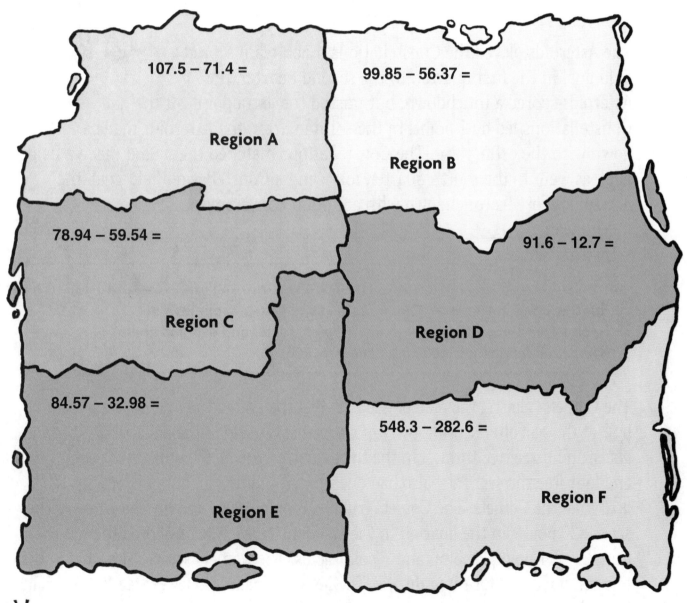

Region A
$107.5 - 71.4 =$

Region B
$99.85 - 56.37 =$

Region C
$78.94 - 59.54 =$

Region D
$91.6 - 12.7 =$

Region E
$84.57 - 32.98 =$

Region F
$548.3 - 282.6 =$

 Mary traveled to two regions. Their difference is 24.08. What two regions did she visit?

Sums & Differences

> ### Point-scoring in the Inter-Galaxy Football League
> Touchdown . . . . .6 points
> Touchdown with an extra point . . . . .7 points
> Touchdown with a 2-point conversion . . . . .8 points
> Field Goal . . . . .3 points

The Asteroids played the Constellations. Each team scored a field goal in the first quarter. In the second quarter, the Asteroids scored a touchdown, but missed the extra point. At the half, the Constellations led by 1 point. In the third quarter, the Asteroids made a touchdown with the extra point. The Constellations matched them, and made a field goal, as well. In the fourth quarter, following a Constellation field goal, the Asteroids scored a touchdown with a 2-point conversion.

Who won? _____

By what score? _____

> Point-scoring in the Inter-Galaxy Basketball League consists of
> 1-point free throws, 2-point goals, 3-point goals, and 4-point goals
> (those made without looking at the basket!).

The Comets, playing the Meteors, led 22–9 at the end of the first quarter. They led by 7 at the half after scoring two 4-point goals, two 3-point goals, four 2-point goals, and three free throws. In the third quarter, the Meteors had six 2-point goals and four free throws. They also had one more 4-point goal, but one less 3-point goal than the Comets. The Comets had five 2-point goals and no free-throws. They scored 20 points in the quarter. In the last quarter, each team scored the same number of 4-point, 3-point, and 2-point goals. The Comets scored 31 points in that quarter, including four free throws. The Meteors made two fewer free throws than the Comets.

Who won? _____

By what score? _____

Name _____

Follow the Map

Write a number sentence for each problem. Solve.

A. Hannah's family drove 1,246 miles in 2 days. They drove 879 miles the first day. How far did they drive the second day?	**B.** Joplin is between Wells and Greenville. The distance from Wells to Greenville is 4,128 miles. The distance from Wells to Joplin is 1,839 miles. How far is it from Joplin to Greenville?
C. The Midnight Express travels 6,283 miles. When the train reaches Springfield, it has traveled 2,496 miles. How much farther will the Midnight Express travel?	**D.** Jacob's scout troop is going camping 947.6 miles from home. The bus breaks down after 289.9 miles. How far is the bus from the campgrounds?
E. Jonesburgh is between Johnsonville and Piper. Johnsonville is 8,612 miles from Piper. Piper is 4,985 miles from Jonesburgh. How far is it from Jonesburgh to Johnsonville?	**F.** Lola's family drove 2,391 miles to go to the beach. They drove home using another route that was 3,290 miles. How much longer was the second route?

Name _____

It's a Circus in Here!

 To multiply is to use repeated addition. Basic multiplication facts
are learned by memorizing.

$$3 \text{ groups of } 5 = 5 + 5 + 5 = 3 \times 5 = 15$$

Multiply.

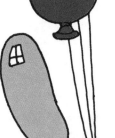
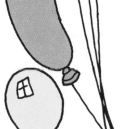

2 x 2 **4**	3 x 3 **9**	9 x 6 **54**	5 x 4 **20**	6 x 7 **42**
6 x 4 **24**	4 x 1 **4**	5 x 8 **40**	9 x 3 **27**	2 x 4 **8**
8 x 6 **48**	9 x 5 **45**	1 x 0 **0**	3 x 5 **15**	9 x 7 **63**
8 x 8 **64**	4 x 7 **28**	9 x 9 **81**	0 x 8 **0**	3 x 4 **12**
5 x 5 **25**	6 x 6 **36**	7 x 7 **49**	5 x 2 **10**	8 x 4 **32**

 **On another piece of paper, draw a picture to match this problem:
There are 6 clowns. Each clown is holding 7 balloons. Then write the
multiplication fact that tells the total number of balloons.**

Scholastic Professional Books

Name _____

Under the Big Top

*The answer to a multiplication problem is called the **product**.
The numbers being multiplied are called **factors**.*

Multiply. Then use each product and the code to answer the riddles.

What happened to the human cannonball at the circus?

___ ___   ___ ___ ___   ___ ___ ___ ___ ___
4 x 6 6 x 3   7 x 7 3 x 4 8 x 8   8 x 3 6 x 8 7 x 9 2 x 9 8 x 7

___ ___ ___   ___ ___ ___ ___ ___   ___ ___
6 x 2 8 x 9 7 x 8   9 x 9 8 x 6 9 x 7 3 x 6 7 x 8   7 x 6 9 x 8

___ ___ ___   ___ ___ ___ ___   ___ ___ ___!
5 x 9 6 x 4 9 x 2   8 x 8 4 x 3 6 x 6 6 x 3   8 x 7 2 x 6 5 x 5

What happened to the kid who ran away with the circus?

___ ___   ___ ___ ___
3 x 8 2 x 9   4 x 6 3 x 4 8 x 7

___ ___   ___ ___ ___ ___ ___
9 x 5 6 x 7   9 x 3 7 x 9 8 x 6 9 x 8 5 x 8

___ ___   ___ ___ ___ ___!
6 x 8 5 x 9   3 x 9 2 x 6 5 x 3 9 x 6

A = 12	H = 24	O = 42	V = 21
B = 27	I = 48	P = 16	W = 49
C = 15	J = 4	Q = 28	X = 1
D = 56	K = 54	R = 63	Y = 25
E = 18	L = 8	S = 64	Z = 2
F = 81	M = 36	T = 45	
G = 40	N = 72	U = 0	

Come to Costa Rica

 To multiply with a 2-digit factor, follow these steps.

1. Multiply the ones column.

$$\begin{array}{r} 4\,2 \\ \times 3 \\ \hline 6 \end{array}$$

2. Multiply the bottom factor in the ones column with the top factor in the tens column.

$$\begin{array}{r} 4\,2 \\ \times 3 \\ \hline 1\,2\,6 \end{array}$$

Multiply. Use the code to fill in the blanks below.

I. 82 × 4	**O.** 91 × 9	**S.** 21 × 8	**H.** 92 × 3	**J.** 73 × 2
E. 71 × 7	**L.** 53 × 3	**R.** 90 × 8	**C.** 61 × 6	**N.** 11 × 5
A. 32 × 4	**F.** 41 × 9	**T.** 70 × 7	**E.** 52 × 4	**P.** 40 × 8

490 276 208
‾‾‾   ‾‾‾   ‾‾‾

366 128 320 328 490 128 159
‾‾‾   ‾‾‾   ‾‾‾   ‾‾‾   ‾‾‾   ‾‾‾   ‾‾‾

819 369   366 819 168 490 128
‾‾‾   ‾‾‾   ‾‾‾   ‾‾‾   ‾‾‾   ‾‾‾   ‾‾‾

720 328 366 128   328 168
‾‾‾   ‾‾‾   ‾‾‾   ‾‾‾   ‾‾‾   ‾‾‾

168 128 55   146 819 168 497 .
‾‾‾   ‾‾‾   ‾‾   ‾‾‾   ‾‾‾   ‾‾‾   ‾‾‾

 Costa Rica is in Central America. If a Costa Rican farmer sells 63 pounds of coffee every day for 3 days. How much will he sell altogether?

Name _____

The Faraway Country

To multiply with a 2-digit factor that requires regrouping, follow these steps.

1. Multiply the ones.
   Regroup if needed.
   $7 \times 3 = 21$

2. Multiply the bottom factor in the ones column with the top factor in the tens column. Add the extra tens.
   $6 \times 3 = 18 \qquad 18 + 2 = 20$

Multiply.

A.
```
    48        24        73
  x  3      x  7      x  4
```

B.
```
    57        63        56
  x  7      x  9      x  3
```

C.
```
    98        64        57        35        23        82
  x  2      x  8      x  8      x  9      x  8      x  6
```

D.
```
    95        77        83        96        28        96
  x  9      x  6      x  9      x  8      x  4      x  5
```

 Switzerland is famous for the magnificent Swiss Alps. Waterfalls are formed by many of the mountain streams. The highest waterfall is Giessbach Falls. To find out how many meters high this waterfall is, add the products in Row A.

Name _____

A Multiplication Puzzler

Multiply. Circle each product in the puzzle. The products will go across and down.

A.   32   56   70   65   68
     x 8   x 8   x 5   x 4   x 5

B.   81   89   60   69   96
     x 3   x 6   x 5   x 4   x 2

C.   49   78   72   68   24
     x 6   x 4   x 8   x 9   x 9

D.   43   97   91   79   49
     x 5   x 3   x 2   x 3   x 3

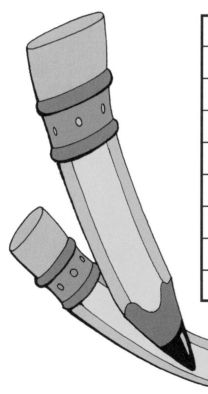

6	1	2	9	6	8	2	3	7
9	3	6	3	1	4	7	2	3
7	1	2	5	6	0	6	1	5
2	8	3	0	9	5	4	5	7
6	2	4	3	2	3	2	1	6
0	7	4	3	4	0	6	9	3
1	6	8	1	3	3	1	2	0
7	5	2	9	1	0	4	3	5
5	3	4	3	8	0	2	9	4

Scholastic Professional Books

The Big City

To multiply with a 3-digit factor that requires regrouping, follow these steps.

1. Multiply the ones. Regroup if needed.	2. Multiply the tens in the top factor. Add the extra tens. Regroup if needed.	3. Multiply the hundreds in the top factor. Add the extra hundreds.

```
     1
   4 7 3
 x     6
 ------
       8
```

```
    4 1
   4 7 3
 x     6
 ------
     3 8
```

```
    4 1
   4 7 3
 x     6
 ------
   2,838
```

Multiply.

A.

463	923	194	630	494	604
x 3	x 4	x 8	x 5	x 2	x 4

B.

325	817	293	168	208	196
x 7	x 6	x 9	x 3	x 8	x 6

C.

305	815	980	155	626	126
x 2	x 5	x 7	x 9	x 3	x 6

A subway train travels 296 miles daily. How far does the train travel in a week?

A Changing Reef

 To multiply with zeros, follow these steps.

9 0	9 x 2 = 18	9 0	9 x 2 = 18	9 0 0	9 x 2 = 18
x 2	Add a zero in the ones place to make 180.	x 20	Add 2 zeros—one in the ones place and one in the tens place.	x 20	Add 3 zeros—one in the ones place, one in the tens place, and one in the hundreds place.

Multiply.

A.

80	60	900	40	120	200
x 7	x 50	x 30	x 11	x 2	x 60

B.

70	120	60	700	50	30
x 7	x 300	x 90	x 60	x 70	x 12

C.

600	40	30	90	200	50
x 80	x 12	x 8	x 50	x 120	x 8

fringing reef

barrier reef

atoll

 The formation of a coral reef starts growing around the top of an undersea volcano forming a fringing reef. As the the volcano sinks, it leaves behind a barrier reef. When the volcano sinks below the ocean's surface, an atoll is left. On another piece of paper, write three problems with products to match those on the pictures.

Ship Shape

What are the cheapest
ships to buy?

What To Do

To find the answer to the riddle,
solve the multiplication problems.
Then, match each product with a
letter in the Key below. Write the
correct letters on the blanks below.

① 100 x 23 = _____

② 200 x 17 = _____

③ 300 x 31 = _____

④ 400 x 44 = _____

⑤ 500 x 19 = _____

⑥ 600 x 27 = _____

⑦ 700 x 35 = _____

⑧ 800 x 18 = _____

⑨ 900 x 50 = _____

Key

3,200 . . . . D	16,200 . . . . B	16,700 . . . . H
17,600 L	3,600 . . . . K	24,500 . . . . O
10,500 I	3,400 . . . . T	12,600 . . . . Y
45,000 . . . . A	9,300 . . . . E	14,400 . . . . A
15,300 . . . . R	9,500 . . . . S	2,300 . . . . S

Riddle
Answer:

" __ __ __ __ " __ __ __ __ __
  ⑤ ⑨ ④ ③   ⑥ ⑦ ⑧ ② ①

Caught in the Web

Why did the
spider join the
baseball team?

What To Do

To find the answer to the riddle,
solve the multiplication problems. Then, match each product
with a letter in the Key below.
Write the correct letters on the
blanks below.

1 1,000 x 11 = _____

2 2,000 x 12 = _____

3 3,000 x 10 = _____

4 4,000 x 14 = _____

5 5,000 x 20 = _____

6 6,000 x 24 = _____

7 7,000 x 30 = _____

8 8,000 x 32 = _____

9 9,000 x 40 = _____

10 7,500 x 50 = _____

Key

56,000 .... H	65,000 .... M	30,000 C
11,000 I	144,000 .... T	375,000 C
265,000 .... B	25,000 .... N	10,000 .... Y
360,000 .... F	256,000 L	100,000 .... A
210,000 .... E	90,000 .... Q	24,000 .... S

Riddle
Answer: **TO** _____ " _____ "

Purple Blossoms

Solve the problems. ◆ If the answer is between 1 and 250, color the shape yellow. ◆ If the answer is between 251 and 4000, color the shape purple. ◆ If the answer is between 4,001 and 9,000, color the shape pink. ◆ Finish by coloring the other shapes with colors of your choice.

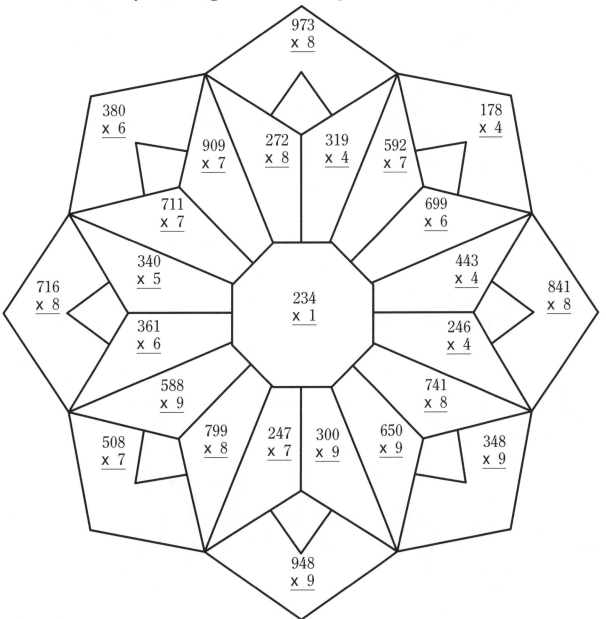

Taking It Further: I am an even number. I have three digits and they are all the same. If you multiply me by 4, all of the digits in the product are 8. What number am I? _____

Stallions in the Stable

Multiply. Use the products to put each stallion back where he belongs. Write the horse's name on the stall door.

| 11,284 | 22,635 | 7,161 | 20,130 | 72,648 | 7,692 |

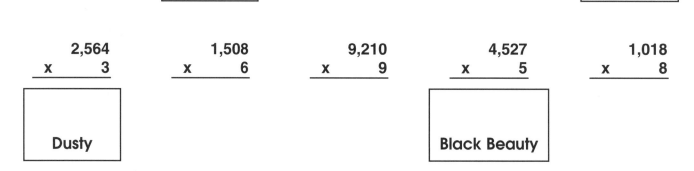

3,458	4,026	2,716	1,459	5,642
x 2	x 5	x 7	x 4	x 2
	Lola's Lad			Stormy

2,564	1,508	9,210	4,527	1,018
x 3	x 6	x 9	x 5	x 8
Dusty			Black Beauty	

1,809	2,387	9,081	7,186	7,130
x 7	x 3	x 8	x 4	x 6
	Midnight	Lightning		

Scholastic Professional Books

Name _____

Stop Horsing Around!

To multiply with a 2-digit factor that requires regrouping, follow these steps.

1. Multiply by the ones digit.	2. Place a zero in the ones column..	3. Multiply by the tens digit.	4. Add to find the product.

```
     3              3              3              1
    46             46             46             3
  x 26           x 26           x 26            46
  ----           ----           ----          x 26
   276            276            276           ----
                    0          + 920            276
                                              + 920
                                              -----
                                              1,196
```

Multiply. Then use the code to answer the riddle below.

G.	T.	S.	I.	A.	D.
32	67	53	96	83	49
x 48	x 14	x 27	x 52	x 33	x 72

M.	E.	N.	R.	K.	H.
39	56	83	75	96	84
x 28	x 15	x 24	x 46	x 51	x 62

What horses like to stay up late?

___ ___ ___ ___ ___ ___ ___ ___ ___ ___!
1,992 4,992 1,536 5,208 938 1,092 2,739 3,450 840 1,431

 Each of Farmer Gray's 24 horses eat 68 pounds of hay. How many pounds of hay do the horses eat altogether?

Name _____

Famous Landmarks

Which of these landmarks is the tallest? Multiply. Write the ones digit of each product in order to find the height of each landmark. Circle the tallest landmark.

Gateway Arch

73	49	55
x 42	x 27	x 72

= _____ feet tall

Empire State Building

67	25	76
x 42	x 97	x 14

= _____ feet tall

83	48	79
x 81	x 45	x 65

= _____ feet tall

Statue of Liberty

76	65	83
x 86	x 56	x 37

= _____ feet tall

Space Needle

 The Sears Tower in Chicago is 110 stories tall. If 55 people work on each floor, how many total people work in the building?

Soccer Balls

Solve the problems, then choose two colors that you like. ◆ Write the
name of one of the colors on each line below. ◆ Color the design. If the
answer is even, color the shape _____. If the answer
is odd, color the shape _____. ◆ Finish the design by
coloring the other shapes with the colors of your choice.

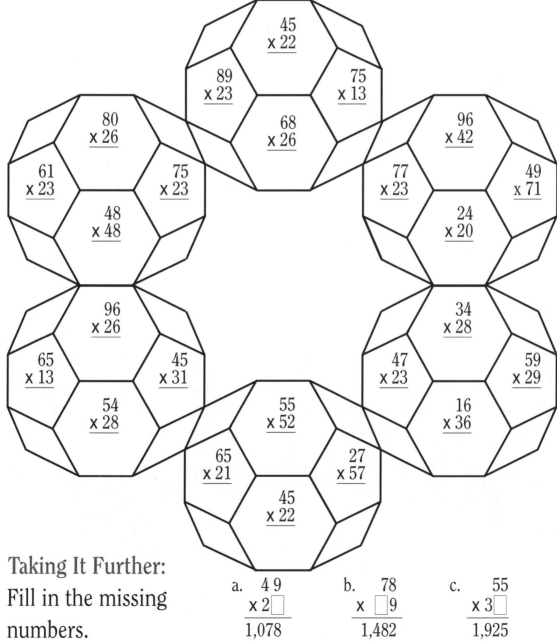

45
x 22

89
x 23

75
x 13

80
x 26

68
x 26

96
x 42

61
x 23

75
x 23

77
x 23

49
x 71

48
x 48

24
x 20

96
x 26

34
x 28

65
x 13

45
x 31

47
x 23

59
x 29

54
x 28

55
x 52

16
x 36

65
x 21

27
x 57

45
x 22

Taking It Further:
Fill in the missing
numbers.

a.   4 9
   x 2☐
  1,078

b.   78
  x ☐9
  1,482

c.   55
  x 3☐
  1,925

In the Wink of an Eye

Solve the problems. If the answer is even, connect the dot beside each
problem to the heart on the right- and left-hand sides of the circle. If
the answer is odd, do nothing. Two lines have been drawn for you.

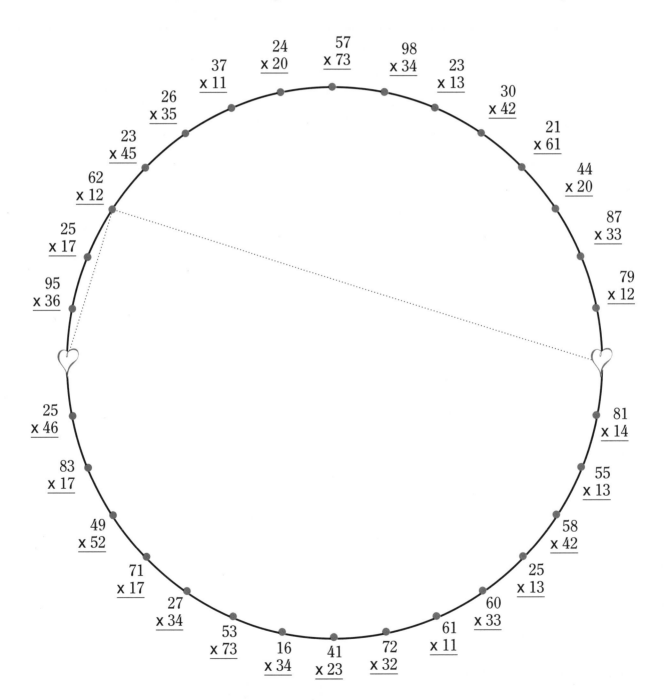

Name _____

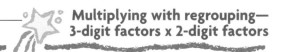
Monumental Multiplication

Multiply.

A.
```
   362        602        452        283        918        473
x   43     x   18     x   22     x   13     x   27     x   55
```

B.
```
   540        417        308
x   38     x   56     x   61
```

C.
```
   692        586        918
x   34     x   37     x   86
```

D.
```
   467        598        861
x   42     x   29     x   73
```

 **The Washington Monument has 898 steps. If 42 people climb to the top, how many
steps have they climbed altogether?**

The Music Store

When a multiplication problem involves money, the product must have a dollar sign and a decimal point. The decimal point is placed between the ones digit and the tenths digit.

```
        6
        2
     $3.71
   x    94
   ───────
     14.84
  + 333.90
   ───────
   $348.84
```

Remember to use a dollar sign and a decimal point.

Multiply. Then use the code to answer the riddle below.

| N. $1.94 x 23 | M. $0.79 x 25 | I. $2.06 x 64 | O. $0.68 x 45 |

| A. $3.68 x 32 | T. $9.54 x 19 | F. $0.88 x 72 | D. $0.93 x 94 |

| E. $8.15 x 67 | S. $7.43 x 92 | R. $0.87 x 75 | H. $6.92 x 83 |

Where do musicians buy instruments?

___ ___   ___ ___ ___
$117.76 $181.26 $181.26 $574.36 $546.05

___ ___ ___ ___   ___ ___ ___
$63.36 $131.84 $63.36 $546.05 $117.76 $44.62 $87.42

___ ___ ___ ___   ___ ___ ___ ___ ___!
$87.42 $131.84 $19.75 $546.05 $683.56 $181.26 $30.60 $65.25 $546.05

Price your favorite CD. Imagine that you buy one for each of your classmates. How much would you spend?

The Corner Candy Store

Word problems that suggest equal groups often require multiplication.

Write a number sentence for each problem. Solve.

A. Sam bought 4 candy bars at $1.23 each. How much did Sam spend altogether?	**B.** Mr. Johnson, the store owner, ordered 48 boxes of jawbreakers. Each box contained 392 pieces of candy. How many jawbreakers did Mr. Johnson order?
C. Carly's mom sent her to the candy store with 29 party bags. She asked Carly to fill each bag with 45 pieces of candy. How many pieces of candy will Carly buy?	**D.** Thirty-five children visited the candy store after school. Each child spent 57¢. How much money was spent in all?
E. Mr. Johnson keeps 37 jars behind the candy counter. Each jar contains 286 pieces of candy. How many pieces of candy are behind the counter altogether?	**F.** Nick bought each of his 6 friends a milk shake. Each milk shake cost $2.98. How much did Nick spend in all?

What's on the Tube?

 To divide means to make equal groups. Since multiplication also depends on equal groups, you can use the multiplication facts to help you learn the division facts.

Basic division facts are problems you will learn by memory. Divide.

A. 4)24   4)36   7)56   5)25   9)81   8)24

B. 5)45   8)72   4)28   6)42   6)36   1)9

C. 3)12   7)21   6)48   3)24   8)32   7)63

D. 8)64   7)49   5)30   9)27   6)6   3)15

Divide to learn an interesting fact.

In what year was television invented?

 3)3   8)72   7)14   8)64

 Research to find the year something else was invented. On another piece of paper, write four division facts with the year hidden in their quotients.

Television Division

 Each part of a division problem has a name.

$$5 \leftarrow \text{quotient}$$
$$\text{divisor} \rightarrow 9\,\overline{)45} \leftarrow \text{dividend}$$

Divide.

A.

$6\,\overline{)24}$ $9\,\overline{)63}$ $4\,\overline{)12}$

$9\,\overline{)45}$ $3\,\overline{)18}$ $8\,\overline{)56}$

$8\,\overline{)64}$ $8\,\overline{)40}$ $9\,\overline{)72}$

B.

$7\,\overline{)35}$ $9\,\overline{)36}$ $7\,\overline{)21}$

$4\,\overline{)32}$ $5\,\overline{)20}$ $6\,\overline{)36}$

$3\,\overline{)9}$ $7\,\overline{)56}$ $9\,\overline{)81}$

C.

$8\,\overline{)48}$ $5\,\overline{)25}$ $9\,\overline{)27}$

$7\,\overline{)49}$ $9\,\overline{)54}$ $4\,\overline{)36}$

$5\,\overline{)15}$ $7\,\overline{)63}$ $5\,\overline{)30}$

D.

$6\,\overline{)54}$ $3\,\overline{)27}$ $6\,\overline{)42}$

$3\,\overline{)21}$ $6\,\overline{)18}$ $4\,\overline{)28}$

$7\,\overline{)28}$ $5\,\overline{)40}$ $7\,\overline{)42}$

 On another piece of paper, write nine division facts with a quotient of 8.

Patchwork Diamonds

Solve the problems. ◆ If the answer is between 1 and 6, color the shape green. ◆ If the answer is between 7 and 12, color the shape red. ◆ Finish the design by coloring the other shapes with the colors of your choice.

Taking It Further: Jamie is making a quilt with 70 diamond-shaped pieces. If 7 pieces make 1 square, how many squares will her quilt have?

Mirror Image

Solve the problems. Then connect the dot beside each problem to the dot beside its answer.

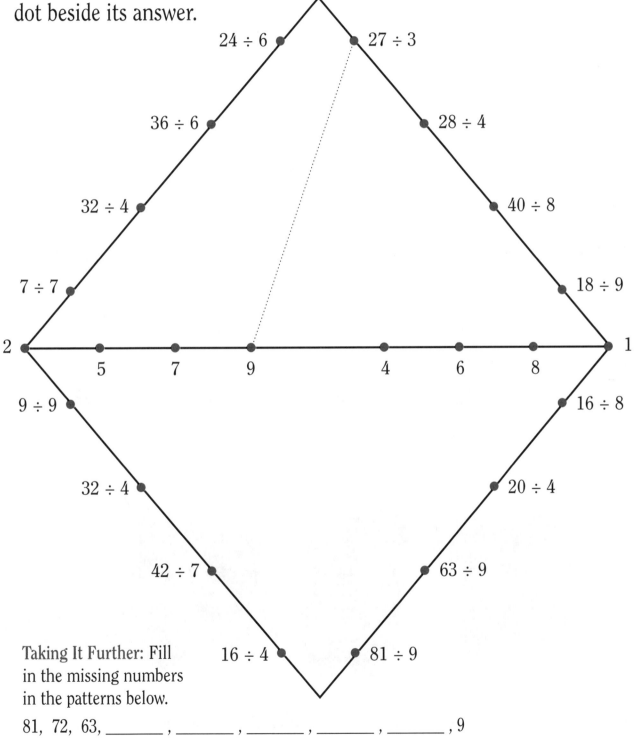

$24 \div 6$

$27 \div 3$

$36 \div 6$

$28 \div 4$

$32 \div 4$

$40 \div 8$

$7 \div 7$

$18 \div 9$

2

5   7   9   4   6   8

1

$9 \div 9$

$16 \div 8$

$32 \div 4$

$20 \div 4$

$42 \div 7$

$63 \div 9$

Taking It Further: Fill
in the missing numbers
in the patterns below.

$16 \div 4$

$81 \div 9$

81, 72, 63, _____ , _____ , _____ , _____ , _____ , 9

63, 56, 49, _____ , _____ , _____ , _____ , _____ , 7

A Barrel of Monkeys

 To divide with zeros, follow these samples.

```
    80    64 ÷ 8 = 8              800    64 ÷ 8 = 8
8 ) 640   0 ÷ 8 = 0           8 ) 6400   0 ÷ 8 = 0
          Add a zero to                  0 ÷ 8 = 0
          make 80.                       Add 2 zeros to
                                         make 800.
```

Divide.

A.   6) 420   9) 8100   6) 540   5) 4500   3) 2400

B.   3) 1800   4) 320   8) 7200   7) 560   5) 400

C.   3) 150   4) 360   6) 4800   6) 360   8) 640

90   900   9

 Write three problems with quotients to match those on the barrels.

Name _____

No Way!

To divide with remainders, follow these steps.

1. Does 8 x __ = 34? No!

$8 \overline{)34}$

2. Use the closest smaller dividend.
8 x 4 = 32

$8 \overline{)34}^{4}$
32

3. Subtract to find the remainder.

$8 \overline{)34}^{4}$
-32
2

4. The remainder is always less than the divisor.

$8 \overline{)34}^{4\ R2}$
-32
2

Divide. Then use the code to complete the riddle below.

E. $9\overline{)84}$	**L.** $3\overline{)29}$	**S.** $7\overline{)67}$	**O.** $5\overline{)24}$
T. $6\overline{)23}$	**N.** $6\overline{)47}$	**P.** $6\overline{)39}$	**I.** $7\overline{)52}$
O. $4\overline{)19}$	**A.** $8\overline{)70}$	**T.** $3\overline{)26}$	**S.** $9\overline{)55}$
H. $4\overline{)23}$	**!** $7\overline{)45}$	**R.** $5\overline{)27}$	**N.** $8\overline{)79}$

Emily: **Yesterday I saw a man at the mall with very long arms. Every time he went up the stairs he stepped on them.**

Jack: **Wow! He stepped on his arms?**

Emily: ___ ___ , ___ ___ ___ ___ ___ ___
7 R5 4 R4   4 R3 9 R7   8 R2 5 R3 9 R3

___ ___ ___ ___ ___ ___ ___
9 R4 3 R5 8 R6 7 R3 5 R2 6 R1 6 R3

Scholastic Success With Addition, Subtraction, Multiplication & Division • Grade 4   311

Honeycomb

Solve the problems. ◆ If the answer has a remainder between 1 and 4, color the shape black. ◆ If the answer has a remainder between 5 and 8, color the shape red. ◆ Finish the design by coloring the other shapes with the colors of your choice.

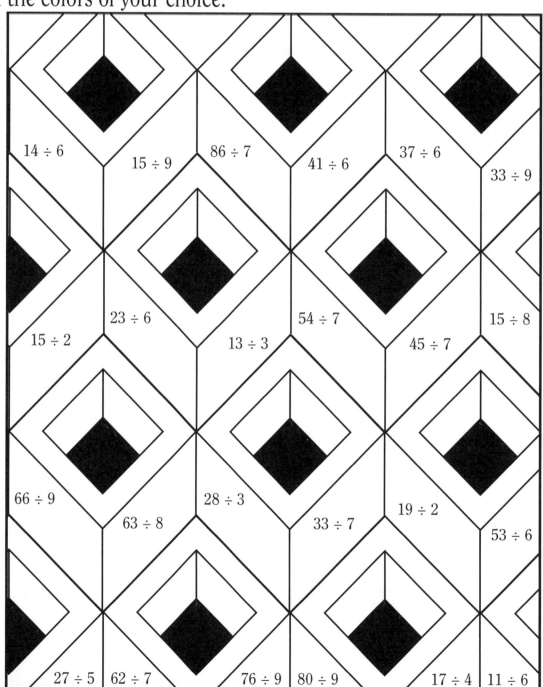

$14 \div 6$ $15 \div 9$ $86 \div 7$ $41 \div 6$ $37 \div 6$ $33 \div 9$

$23 \div 6$ $54 \div 7$ $15 \div 8$

$15 \div 2$ $13 \div 3$ $45 \div 7$

$66 \div 9$ $28 \div 3$ $19 \div 2$

$63 \div 8$ $33 \div 7$ $53 \div 6$

$27 \div 5$ $62 \div 7$ $76 \div 9$ $80 \div 9$ $17 \div 4$ $11 \div 6$

Division Decoder

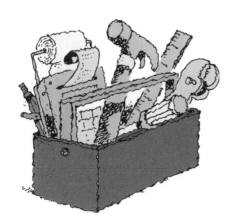

Riddle: What kind of tools do you use for math?

Find each quotient. Then use the Decoder to solve the riddle by filling in the spaces at the bottom of the page.

Decoder

8	I
3 remainder 2	L
7	W
8 remainder 1	S
6	U
9	A
15 remainder 3	B
4	L
2 remainder 3	D
9 remainder 2	T
1	F
7 remainder 6	N
6 remainder 6	I
2	E
11	O
15 remainder 2	P
2 remainder 5	X
10	C
5	R

❶ 8 ÷ 2 = _____

❷ 10 ÷ 5 = _____

❸ 24 ÷ 4 = _____

❹ 50 ÷ 10 = _____

❺ 72 ÷ 9 = _____

❻ 32 ÷ 10 = _____

❼ 48 ÷ 7 = _____

❽ 29 ÷ 3 = _____

❾ 65 ÷ 8 = _____

❿ 92 ÷ 6 = _____

"M __ __ __ __ " __ __ __ __ __ __
    3 1 8 5   10 6 7 2 4 9

Scholastic Professional Books

Mousing Around

To divide with a 3-digit dividend, follow these steps.

1.
```
      6
7 ) 427
      42
```
7 x ___ = 42
7 x 6 = 42

2.
```
      6
7 ) 427
   - 42↓
      07
```
Subtract.
Bring down the ones digit.

3.
```
      61
7 ) 427
   - 42↓
      07
    -  7
       0
```
7 x ___ = 7
7 x 1 = 7
Subtract.

Divide. Then use the code to answer the riddle below.

T. 4) 208   U. 6) 306   H. 9) 819   C. 3) 246   A. 4) 368

E. 8) 648   O. 7) 497   S. 4) 248   N. 2) 168   D. 4) 288

C. 4) 328   I. 3) 159   W. 5) 305   M. 9) 279   ! 4) 88

Why did the cat hang out near the computer?

___ ___   ___ ___ ___ ___ ___ ___   ___ ___
53 52   61 92 84 52 81 72   52 71

___ ___ ___ ___ ___   ___ ___ ___
82 92 52 82 91   52 91 81

___ ___ ___ ___ ___ ___
31 71 51 62 81 22

On another piece of paper, design a mouse pad. Include at least three division problems and their quotients in your design.

Scholastic Professional Books

Surfing the Web

 When the divisor has a remainder in the middle of a problem, follow these steps.

1.
```
      10
   8 ) 816
      80
```
8 x ___ = 81
8 x 10 = 80

2.
```
      10      Subtract.
   8 ) 816
    - 80↓     Bring down
   ———        the ones digit.
        16
```

3.
```
      102
   8 ) 816
    - 42↓
   ———
       07    Subtract
     -  7    again.
   ———
        0
```
8 x ___ = 16
8 x 2 = 16

Divide. Use another piece of paper to work the problems.
Then connect each problem to its answer to learn the definitions of some computer terms.

A. 5) 375   browser

B. 6) 492   byte

C. 2) 216   download

D. 3) 246   gigabyte

E. 9) 243   Internet

F. 8) 288   megabyte

G. 4) 424   network

H. 6) 564   program

I. 7) 532   scanner

J. 4) 312   virus

K. 9) 486   web site

82   an amount of data equal to 8 bits

75   a program to help get around the Internet

54   a place on the Internet's World Wide Web where text and pictures are stored

106   a group of computers linked together so they can share information

36   an amount of information equal to 1,048,516 bytes

27   a worldwide system of linked computers

108   to transfer information from a host computer to a personal computer

82   an amount of information equal to 1,024 megabytes

78   a program that damages other programs and data; often transmitted through telephone lines or shared disks

94   instructions for a computer to follow

76   a device that can transfer words and pictures from a printed page into the computer

Flying Carpet

Solve the problems. ◆ If the answer is between 100 and 250, color the shape red. ◆ If the answer is between 251 and 900, color the shape blue. ◆ Finish the design by coloring the other shapes with the colors of your choice.

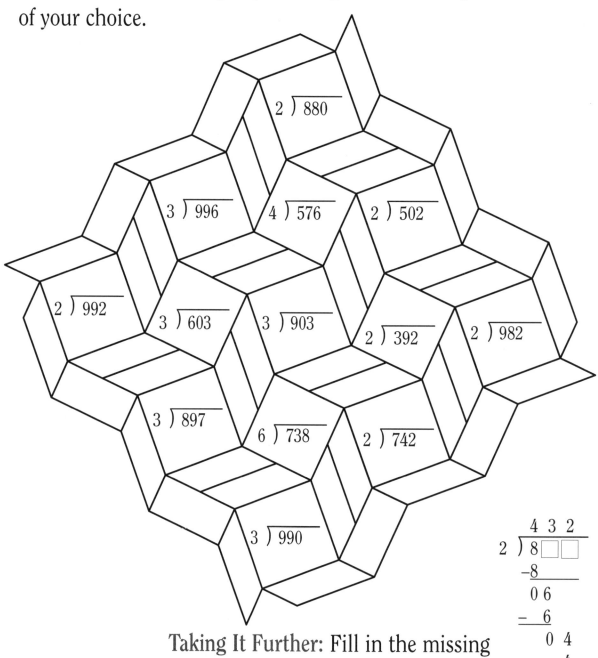

Taking It Further: Fill in the missing digits in the problem to the right.

$$\begin{array}{r} 4\ 3\ 2 \\ 2\overline{)8\square\square} \\ -8 \\ \hline 0\ 6 \\ -\ 6 \\ \hline 0\ 4 \\ -\ 4 \\ \hline 0 \end{array}$$

Scholastic Professional Books

Name _____

Poolside!

 Remember: The remainder is always less than the divisor.

Divide. Then use the code to answer the riddle below.

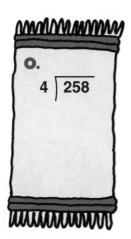
O. $4\overline{)258}$

G. $7\overline{)445}$

K. $6\overline{)573}$

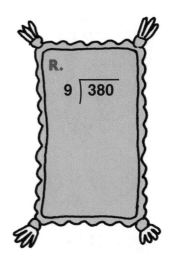
R. $9\overline{)380}$

L. $8\overline{)419}$

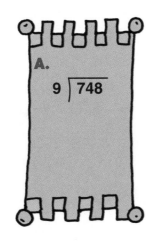
A. $9\overline{)748}$

M. $5\overline{)293}$

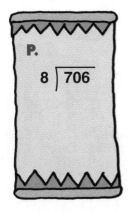
P. $8\overline{)706}$

S. $3\overline{)263}$

T. $6\overline{)356}$

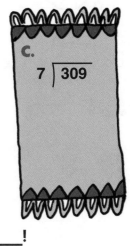
C. $7\overline{)309}$

What kind of pool is not made for swimming?

__ __ __ __ __ __ __ __!
83R1 44R1 83R1 42R2 88R2 64R2 64R2 52R3

Scholastic Professional Books

Summer Days

Divide. Then use the code to answer the riddle below.

Z. 3) 2226   **N.** 5) 2918   **T.** 8) 2099

S. 4) 2992   **B.** 7) 4332   **P.** 9) 3204

D. 6) 2364   **C.** 7) 3800   **U.** 3) 2571

O. 9) 8289   **A.** 5) 4609   **Y.** 8) 5376

What is the best day to go to the beach?

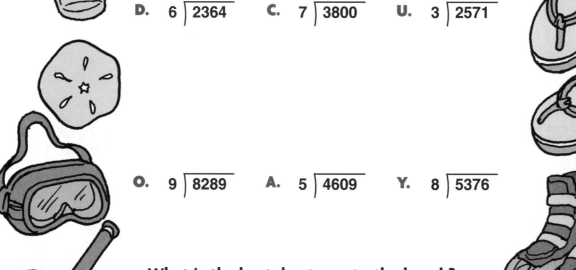

____ ____ ____ ____ ____ ____!

748   857   583R3   394   921R4   672

A year has 365 days. Summer is one of the four seasons. On another piece of paper, divide to find the exact number of days that are in each season. Your answer will tell you why our seasons truly change at a specific hour.

Scholastic Professional Books

Bone Up on Division

 To divide by a 2-digit divisor, follow these steps.

1.
$$15\overline{)330} \quad \begin{array}{c}2\\30\end{array}$$

15 x ___ = 33
Use the closest smaller dividend.
15 x 2 = 30
Put the 2 above the 3 tens.

2.
$$15\overline{)330}$$
$$\underline{-30\downarrow}$$
$$30$$

Subtract.
Bring down the ones digit.

3.
$$15\overline{)330}$$
$$\underline{-30\downarrow}$$
$$30$$
$$\underline{-30}$$
$$0$$

15 x ___ = 30
15 x 2 = 30
Subtract again.

Divide. Write the digit in the ones place with the least amount in each row to find out how many bones an adult human body has.

A. $13\overline{)559}$ $16\overline{)208}$ $39\overline{)468}$ $23\overline{)874}$

B. $31\overline{)682}$ $46\overline{)690}$ $26\overline{)858}$ $47\overline{)940}$

C. $35\overline{)630}$ $27\overline{)486}$ $28\overline{)756}$ $18\overline{)828}$

_____ _____ _____ bones

 How many bones are in a newborn baby's body?
Divide to find out: 8,750 ÷ 25 =

Name _____

Let's Go to the Show

 Look at each sample to learn how to finish dividing when there is a zero in the quotient.

Sample 1:

```
        306
    8 ) 2448
      - 24 ↓
         04 ↓
       -  0 ↓
          48
       -  48
```

8 x ___ = 4
Since there is no number, record a 0 in the quotient.
Subtract and bring down the 8.
Continue to divide.

Sample 2:

```
        680
    6 ) 4080
      - 36 ↓
        048 ↓
      -  48 ↓
          00
```

Sample 3:

```
         20 R9
    44 ) 889
       - 88 ↓
          09
        -  0
           9
```

Divide. Then use the code to answer the riddle below.

S. 3) 1812   **U.** 4) 3632   **W.** 18) 910   **X.** 25) 3250

G. 17) 356   **B.** 6) 1848   **R.** 39) 786   **J.** 8) 7216

A. 7) 4207   **E.** 27) 562   **Y.** 9) 2880   **T.** 9) 6345

What is the name of the movie about frogs in outer space?

___ ___ ___ ___   ___ ___ ___ ___ ___!
604 705 601 20R6   50R10 601 20R6 705 604

 Imagine that you have popped 1,422 pieces of popcorn for you and your 6 friends. How many pieces would each person get?

Scholastic Success With

MATH

Comparing & Ordering Numbers

Use the digits in the box to answer each number riddle.
You cannot repeat digits within a number.

1 8 3 4 9 6 2 7

 I am the number that is 100 greater than 3,362.
What number am I? _____

 I am the number that is 40 less than the largest number
you can make using five of the digits.
What number am I? _____

 I am the largest number you can make that is greater than
8,745 but less than 8,750.
What number am I? _____

 I am the number that is 5,000 greater than the smallest
number you can make using six of the digits.
What number am I? _____

 I am the smallest number you can make that is greater
than 617,500.
What number am I? _____

 I am the largest number you can make that is less than
618,400 but greater than 618,300.
What number am I? _____

Sign It!

✏ There are signs with numbers on them almost everywhere you look! They're on street corners and on highways. What if those numbers were written out as words?

Take a look at the street signs below. They all have numbers on them. Each sign has a blank sign next to it. Write the numbers as words on each blank sign. We've done the first one for you.

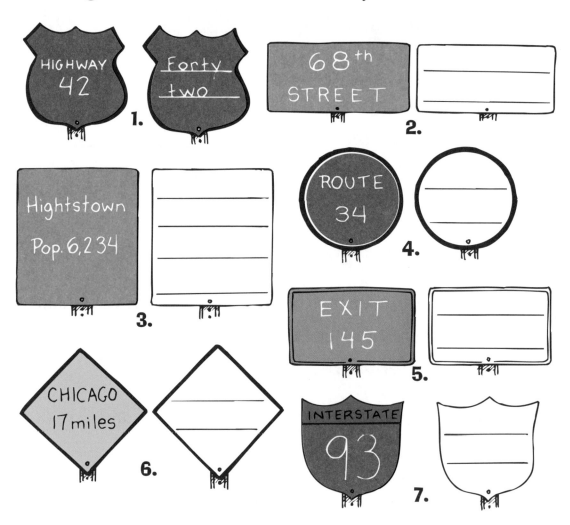

HIGHWAY 42

Forty two
1.

68th STREET
2.

Hightstown Pop. 6,234
3.

ROUTE 34
4.

EXIT 145
5.

CHICAGO 17 miles
6.

INTERSTATE 93
7.

 Try writing other numbers as words, such as your address, area code, age, or shoe size.

Mystery Number

Use the digits in the box to answer each number riddle. Digits appear only once in an answer. Each answer may not use all digits.

2 4 9 6 7 3

1 When you subtract a 2-digit number from a 3-digit number, the difference is 473.
What are the numbers? _____

2 The sum of these two numbers is 112.
What are the numbers? _____

3 The sum of these two numbers is 519.
What are the numbers? _____

4 The difference between these two 3-digit numbers is 263.
What are the numbers? _____

5 The sum of these three 2-digit numbers is 184.
What are the numbers? _____

6 The difference between two 3-digit numbers is a palindrome between 200 and 300.
What are the numbers? _____

What Number Am I?

Use the digits in the box to answer each number riddle.
You cannot repeat digits within a number.

1 2 3 4 5 6 7 8 9

 I am the largest 4-digit odd number you can make.
What number am I? _____

 I am the smallest 5-digit even number you can make.
What number am I? _____

 I am the largest 5-digit even number you can make that has
a 3 in the thousands place.
What number am I? _____

 I am the smallest 5-digit number you can make that has all
odd digits.
What number am I? _____

 I am the largest 6-digit number you can make that has a 1
in the thousands place and a 5 in the ten-thousands place.
What number am I? _____

 I am the smallest 6-digit even number you can make that
has a 6 in the hundreds place.
What number am I? _____

A Place for Every Number

Look at the numbers in 243. Each number in the group has its own "place" and meaning. For instance, the 2 in 243 is in the hundreds place. That stands for 2 hundreds or 200. The 4 is in the tens place, meaning 4 tens or 40. And the 3 is in the ones place, meaning 3 ones or 3.

DIRECTIONS:

Use a place value chart to put the numbers in this crossnumber puzzle in their places.

ACROSS

A. 3 hundreds 2 tens 6 ones
C. 8 tens 1 one
E. 6 tens 4 ones
F. 4 tens 7 ones
H. 5 hundreds 2 tens 6 ones
J. 9 tens 3 ones
K. 8 tens 9 ones
M. 5 hundreds 4 tens 2 ones
O. 2 thousands 8 hundreds 3 tens 1 one
Q. 9 tens 8 ones
S. 6 hundreds 6 tens 4 ones

DOWN

A. 3 tens 6 ones
B. 2 thousands 4 hundreds 5 tens 7 ones
D. 1 hundred 4 tens 9 ones
G. 7 tens 3 ones
I. 6 thousands 8 hundreds 5 tens 1 one
L. 9 tens 4 ones
N. 2 hundreds 9 tens 6 ones
P. 3 tens 5
R. 8 tens 4 ones

 Make a list of 10 numbers written out in the same way as the clues above. Ask a classmate to write each of those numbers in their own place value box.

Bee Riddle

**Riddle: What
did the farmer
get when he
tried to reach
the beehive?**

Round each number. Then use the Decoder to
solve the riddle by filling in the spaces at the
bottom of the page.

Decoder

400	A
800	W
30	O
10	Y
25	E
500	I
210	J
20	L
40	C
700	U
90	S
100	T
600	G
95	F
50	N
550	V
300	Z
7	H
200	Z

❶ Round 7 to the nearest ten _____

❷ Round 23 to the nearest ten _____

❸ Round 46 to the nearest ten _____

❹ Round 92 to the nearest ten _____

❺ Round 203 to the nearest hundred _____

❻ Round 420 to the nearest hundred _____

❼ Round 588 to the nearest hundred _____

❽ Round 312 to the nearest hundred _____

❾ Round 549 to the nearest hundred _____

❿ Round 710 to the nearest hundred _____

A "**B** __ __ __ __ " __ __ __ __ __ __

  10 5 8 1   4 9 7 3 6 2

Scholastic Professional Books

When to Estimate

Estimation is a great way to solve many problems.
But some problems need an exact answer. How can you decide?

Read each question below. Think about what kind of answer you need.
Then circle Estimate or Exact Answer.

1. How much sugar do you need to make cookies?   Estimate   Exact Answer

2. How much money could your school play earn?   Estimate   Exact Answer

3. How many plates will you need to serve dinner?   Estimate   Exact Answer

4. How much money will three new tapes cost?   Estimate   Exact Answer

5. How long will it take to get to the airport?   Estimate   Exact Answer

6. How much money is in a bank account?   Estimate   Exact Answer

7. How long would it take you to run a mile?   Estimate   Exact Answer

8. How many kids are in your class?   Estimate   Exact Answer

How Would You Estimate . . .

On another sheet of paper, write about how you would estimate each of these.

...the height of a tree?

...how long it would take to walk from Miami to Seattle?

...how much water you use in a year?

...the number of gumballs in a gumball machine?

...the number of students in your school?

...how much one million pennies would weigh?

Super Seven

How can you make the number seven even?

Find the answer by completing the next step in the pattern. Then use the Decoder to solve the riddle by filling in the blanks at the bottom of the page.

1 10, 7, 4, ___

2 19, 13, 8, ___

3 42, 40, 36, 30, ___

4 56, 54, 50, 42, ___

5 33, 32, 34, 33, 35, ___

6 117, 97, 77, ___

7 205, 175, 150, 130, ___

8 344, 274, 214, 164, ___

9 760, 660, 540, 400, 240, ___

10 512, 490, 457, 413, 358, 292, ___

Decoder

5	B
1	A
97	D
215	Y
22	W
124	H
31	I
2	P
115	A
120	C
50	N
4	E
60	S
232	M
26	T
100	R
32	F
57	E
34	K

TA __ __   __ __ __ __ __   __ __ __   " __ ".
   5 2   7 3 1 10   4 8 6   9

Scholastic Professional Books

Pansy's Picture Patterns

✐ Pansy Pattern has lots of hobbies. Her favorite hobby, though, is drawing patterns. There's just one problem. Sometimes Pansy forgets to draw the complete pattern. Maybe you can help. Try filling in the missing pieces in the patterns below.

1.

2.

3.

4.

5.

Draw a picture pattern of your own. Ask a classmate to fill in the missing pictures.

Root for the Home Team!

Riddle: What do cheerleaders like to drink?

Use the coordinates to identify points on the graph. Then use the point names to solve the riddle by filling in the blanks at the bottom of the page.

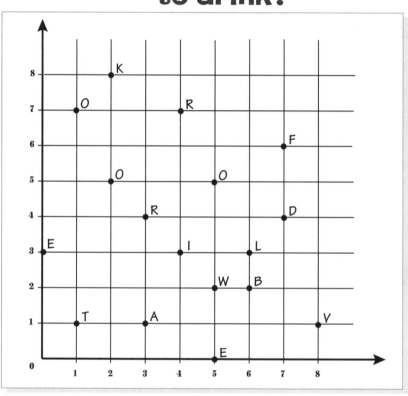

❶ (1,1) _____   ❻ (2,5) _____

❷ (3,4) _____   ❼ (0,3) _____

❸ (4,7) _____   ❽ (1,7) _____

❹ (6,2) _____   ❾ (7,6) _____

❺ (5,5) _____   ❿ (5,0) _____

LOTS __ __   __ __ __ __   __ __ __ __

      5   9   2   6   8   1   4   7   10   3

Bewitching Math

Solve the problems. Then connect the dot above each problem to the dot beside its answer. The first line has been drawn for you. Some dots will not be used.

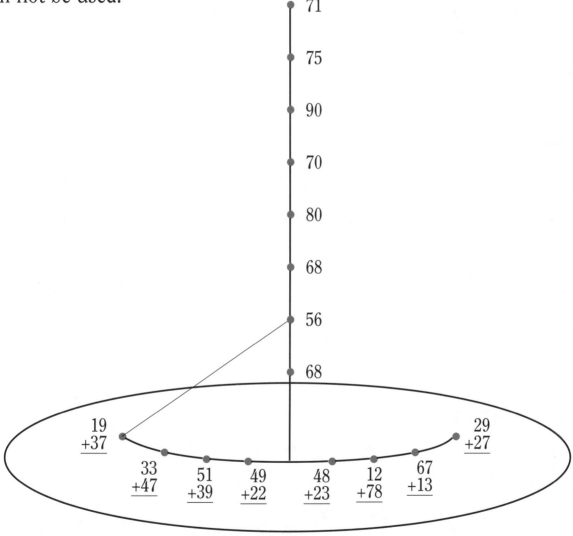

71

75

90

70

80

68

56

68

19
+37

29
+27

33
+47

51
+39

49
+22

48
+23

12
+78

67
+13

Taking It Further: Fill in the missing numbers in the problems below.

a. $\begin{array}{r} 2\square \\ +27 \\ \hline 50 \end{array}$

b. $\begin{array}{r} 53 \\ +2\square \\ \hline 82 \end{array}$

c. $\begin{array}{r} 56 \\ +1\square \\ \hline 73 \end{array}$

d. $\begin{array}{r} 28 \\ +57 \\ \hline \square\square \end{array}$

e. $\begin{array}{r} 43 \\ +\square 7 \\ \hline 90 \end{array}$

f. $\begin{array}{r} 45 \\ +\square\square \\ \hline 71 \end{array}$

Food Fractions

ACTIVITY GOAL

Identify the fraction represented in each shape to complete a riddle.

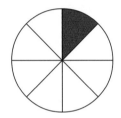

HELPFUL HINT!

• The **denominator** of each fraction represents the total amount of parts in the shape. The shaded parts represent the **numerator**. A food item can help illustrate this strategy.

EXAMPLE

There are 8 slices of pie shown here (/8) the denominator. The shaded area represents how many pieces of the pie you can eat (1/) the numerator. The fraction represented in this picture is 1/8.

TRY THIS!

Draw a pizza on another piece of paper, then cut out the circle. Cut the pizza into six equal pieces. Using your paper pizza, make the following fractions: 1/2, 2/6, 5/6, 1/3.

Now divide your pizza between you and two imaginary friends. Did you each get the same amount? _____

MORE SWEET FUN!

Color **1/3** of these **12** pieces of candy. What fraction of the candy is left? _____

Now that you've reviewed fractions, duck into action and name a few fractions to solve the riddle on the following page!

Duck Into Action With Fractions

✏ Why don't ducks like to get mail? Fractions can help you find the answer. Each of the shapes below represent a fraction and a letter. To figure out each fraction, compare the number of shaded spaces in the shape to the total number of spaces.

Example: 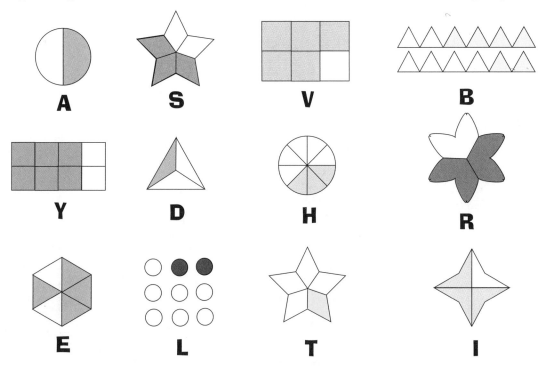 is the same as 2/6. Next, write the letter that is underneath each shape on the corresponding blank below. You will use some letters several times. Now get quacking!

Why don't ducks like to get mail?

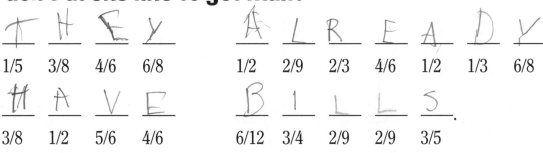

T	H	E	Y		A	L	R	E	A	D	Y
1/5	3/8	4/6	6/8		1/2	2/9	2/3	4/6	1/2	1/3	6/8

H	A	V	E		B	I	L	L	S
3/8	1/2	5/6	4/6		6/12	3/4	2/9	2/9	3/5

 Draw several shapes of your own. Shade in parts of the shape to represent a fraction. Trade shapes with a classmate and identify the fractions shown.

Scholastic Professional Books

Into Infinity

Solve the problems. Then rename the answers in lowest terms.

If the answer is $\frac{1}{4}$, $\frac{1}{8}$, or $\frac{1}{16}$, color the shape purple.

If the answer is $\frac{1}{2}$, $\frac{1}{3}$, or $\frac{1}{7}$, color the shape blue.

If the answer is $\frac{2}{3}$, $\frac{3}{4}$, or $\frac{7}{8}$, color the shape green.

If the answer is $\frac{3}{5}$, $\frac{4}{5}$, or $\frac{5}{7}$, color the shape yellow.

If the answer is $\frac{9}{10}$ or $\frac{11}{12}$, color the shape red.

Finish the design by coloring the other shapes with colors of your choice.

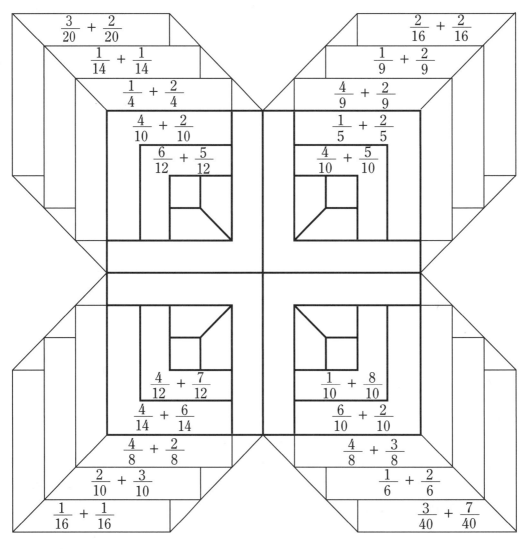

Scholastic Professional Books

Trefoil

Solve the problems. ◆ Rename the answers in lowest terms. ◆ If the answer is $\frac{1}{2}$ or greater, color the shape red. ◆ If the answer is less than $\frac{1}{2}$, color the shape blue. ◆ Finish the design by coloring the other shapes with the colors of your choice.

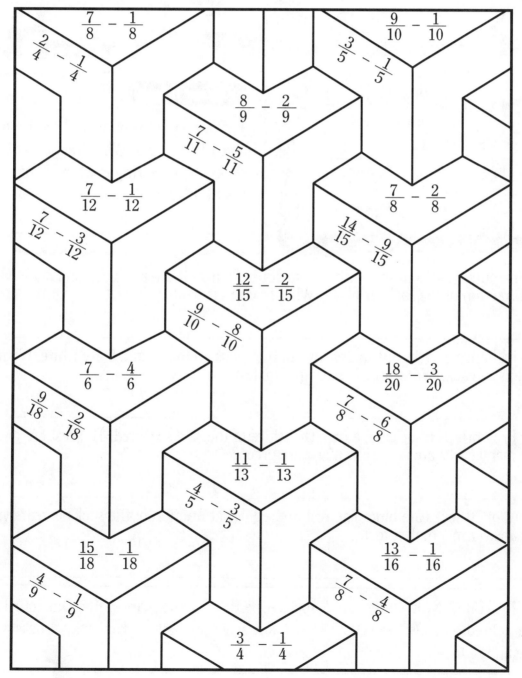

White Socks, Black Socks

Figure it out!

1. Rowena Pig is wearing 1 white sock and 1 black sock. What fraction of the socks she's wearing is white? What fraction is black?

_____

2. Rowena puts 7 socks in the washing machine. Four of them are black and 3 are white. What fraction of the socks is black? What fraction is white?

_____

3. Rowena hangs 8 socks out to dry. Two of the socks are black and 6 are white. What fraction is black? Write your answer in simplest form.

_____

4. Judy Frog brings 6 socks on a trip. One third of the socks are red. The rest are green. How many socks are red? How many are green?

_____

5. Six out of 10 socks are blue. The rest are red. What fraction of the socks is red? Write your answer in simplest form.

_____

SUPER CHALLENGE: Judy has 12 socks. One third of them are white. One fourth of them are red. The rest are yellow. How many socks are yellow? How many socks are white and red?

Scholastic Professional Books

Decimals Around the Diamond

Baseball fans always argue who the best player was. Some say it was Ken Griffey, Jr. Others insist it was Cal Ripkin, Jr. Still others claim it was Barry Bonds. Everybody seems to have a favorite!

When it comes to finding the best hitter, though, no one can argue with batting averages. The batting average shows how often a baseball player gets a hit. It is a 3-digit decimal number, and looks like this: .328, .287, .311, .253. The larger the batting average is, the better the hitter is.

Decimals are numbers between 0 and 1. They are written to the right of the ones place. Decimals always have a decimal point to the left of them.

Rank	Player (Team)	1995 Batting Average
	Cal Ripken, Jr. (Baltimore Orioles)	.262
	Barry Bonds (San Francisco Giants)	.294
	Mo Vaughn (Boston Red Sox)	.300
	Barry Larkin (Cincinnati Reds)	.319
	Kirby Puckett (Minnesota Twins)	.314
	Tony Gwynn (San Diego Padres)	.368
	Ken Griffey, Jr. (Seattle Mariners)	.258
	Mike Piazza (Los Angeles Dodgers)	.346
	Frank Thomas (Chicago White Sox)	.308
	David Justice (Atlanta Braves)	.253

What to Do:

Read the chart of baseball players' batting averages from 1995. Rank the batting averages. This means number the batting averages in order from highest to lowest. (See Home Plate for help.) Write the numbers 1 to 10 in the boxes next to the names—1 for the highest average, 10 for the lowest. Ready? Play ball!

HOME PLATE

To rank decimal numbers:
- Start at the left.
- Compare the digits in the same place.
- Find the first place where the digits are different.
- The number with the smaller digit is the smaller number. Example: Rank .317 and .312

.317

.312

So .312 is smaller than .317.

Scholastic Professional Books

Across-and-Down Decimals

Complete the crossnumber puzzle as if it were a crossword puzzle. Give each digit and decimal point its own square. Remember to align the decimal points and add any necessary zeros, then proceed as if you were adding whole numbers.

ACROSS

A.	1.3 + 2.4
C.	2.2 + 2.18
E.	.3 + .25
F.	.3 + .3
G.	.56 + .34
J.	.4 + .17
K.	6.93 + .23
L.	1.18 + 3.12

DOWN

A.	1.44 + 1.7
B.	23.11 + 53.18
C.	2.25 + 2.25
D.	6.5 + 1.6
F.	.1604 + .11
H.	20.8 + 3.5
I.	1.367 + .333
J.	.2 + .16

Change Arranger

When you make change, always start with the price. Count on from the price. Start with the coins that have the least value. Write the change from these purchases.

1. LAWN GAME

AMOUNT GIVEN $ 5.00

PRICE 3.45

CHANGE $ 245

2. YO-YO

AMOUNT GIVEN $ 3.00 2 9

PRICE 2.77

CHANGE $ 0.23

3. BIKE HELMET

AMOUNT GIVEN $10.00 99 9

PRICE 7.55

CHANGE $ 92.45

4. SOAP BUBBLES

AMOUNT GIVEN $2.00 1 9

PRICE 1.52

CHANGE $ 0.48

5. VIDEO GAME

AMOUNT GIVEN $20.00 19 9

PRICE 7.30

CHANGE $ 12.70

6. ACTION TOY

AMOUNT GIVEN $10.00 99 9

PRICE 6.49

CHANGE $ 13.51

7. SUNGLASSES

AMOUNT GIVEN $4.00 3 9

PRICE 3.68

CHANGE $ 0.32

8. BACKPACK

AMOUNT GIVEN $20.00 19 9

PRICE 9.35

CHANGE $ 10.65

9. JUMP ROPE

AMOUNT GIVEN $4.00 3 9

PRICE 3.17

CHANGE $ 0.83

10. MARKERS

AMOUNT GIVEN $5.00 4 9

PRICE 2.43

CHANGE $ 2.57

Scholastic Professional Books

Money Magic Puzzle

Round your answers to the nearest dollar. Circle the correct amount, then fill in the puzzle.

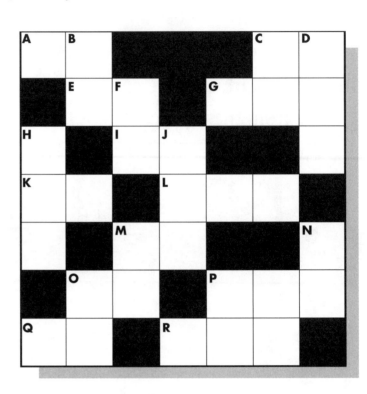

ACROSS:

A.	$16.98 + $18.99	$36	$26
C.	$24.85 + $29.99	$65	$55
E.	$21.99 + $8.95	$31	$41
G.	$218.04 + $67.90	$286	$386
I.	$53.75 + $40.98	$105	$95
K.	$7.99 + $19.70	$28	$22
L.	$99.98 + 99.57	$300	$200
M.	$65.75 + $20.90	$87	$97
O.	$9.69 + $32.99	$40	$43
P.	$588.95 + $14.90	$704	$604
Q.	$3.75 + $9.99	$13	$14
R.	$428.70 + $50.90	$480	$520

DOWN:

B.	$28.59 + $33.95	$69	$63
C.	$39.25 + $18.70	$58	$42
D.	$376.35 + $184.50	$521	$561
F.	$7.28 + $11.69	$19	$16
H.	$199.80 + $224.99	$525	$425
J.	$399.95 + $126.99	$527	$566
M.	$5.85 + $76.95	$83	$75
N.	$39.80 + $13.99	$54	$62
O.	$26.98 + $16.89	$44	$49
P.	$48.95 + $18.99	$68	$66

Time for Play

✏ The dogs in the neighborhood play in the park at the same time every day. Today, some are running around trees and others are playing catch with their owners. But most of them are busy doing something else—chasing another dog! What time were they chasing the dog? Equivalent measurements can help you find the answer.

DIRECTIONS:

• There are two answers next to each question. Circle the letter after the correct answer.
• When you've finished, write each circled letter in the blanks below the riddle. Be sure to write the letters in order.

1.	How many weeks are in a year?	34	**L**	52	**T**
2.	How many inches are in a foot?	12	**W**	36	**A**
3.	How many centimeters are in a meter?	100	**E**	1000	**O**
4.	How many nickels are in a dollar?	40	**M**	20	**N**
5.	How many days are in a year?	365	**T**	245	**S**
6.	How many inches are in a yard?	36	**Y**	24	**B**
7.	How many ounces are in a pound?	16	**A**	12	**I**
8.	How many hours are in a day?	48	**C**	24	**F**
9.	How many years are in a decade?	50	**H**	10	**T**
10.	How many cups are in a pint?	2	**E**	4	**U**
11.	How many quarts are in a gallon?	4	**R**	8	**D**
12.	How many feet are in a mile?	5,280	**O**	2,160	**G**
13.	How many seconds are in a minute?	30	**J**	60	**N**
14.	How many millimeters are in a meter?	1,000	**E**	1500	**P**

What time is it when twenty dogs run after one dog?

— — — — — — — — — — — — — — —

Come up with an equivalent measurement problem of your own.

Measure by Measure

✏ Josie is surrounded by all kinds of measuring tools. But she's not sure which tool does what! Sure, she knows that a ruler measures the length of something. But she doesn't realize that all the other tools around her are used for measuring things too. Try giving Josie a hand.

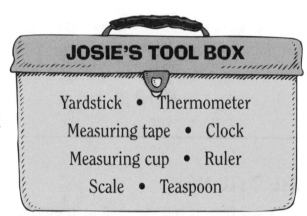

JOSIE'S TOOL BOX

Yardstick • Thermometer
Measuring tape • Clock
Measuring cup • Ruler
Scale • Teaspoon

DIRECTIONS:

Take a look at the list of measuring tools in Josie's Tool Box. Use the list to answer the questions below.

1. What tool could Josie use to measure the weight of a pumpkin? _____

2. What tool could Josie use to measure the width of her math book?

_____

3. Josie plans to watch one of her favorite television shows. What tool could help her measure the length of each commercial that appears during that show?

_____

4. Josie has an awful cough. What tool could she use to measure the amount of cough syrup she should take? _____

5. If Josie's mom wants to find out Josie's temperature, which tool could she use?

_____

6. Say Josie wanted to make a cake. What tool could she use to measure the milk she needs to put in the cake mix? _____

7. What tool could Josie use to measure the height of her brother's tree house?

_____

8. What tool could Josie give her dad to measure the length of their living room?

_____

 Choose four of the measuring tools in Josie's Tool Box. Make a list of things you could measure with each of those tools.

Picnic Area

What to Do:
Area measures the number of square units inside a shape. Find the area of each ant family's picnic blanket by counting the number of squares on the blanket. Then answer the following questions.

Remember—area is measured in square units, such as square centimeters. My blanket's area is four square units.

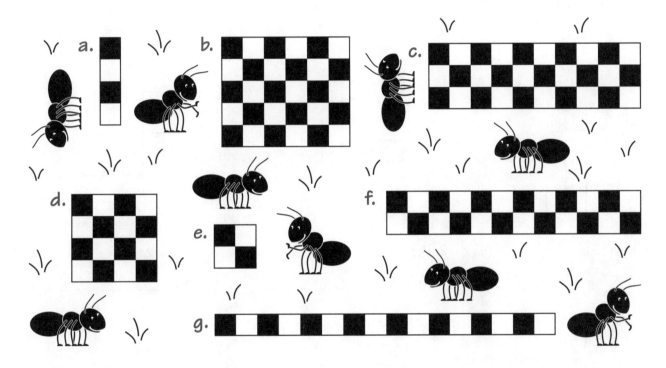

1. Which pairs of blankets have the same area?

   _____ and _____

   _____ and _____

   _____ and _____

2. Which two blankets can you put together to make a rectangle with an area of 20?

   _____

3. Which three blankets can you put together to make a rectangle with an area of 50?

   _____

4. What is the total area of all of the ants' blankets?

   _____

Perimeter and Area Zoo

A shape doesn't have to be a square or a rectangle to have perimeter and area. The animals in this zoo are different shapes. Can you find each animal's perimeter and area?

Remember: To find perimeter, count the sides of the units. To find area, count the number of whole units.

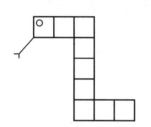

1. Perimeter _____

   Area _____

2. Perimeter _____

   Area _____

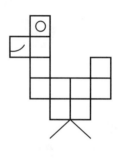

3. Perimeter _____

   Area _____

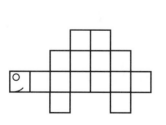

4. Perimeter _____

   Area _____

5. Perimeter _____

   Area _____

6. Perimeter _____

   Area _____

Scholastic Professional Books

Angles from A to Z

Angles are hiding everywhere—even in the words you're reading now. When two straight lines meet, they make an angle. There are three kinds of angles:

- The corner of a square or rectangle makes a right angle.

- Angles that are smaller than right angles are called acute angles.

- Angles that are larger than right angles are called obtuse angles.

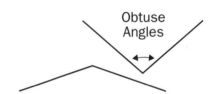

Take a look at the letters below. Circle each angle you see in the letters. Tell whether it is right, acute, or obtuse.

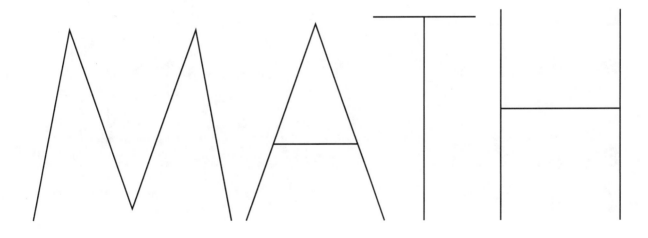

Flying Through the Air

What is the last thing that the trapeze flier wants to be?

Find the symmetrical shapes. Then use the Decoder to solve the riddle by filling in the blanks at the bottom of the page.

1. ▯ _____

2. ◁ _____

3. ◖ _____

4. ⚡ _____

5. ⊏ _____

6. ⊂ _____

7. ⌇ _____

8. ⊐ _____

9. ⚡ _____

10. ⊐ _____

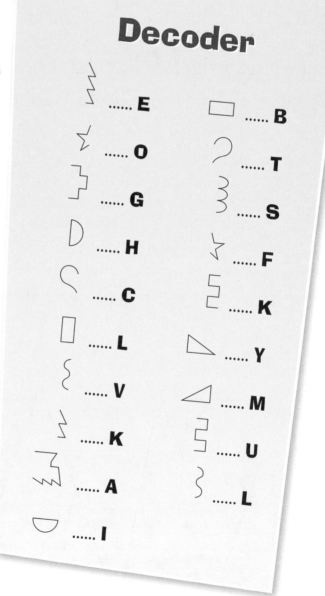

Decoder

⚡ ...... E   ▭ ...... B

⚡ ...... O   ? ...... T

⊐ ...... G   ⌇ ...... S

◖ ...... H   ⚡ ...... F

⊂ C   ⊐ ...... K

▯ L   △ ...... Y

⊂ V   ◁ ...... M

⚡ ...... K   ⊐ ...... U

⚡ ...... A   ⌇ L

◖ I

___ ___ ___   ___ ___ ___ ___   ___ ___ ___
 6   3   9   4   10 1   7   5   8   2

Shape Up!

✏ How well do you know geometric shapes? Here's your chance to test yourself. Take a look at the shape in each statement. Fill in the blank spaces with the correct answers. When you're done, write the letters in the shaded squares on the spaces provided to solve the riddle.

What did the alien eat for lunch?

1. An ⬡ has __ ▢ __ __ ▢ sides.

2. This triangle has an angle that is the opposite of obtuse.

   It's an ▢ __ __ ▢ ▢ angle. ◺

3. The __ __ __ ▢ __ __ __ __ __ of this rectangle is fourteen.

4. The ▢ ▢ __ __ of this rectangle is twelve. ³⬜⁴ ³⬜⁴

5. This shape ⬜ is a ▢ __ __ __ __ __.

6. This shape ▱ is a __ __ ▢ __.

7. This shape △ is a __ __ __ ▢ __ __ __.

8. This shape ◯ is a __ __ ▢ __ __ __.

9. These shapes ⬡⬠⬡ have many sides.

   They are called __ __ __ __ __ __ __ ▢.

What did the alien eat for lunch?

__ __ __ __ __ __   __ __ __ __ __ __ __ __ __.

 Draw a geometric shape not included in this activity on a piece of paper. Give it to a friend. See if he or she can name the shape.

Name _____

Terrific Tessellations

What do math and art have in common? Everything—if you're making tessellations!

A tessellation (tess-uh-LAY-shun) is a design made of shapes that fit together like puzzle pieces. People use tessellations to decorate walls and floors, and even works of art.

This sidewalk is formed from rectangles.

Hexagons form this beehive.

Here is a tessellation made from more than one shape.

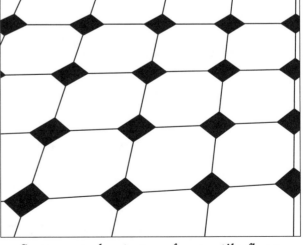

Squares and octagons form a tile floor.

Terrific Tessellations

You Need:
heavy paper ◆ scissors
tape ◆ crayons

What to Do:
Here's how you can make your own tessellation.

1. Start with a simple shape like a square. (Cut your shape from the heavy paper). Cut a piece out of side A . . .

2. . . . and slide it over to side B. Make sure it lines up evenly with the cut out side, or your tessellation won't work. Tape it in place on side B.

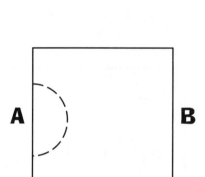

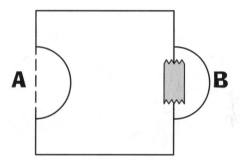

3. If you like, do the same thing with sides C and D. Now you have a new shape.

4. Trace your new shape on paper. Then slide the shape so it fits together with the one you just traced. Trace it again. Keep on sliding and tracing until your page is filled. Decorate your tessellation.

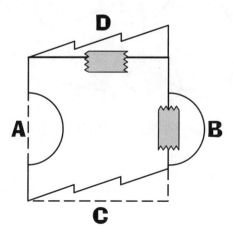

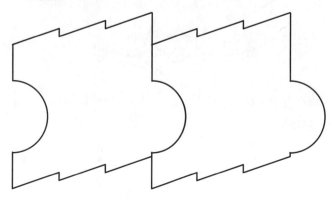

Kaleidoscope of Flowers

If the number has a 5 in the ones place, color the shape green.
If the number has a 5 in the tenths place, color the shape pink.
If the number has a 5 in the hundredths place, color the shape yellow.
Finish the design by coloring the other shapes with colors of your choice.

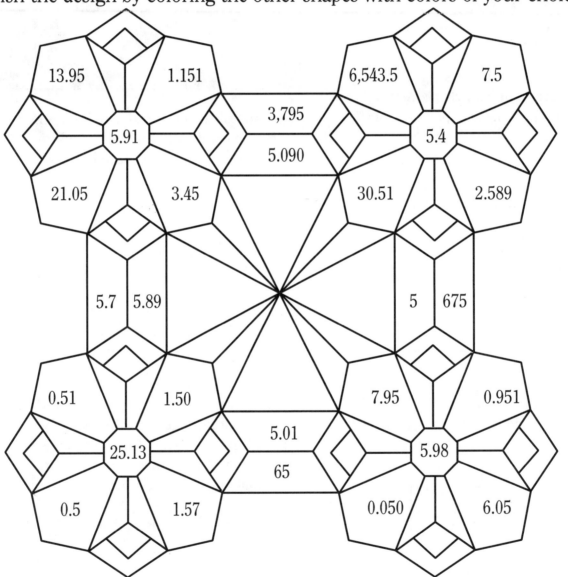

Taking It Further: Place the following decimals in the correct places on the lines below the dots: 4.9, 1.7, 2.5, and 0.2.

Scholastic Professional Books

What Is a Map?

A map is a flat drawing of a part or all of Earth. A map shows a place from above much as a picture taken high in the sky or from space does. In fact, mapmakers study aerial photographs to help them make more accurate maps.

map reader's **Tip**

Another word for mapmaker is cartographer. This word comes from the Latin word *carta*, which means "paper" and the Greek word *graphia*, which means "to write."

Since a map shows a large area in a small space, mapmakers use **symbols** to stand for buildings, roads, cities, and other things. A symbol is a drawing or color that represents something else. You can find out what each symbol means by checking the map key or legend.

Study the map key for the map on page 355. Then answer the questions.

1. This symbol --·--·-- stands for _____ .

2. The capital of Wyoming is _____ .

3. Las Vegas is a city in _____ .

4. Two states that share a border with Canada are _____ and _____ .

5. Boise is the capital of _____ .

Scholastic Professional Books

Mountain States

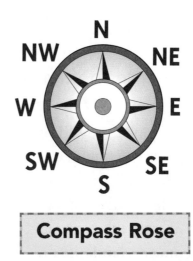

Compass Rose

A map also has a symbol called a **compass rose** that shows directions. The four main directions are north, south, east, and west. These are called the **cardinal directions**. A compass rose might show **intermediate directions** too. They are northeast, southeast, southwest, and northwest. Often, abbreviations are used to show the directions on a compass rose.

Use the compass rose to answer these questions.

6. The direction between east and south is _____ .

7. The letters NW stand for _____ .

8. Colorado is _____ of Idaho.

9. Montana is _____ of Wyoming.

10. A plane traveling from the capital of Idaho to the capital of Nevada would go in a _____ direction. Draw its route on the map.

Globes and Hemispheres

As you know, Earth is a large, round planet. To see all of Earth, you would have to orbit it in a spacecraft! An easier way to see Earth is to look at a small model called a globe.

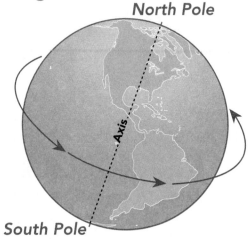

A globe shows Earth's four oceans and seven continents. A globe also shows how Earth turns on an imaginary center line called an **axis**. At the ends of this line are the North and South poles. Pole means "end." These poles help you find directions on Earth. North is toward the North Pole, and south is toward the South Pole.

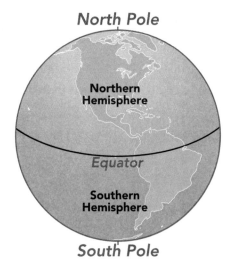

Another imaginary line on a globe is called the **equator**. The equator runs around the center of Earth and divides it into two halves called **hemispheres**. The northern half is called the Northern Hemisphere, and the southern half is called the Southern Hemisphere.

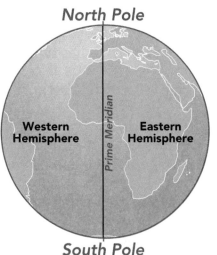

Still another imaginary line divides Earth into the Eastern and Western hemispheres. This line is called the **Prime Meridian**. This line runs from the North Pole to the South Pole.

Northern Hemisphere

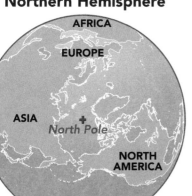

Southern Hemisphere

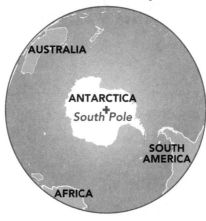

Western Hemisphere

Eastern Hemisphere

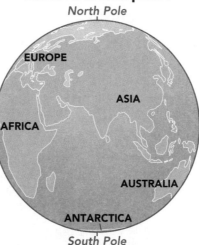

Here are four views of a globe showing the four hemispheres. Use the pictures on these pages to answer these questions.

1. How many hemispheres does Earth have? _____

2. What is the hemisphere nearest the South Pole? _____

3. What line divides the Eastern and Western hemispheres? _____

4. In which direction is the North Pole from the equator? _____

5. What line divides the Northern and Southern hemispheres? _____

6. What is Earth's axis? _____

7. Name one continent in the Northern Hemisphere. _____

8. Name one continent in the Eastern Hemisphere. _____

Map Projections

A globe is the best way to represent Earth, but globes are not easy to put in your pocket and carry around. Also, you cannot see all of a globe at one time. So mapmakers have developed flat maps that show all of Earth. The different ways of drawing the round Earth on flat maps are called **projections**. You can see two different projections on these pages.

No flat map can show Earth perfectly. Look at the Mercator projection. It was developed in 1569 by Gerardus Mercator. A Mercator map shows the true shapes of Earth's land, but it distorts sizes, especially near the poles. On a Mercator map, Greenland looks as big as South America. In fact, South America is eight times bigger than Greenland!

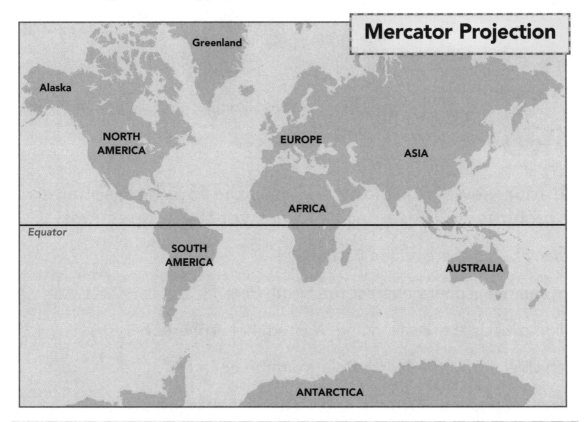

Mercator Projection

Greenland

Alaska

NORTH AMERICA

EUROPE

ASIA

AFRICA

Equator

SOUTH AMERICA

AUSTRALIA

ANTARCTICA

map reader's **Tip**   Other types of projections on world maps include **Mollweide**, **Polar**, and **Interrupted** projections.

Scholastic Professional Books

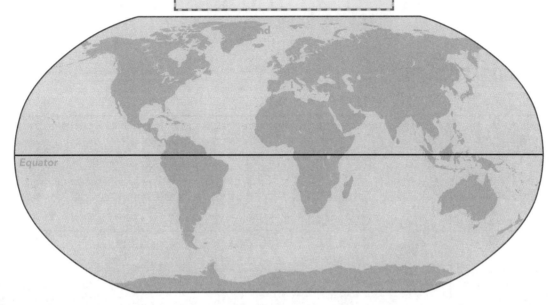

Robinson Projection

The map above shows the Robinson projection. It is used by many geographers today. The land sizes are more accurate on this map, but the shapes get distorted near the outer edges. Compare the shape of Alaska on the two maps. Use the maps to answer the questions.

1. How is a world map different from a globe? _____

2. On which map does Antarctica look bigger? _____

3. Which map is more like a globe? _____

4. On which map does the distance from

   Greenland to Antarctica look greater? _____

5. Which map looks more like a peeled orange? _____

   Why do you think this is so? _____

word scramble
There are five types of map projections named in this lesson. Can you unscramble them?

LAROP   **RATROMEC**   **PETDURNITRE**   **ILEMDEWLO**   **BOSNIRON**

_____ _____ _____ _____ _____

Using a Map Grid and Index

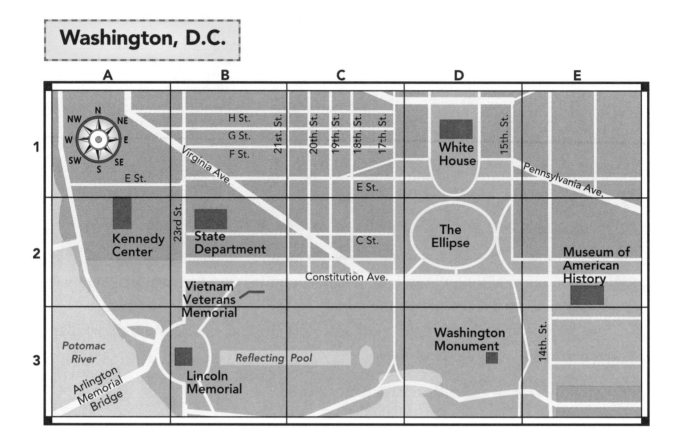

Washington, D.C.

S ometimes mapmakers place a pattern of lines called a **grid** over a map. The squares formed by the grid are marked with letters and numbers. On this map the letters run across the top; the numbers run down the side. The first square in the top left corner of the map is A1. Can you find it? What is the name of the square immediately to the right of A1?

Use the map to answer these questions.

1. What landmark is in D3? _____

2. In which grid square is the White House? _____

3. What avenue runs from A1 to C2? _____

4. In which grid squares is Pennsylvania Avenue? _____

5. What body of water do you see in A2? _____

Scholastic Professional Books

map reader's **Tip**

Index

Arlington Memorial Bridge	A3
The Ellipse	D2
Kennedy Center	A2
Lincoln Memorial	B3
Museum of American History . . .	E2
Reflecting Pool	B3, C3
State Department	B2
Vietnam Veterans Memorial	B2
Washington Monument	D3
White House	D1

The D.C. in the city's name stands for District of Columbia. Washington, D.C., is not part of a state, but rather a "federal district." A mayor and city council make laws, but the U.S. Congress has final authority over Washington, D.C.'s government.

Suppose you are visiting Washington, D.C., and want to see some of its sights. A **map index** can help you locate different places. A map index is an alphabetical listing of place names on a map. This index gives the grid square or squares for each place.

Use the index to answer these questions.

6. You are at the Museum of American History.

What is your grid location?_____

7. In which square would you look for the State Department?_____

8. What place is listed after the Reflecting Pool on the index?_____

9. What is the grid location of the Lincoln Memorial? _____

10. You are going to a concert at the Kennedy Center.

Where can you find it on the map? _____

Understanding Latitude

You know that the equator is an imaginary line that runs around the middle of Earth. Mapmakers create other imaginary lines on globes and maps as well. Look at the lines on this globe. These lines run parallel to the equator and are called parallels or lines of **latitude**. You can use lines of latitude to measure places north and south of the equator.

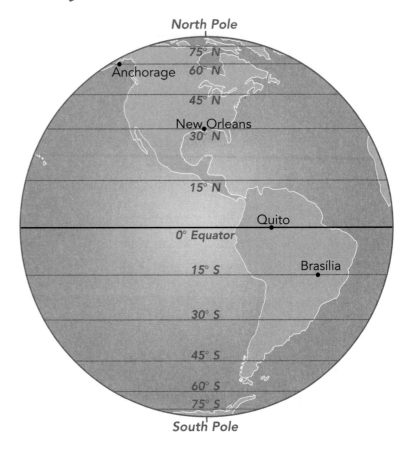

Lines of latitude are measured in degrees, shown by the symbol °. For example, the equator is 0°. Parallels north of the equator are marked in degrees north (N), and parallels south of the equator are marked in degrees south (S). The North Pole is at 90° north and the South Pole is at 90° south. Use the map to answer these questions.

1. Find the 60°N latitude line. What city is located there? _____

2. At what degree of latitude is New Orleans? _____

3. Look at the Southern Hemisphere. What city is at 15°S? _____

4. Quito, a city in Ecuador, is at 0°.
   What is another name for this line of latitude? _____

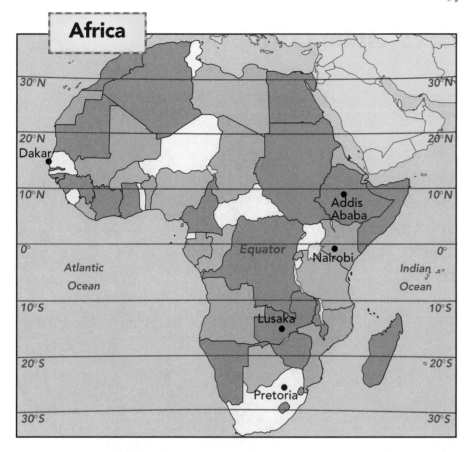

Scholastic Professional Books

map reader's **Tip**

The distance between two parallels that are one degree apart is about 69 miles or 111 kilometers. This distance varies slightly because the Earth is not a perfect sphere.

Most maps do not show every line of latitude. Look at the globe on page 362 again. It shows the lines of latitude for every 15 degrees. How many degrees apart are the lines of latitude on this map of Africa?

5. What city is almost on the equator? _____

6. Find the line of latitude marked 10°N. What city is located near this parallel? _____

7. Is Dakar in the northern or southern latitudes? _____

8. Find a city at about 15°S. About how many degrees north of Pretoria is it? _____

9. Most of Africa is between _____ and _____ lines of latitude.

10. All in all, Africa covers about _____ degrees of latitude.

Understanding Longitude

You know that lines of latitude measure the distance north and south on a globe. Lines of **longitude** measure Earth in degrees from east to west.

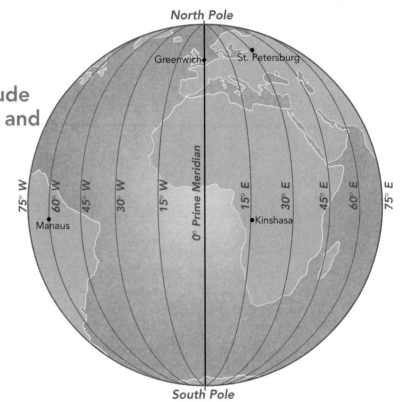

These lines are also called meridians. You read that the Prime Meridian divides Earth into the Eastern and Western hemispheres. The Prime Meridian is 0°. From the Prime Meridian to 180° longitude is exactly halfway around Earth.

1. In which direction do lines of longitude run? _____

2. Find the 15°W longitude line. What does the W stand for? _____

3. Find the 60°W longitude line. What city is located there? _____

4. At what degree of longitude is St. Petersburg? _____

5. Find a city in Africa at 15°E longitude. _____

6. Greenwich, a city in England, is at 0°.

   What is another name for this line of longitude? _____

7. Why can't you see 90° W longitude on this globe? _____

8. Most of Africa is between _____ and _____ lines of longitude.

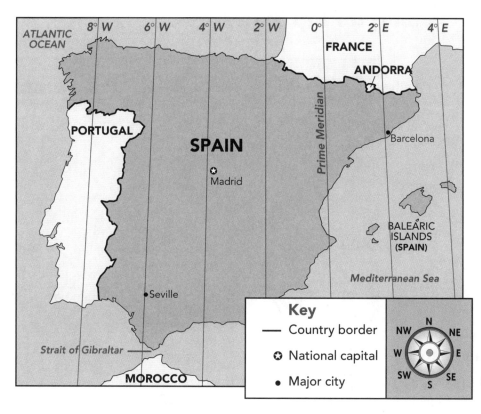

map reader's Tip

Unlike latitude, lines of longitude are not all the same distance apart from each other. They are farthest apart at the equator. At the North and South poles, they all come together.

Most maps do not show every line of longitude. The globe on page 364 shows the lines of longitude for every 15 degrees. How many degrees apart are the lines of longitude on this map of Spain?

Write True or False before each statement.

_____ **9.** Spain is entirely in the west longitudes.

_____ **10.** The Prime Meridian runs through Spain.

_____ **11.** Madrid is at about 4°W longitude.

_____ **12.** Spain covers less than 20 degrees of longitude.

word search

Find the following words from this lesson: **meridian, longitude, north, south, east, west, earth.**

```
L H E T M J J O Z
F C S E E A R T H
V I O U R T S A E
E D U T I G N O L
J N T X D B E Z Q
U E H D I C S A N
F K R S A W E S T
H T R O N I X P O
```

Using a Map Scale

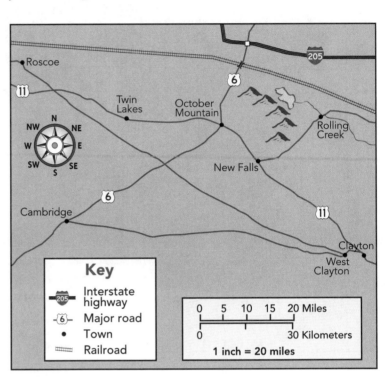

When you are traveling, it is useful to know how far you have to go. To show distances accurately on a map, mapmakers use a **scale**. A map scale helps you measure distance on a map. Look at the scale on this map. It shows that one inch equals twenty miles. That means that one inch on the map stands for twenty miles on Earth.

Use a ruler to measure distances on the map. Circle the correct answers.

1. From Twin Lakes to October Mountain, it is about _____.

    a. 20 miles   b. 40 miles   c. 50 miles

2. Between Clayton and New Falls there are _____.

    a. 20 miles   b. 30 miles   c. 40 miles

3. The distance from Cambridge to West Clayton is _____.

    a. 20 miles   b. 60 miles   c. 80 miles

4. The distance between Roscoe and West Clayton is less than _____.

    a. 100 miles   b. 20 miles   c. 60 miles

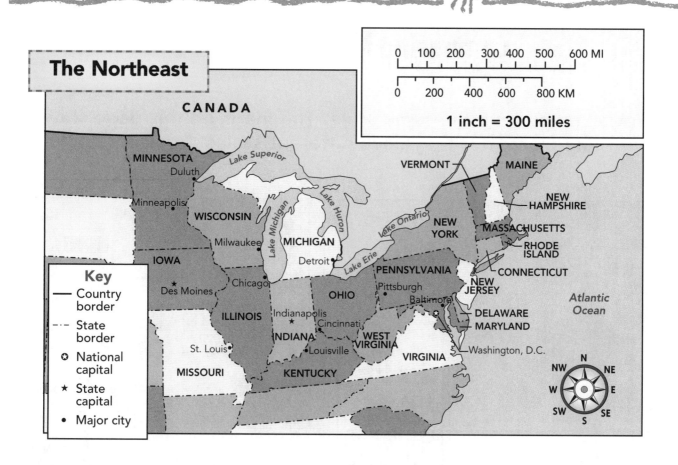

The Northeast

0   100 200   300 400 500   600 MI

0   200   400   600   800 KM

1 inch = 300 miles

CANADA

MINNESOTA
Duluth

Lake Superior

VERMONT

MAINE

Minneapolis

WISCONSIN

Lake Michigan

Lake Huron

NEW
HAMPSHIRE

Milwaukee

MICHIGAN

Lake Ontario

NEW
YORK

MASSACHUSETTS

IOWA

Detroit

Lake Erie

RHODE
ISLAND

Des Moines

Chicago

PENNSYLVANIA

CONNECTICUT

Pittsburgh

NEW
JERSEY

OHIO

ILLINOIS

Indianapolis

Baltimore

Atlantic
Ocean

Cincinnati

DELAWARE

INDIANA

WEST
VIRGINIA

MARYLAND

St. Louis

Louisville

Washington, D.C.

VIRGINIA

MISSOURI

KENTUCKY

Key

— Country
   border

- - - State
   border

⊕ National
   capital

★ State
   capital

• Major city

N
NW   NE
W   E
SW   SE
S

A map scale usually shows distance in both miles and kilometers. A kilometer is a measurement in the metric system. A mile is a longer distance than a kilometer. On this map scale you can see that 300 miles is a longer distance than 400 kilometers. Notice that the abbreviation for miles is MI and the abbreviation for kilometers is KM. Use the map to answer these questions.

5. How many miles does one inch represent on this map? _____

6. How many miles is it from St. Louis to Cincinnati? _____
About how many kilometers is this? _____

7. About how many miles is it from Milwaukee to Pittsburgh? _____

8. How many kilometers is it between
Minneapolis and Des Moines? _____

9. About how many kilometers is it from
Indianapolis to Washington, D.C.? _____

Comparing Maps and Scales

Not all maps have the same scale. The maps on this page show the same place, but they have different scales.

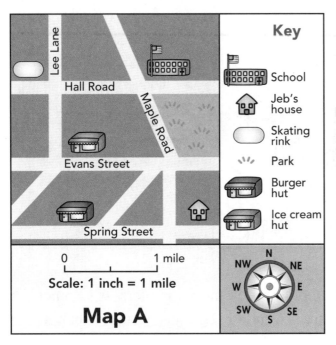

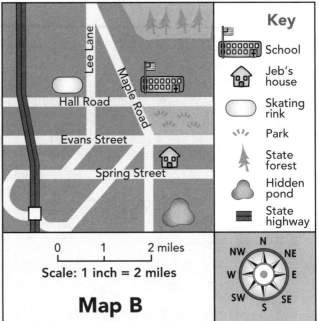

Use the map to answer these questions.

1. What does one inch stand for on the Map A scale? _____

2. How many miles does one inch stand for on Map B? _____

3. How long is Hall Road on Map A? _____

   How long is it on Map B? _____

4. Which map shows a smaller area? _____

5. Which map shows a larger area? _____

6. Which map would be more useful for getting from the state highway to

   Jeb's house? _____

Scholastic Professional Books

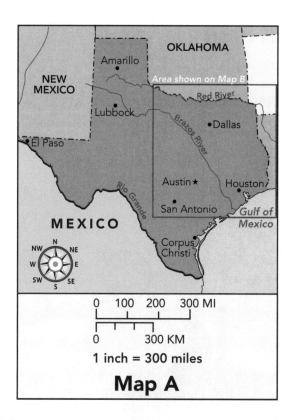

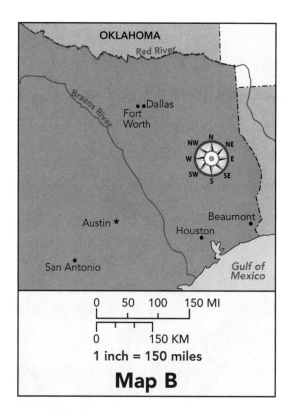

The maps on this page are the same size, but they show areas of different sizes. One map shows the whole state of Texas. The other map shows just the eastern part of the state.

Use the maps to answer the questions.

7. How many miles does one inch stand for on each map? _____

8. Why isn't El Paso on Map B? _____

9. Name two cities on Map B that are not shown on Map A. _____

10. About how many miles is it between El Paso and Lubbock? _____

11. Which map would you use if you were driving all the way across the state of Texas? _____

A Vegetation Map

The different kinds of trees and plants that grow in an area are called vegetation. This map shows **vegetation** on the continent of Africa.

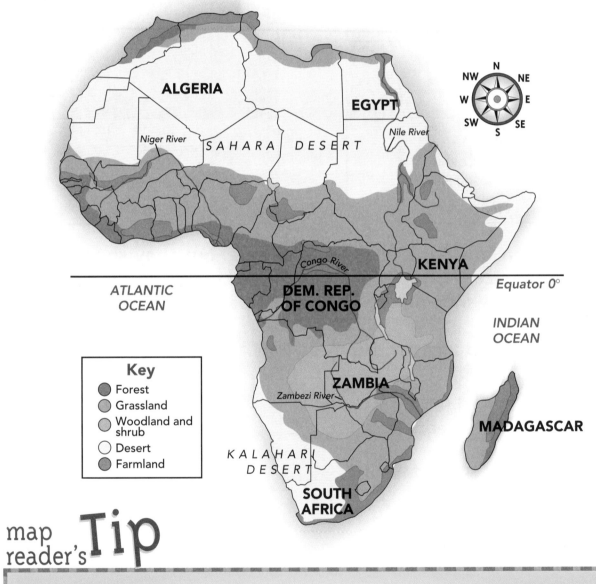

map reader's **Tip**

The cacao tree is one special kind of vegetation that grows in the West African countries of Ghana, Ivory Coast, and Nigeria. The seeds from these trees produce most of the world's chocolate.

Scholastic Professional Books

Use the map to answer these questions.

1. What does this symbol ◯ stand for? _____

2. Deserts cover two-fifths of Africa.

   In what part of Africa do you find the largest desert? _____

3. Would you expect the population in Africa's desert regions to be large

   or small? Why? _____

4. Grasslands also cover much of Africa.

   What is the symbol for this vegetation on the map? _____

5. How would you describe the vegetation in Zambia? _____

6. Name two African nations that are mostly desert. _____

Crossword Puzzle

Use the map to complete this puzzle.

Across

3. desert in southern Africa

4. land where crops are grown

5. a river that runs through large forests

6. a country with farmland and desert

Down

1. land that is very dry

2. a river that flows through a desert

3. a country in the east that is almost all grassland

4. land along the Congo River

Looking at Landforms

As you know, Earth's surface has both land and water. The pictures on this page show some of the landforms found on Earth. Read each of these descriptions. Then write the name of the correct landform on each line under the picture.

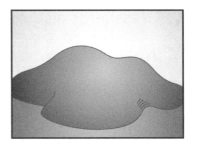

1. _____

A **canyon** is a deep, narrow valley with high, steep sides.

A **mountain** is high, steep, rugged land that rises sharply from the surrounding area.

A **hill** is an area of raised land that is lower and more rounded than a mountain.

A **plain** is a broad area of open, flat land.

A **plateau** is a large area of high, flat land.

A **valley** is the land that lies between hills or mountains.

A **volcano** is a mountain with a cone shape that is formed by lava that erupts from a crack in the Earth's surface.

2. _____

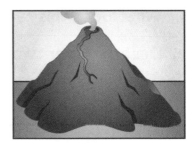

3. _____

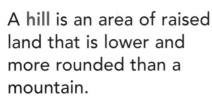

4. _____

5. _____

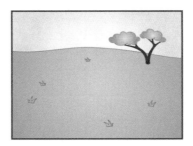

6. _____

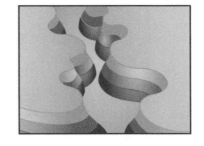

7. _____

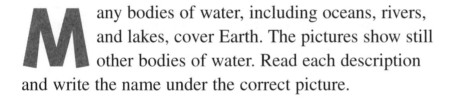

Many landforms are formed where land and water come together. The pictures on this page show some examples. Read the description of each one. Then write the name of each landform under the correct picture.

A **cape** is a small, narrow point of land that sticks out into a body of water.

A **peninsula** is an area of land that is surrounded by water on three sides.

An **isthmus** is a narrow strip of land that connects two large areas of land.

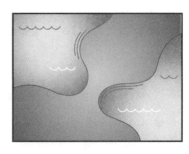

8. _____

9. _____

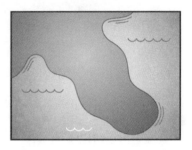

Many bodies of water, including oceans, rivers, and lakes, cover Earth. The pictures show still other bodies of water. Read each description and write the name under the correct picture.

A **strait** is a narrow channel that connects two larger bodies of water.

A **gulf** is an arm of an ocean or sea that is partly enclosed by land.

A **bay** is a smaller body of water partly enclosed by land.

10. _____

11. _____

12. _____

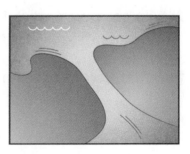

13. _____

A Profile and Contour Map

You know that mountains are high, but how high are they?
The drawing on this page shows the **profile**, or side view,
of two mountains.

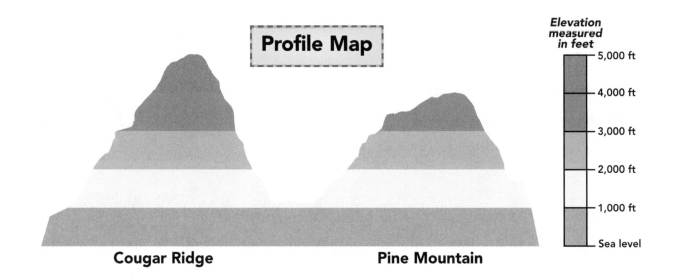

Profile Map

Cougar Ridge   Pine Mountain

Elevation
measured
in feet
— 5,000 ft
— 4,000 ft
— 3,000 ft
— 2,000 ft
— 1,000 ft
— Sea level

The key tells you the **elevation** of different parts of the mountains. Elevation is
the height of any place on land above **sea level**. Sea level is the average height
of the ocean's surface. It is zero elevation. Land that rises 500 feet higher than
sea level has an elevation of 500 feet.

1. What does the color yellow stand for on the mountains?_____

2. Which mountain is higher?_____
   What is its elevation? _____

3. What color represents an elevation of 800 feet? _____

4. Forest rangers are building a hut at the top of Pine Mountain.
   At what elevation will it be? _____

5. Suppose you are climbing Cougar Ridge
   and are halfway to the top. What is the elevation? _____

Scholastic Professional Books

Cougar Ridge | **Contour Map** | **Pine Mountain**

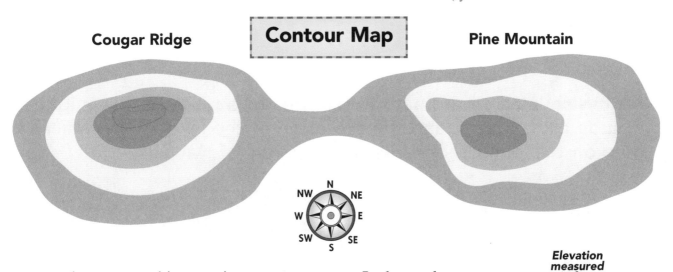

T he map on this page is a **contour map**. It shows the same mountains as the profile on page 374, but it shows the view from above. The lines on the contour map show the elevations of different parts of the mountains. When the lines on a contour map are close together, they show that the land is steep. When the lines are far apart, they show a more gradual slope.

Imagine you are a mountain guide planning treks up these mountains. Draw the following routes on the contour map.

Elevation measured in feet

- 5,000 ft
- 4,000 ft
- 3,000 ft
- 2,000 ft
- 1,000 ft
- Sea level

6. For expert hikers draw a dotted line up the steepest side of Cougar Ridge Mountain. Write the elevation at the top.

7. Mark a point halfway up this mountain with an X so the hikers can take a rest.

8. For the beginning hikers draw a double line up the least steep side of Pine Mountain. Write the elevation at the top.

9. For an all-day hike draw a continuous line from the lowest point on the map to the highest point on the map.

map reader's **Tip**

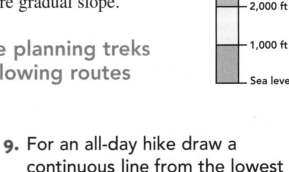

Some land on Earth is actually below sea level. For example, Death Valley in California is 282 feet below sea level. It is the lowest land in the Western Hemisphere.

Scholastic Professional Books

A Physical Map

A **physical map** shows natural features of a place. These might include lakes, rivers, and the elevation of the land. The physical map on this page shows the main islands of Hawaii.

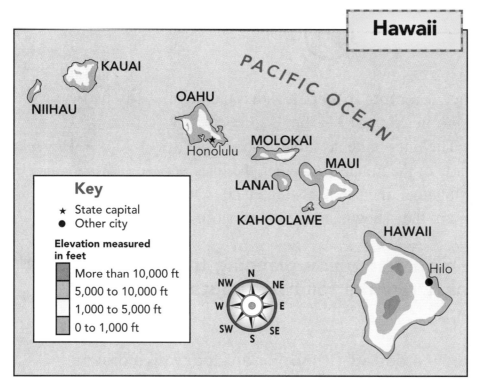

map reader's Tip

The islands of Hawaii were formed by volcanoes. Most of these volcanoes are no longer active, but Mauna Loa and Kilauea on the island of Hawaii still erupt sometimes.

1. What elevation does the color green stand for? _____

2. Which island has the highest elevation? _____

3. What landforms would you expect to see on the highest island? _____

4. Find Hawaii's capital, Honolulu. What is the elevation of this city? _____

5. Which islands are less than 5,000 feet high? _____

_____

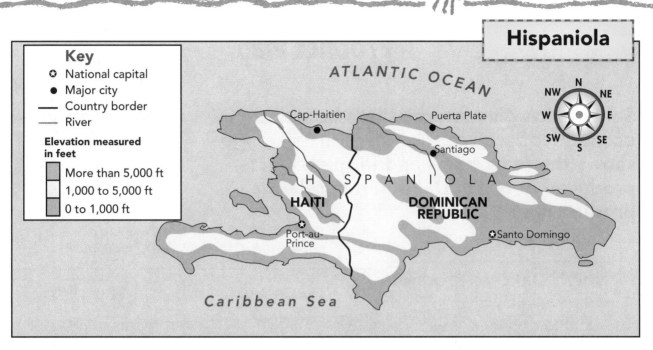

Hispaniola

Key
- ✪ National capital
- ● Major city
- — Country border
- — River

Elevation measured in feet
- More than 5,000 ft
- 1,000 to 5,000 ft
- 0 to 1,000 ft

ATLANTIC OCEAN

Cap-Haitien
Puerta Plate
Santiago

H I S P A N I O L A

HAITI

DOMINICAN REPUBLIC

Port-au-Prince

Santo Domingo

Caribbean Sea

Here is another physical map. It shows the two countries on the island of Hispaniola in the Caribbean Sea.

1. What are the two countries shown on this map? _____

2. What color is used to show elevations at sea level on this map? _____

3. In which country do you find the highest elevation?
   What landform would you expect to find there?_____

4. Find Santo Domingo, the capital of the Dominican Republic.
   What is the elevation of this city?_____

5. Find the border between the two countries.
   What is the elevation for most of it? _____

6. Rivers flow from high land to lower land. Find the rivers on this map.
   In which direction are they flowing? _____

map reader's **Tip**

Hispaniola is the second largest island (after Cuba) in the West Indies. The explorer Christopher Columbus landed on Hispaniola in 1492.

Scholastic Professional Books

A Product Map

Some maps give information about the economy of a place. The map on this page shows the main crops and farm products produced in North Dakota. It is called a **product map**.

North Dakota is a leading producer of flax, which is used to make paint.

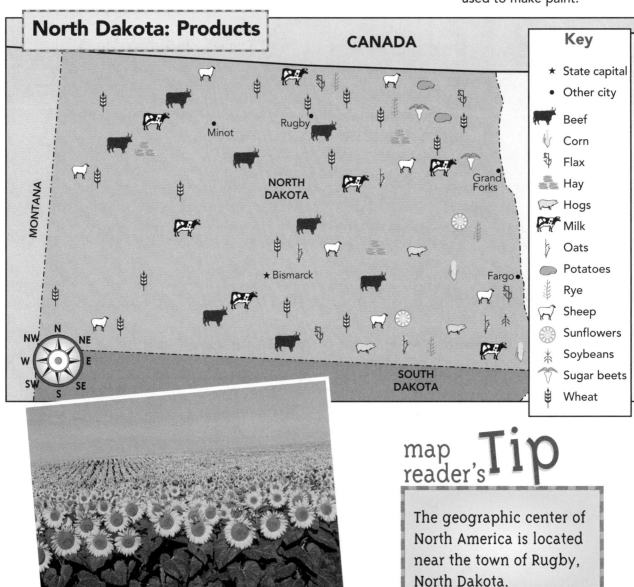

North Dakota: Products

CANADA

MONTANA

NORTH
DAKOTA

Minot

Rugby

Grand
Forks

★ Bismarck

Fargo

SOUTH
DAKOTA

NW N NE
W E
SW S SE

Key

★ State capital
• Other city
🐄 Beef
🌾 Corn
Flax
Hay
🐖 Hogs
🐄 Milk
Oats
Potatoes
Rye
🐑 Sheep
☀ Sunflowers
Soybeans
Sugar beets
🌾 Wheat

Many farmers grow sunflowers for their oil and seeds.

map reader's **Tip**

The geographic center of North America is located near the town of Rugby, North Dakota.

Scholastic Professional Books

Write TRUE or FALSE on the line next to each sentence.

_____ **1.** More crops are grown in the western part of the state than the eastern part.

_____ **2.** Wheat and other grains such as rye and oats are grown in many parts of the state.

_____ **3.** ![hay symbol] is the symbol for hay on this map.

_____ **4.** Fruit is an important farm product in North Dakota.

_____ **5.** Some farmers in the state raise dairy cows.

_____ **6.** Steaks are probably a big meat product in North Dakota.

_____ **7.** Sunflowers grow mostly in the southeastern part of the state.

_____ **8.** The soil in North Dakota is probably fertile.

Creating symbols

Product maps use many different symbols. Imagine you are creating a product map for another state. Draw symbols for each of the following products.

grapes	mushrooms	carrots

lettuce	strawberries	lemons

A History Map

Most maps show what the world is like today. But some maps can show you what a place was like long ago. These are called history maps.

A

1 SCOTLAND STREET

2 PRINCE GEORGE STREET

3 College of William and Mary

4 BOUNDARY STREET

The map on these pages shows Colonial Williamsburg in Virginia. Some people call this community a "living museum." That's because Colonial Williamsburg was rebuilt to show how people lived in 1775. Looking at this map is like stepping back in time.

Glossary of Colonial Terms

apothecary . . . . pharmacy or drugstore
blacksmith . . . . . maker of iron tools, knives, and horsehoes
cooper . . . . barrelmaker
gaol . . . . jail
milliner . . . . hatmaker
rural trades . . . . farm equipment
tavern . . . . restaurant
wheelwright . . . . wheelmaker
windmill . . . . . . grinder of grain into flour

Use the glossary and grid to answer the questions. List the name and grid location of each place.

1. You drop off your horse's harness for repair. _____

2. You pick up some medicines for your mother. _____

3. You order a barrel for your father. _____

4. You drop off an ad for the newspaper. _____

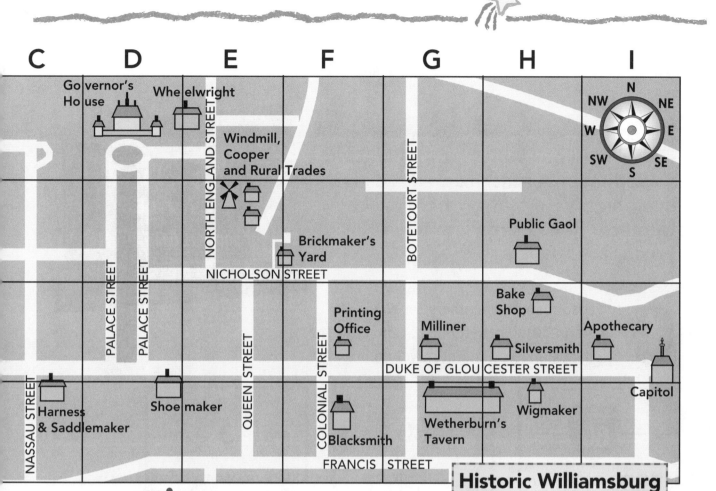

map reader's Tip

Williamsburg was the capital of Virginia from 1699 to 1780. Today, Virginia's capital is Richmond.

5. You leave a basket of corn to be ground into corn meal. _____

6. You join your father for dinner. _____

7. You stop to look at hats in a store window. _____

8. You help your father take a horse to get new shoes. _____

9. Mmmm. You can't resist those baked apple pies! _____

10. You buy a candlestick for your sister's wedding. _____

A Road Map

Have you ever taken a vacation by car? Then your family probably used a **road map**. A road map shows the main highways that go from place to place. It also shows smaller, secondary roads.

O n a road map, the numbers for roads are shown in different symbols. Some kinds of highways that you might travel on are:

interstate highway

U.S. highway

state or county road

1. What interstate highway runs east and west across Iowa? _____

2. If you travel from Cedar Rapids to Waterloo, what interstate can you take? _____

3. Interstate 29 connects Iowa with which two other states. _____

4. What does this symbol ─(3)─ stand for? _____

5. Name two routes you could take from Dubuque to South Dakota. _____

6. On which highways is Ames? _____

7. What cities does Interstate 35 run through? _____

8. Describe the best route from Council Bluffs to Mason City. _____

Scholastic Professional Books

map reader's Tip

"Inter" means between or among. Interstate highways cross between states. Interstate routes that go east and west have even numbers. North-south interstate routes have odd numbers.

Iowa: Highways

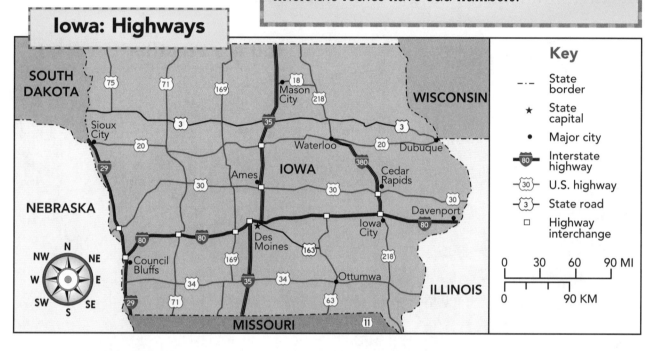

Key

– · –	State border
★	State capital
•	Major city
🛡80	Interstate highway
30	U.S. highway
3	State road
□	Highway interchange

0   30   60   90 MI

0   90 KM

E-Z Trip Planner

Imagine you are planning a trip from Davenport to Sioux City. Use the E-Z Trip Planner to list the highways you will travel on. Don't forget to pick a place for a lunch break!

Highway	Direction
Lunch break	

A Weather Map

What's the weather like today? One way to find out is to look out the window. Another way to check the weather is to look at a weather map like the one shown here.

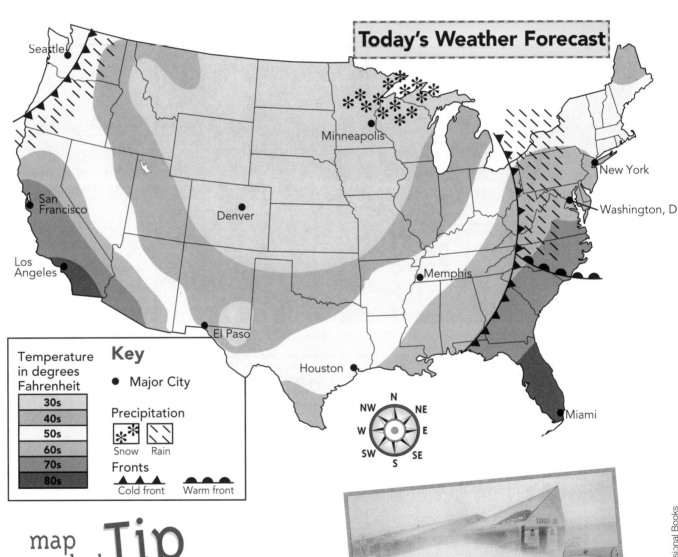

Today's Weather Forecast

Seattle

San Francisco

Los Angeles

El Paso

Minneapolis

Denver

Houston

Memphis

New York

Washington, D

Miami

Key

Temperature in degrees Fahrenheit

| 30s |
| 40s |
| 50s |
| 60s |
| 70s |
| 80s |

• Major City

Precipitation

Snow   Rain

Fronts

▲▲▲ Cold front   ●●● Warm front

N
NW   NE
W   E
SW   SE
S

map reader's **Tip**

The symbols that are used to show warm and cold fronts on a weather map were created by the Norwegian scientist Wilhelm Bjerknes in the 1920s.

Weather like this can make it dangerous to be outside.

Scholastic Professional Books

A cold front is a zone of cold air moving in as warm air retreats. A cold front usually means clouds and showers. A warm front is a zone of warm air advancing as cold air retreats. Clouds and rain often occur just ahead of a warm front. Weather systems usually move from west to east across North America.

1. In which part of the country is there a warm front? _____

2. What is the temperature in Seattle today? _____

3. What city is about to get snow? _____

4. Name two cities with temperatures in the 80s. _____

5. If you were in Denver today, how would you dress? _____

6. What kind of weather is heading toward Washington, D.C.?_____

7. Is it cooler in San Francisco or Los Angeles today? _____

8. You live in Memphis and are planning a hike.

Will you have good weather for this activity? _____

Weather or Not

Find the area of your hometown on the weather map. Then fill out the chart below with your prediction for the weather for today and the next two days. Use the symbols provided.

Today	Tomorrow	Day After Tomorrow

Name _____

A Climate Map

Weather changes from day to day, but climate remains more or less the same.

Climate is the pattern of weather that an area has over a period of time. Does an area get a lot of rain during the year? Is it mostly hot or mostly cold? The map shown here is a climate map. It shows the different kinds of climate regions in the United States.

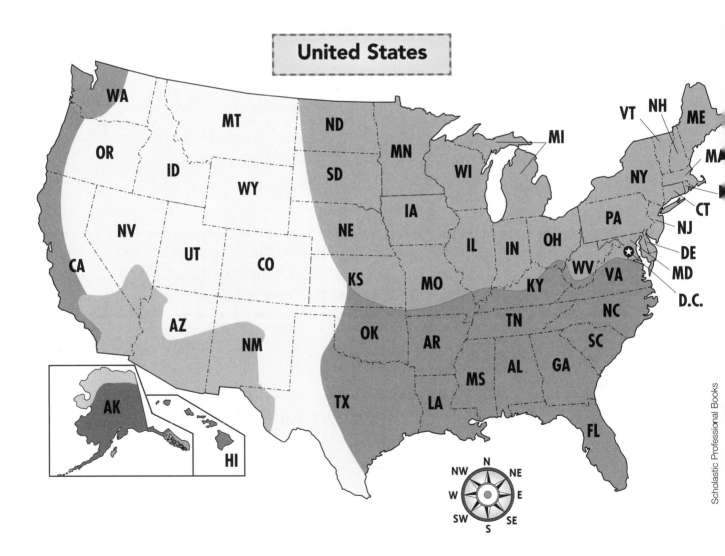

map reader's Tip

Different factors affect climate. Elevation is one. Another is latitude or how far a place is from the equator. Landforms also affect climate.

Map Key

☐ Cool summers/ cold winters; Very dry

☐ Cool summers/ cold winters; Wet

☐ Cool summers/ mild winters; Wet

☐ Warm or hot summers/ cold winters; Dry

☐ Warm or hot summers/ mild winters; Dry or very dry

☐ Warm or hot summers/ cold winters; Wet

☐ Hot summers/ mild or warm winters; Wet

1. How would you describe the climate in the northeastern part of the United States?

_____

_____

2. Find an area where summers are hot and winters are mild. Where is it?_____

3. How many kinds of climates does Texas have? _____

4. Describe one climate in Alaska. _____

_____

_____

5. What is the climate like along most of the west coast?

_____

_____

6. What kind of climate does this color ☐ represent?_____

_____

7. In general, is the western part of the country drier or wetter than the eastern part? _____

8. Find your state. What is its climate like? _____

Scholastic Professional Books

A News Map

News maps help readers locate and understand events around the globe. Here is the first paragraph of a news story and a map that goes with it.

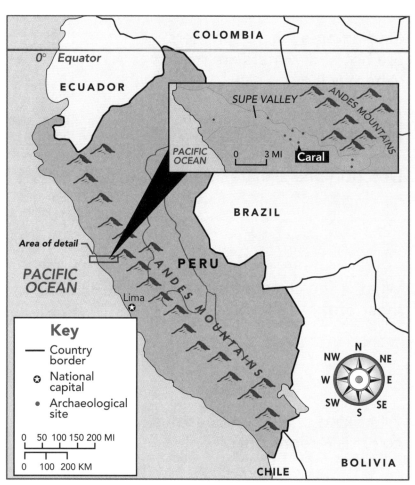

Oldest City in the Americas

Researchers working at an archaeological site in Peru say that they think it is the oldest city in the Americas. The site, called Caral, dates back to 2600 B.C. Scientists used radiocarbon dating of plant fibers from the site to determine its age. They believe that a civilization existed at Caral for five centuries. Until now, scientists thought that the earliest civilization in Peru was on the coast.

1. In which direction is Caral from Lima?_____

2. What is the symbol for an archaeological site? _____

3. In which valley is Caral?_____

4. In which mountain range is the valley located? _____

5. Is Caral on the ocean or inland? _____

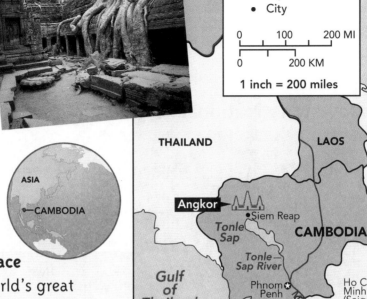

This news story takes place in another part of the world, the country of Cambodia in Southeast Asia.

Temples and Trees Embrace

Angkor was one of the world's great cities between the ninth and fifteenth centuries. Its huge temples were famous. When the empire at Angkor collapsed, the jungle crept in and the temples lay hidden by trees and undergrowth. Although the temples were rediscovered by explorers many years later, only part of the jungle was cleared away. Today, efforts are being made to restore the beautiful temples. But in many cases the trees have become part of the buildings.

6. What countries border Cambodia on the north? _____

What country borders Cambodia on the east? _____

7. What city is Angkor near? _____

8. In which direction is Angkor from Phnom Penh? _____

9. About how far is Angkor from the Mekong River? _____

10. What body of water is Angkor near? _____

Planning With a Map

The map on this page shows Yellowstone National Park, one of the most popular parks in our country. It's a great place to take a vacation!

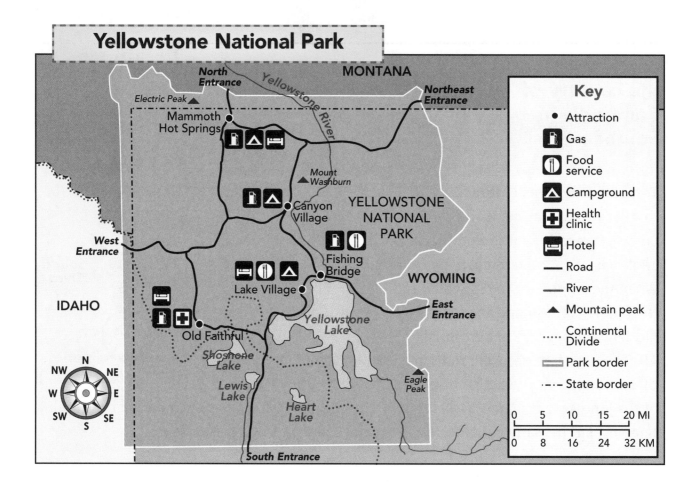

1. Yellowstone is located in three different states. What are they? _____

2. How many road entrances are there to the park? _____

3. Old Faithful Geyser is the park's most famous attraction.

   In which direction is the geyser from Yellowstone Lake? _____

map reader's Tip

The Continental Divide runs through Yellowstone Park. Rain that falls on the west side of this line flows to the Pacific Ocean. Rain that falls on the east side of this line flows to the Atlantic Ocean.

Handy Dandy Planning Guide

Use the guide below to plan a three-day visit to Yellowstone Park.

	Day 1	Day 2	Day 3
Sights to See			
Places to Swim or Fish			
Mountain to Hike			
Hotel			

4. Which river flows out of the north end of the park? _____

5. What is the largest lake in the park? _____

6. Look at the scale on this map. About how many miles is it from the east side of the park to the west side? _____

Maps and Charts

Sometimes maps don't provide all the information you need. The chart on page 393 tells what the abbreviations in the map below stand for. It also provides the nickname of each state.

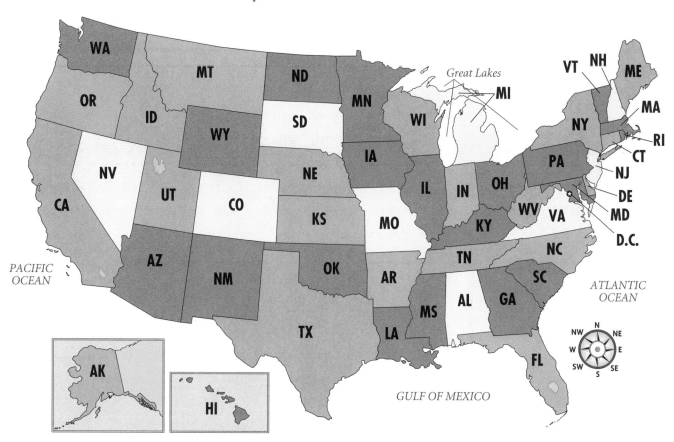

Use the map and the chart to answer these questions.

1. What two states bordering the Great Lakes have nicknames that are animals? _____

2. What is the abbreviation of the Mountain State? _____

3. Which ocean does the Ocean State border? _____

4. What is the nickname of Nebraska? _____

   What does this tell you about the crops grown there? _____

Scholastic Professional Books

STATE NAME	ABBREVIATION	NICKNAME	STATE NAME	ABBREVIATION	NICKNAME
Alabama	AL	Heart of Dixie	Montana	MT	Treasure State
Alaska	AK	The Last Frontier	Nebraska	NE	Cornhusker State
Arizona	AZ	Grand Canyon State	Nevada	NV	Silver State
Arkansas	AR	Land of Opportunity	New Hampshire	NH	Granite State
California	CA	Golden State	New Jersey	NJ	Garden State
Colorado	CO	Centennial State	New Mexico	NM	Land of Enchantment
Connecticut	CT	Constitution State	New York	NY	Empire State
Delaware	DE	First State	North Carolina	NC	Tar Heel State
Florida	FL	Sunshine State	North Dakota	ND	Peace Garden State
Georgia	GA	Peach State	Ohio	OH	Buckeye State
Hawaii	HI	The Aloha State	Oklahoma	OK	Sooner State
Idaho	ID	Gem State	Oregon	OR	Beaver State
Illinois	IL	Prairie State	Pennsylvania	PA	Keystone State
Indiana	IN	Hoosier State	Rhode Island	RI	Ocean State
Iowa	IA	Hawkeye State	South Carolina	SC	Palmetto State
Kansas	KS	Sunflower State	South Dakota	SD	Coyote State
Kentucky	KY	Bluegrass State	Tennessee	TN	Volunteer State
Louisiana	LA	Pelican State	Texas	TX	Lone Star State
Maine	ME	Pine Tree State	Utah	UT	Beehive State
Maryland	MD	Free State	Vermont	VT	Green Mountain State
Massachusetts	MA	Bay State	Virginia	VA	Old Dominion
Michigan	MI	Wolverine State	Washington	WA	Evergreen State
Minnesota	MN	North Star State	West Virginia	WV	Mountain State
Mississippi	MS	Magnolia State	Wisconsin	WI	Badger State
Missouri	MO	Show Me State	Wyoming	WY	Equality State

5. Which state in the northwest probably has a lot of pine trees? _____

   Which state in the northeast is similar? _____

6. Which state on the Gulf of Mexico
   has a nickname that is a bird? _____

7. Why do you think Florida is called the Sunshine State? _____

Name _____

Map Review 1

South America: Vegetation

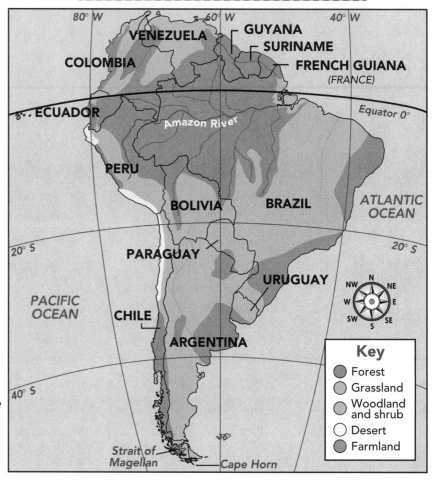

1. Find the equator. What degree latitude is it? _____

2. Name three countries that the equator runs through.

   _____

   _____

   _____

3. Look at the other lines of latitude. In which hemisphere is most of South America?

   _____

4. At about what longitude is the westernmost part of Ecuador? _____

5. What does this symbol ⬤ stand for? _____

6. Where are the deserts in South America? _____

7. How would you describe the vegetation in Guyana? _____

8. In which part of Brazil would you expect to find the Amazon Rain Forest? _____

Scholastic Professional Books

Map Review 2

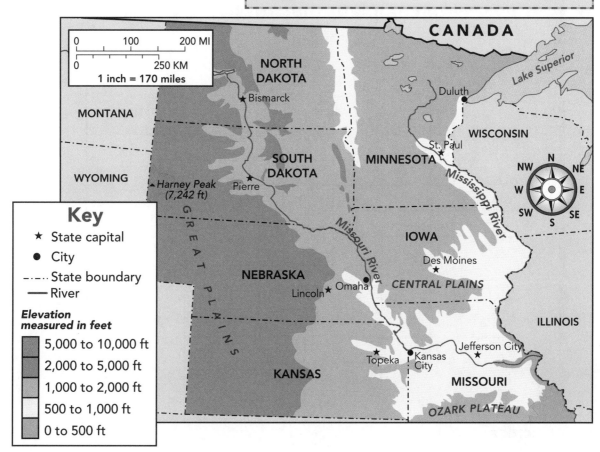

Physical Map of the Plains States

Key
★ State capital
● City
-·-·- State boundary
— River

Elevation measured in feet
5,000 to 10,000 ft
2,000 to 5,000 ft
1,000 to 2,000 ft
500 to 1,000 ft
0 to 500 ft

0   100   200 MI
0   250 KM
1 inch = 170 miles

CANADA

MONTANA

NORTH DAKOTA
★Bismarck

WYOMING

SOUTH DAKOTA
▲Harney Peak (7,242 ft)   ★Pierre

MINNESOTA
St. Paul

Lake Superior
•Duluth

WISCONSIN

GREAT PLAINS

NEBRASKA
Lincoln★ •Omaha

Missouri River

Mississippi River

IOWA
Des Moines★

CENTRAL PLAINS

ILLINOIS

KANSAS
Topeka★ •Kansas City

Jefferson City★

MISSOURI

OZARK PLATEAU

1. What is the elevation of Bismarck, North Dakota? _____

2. What does this symbol ☐ stand for? _____

3. Where is the highest land in South Dakota? _____

4. At what elevation are the Great Plains? _____

5. Are the Great Plains higher or lower than the Central Plains? _____

6. At what elevation is the land along
   the eastern border of Missouri? _____

Thinking About Maps

Use what you have learned about maps
to complete the crossword puzzle.

Across

4. a way to measure distance on a map
5. half of Earth
8. a map that is a side view
9. a drawing that stands for something on a map
10. 0° latitude

Down

1. plants that grow in a place

2. A mountain is a kind of _____.
3. the pattern of weather in a place
4. a narrow channel of water
6. the height of land above sea level
7. an area of high, flat land
9. there are 50 of these

Glossary

axis
An axis is an imaginary center line on which Earth turns.

canyon
A canyon is a deep, narrow valley with high, steep sides.

cape
A cape is a small, narrow point of land that sticks out into a body of water.

cardinal directions
Cardinal directions are the four main directions—north, south, east, and west.

climate
Climate is the kind of weather that an area has over a period of time.

compass rose
A compass rose is a symbol that shows directions.

contour map
A contour map has lines that show the elevations of different parts of land.

elevation
Elevation is the height of land above sea level.

equator
The equator is an imaginary line that runs around the center of Earth and divides it into the Northern and Southern hemispheres. The equator is 0° latitude.

grid
A grid is a pattern of lines that form squares.

gulf
A gulf is an arm of an ocean or sea that is partly enclosed by land.

hemisphere
A hemisphere is half of Earth. Earth can be divided into Northern and Southern hemispheres or Eastern and Western hemispheres.

intermediate directions
Intermediate directions are directions between the four main directions. They are northeast, southeast, southwest, and northwest.

isthmus
An isthmus is a narrow strip of land that connects two large areas of land.

latitude
Lines of latitude run around Earth parallel to the equator. They are marked in degrees north and south.

longitude
Lines of longitude are meridians that measure Earth in degrees from east to west.

map index
A map index is an alphabetical listing of place names on a map. A map index gives the grid square for each place.

peninsula
A peninsula is an area of land that is surrounded by water on three sides.

physical map
A physical map shows natural features of Earth.

plateau
A plateau is a large area of high, flat land.

Prime Meridian
The Prime Meridian is an imaginary line at 0° longitude. The Prime Meridian divides Earth into Eastern and Western hemispheres.

profile map
A profile map shows the side view of a place.

product map
A product map shows the products produced in a region.

projections
Map projections are different ways of showing Earth on a flat surface.

road map
A road map shows the main roads and highways that go from place to place in an area.

scale
A map scale helps you measure distance on a map.

sea level
Sea level is the average height of the ocean's surface. It is zero elevation.

strait
A strait is a narrow channel that connects two larger bodies of water.

symbol
A symbol is a drawing or color that represents something else.

vegetation
Vegetation is the different kinds of trees and plants that grow in an area.

volcano
A volcano is a mountain with a cone shape that is formed by lava that erupts from a crack in Earth's surface.

Scholastic Professional Books

Answer Key

READING COMPREHENSION

Pages 12–13
Answers will vary. Sample main ideas: Letter one—Except for the bugs, Tyler and his new friends are having fun at camp.; Letter two—Tyler's mom is worried about his bug bites, and she wants him to start being nice to the other campers.; Letter Three—Tyler is having a great time at camp, has some new friends, and is having fun playing tricks on other campers.; Letter four—Steven is sad he could not go to camp and remembers the fun he had at camp last year.

Pages 14–15
1. b; 2. c; 3. c; 4. Answers will vary. 5. Answers will vary. Sample answers: The course for the Tour de France changes each year. The course is always over 2,000 miles long. 6. Armstrong faced the challenges of battling cancer and competing in the Tour de France. Opinions will vary.

Pages 16–17
1. between Virginia and Maryland on the Potomac River; 2. Answers will vary. Possible answers: capital of the United States, symbol of our country's history, home of many important historic landmarks; 3. George Washington, Abraham Lincoln, Thomas Jefferson, and Franklin D. Roosevelt; 4. Americans who fought in the Korean War and Vietnam War; 5. The National World War II Memorial; 6. to honor Americans who fought in World War II; 7. about four years—1941–1945; 8. Rainbow Pool, two giant arches, ring of stone columns, wall covered with stars; 9. Americans who died fighting in World War II; 10. Bob Dole; 11. the value of freedom; 12. many business, private groups, and schools

Pages 18–19
1. formal; 2. residence; 3. reception; 4. entertained; 5. adorned; 6. guide; 7. wing; 8. mansion; 9. tour; 10. incredible; 11. huge; 12. visitors; 13. vary; five hundred seventy

Pages 20–21
1. classed; 2. unique; 3. fascinating; 4. strike; 5. enamored; 6. eventually; 7. accumulated; 8. carting; 9. slinky; 10. creature; 11. Cassidy loves large, dangerous snakes. 12. a diamondback rattlesnake

Pages 22–23
1. Southwest: many-storied homes; steep-walled canyons; buttes; Arizona, New Mexico, and southern Colorado; Apache and Navajo; Both: made pottery; hunting; excellent craftspeople; corn, beans, and squash; Eastern Woodlands: wigwams and longhouses; fishing; cold winters, warm summers; Iroquois and Cherokee; bordered what is now Canada; 2. large, multiply-family dwellings; 3. The northern parts had cold winters.

Pages 24–25
1. Arizona: Tonto National Forest, Phoenix, very hot, Apache Trail, Grand Canyon; Massachusetts: Old State House, Freedom Trail, mild climate, Boston, Cape Cod; 2. building sandcastles, beach, Meteor Crater, Freedom Trail; 3. Their parents love hot weather. Zach and Emily do not. 4. You can walk on the Freedom Trail; you must drive along the Apache Trail. 5. Emily likes to boogie board, and Zach likes to body surf. 6. Zach thinks he might be able to find the missing object. Emily thinks he is crazy to think he might find it.

Pages 26–27
1. Picture order: 5, 1, 6, 3, 4, 2, Sentences will vary.
2.

a	p	r	t	e	i	c
c	o	l	e	s	a	b
m	u	s	i	i	n	l
g	l	y	l	c	p	r
e	d	e	i	t	c	e
o	d	v	s	e	b	r
i	s	l	l	i	o	n

Pages 28–29
1. 7, 3, 4, 2, 1, 5, 6; 2. Answers will vary. 3. prank, party, delicious; 4. because water makes the chocolate lose its creaminess; 5. tortilla, apricot jam, green fruit roll, cashews, chocolate chips; 6. Maria "sweetly" tricked her friends on April Fools' Day. 7. vanilla ice cream, marshmallow fluff, yellow pudding; 8. black olives, green peppers, mushrooms

Pages 30–31
1. hard worker, brave, fast-thinking, quick-acting; 2. scared, helpless, sick, alarmed; 3. Answers will vary. 4. Both: good students; Lindsay: persistent, courageous; Erica: frightened, grateful, appreciative; 5. Henry Heimlich; 6. Mount Waialeale; 7. just under 2"; 8. Answers will vary.

Pages 32–33
1. positive: He sees his friend, Eric., He learns Home Run Harvey is the coach.; negative: He could not play baseball with his friends., He sees a player on his new team strike out. 2. He would not get to see his friends and have Coach Dave whom he loved. 3. when he saw Eric; 4. Answers will vary. 5. excited, remorseful; 6. What Juan thought was going to be a negative experience soon looked like it could be a positive one. 7. Answers will vary.

Pages 34–35
1. Tuesday and Wednesday; 2. Monday; 3. Answers will vary. Suggested answers: go to the movies, go to the mall, go bowling, go to a museum, go to the library; 4. Wednesday, Thursday, Friday; 5. Answers will vary. Possible answer: They are probably not pleased. They want to do all kinds of outdoor activities, and it is going to be cold and rainy. 6. no clouds with a high of 82; It is the best forecast for doing outside activities. 7. lingering; 8. athletic, energetic; 9. goggles, sunglasses, cooler with drinks, sunscreen; 10. Paragraphs will vary.

Pages 36–37
main characters: the colonists; setting: east coast of America; problem: The colonists wanted their independence from Britain. solution: Delegates met to try to help gain independence from Britain. When their efforts did not work, they agreed to go to war.

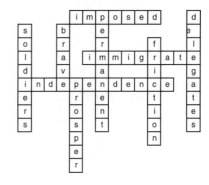

Scholastic Professional Books

Pages 38–39
1. B, C, A; 2. a. E, C; b. C, E; c. E, C; d. E, C;
3. Since it was a beautiful day, Janie and
Jake's mom was taking them to the beach.
4. Janie: because Hayley had recently had
Janie over to play; Jake: because he
and Charlie went everywhere together;
5. Answers will vary.

Page 40
1. Pluto; 2. Jupiter; 3. Uranus; 4. Neptune;
5. Earth; 6. Saturn; 7. Mercury; 8. Mars;
9. Venus

Page 41
Grant: Washington; Spencer: Arizona; Kara:
Pennsylvania; Jack: Massachusetts; All live in
Maine.

Pages 42–43
1. to run errands and shop;
2. Answers will vary.

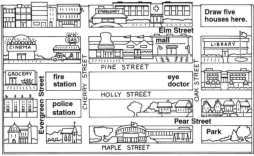

Pages 44–45
Chart: Dairy—milk, yogurt, ice cream,
cheese, milkshake; Vegetables—carrots,
peas, corn, broccoli, cauliflower; Grains—
oatmeal, wheat bread, rice, crackers, pasta;
Fruits—banana, apple, grapes, strawberries,
pear; Meat & Fish—chicken nuggets, ham,
hamburger, fish sticks, pork chops;
Fats/Sweets—chocolate chip cookies, candy
bar, doughnuts, chocolate cake, cheesecake;
1. She eats right and exercises.
2. hamburger, chicken, ribs;
3. Answers will vary. 4. E, C;
5. Katie: banana, oatmeal; Jimmy: candy bar,
ham, corn; Toni: chocolate chip cookies,
chicken nuggets, carrots; Anna: fish sticks,
pear

Page 46
1. spring; 2. Mother's Day; 3. because they
are having a sale; 4. Answers will vary.
Possible answer: It was spring. Many people
shop for plants in the spring, so a sale would
not be needed. 5. because they are buy one
get one free; 6. because the sale ends
Tuesday

Page 47
1. They love it. 2. They are sad., They do not
they will do without their good friends. 3.
They think it sounds like a fun, interesting
part of the country.
4.

Pages 48–49
1. Most whales are enormous
creatures.
2. Whales might look a lot like fish, but
the two are very different. 3. Whales
can be divided into two groups—
baleen and toothed. 4. Blubber is very
important to whales and has many
purposes. 5. Most whales are
enormous creatures. Whales might
look a lot like fish, but the two are very
different. Whales can be divided into
two groups—baleen and toothed. Blubber is
very important to whales and has many
purposes. 6. Whale: can hold breath for long
time, tail fin sideways, lungs; Fish: gills, live
in ponds, tail fin up and down; Both: live in
oceans, people love to watch

Pages 50–51
1. O, O, F, O, F, F, F, O; 2. Answers will vary.
3. Answers will vary. 4. brave, strong, daring,
athletic; 5. climbing poles, ice axes, breathing
masks; 6. Answers will vary. 7. Answers will
vary.

Pages 52–53
1. to entertain; 2. Working is not what the
author would choose to do. 3. The author
wants to escape from worries and be free
like animals. 4. worries, chores, homework;
5. bird: fly, float, sing, play, soar; dolphin:
splash, play, dive, flip; bear: jump, climb,
sleep, run, play, fish; dog: play ball, jump,
run, roll over, fetch, rest, catch;
6. F, O, F, F, O

Page 54
1. to persuade; 2. Answers will vary.
3. Answers will vary. Possible reasons:
Students would get around more quickly.,
Students would learn more., It would lead to
better health. 4. Answers will vary.

TESTS: READING

Test 1: Pages 57–60
Sample: 1.D 2.C

Passage A
1.D 2.A 3.D

Passage B
1.C 2.A 3.C

Passage C
1.C 2.D 3.A 4.B

Passage D
1.A 2.B 3.D

Passage E
1.A 2.D 3.D 4.B

Vocabulary
Synonyms
Sample: A
1.C 2.B 3.B 4.C
5.D 6.B 7.A
Antonyms
Sample: C
1.C 2.D 3.D 4.C
5.A 6.B 7.A

Test 2: Pages 61–64
Sample: 1.D 2.C

Passage A
1.C 2.D 3.B

Passage B
1.C 2.D 3.B

Passage C
1.B 2.A 3.C 4.C

Passage D
1.B 2.C 3.B

Passage E
1.B 2.C 3.D

Vocabulary
Synonyms
Sample: C
1.B 2.B 3.C 4.D
5.B 6.D 7.B

Antonyms
Sample: C
1.D 2.D 3.A 4.C
5.C 6.C 7.A

Test 3: Pages 65–68
Sample: 1.D 2.A

Passage A
1.B 2.D 3.C

Passage B
1.B 2.B 3.D

Passage C
1.C 2.A 3.B 4.D

Passage D
1.A 2.B 3.D 4.C

Passage E
1.B 2.C 3.A

Vocabulary
Synonyms
Sample: B
1.C 2.A 3.B 4.B
5.D 6.D 7.B

Antonyms
Sample: A
1.C 2.D 3.A 4.D
5.B 6.C 7.D

Test 4: Pages 69–72
Sample: 1.D 2.C

Passage A
1.C 2.B

Passage B
1.A 2.D 3.A

Passage C
1.C 2.B 3.B

Passage D
1.A 2.D 3.D

Passage E
1.C 2.C 3.B

Vocabulary
Synonyms
Sample: D
1.D 2.A 3.B 4.C
5.D 6.B 7.A

Antonyms
Sample: A
1.D 2.C 3.A 4.B
5.D 6.B 7.A

Test 5: Pages 73–76
Sample: 1.B 2.A

Passage A
1.D 2.A 3.C

Passage B
1.A 2.D 3.C

Passage C
1.B 2.B 3.D

Passage D
1.C 2.B 3.B

Passage E
1.B 2.B 3.C

Vocabulary
Synonyms
Sample: A
1.C 2.B 3.D 4.B
5.D 6.D 7.C

Antonyms
Sample: B
1.B 2.B 3.A 4.B
5.A 6.D 7.C

Test 6: Pages 77–80
Sample: 1.B 2.D

Passage A
1.A 2.C 3.A

Passage B
1.C 2.A 3.C

Passage C
1.D 2.A 3.C

Passage D
1.C 2.B 3.A

Passage E
1.C 2.D 3.B

Vocabulary
Synonyms
Sample: A
1.D 2.B 3.C 4.B
5.A 6.A 7.D

Antonyms
Sample: B
1.B 2.A 3.B 4.D
5.B 6.D 7.C

Test 7: Pages 81–84
Sample: 1.B 2.C

Passage A
1.C 2.C 3.B

Passage B
1.D 2.C

Passage C
1.D 2.B

Passage D
1.C 2.D 3.A

Passage E
1.A 2.B 3.A 4.D

Passage F
1.B 2.A 3.B

Vocabulary
Synonyms
Sample: A
1.B 2.C 3.B 4.D
5.D 6.B 7.A

Multiple Meanings
Sample: C
1.B 2.D 3.B 4.A

Test 8: Pages 85–88
Sample: 1.B 2.A

Passage A
1.C 2.B 3.A 4.C

Passage B
1.C 2.A 3.D

Passage C
1.D 2.C 3.B 4.C 5.D

Passage D
1.D 2.A 3.C 4.B

Passage E
1.B 2.D 3.B

Vocabulary
Synonyms
Sample: A
1.C 2.B 3.D 4.C
5.A 6.A 7.A

Antonyms
Sample:B
1.B 2.A 3.D 4.A
5.C 6.C 7.B

Test 9: Pages 89–92
Sample: 1.B 2.B

Passage A
1.B 2.C 3.A

Passage B
1.B 2.D 3.C

Passage C
1.C 2.B 3.D 4.B

Passage D
1.D 2.A 3.C

Passage E
1.C 2.B 3.D

Vocabulary
Synonyms
Sample: B
1.A 2.D 3.C 4.A
5.B 6.A 7.D

Antonyms
Sample: C
1.A 2.D 3.A 4.A
5.A 6.A 7.D

Test 10: Pages 93–96
Sample: 1.C 2.C

Passage A
1.B 2.C

Passage B
1.A 2.C 3.B

Passage C
1.C 2.A 3.C

Passage D
1.B 2.A 3.D

Passage E
1.C 2.A 3.B 4.B

Vocabulary
Synonyms
Sample: A
1.D 2.B 3.D 4.B
5.D 6.B 7.C

Antonyms
Sample: A
1.B 2.B 3.D 4.A
5.A 6.A 7.B

Test 11: Pages 97–100
Sample: 1.B 2.D

Passage A
1.A 2.D 3.C

Passage B
1.B 2.A 3.A 4.D

Passage C
1.A 2.C 3.D 4.D

Passage D
1.A 2.D 3.A 4.C

Passage E
1.A 2.B 3.C 4.A

Vocabulary
Synonyms
Sample: C
1.D 2.A 3.C 4.B
5.A 6.C 7.A

Antonyms
Sample: A
1.C 2.B 3.D 4.D
5.A 6.B 7.B

Test 12: Pages 101–104
Sample: 1.D 2.A

Passage A
1.D 2.D 3.C

Passage B
1.B 2.D 3.B

Passage C
1.B 2.D 3.A

Passage D
1.B 2.D 3.C 4.A

Passage E
1.D 2.C 3.A 4.B

Vocabulary
Sample: C
1.D 2.A 3.C 4.D 5.C
6.A 7.B 8.B 9.C

Test 13: Pages 105–108
Sample: 1.A 2.C

Passage A
1.B 2.B 3.A 4.C

Passage B
1.B 2.D 3.D

Passage C
1.A 2.D 3.A 4.B 5.A

Passage D
1.C 2.B 3.D 4.A

Passage E
1.A 2.B 3.D 4.A

Vocabulary
Sample: B; B
1.B 2.B 3.C 4.D
5.B 6.C 7.B

Antonyms
Sample: C
1.D 2.C 3.B
4.A 5.C 6.B

Test 14: Pages 109–112
Sample: 1.A 2.B

Passage A
1.C 2.A 3.D

Passage B
1.B 2.A 3.B

Passage C
1.C 2.B 3.A

Passage D
1.A 2.D 3.D

Passage E
1.B 2.B 3.D

Vocabulary
Synonyms
Sample: B
1.A 2.B 3.B 4.B
5.D 6.A 7.B

Antonyms
Sample: B
1.A 2.C 3.B 4.B
5.B 6.C 7.A

Test 15: Pages 113–116
Sample: 1.D 2.A

Passage A
1.D 2.B 3.A

Passage B
1.C 2.A 3.A

Passage C
1.C 2.A 3.D

Passage D
1.C 2.D 3.B

Passage E
1.D 2.B 3.C 4.C

Vocabulary
Sample: C
1.B 2.C 3.A 4.C 5.A 6.B 7.B 8.D
9.B 10.D 11.A 12.C 13.B

GRAMMAR

Page 119
A. 1. declarative
   2. interrogative
   3. imperative
   4. imperative
   5. exclamatory
   6. interrogative
B. 1. incomplete
   2. complete
   3. complete
   4. incomplete
   5. complete
C. 1. Sarah stood at the edge of the square.
   2. The sword slid out of the stone.

Page 120
A. 1. interrogative, ?
   2. exclamatory, !
   3. imperative, .
   4. declarative, .
B. 1. listened, declarative
   2. play, interrogative
   3. pass, imperative
   4. won, exclamatory
C. Answers will vary.

Page 121
1. b   3. c   5. c   7. c   9. a
2. b   4. a   6. b   8. a   10. b

Page 122
A. 1. A small family | lived on a faraway planet.
   2. The family's two children | played near the space launch.
   3. The little girl | dreamed about life on Earth.
   4. Huge spaceships | landed daily on the planet.
   5. The spaceship mechanics | repaired huge cargo ships.
   6. Twinkling stars | appeared in the black sky.
B. 1. The planet's inhabitants | lived in underground homes.
   2. A special machine | manufactures air inside the family's home.
   3. The athletic girl | jumped high into the air.
   4. Many toys and games | cluttered the children's playroom.
   5. The children's father | described weather on Earth.
C. 1. (The underground home) contained large,comfortable rooms.
   2. (The playful child) rolled his clay into a ball.

Page 123
A. 1. My whole family
   2. The warm, sunny day in the park
   3. My cousin Fred
   4. Everyone
   5. The people in

Page 124

B. 1. watched the space shuttle on TV this morning.
   2. rocketed into space at 6:00 a.m.
   3. released a satellite into space.
   4. circled Earth for three days.
   5. landed smoothly on Monday at noon.
C. Answers will vary.

Page 124
1. b   3. a   5. b   7. a   9. b
2. c   4. c   6. b   8. c   10. c

Page 125
A. 1. Pig One, Pig Two, and Pig Three
   2. bears, rabbits, and pigs
   3. Carrots, beets, and squash
   4. Teddy and Osito
   5. brothers and sisters
B. 1. cleaned and peeled
   2. laughed and giggled
   3. waited and watched
   4. weeds and waters
   5. writes and edits
C. 1. buys and reads, CP
   2. authors and illustrators, CS

Page 126
A. 1. teacher, students; The teacher and her students visited the ocean.
   2. Seagulls, Pelicans; Seagulls and pelicans flew overhead.
   3. Seashells, Seaweed; Seashells and seaweed littered the sand.
   4. Carlos, Tanya; Carlos and Tanya ran on the beach
B. 1. paints, draws; The artist paints and draws sea life.
   2. collect, decorate; I collect and decorate driftwood.
   3. swim, dive; Seals swim and dive near the pier.

Page 127
A. 1. a   2. b   3. a   4. c   5. b
B. 1. c   2. a   3. c   4. b   5. b

Page 128
A. 1. simple   3. compound 5. simple
   2. compound 4. simple   6. compound
B. 1. Connor had seen many parks in his life, but he never had seen a park like this one.
   2. Dad brought a pair of binoculars, and Nate used them to look for animals.
   3. He saw his first live bear, and the hair stood up on his arms.
   4. It was an exciting moment, but it only lasted a second.
   5. The bear was no bear at all, and Felicia was embarrassed.
   6. He hadn't seen a bear, but he kept looking.

Page 129
A. 1. One day we were in the park, (and) we saw two ducks swimming by.
   2. We watched the ducks for a while, (but) they disappeared into the tall grass.
   3. The ducks might have gone to a nest, (or) they could have swum to the shore.
   4. We walked along the grassy bank, (but) we could not find them anywhere.
   5. We sat down on the dock, (and) out came the ducks again.
   6. One adult duck led six ducklings around the pond, (and) the other adult followed behind the babies.
B. 1. but   3. and   5. or
   2. but   4. and
C. Answers will vary.

Page 130
A. 1. b   2. b   3. a   4. b   5. a
B. 1. a   2. b   3. a   4. b   5. c

Page 131
A. 1. farmer, house, road
   2. farmer, wheat, soybeans, corn
   3. fields, crop
   4. crops, rows
   5. plants, farmer, weeds, bugs
B. 1. John Vasquez, Tulsa, Oklahoma
   2. Vasquez Farm, Rising J Horse Ranch
   3. Mr. Vasquez, Sally
   4. Joker
   5. October, Vasquez Farm, Harvest Celebration
C. 1. the street, park
      We walked down Oak Street to Blair Park.
   2. aunt, the city
      My Aunt Ellen lives in Denver.

Page 132
A. 1. (story, celebrations); *Atlanta Constitution*
   2. (movie, poodles); *Three Dogs on a Summer Night*
   3. (campfire); "She'll Be Comin' 'Round the Mountain"
   4. (friend, grandparents); August, John, Germany
   5. (family, beach); Memorial Day
B. Common nouns: newspaper, city, day, magazine, park, book, month
   Proper nouns: The Sun News, Chicago, Tuesday, Cobblestone, Yellowstone National Park, Young Arthur, July

Page 133
1. b   3. b   5. a   7. b   9. a
2. c   4. c   6. c   8. c   10. a

Page 134
A. 1. door, cap, bat, game   4. team
   2. bat, shoulder   5. day, foul, homer
   3. fence, dugout
B. 1. uncles, feet   4. brothers, sisters, cousins
   2. bases   5. teams, playoffs
   3. players
C. 1. (season); teams, players; awards
   2. (hitter), (catcher), (teammate); games
   3. (mother), (father), (assembly); parents
   4. (glove); achievements

Page 135
A. 1. (homework), (night), (story); friends
   2. (home); friends
   3. (cat); dogs, birds, pals
   4. adventures, pets, buddies
   5. (teacher), (story); classes
B. Singular nouns:
   1. chair   3. tooth   5. foot
   2. mouse   4. sheep   6. man
   Plural Nouns:
   1. chairs   3. teeth   5. feet
   2. mice   4. sheep   6. men
C. Answers will vary.

Page 136
1. b   3. b   5. c   7. b   9. a
2. c   4. a   6. c   8. a   10. b

Page 137
A. 1. The fourth graders; (they)
   2. Ada; (she)
   3. Juan, Jill, and I; (We)
B. 1. the author; her
   2. the fourth graders; them
   3. information; it
C. 1. (I), you   2. (You), me   3. (he), us

Page 138
A. 1. We; S   4. I; S   7. them; O
   2. us; O   5. it; O   8. She; S
   3. You; S   6. her; O
B. 1. They sent a postcard to us.
   2. It was addressed to him.
C. Answers will vary.

Page 139
A. 1. a   2. c   3. b   4. a   5. b
B. 1. a   2. b   3. a   4. b   5. b

Page 140
A. 1. my   3. their   5. her   7. Our
   2. his   4. my   6. your
B. 1. My   3. her   5. our
   2. their   4. his   6. my

Page 141
A. 1. mine   3. yours   5. her
   2. your   4. ours
B. 1. our   4. my   7. your
   2. her   5. his   8. our
   3. their   6. My or His
C. Answers will vary.

Page 142
1. d   3. b   5. d   7. b   9. c
2. c   4. c   6. b   8. d   10. a

Page 143
A. 1. wrote   4. weave   7. tie   10. wished
   2. painted   5. knits   8. learned
   3. twisted   6. stretched   9. made
B. 1. hopped   3. slurped
   2. pounded   4. sewed
C. Answers will vary.

Page 144
A. 1. use   3. imagine   5. amazes
   2. tie   4. invented
B. 1. lounge   3. gulp   5. staple
   2. gallop   4. drag

Page 145
A. 1. b   3. a   5. a
   2. c   4. b
B. 1. b   3. a   5. a
   2. b   4. b

Page 146
A. 1. past   5. present   9. future
   2. past   6. future   10. present
   3. future   7. present   11. past
   4. past   8. past
B. 1. Gum acted as an eraser.
   2. Unfortunately, pure rubber cracked in
      cold weather.
   3. Goodyear licensed the process to shoe
      companies.

Page 147
A. 1. wears   4. hurt   7. buys
   2. make   5. cause   8. want
   3. teaches   6. places
B. With Most Singular subjects: laces,
   designs, reaches, erases
   With Plural Subjects: lace, design, reach,
   erase

Page 148
A. 1. c   2. a   3. c   4. b   5. c
B. 1. a   2. c   3. b   4. a   5. c

Page 149
A. 1. will happen   6. will handle
   2. has equipped   7. was talking
   3. was polishing   8. had helped
   4. had tinkered   9. is wearing
   5. was gathering   10. will need
B. 1. had (asked); past
   2. will (drop); future
   3. is (learning); present
   4. will (enjoy); future
   5. has (eaten); past
   6. are (taking); present

Page 150
A. 1. was cooking   4. is tasting
   2. had added   5. will add
   3. have prepared   6. have arrived
B. 1. will bake   4. had planted
   2. has picked   5. have tossed
   3. is picking   6. are planning
C. Answers will vary.

Page 151
1. a   3. c   5. b   7. b   9. a
2. a   4. a   6. c   8. b   10. c

Page 152
A. 1. (I) am (reader)
   2. (books) are (nonfiction)
   3. (bookstore) is (one)
   4. (books) are (interesting)
   5. (owner) is (knowledgeable)
   6. (name) is (Terry Baldes)
   7. (Mr. Baldes) was (inventor, scientist)
   8. (windows) were (attractive)
   9. (event) was (appearance)
  10. (friends) are (admirers)
B. 1. is   3. were   5. were
   2. was   4. are
C. Answers will vary.

Page 153
A. 1. was, S   5. were, P   9. were, P
   2. were, P   6. are, P   10. was, S
   3. are, P   7. is, S   11. am, S
   4. is, S   8. are, P
B. 1. is   2. are   3. are   4. is
C. Answers will vary.

Page 154
1. c   3. c   5. a   7. a   9. b
2. b   4. b   6. b   8. b   10. a

Page 155
A. 1. bought   4. rode   7. took
   2. made   5. shook   8. thought
   3. came   6. heard   9. broke
B. 1. heard   4. broke   7. shook
   2. made   5. rode
   3. bought   6. came

Scholastic Professional Books

Page 156

A. 1. have chosen   6. have gone
    2. has brought   7. had heard
    3. have eaten   8. have ridden
    4. has hidden   9. has bought
    5. had taken

B. 1. heard   4. ridden   7. brought
    2. taken   5. chosen
    3. gone   6. bought

Page 157

A. 1. b   2. a   3. c   4. a   5. b
B. 1. a   2. c   3. a   4. b   5. c

Page 158

A. 1. (colorful), (dark); many
    2. (small); few
    3. (strange), (unusual); one
    4. (mysterious)
    5. (big), (dark); four
    6. (rare), (new)
    7. (tiny), (large), (cold)
    8. (amazing); several

B. Sample answers are given.
    1. small, mysterious
    2. big, large
    3. sandy, small, long
    4. new
    5. underwater, several, many

C. Answers will vary.

Page 159

A. Sample answers are given.
    1. big, hungry
    2. fuzzy, orange, little
    3. missing, tasty
    4. plastic, red; red-headed, young
    5. more, tasty, good

B. 1. gray, shaggy, dark   4. soft, shady
    2. some, droopy   5. enormous, large
    3. little, quiet

C. Answers will vary.

Page 160

1. a   3. b   5. a   7. a   9. b
2. c   4. b   6. b   8. a   10. c

Page 161

A. 1. older   4. quieter   7. brightest
    2. loudest   5. higher   8. saddest
    3. biggest   6. softer

B. 1. hottest; more than two
    2. warmer; two
    3. colder; two
    4. tallest; more than two
    5. longer, two
    6. friendliest; more than two
    7. younger; two
    8. liveliest; more than two

Page 162

1. funniest   7. more challenging
2. funnier   8. most challenging
3. busier   9. more tiring
4. busiest   10. most tiring
5. more exciting   11. more delicious
6. most exciting   12. most delicious

Page 163

1. a   3. b   5. a   7. a   9. a
2. b   4. a   6. b   8. a   10. b

Page 164

A. 1. (of) mountains, rivers, and lakes.
    2. (on) the walls (of) his room
    3. (at) the scenes (in) the pictures
    4. (on) a camping trip
    5. (in) a backpack and knapsack
    6. (from) his father's mug
    7. (in) the mountains (for) hours
    8. (at) the Lost Lake
    9. (on) their journey
    10. (at) a quiet place (for) the night
    11. (in) a tent
    12. (from) the wind and rain
    13. (to) his father
    14. (on) their camping trip

B. 1. Answers will vary.

Page 165

A. 1. in   3. on   5. at
    2. with   4. for   6. into
B. Answers will vary.
C. Answers will vary.

Page 166

1. a   3. b   5. c   7. a   9. c
2. c   4. a   6. c   8. b   10. b

Page 167

A. 1. Tucker, lives; present
    2. It, opens; present
    3. Tucker, collected; past
    4. mouse, filled; past
    5. Tucker, sits; present
    6. He, watches; present
    7. boy, worked; past
    8. They, sell; present

B. 1. crowd, passes; singular
    2. Trains, run; plural
    3. Papa, waits; singular
    4. station, feels; singular
    5. People, rush; plural
    6. Mama, Papa, make; plural

Page 168

A. 1. Crickets, (make)
    2. males, (produce)
    3. I, (listen)
    4. You, (hear)
    5. Mario, (finds)
    6. mother, (calls)

B. 1. Mario wants the cricket for a pet.
    2. He wishes for a pet of his own.
    3. Crickets seem like unusual pets to his mother.
    4. Maybe insects scare her!

Page 169

A. 1. b   3. a   5. a
    2. b   4. b
B. 1. c   3. c   5. b
    2. a   4. b

Page 170

A. 1. "I really like tall tales!"
    2. "Davy Crockett is my favorite character,"
    3. "Who likes Sally Ann Thunder Ann Whirlwind?"

B. 1. "I am a big fan of hers."
    2. I added, "Sally can even sing a wolf to sleep."
    3. "How did Sally tame King Bear?"
    4. "Sally really ought to be in the movies,"

C. 1. "What kind of person is Sally?" asked Davy Crockett.
    2. The schoolman replied, "Sally is a special friend."
    3. "She can laugh the bark off a pine tree," added Lucy.
    4. The preacher said, "She can dance a rock to pieces."
    5. "I'm very impressed!" exclaimed Davy.

D. Answers will vary.

Page 171

A. 1. "Well,   3. "Yes,
    2. "Oh, Ed,   4. "Thank you,

B. 1. "Kim, your posters for the talent contest are terrific!"
    2. She replied, "Thank you, Doug, for your kind words."
    3. Our teacher asked, "Meg, will you play your guitar or sing?"
    4. "Oh, I plan to do both," said Meg.
    5. "Will you perform your juggling act this year Roberto?"
    6. "No, I want to do a comedy routine,"

C. 1. "Kit, which act did you like best?" asked Mina.
    2. He replied, "Oh, I enjoyed the singing pumpkins and the tap dancing elephants."
    3. "Well, I liked the guitar player," said Mina.

D. Answers will vary.

Page 172

1. b	3. b	5. a	7. a	9. a
2. a	4. c	6. b	8. c	10. b

Page 173

A. 1. shouted, (Later)
   2. hit, (Yesterday)
   3. got, (soon)
   4. tried, (earlier)
   5. went, (Then)

B. 1. fell, (everywhere)
   2. piled, (up)
   3. were trapped, (inside)
   4. tunneled, (out)
   5. traveled, (there)

C. 1. never, when   3. inside, where
   2. underground, where   4. Soon, when

Page 174

A. 1. talked, (happily)
   2. squawked, (sharply)
   3. greeted, (warmly)
   4. guided, (expertly)
   5. wrote, (regularly)
   6. recorded, (faithfully)
   7. responded, (personally)
   8. looked, (eagerly)
   9. jumped, (quickly)
   10. snorkeled, (easily)
   11. saw, (clearly)
   12. gazed, (intently)
   13. surrounded, (Swiftly)
   14. chased and nipped, (playfully)

B. Sample answers are given.
   1. bellowed loudly.
   2. swam gracefully.

Page 175

A. 1. a   2. b   3. b   4. c   5. a
B. 1. c   2. b   3. a   4. a   5. b

WRITING

Page 178

Sentences will vary.

Page 179

A. (left to right) S, P; S, P; P, P; S, P; S, S;
P, S; P, P; S, S; B. 1. Half a loaf is better than
none. 2. One good turn deserves another.
3. One rotten apple spoils the whole barrel.
4. The show must go on. 5. Every cloud has
a silver lining. 6. The early bird catches the
worm. 7. A rolling stone gathers no moss.
8. Haste makes waste.

Pages 180–181

1. S; 2. E; 3. S; 4. Q; 5. C; 6. E; 7. C; 8. E;
9. Q; 10. C; 11. S; 12. Q; Sentences will vary.

Page 182

1. Did you know that the whale shark can
grow to a length of 60 feet? 2. That's about
as long as two school buses parked end to
end! 3. These huge creatures are not a threat
to humans like some other sharks are.
4. Whale sharks float near the surface to
look for plankton and tiny fish. 5. Imagine
how amazing it must be to swim alongside
a whale shark. 6. There are an estimated
20,000 known species of fish in the world.
7. Is the dwarf pygmy goby the smallest of
all these species? 8. This species of goby is
less than a half-inch long when it is fully
grown! 9. This tiny fish makes its home in
the massive Indian Ocean.

Page 183

1. Are numbers that cannot be divided evenly
by 2 called odd numbers? 2. Can all even
numbers be divided evenly by 2? 3. Is 0
considered an even number? 4. Are numbers
that have 0, 2, 4, 6, or 8 in the ones place
even numbers? 5. Do odd numbers end in 1,
3, 5, 7, or 9? 6. Is the number 317,592 an
even number because it ends in 2? 7. Is the
sum always an even number when you add
two even numbers? 8. Is the sum of two odd
numbers also an even number? 9. Does the
same rule apply if you subtract an odd
number from an odd number? 10. Can you
figure out all the rules for working with odd
and even numbers?

Page 184

Think about the fastest car you've ever seen
in the Indianapolis 500 race. That's about
how fast a peregrine falcon dives. It actually
reaches speeds up to 175 miles an hour.
How incredibly fast they are! Peregrine
falcons are also very powerful birds. Did you
know that they can catch and kill their prey in
the air using their sharp claws? What's really
amazing is that peregrine falcons live in both
the country and in the city. Keep on the
lookout if you're ever in New York City.
Believe it or not, it is home to a very large
population of falcons.

Page 185

Answers will vary.

Page 186

Sentences will vary.; The simple sentence
will be: The team cheered.

Page 187

Answers and sentences will vary.

Page 188

1. My sister Annie has always participated in
sports, and many say she's a natural athlete.
2. Soccer, basketball, and softball are fun,
but she wanted a new challenge. 3. My sister
talked to my brother and me, and we were
honest with her. 4. I told Annie to go for it,
but my brother told her to stick with soccer or
basketball. 5. Will Dad convince her to try
skiing, or will he suggest ice skating?

Page 189

1. The Caspian Sea, the world's largest lake,
covers an area about the same size as
Montana. 2. The Komodo dragon, a member
of the monitor family, can grow to a length of
10 feet. 3. Our closest star, the sun, is
estimated to be more than 27,000,000°F.
4. Ronald W. Reagan, our nation's 40th
president, worked as a Hollywood actor for
almost 30 years. 5. Georgia, the state that
grows the most peanuts, harvests over 1.3
billion pounds each year. 6. Hank Aaron,
major league baseball's all-time home-run
hitter, broke Babe Ruth's record in 1974.

Page 190

1. My brothers built a tree house in the old
oak tree in our backyard. 2. Jim made a
sturdy rope ladder for the tree house. 3. Kyle
bought a gallon of brown paint. 4. Kyle and
Jim finished painting the walls in an hour.
5. Jim painted a "no trespassing" sign on the
tree house door. 6. A curious squirrel leaped
from a branch into their tree house. 7. The
unexpected visitor startled my unsuspecting
brothers. 8. The frightened squirrel leaped
out of the tree house in a big hurry.

Scholastic Professional Books

Page 191

1. While I waited for my parents to get home, I watched a movie. 2. My brother was in his room because he had homework to do. 3. Before the movie was over, the power went out. 4. Since this happens all the time, I wasn't concerned. 5. I didn't mind the dark at first until I heard a scratching sound. 6. When I found my flashlight, I started to look around. 7. I was checking the living room when I caught Alex trying to hide.

Page 192

Sentences will vary.

Page 193

1. I'd like a bike, a pair of in-line skates, and a snowboard for my birthday. 2. Well, my friend, you can't always have what you want when you want it. 3. No, but I can always hope! 4. My friends and I skate all year long and snowboard during the winter. 5. I used to like skateboarding, but now I prefer snowboarding and in-line skating. 6. What sports, games, or hobbies do you enjoy most, Jody? 7. I learned to ski last year, and now I'm taking ice-skating lessons. 8. Skiing, ice skating, and skateboarding are all fun things to do. 9–12: Examples will vary.

Page 194

1. While Gina answered the phone, Marta watched for the bus. 2. Just as Gina said, "Hello," the caller hung up. 3. Unless they hurried, the girls were going to miss the one o'clock show. 4. By the time they got to the corner, the bus had already come and gone. 5. After the girls had waited a half hour, the next bus to town finally showed up. 6. Since they missed the earlier show, the girls decided to catch the four o'clock show. 7. Since Gina bought the tickets first, they wouldn't have to stand in line later. 8. Even though it was early, Gina and Marta were at the theater by three o'clock. 9. Once they were inside, they bought a tub of popcorn and drinks.

Page 195

Possible sentences: 1. Did you know that the United States is the top meat-eating country in the world? Each person consumes about 260 pounds of meat each year. Beef is the most commonly eaten meat. 2. Have you ever noticed that Abraham Lincoln faces right on a penny? He is the only president on a U.S. coin who does. Sacagawea faces right on the new dollar coin, but she was not a president. 3. It would be fantastic to have a robot to do all my chores, help do my homework, and play games. I really think the day will come. Unfortunately, it won't come soon enough for me.

Page 196

How would **you** like to go to school on Saturdays? If you lived in the **country** of Japan, that's just where you'd be each Saturday morning. I have a **friend** who lives in Japan. Yuichi explained that **students** attend classes five and one-half **days** a week. The **half** day is on Saturday. I was also surprised to **learn** that the Japanese school **year** is one of the longest in the world—over 240 days. It begins in the **month** of April. While we have over two months off each **summer**, students in Japan get their **vacation** in late July and August. School then **begins** again in fall and ends in March. The people of **Japan** believe that a good **education** is very important. Children are required to attend school from the age of six to the **age** of fifteen. They have elementary and middle **schools** just like we do. Then most **students** go on to **high** school for another three years. Yuichi says that students work very **hard** because the standards are so high. He and some of his friends even **take** extra classes after school. They all want to get into a good **college** someday.

Page 197

Starting Over

Today started off badly and only got worse. Everyone in my family woke up late this morning. I had only 15 minutes to get ready and catch the bus. I dressed as fast as I could, grabbed an apple and my backpack, and raced to get to the bus stop on time. Fortunately, I just made it. Unfortunately, the bus was pulling away when several kids pointed out that I had on two different shoes. At that moment, I wanted to start the day over.

Pages 198

Sentences and topics will vary.

Page 199

Topic sentences will vary.

Page 200

Topic sentences will vary.

Page 201

Topic sentence: Tony Hawk is an extraordinary skateboarder.

Supporting sentences: He turned professional when he was only 14 years old. Now in his thirties, Tony has won more skateboarding contests than anyone else has. He even made history in 1999 by landing a trick called the "900" at the Summer X Games.

Closing sentence: Tony Hawk may just be the greatest skateboarder in the world. Paragraphs will vary.

Page 202

Topic sentence: Yesterday our science class went on a field trip to a pond.

Unrelated supporting sentences: Next month we're going to the ocean.; That will be fun.; One of the boys accidentally fell in.; He was really embarrassed.

Page 203

Supporting sentences will vary.

Page 204

Paragraphs will vary.

Page 205

1. O; 2. F; 3. F; 4. O; 5. F; 6. O; Fact and opinion sentences will vary.

Page 206

Paragraphs will vary.

Page 207

Responses and paragraphs will vary.

Page 208

Responses will vary.

Page 209

1. Max had forgotten to check the pot of stew heating up on the stove. 2. Effects: the stew boiled over; the bottom of the pot was scorched; smoke filled the kitchen; dinner was ruined; and Max was in trouble; Paragraphs will vary.

Page 210

Paragraphs will vary.

Page 211

Overused words in paragraph: good, nice, little, big, bad, hard, afraid, sad; Synonyms will vary.

Page 212

Verbs: 1. went; 2. ran; 3. blew; 4. cleaned; 5. laughed; 6. ate; 7. liked; 8. slept; 9. looked; Synonyms will vary.; Exact verbs and sentences will vary.

Page 213

Responses will vary.

Page 214

Responses will vary.

Page 215

Responses will vary.

Page 216

Responses will vary.

Page 217

Responses will vary, but all should include commas and quotation marks around the direct words of speakers.

Pages 218–219

1. Chester Greenwood; 2. 3; 3. Who was Chester Greenwood?; 4. 5; Outlines will vary.

Page 220

Responses will vary.

CHARTS, TABLES & GRAPHS

Mathematics

Page 222
1. c
2. b
3. d
4. a
5. b

Page 223
1. 60 in.
2. 24 pounds
3. Teresita and Pablo
4. Size 5
5. The sizes get larger, or the numbers increase.

Page 224
1. b
2. a
3. c
4. d

Page 225
1. a
2. d
3. b
4. d

Page 226
1. a
2. a
3. b
4. c

Page 227
1. Computer
2. 30
3. Automobile and telephone
4. 20

Page 228
1. a
2. c
3. b
4. b

Page 229
1. 2
2. Vermont
3. 1
4. 16

Page 230
1. b
2. d
3. b
4. c

Page 231
1. 5
2. 3
3. Nature
4. 31
5. The Science badge is probably most difficult because it has been earned by the fewest scouts.

Page 232

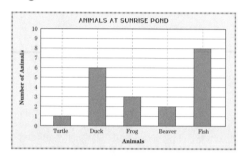

Page 233
1. Science museum
2. 5
3. Water park and amusement park
4. Amusement park
5. Example: The water park would get the fewest votes; the science museum would get a lot more votes.

Page 234
1. d
2. a
3. d
4. b
5. c

Page 235
1. 21
2. Thursday
3. 8
4. 29
5. About 13 books

Page 236
1. 16 in.
2. 5 in.
3. 20 sq. in.
4. 3.5 in.
5. Example: The area of a square increases rapidly as the sides of the square become longer.

Reading/Language Arts

Page 237
1. c
2. a
3. d
4. c
5. a

Page 238
1. Hiking, camping
2. 4
3. Lilac Lake and Mead Canyon
4. Mead Canyon
5. Underwood Park

Page 239
1. a
2. c
3. b
4. c

Page 240
1. Amy Grows Up
2. $2.95
3. 5
4. Dinosaur Dig, $4.50

Page 241
1. b
2. a
3. d
4. d

Page 242
1. c
2. a
3. b
4. d

Social Studies

Page 243
1. 2
2. July
3. 5
4. Spring
5. April

Page 244
1. c
2. b
3. d
4. c
5. a

Page 245
1. Verrazano-Narrows
2. Mackinac Straits, Michigan
3. California, 1937
4. 3,500 feet
5. Delaware Memorial and Tacoma Narrows

Page 246
1. Olympia
2. 1890
3. Oregon
4. Lark Bunting
5. Oregon
6. Sagebrush
7. Idaho and Nevada both have the mountain bluebird.

Page 247
1. Logs are chipped into small pieces.
2. Wood pulp is cleaned and beaten into slush.
3. Step 4, Screen
4. Heat is used to cook the wood chips and to dry the web.

Page 248
1. 60 houses
2. Franklin County
3. Langham County
4. 25 houses
5. The answer should show $4\frac{1}{5}$ house symbols.

Page 249
1. c
2. d
3. b
4. c
5. b

Page 250
Examples of Correct Responses:
1.

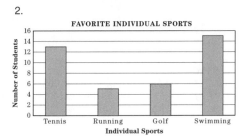

2.

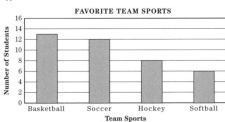

Page 251
1. b
2. d
3. d
4. b
5. a
6. c

Page 252
1. About 1200
2. About 400
3. About 2400
4. 1940–1960
5. Example: The population grew steadily from 1900 to 1980, and then it began to decline.
6. Probably between 2,000 and 2,200

Page 253
1. a
2. c
3. d
4. c
5. Example: Winding became unnecessary in 1930 when electric clocks were invented.

Science

Page 254
1. 5:26 am
2. August 4
3. June 23
4. 10 minutes
5. July 14
6. The sun rises later each day and sets earlier.

Page 255
1. 68˚F, 42˚F
2. Tuesday
3. Friday and Saturday
4. Partly cloudy
5. 1.5 inches
6. Example: It was warm until Wednesday, and then it got cooler each day. It got cloudy and rainy on Thursday and Friday.

Page 256
1. b
2. c
3. b
4. d
5. a

Page 257
1. Ana
2. Earl
3. Hanna
4. Danielle
5. Example: In each year, names alternate between male and female. In even-numbered years, the first name is male. In odd-numbered years, the first name is female.

Page 258
1. 50 mph
2. 25 mph
3. Cheetah
4. 40 mph
5. Elephant, deer, zebra, lion, cheetah

Page 259
1. c
2. d
3. a
4. c
5. a

Page 260
1. 37°F
2. 64°F
3. July
4. January
5. 47°F
6. Example: The average temperature rises steadily each month from January through July, and then it drops steadily from July through December.

ADDITION, SUBTRACTION, MULTIPLICATION & DIVISION

Page 262
1. 19; 2. 42; 3. 54; 4. 35; 5. 66
6. 165; 7. 245; 8. 368; 9. 768; 10. 1,323
What sickness can't you talk about until it's cured? Laryngitis

Page 263
102 + 49 = 151; 311 + 219 = 530
315 + 669 = 984; 452 + 266 = 718
167 + 267 = 434; 202 + 179 = 381
177 + 114 = 291; 372 + 109 = 481
345 + 166 = 511; 201 + 99 = 300
99 + 246 = 345; 397 + 119 = 516
245 + 345 = 590; 548 + 328 = 876
756 + 145 = 901
219 + 79 = 298
Taking It Further: 750, 900, 1,050

Page 264
A. 13, 14; B. 18, 14; C. 16, 12; D. 15,14;
E. 15, 15; F. 15, 13; G. 17, 17; H. 19, 15;
I. 17, 14; J. 15, 20; K. 20, 22; (6 + 3) + 7=16 pieces

Page 265

18	18	17	19	15
16	18	15	15	17
17	18	18	16	16
17	22	18	15	19
17	15	18	18	18

Page 266
A. 3,569, 9,876; B. 9,982, 7,949, 7,860, 91,798; C. 86,992, 90,749, 89,994, 77,787; D. 581,998, 774,862, 567,990, 694,939, 959,596; 29,028 feet

Page 267
A. 15,981, 19,341, 10,397, 8,990; B. 12,349, 12,188, 11,929,10,984; C. 18,990, 16,767, 20,320, 16,971; D. 17,759, 15,984, 14,487, 18,510; 39,661 feet

Page 268
Z. 1,371; B. 632; R. 1,211; Q. 1,522; S. 1,201; X. 761; I. 9,107; C. 4,053; Y. 10,155; A. 14,024; Y. 9,122; L. 103,468; P. 76,076; E. 82,373; F. 92,228; D. 539,396; Q. 651,951; R. 1,059,472; THEY ARE BIRDS OF PREY.

Page 269
H. 9,122; L. 12,548; I. 18,975; A. 17,531; E. 10,322; O. 17,200; C. 18,506; T. 14,123; M. 13,590; N. 130,752; U. 111,110; Y. 182,920; R. 136,131; THE BALD EAGLE IS FOUND ONLY ON THE NORTH AMERICAN CONTINENT.

Page 270
W. 7,901; T. 12,300; P. 7,148; N. 12,885; O. 11,695; E. 15,019; H. 15,994; R. 10,404; S. 9,207; ! 9,816; A. 8,915; U. 11,303; ONE WEARS TROUSERS. THE OTHER PANTS!

Page 271
A. 6,741 + 3,382 = 10,123, 9,443 + 9,817 = 19,260, 4,578 + 5,361 = 9,939, 2,227 + 6,973 = 9,200; B. 3,841 + 4,064 = 7,905, 7,024 + 9,438 = 16,462, 9,810 + 9,385 = 19,195, 7,426 + 7,923 = 15,349; C. 1,773 + 158 = 1,931, 3,654 + 6,474 = 10,128, 4,284 + 3,821 = 8,105, 8,863 + 2,317 = 11,180; D. 3,948 + 9,265 = 13,213, 9,759 + 8,724 = 18,483, 7,558 + 9,948 = 17,506, 4,595 + 6,628 = 11,223; 38,369 + 42,510 = 80,879 pieces

Page 272
A. $92.83; G. $92.53; U $114.60; O. $63.87; B. $72.25; N. $170.78; E. $157.35; R. $69.37; M. $168.72; C. $765.09; S. $980.05; T. $670.09; D. $477.07; Y. $616.34; F. $1,216.40; W. $1,000.68; BECAUSE MONEY DOESN'T GROW ON TREES!

Page 273
1. 1,804; 2. 689; 3. 1,063; 4. 2,133; 5. 3,489
6. 8,234; 7. 7,538; 8. 8,292; 9. 5,429
10. 10,439
What's the best thing to eat in a bathtub? Sponge cake

Page 274
1. Deluxe Scraps
2. Kibble or Mouse Crumbs
3. Mouse Crumbs
4. Table Scraps and Mouse Crumbs
5. Crumbs & Cheese and Deluxe Scraps
Super Challenge: Woovis can't buy three items with $5. The cheapest three items cost a combined $5.67.

Page 275
A. $69.95; B. $118.00; C. $23.88; D. $18.58; E. $178.75; F. $5.25

Page 276
N. 3; T. 10; B. 9; L. 15; U. 14; E. 7; D. 0; O. 1; L. 8; I. 6; W. 5; D. 12; R. 11; N. 13; I. 16; O. 2; H. 4; TWO HUNDRED BILLION

Page 277
2237 m.p.h.; A. 5, 5; B. 2, 9; C. 9, 9; D. 8, 2; E. 1, 6; F. 5, 8; G. 3, 2; H. 9, 8; I. 6, 7; J. 3, 9

Page 278
5,104, 9,221, 4,732, 6,528; 803, 1,161,
3,106, 3,114; 9,159, 112, 2,106, 236; 1,515,
337, 8,613, 241

Page 279
464, 63, 416; 73, 179, 699; 240, 164, 119;
506, 376; 479 is left standing.

Page 280
E. 3,338; E. 4,729; H. 2,579; T. 4,818;
A. 8,858; R. 3,689; H. 7,046; N. 857;
C. 2,491; B. 3,875; E. 5,252; L. 5,583;
S. 874; I. 1,988; IN THE BLEACHERS!

Page 281
First Column: 5,708, 4,834, 1,052, 491, 3;
Second Column: 7,187, 5,708, 2,812, 1,034, 7;
Third Column: 8,245, 6,879, 2,980, 1,383, 4;
Fourth Column: 4,609, 2,656, 818, 126, 9;
Panthers

Page 282
E. 51,411; I. 3,228; R. 41,164; E. 2,497;
P. 30,702; H. 9,166; T. 7,805; L. 13,041;
A. 6,748; G. 16,378; S. 11, 907; ! 9,477;
HE'S A LIGHT SLEEPER!

Page 283
8,604; 26,416; 41,658; 73,278; 4,316; 9,156;
9,493; 5,289

Page 284
Across: 2. 1807; 6. 90,213; 8. 35,975;
9. 1,321; 10. 17,496; 11. 2,072; 12. 686,552;
14. 1,829; 15. 6,317; Down: 1. 3,131;
3. 6,956; 4. 7,761; 5. 45,044; 7. 37,127;
10. 12,697; 13. 666,372

Page 285
A. 36.1; B. 43.48; C. 19.40; D. 78.9; E. 51.59;
265.7; Mary visited Regions B and C.

Page 286
Asteroids, 24–23; Comets, 98–96

Page 287
A. 367 miles; B. 2,289 miles; C. 3,787 miles;
D. 657.7 miles; E. 3,627 miles; F. 899 miles

Page 288
4, 9, 54, 20, 42; 24, 4, 40, 27, 8; 48, 45, 0,
15, 63; 64, 28, 81, 0, 12; 25, 36, 49, 10, 32;
6 x 7 = 42 balloons

Page 289
HE WAS HIRED AND FIRED ON THE
SAME DAY!; HE HAD TO BRING IT BACK!

Page 290
I. 328; O. 819; S. 168; H. 276; J. 146; E. 497;
L. 159; R. 720; C. 366; N. 55; A. 128; F. 369;
T. 490; E. 208; P. 320; THE CAPITAL OF
COSTA RICA IS SAN JOSE.; 189 pounds
of coffee

Page 291
A. 144, 168, 292; B. 399, 567, 168; C. 196,
512, 456, 315, 184, 492; D. 864, 462, 747,
768, 112, 495; 604 meters

Page 292
A. 256, 448, 350, 260, 340; B. 243, 534, 300,
276, 192; C. 294, 312, 576, 612, 216; D. 215,
291, 182, 237, 147

6	1	2	9	6	8	2	3	7
9	3	6	3	1	4	7	2	3
7	1	2	5	6	0	6	1	5
2	8	3	0	9	5	4	5	7
6	2	4	3	2	3	2	1	6
0	7	4	3	4	0	6	9	3
1	6	8	1	3	3	1	2	0
7	5	2	9	1	0	4	3	5
5	3	4	3	8	0	2	9	4

Page 293
A. 1,389, 3,692, 1,552, 3,150, 988, 2,416;
B. 2,275, 4,902, 2,637, 504, 1,664, 1,176;
C. 610, 4,075, 6,860, 1,395, 1,878, 756;
2,072 miles

Page 294
A.560, 3,000, 27,000, 440, 240, 12,000;
B. 490, 36,000, 5,400, 42,000, 3,500, 360;
C. 48,000, 480, 240, 4,500, 44,000, 400

Page 295
1. 2,300; 2. 3,400; 3. 9,300; 4. 17,600
5. 9,500; 6. 16,200; 7. 24,500; 8. 14,400
9. 45,000
What are the cheapest ships to buy?
"Sale"boats

Page 296
1. 11,000; 2. 24,000; 3. 30,000; 4. 56,000;
5. 100,000; 6. 144,000; 7. 210,000
8. 256,000; 9. 360,000; 10. 375,000
Why did the spider join the baseball team?
To catch "flies"

Page 297
973 x 8 = 7784; 380 x 6 = 2280
909 x 7 = 6363; 178 x 4 = 712
272 x 8 = 2176; 319 x 4 = 1276
592 x 7 = 4144; 711 x 7 = 4977
699 x 6 = 4194; 716 x 8 = 5728
340 x 5 = 1700; 234 x 1 = 234
443 x 4 = 1772; 841 x 8 = 6728
361 x 6 = 2166; 246 x 4 = 984
588 x 9 = 5292; 741 x 8 = 5928
508 x 7 = 3556; 799 x 8 = 6392
247 x 7 = 1729; 300 x 9 = 2700
650 x 9 = 5850; 348 x 9 = 3132
948 x 9 = 8532
Taking It Further: 222

Page 298
6,916, 20,130, 19,012, 5,836, 11,284; 7,692,
9,048, 82,890, 22,635, 8,144; 12,663, 7,161,
72,648, 28,744, 42,780; Stormy, Black
Beauty, Midnight, Lola's Lad, Lightning,
Dusty

Page 299
G. 1,536; T. 938; S. 1,431; I. 4,992; A. 2,739;
D. 3,528; M. 1,092; E. 840; N. 1,992;
R. 3,450; K. 4,896; H. 5,208; NIGHTMARES!;
1,632 pounds

Page 300
3,066, 1,323, 3,960; 630 feet; 2,814, 2,425,
1,064; 454 feet; 6,723, 2,160, 5,135; 305
feet; 6,536, 3,640, 3,071; 601 feet; Gateway
Arch should be circled.; 6,050 people

Page 301

45 x 22 = 990; 89 x 23 = 2047

75 x 13 = 975; 68 x 26 = 1768

80 x 26 = 2080; 61 x 23 = 1403

75 x 23 = 1725; 48 x 48 = 2304

96 x 42 = 4032; 77 x 23 = 1771

49 x 71 = 3479; 24 x 20 = 480

96 x 26 = 2496; 65 x 13 = 845

45 x 31 = 1395; 54 x 28 = 1512

34 x 28 = 952; 47 x 23 = 1081

59 x 29 = 1711; 16 x 36 = 576

55 x 52 = 2860; 65 x 21 = 1365

27 x 57 = 1539; 45 x 22 = 990

Taking It Further: a. 2; b. 1; c. 5

Page 302

57 x 73 = 4161; 98 x 34 = 3332

23 x 13 = 299; 30 x 42 = 1260

21 x 61 = 1281; 44 x 20 = 880

87 x 33 = 2871; 79 x 12 = 948

81 x 14 = 1134; 55 x 13 = 715

58 x 42 = 2436; 25 x 13 = 325

60 x 33 = 1980; 61 x 11 = 671

72 x 32 = 2304; 41 x 23 = 943

16 x 34 = 544; 53 x 73 = 3869

27 x 34 = 918; 71 x 17 = 1207

49 x 52 = 2548; 83 x 17 = 1411

25 x 46 = 1150; 95 x 36 = 3420

25 x 17 = 425; 62 x 12 = 744

23 x 45 = 1035; 26 x 35 = 910

37 x 11 = 407; 24 x 20 = 480

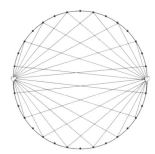

a. 9; b. 7; c. 2; d. 2

Page 303

A. 15,566, 10,836, 9,944, 3,679, 24,786, 26,015; B. 20,520, 23,352, 18,788; C. 23,528, 21,682, 78,948; D. 19,614, 17,342, 62,853; 37,716 steps

Page 304

A. $44.62; M. $19.75; I. $131.84; O. $30.60; A. $117.76; T. $181.26; F. $63.36; D. $87.42; E. $546.05; S. $683.56; R. $65.25; H. $574.36; AT THE FIFE AND DIME STORE!

Page 305

A. $4.92; B. 18,816; C. 1,305; D. $19.95; E. 10,582; F. $17.88

Page 306

A. 6, 9, 8, 5, 9, 3; B. 9, 9, 7, 7, 6, 9; C. 4, 3, 8, 8, 4, 9, D. 8, 7, 6, 3, 1, 5; 1928

Page 307

A. 4, 7, 3, 5, 6, 7, 8, 5, 8; B. 5, 4, 3, 8, 4, 6, 3, 8, 9; C. 6, 5, 3, 7, 6, 9, 3, 9, 6; D. 9, 9, 7, 7, 3, 7, 4, 8, 6; 8 ÷ 1 = 8, 16 ÷ 2 = 8, 24 ÷ 3 = 8, 32 ÷ 4 = 8, 40 ÷ 5 = 8, 48 ÷ 6 = 8, 56 ÷ 7 = 8, 64 ÷ 8 = 8, 72 ÷ 9 = 8

Page 308

14 ÷ 7 = 2; 28 ÷ 7 = 4; 63 ÷ 7 = 9; 49 ÷ 7 = 7

84 ÷ 7 = 12; 70 ÷ 7 = 10; 21 ÷ 7 = 3; 42 ÷ 7 = 6

7 ÷ 7 = 1; 35 ÷ 7 = 5; 77 ÷ 7 = 11; 56 ÷ 7 = 8

70 ÷ 7 = 10; 63 ÷ 7 = 9; 14 ÷ 7 = 2; 28 ÷ 7 = 4

14 ÷ 7 = 2; 7 ÷ 7 = 1; 77 ÷ 7 = 11; 63 ÷ 7 = 9

77 ÷ 7 = 11; 56 ÷ 7 = 8; 7 ÷ 7 = 1; 35 ÷ 7 = 5

Taking It Further: 10 squares

Page 309

24 ÷ 6 = 4; 27 ÷ 3 = 9; 36 ÷ 6 = 6; 28 ÷ 4 = 7

32 ÷ 4 = 8; 40 ÷ 8 = 5; 7 ÷ 7 = 1; 18 ÷ 9 = 2

9 ÷ 9 = 1; 16 ÷ 8 = 2; 32 ÷ 4 = 8; 20 ÷ 4 = 5

42 ÷ 7 = 6; 63 ÷ 9 = 7; 16 ÷ 4 = 4; 81 ÷ 9 = 9

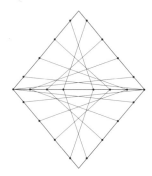

Taking It Further: 54, 45, 36, 27, 18; 42, 35, 28, 21, 14

Page 310

A. 70, 900, 90, 900, 800; B. 600, 80, 900, 80, 80; C. 500, 90, 800, 60, 80

Page 311

E. 9 R3; I. 9 R2; S. 9 R4; O. 4 R4; T. 3 R5; N. 7 R5; P. 6 R3; I. 7 R3; O. 4 R3; A. 8 R6; T. 8 R2; S. 6 R1; H. 5 R3; ! 6 R3; R. 5 R2; N. 9 R7; NO, ON THE STAIRS!

Page 312

14 ÷ 6 = 2R2; 15 ÷ 9 = 1R6; 86 ÷ 7 = 12R2

41 ÷ 6 = 6R5; 37 ÷ 6 = 6R1; 33 ÷ 9 = 3R6

15 ÷ 2 = 7R1; 23 ÷ 6 = 3R5; 13 ÷ 3 = 4R1 54

÷ 7 = 7R5; 45 ÷ 6 = 6R3; 15 ÷ 8 = 1R7

66 ÷ 9 = 7R3; 63 ÷ 8 = 7R7; 28 ÷ 3 = 9R1

33 ÷ 7 = 5R5; 19 ÷ 2 = 9R1; 53 ÷ 6 = 8R5

27 ÷ 5 = 5R2; 62 ÷ 7 = 8R6; 76 ÷ 9 = 8R4

80 ÷ 9 = 8R8; 17 ÷ 4 = 4R1; 11 ÷ 6 = 1R5

Page 313

1. 4; 2. 2; 3. 6; 4. 5; 5. 8; 6. 3 remainder 2

7. 6 remainder 6; 8. 9 remainder 2

9. 8 remainder 1; 10. 15 remainder 2

What kind of tools do you use for math?

"Multi"pliers

Page 314

T. 52; U. 51; M. 91; C. 82; A. 92; E. 81; O. 71; S. 62; N. 84; D. 72; C. 82; I. 53; W. 61; M. 31; ! 22; IT WANTED TO CATCH THE MOUSE!

Page 315

A. 75; B. 82; C. 108; D. 82; E. 27; F. 36; G. 106; H. 94; I. 76; J. 78; K. 54

Page 316

880 ÷ 2 = 440; 996 ÷ 3 = 332; 576 ÷ 4 = 144

502 ÷ 2 = 251; 992 ÷ 2 = 496; 603 ÷ 3 = 201

903 ÷ 3 = 301; 392 ÷ 2 = 196; 982 ÷ 2 = 491

897 ÷ 3 = 299; 738 ÷ 6 = 123; 742 ÷ 2 = 371

990 ÷ 3 = 330

Taking It Further:

```
      432
  2 ) 864
    - 8
    ----
      06
    -  6
    ----
      04
    -  4
    ----
       0
```

Page 317

O. 64 R2; G. 63 R4; K. 95 R3; R. 42 R2; L. 52 R3; A. 83 R1; M. 58 R3; P. 88 R2; S. 87 R2; T. 59 R2; C. 44 R1; A CARPOOL!

Page 318

Z. 742; N. 583 R3; T. 262 R3; S. 748; B. 618 R6; P. 356; D. 394; C. 542 R6; U. 857; O. 921; A. 921 R4; Y. 672; SUNDAY!; 91 R1 days

Page 319

A. 43, 13, 12, 38; B. 18, 15, 33, 10; C. 18, 18, 27, 46; 206 bones; 350 bones

Page 320

S. 604; U. 908; W. 50 R10; X. 130; G. 20 R16; B. 308; R. 20 R6; J. 902; A. 601; E. 20 R22; Y. 320; T. 705; STAR WARTS!; 237 pieces of popcorn

MATH

Page 323
1. 3,462; 2. 98,724; 3. 8,749
4. 128,467; 5. 617,823; 6. 618,397

Page 324
1. forty two; 2. sixty eighth
3. six thousand two hundred thirty four
4. thirty four; 5. one hundred forty five
6. seventeen; 7. ninety three

Page 325
1. 496, 23; 2. 49, 63; or 43, 69
3. 23, 496; or 26, 493; or 93, 426; or 96, 423
4. 732, 469; 5. 23, 64, 97; or 23, 67, 94; or 24, 63, 97; or 24, 67, 93; or 27, 63, 94; or 27, 64, 93; 6. 674, 392

Page 326
1. 9,875; 2. 12,346; 3. 93,876
4. 13,579; 5. 951,876; 6. 123,648

Page 327

Page 328
1. 10; 2. 20; 3. 50; 4. 90; 5. 200
6. 400; 7. 600; 8. 300; 9. 500; 10. 700
What did the farmer get when he tried to reach the beehive?
A "buzzy" signal

Page 329
1. Exact Answer; 2. Estimate
3. Exact Answer; 4. Estimate
5. Estimate; 6. Exact Answer
7. Estimate; 8. Exact Answer
How Would You Estimate...
Answers will vary. Ask students to explain their estimation method in their writing.

Page 330
1. 1; 2. 4; 3. 22; 4. 26; 5. 34
6. 57; 7. 115; 8. 124; 9. 60; 10. 215
How can you make the number seven even?
Take away the "s."

Page 331

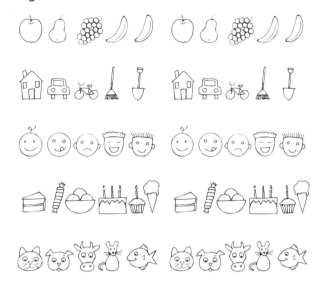

Page 332
1. T; 2. R; 3. R; 4. B; 5. O
6. O; 7. E; 8. O; 9. F; 10. E
What do cheerleaders like to drink?
Lots of root beer

Page 333
19 + 37 = 56; 33 + 47 = 80; 51 + 39 = 90
49 + 22 = 71; 48 + 23 = 71; 78 + 12 = 90
67 + 13 = 80; 29 + 27 = 56

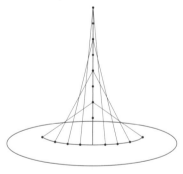

Taking It Further: a. 3; b. 9; c. 7; d. 85; e. 4; f. 26

Pages 334–335
T H E Y   A L R E A D Y
1/5 3/8 4/6 6/8   1/2   2/9 2/3 4/6   1/2   1/3 6/8
H A V E   B I L L S.
3/8 1/2 5/6 4/6   6/12 3/4 2/9 2/9 3/5

Page 336
3/20 + 2/20 = 1/4; 2/16 + 2/16 = 1/4
1/14 + 1/14 = 1/7; 1/9 + 2/9 = 1/3
1/4 + 2/4 = 3/4; 4/9 + 2/9 = 2/3
4/10 + 2/10 = 3/5; 1/5 + 2/5 = 3/5
6/12 + 5/12 = 11/12; 4/10 + 5/10 = 9/10
4/12 + 7/12 = 11/12; 1/10 + 8/10 = 9/10
4/14 + 6/14 = 5/7; 6/10 + 2/10 = 4/5
4/8 + 2/8 = 3/4; 4/8 + 3/8 = 7/8;
2/10 + 3/10 = 1/2; 1/6 + 2/6 = 1/2
1/16 + 1/16 = 1/8; 3/40 + 7/40 = 1/4

Page 337
7/8 - 1/8 = 3/4; 9/10 - 1/10 = 4/5
2/4 - 1/4 = 1/4; 3/5 - 1/5 = 2/5
8/9 - 2/9 = 2/3; 7/11 - 5/11 = 2/11
7/12 - 1/12 = 1/2; 7/8 - 2/8 = 5/8
7/12 - 3/12 = 1/3; 14/15 - 9/15 = 1/3
12/15 - 2/15 = 2/3; 9/10 - 8/10 = 1/10
7/6 - 4/6 = 1/2; 18/20 - 3/20 = 3/4
9/18 - 2/18 = 7/18; 7/8 - 6/8 = 1/8
11/13 - 1/13 = 12/13; 4/5 - 3/5 = 1/5
15/18 - 1/18 = 7/9; 13/16 - 1/16 = 3/4
4/9 - 1/9 = 1/3; 7/8 - 4/8 = 3/8; 3/4 - 1/4 = 1/2

Page 338
1. 1/2 white, 1/2 black
2. 4/7 black, 3/7 white
3. 1/4 black
4. 2 red socks, 4 green socks
5. 2/5 red
Super Challenge: 5 yellow socks, 7 red and white socks

Page 339
Here is the correct ranking from highest to lowest:
1—Tony Gwynn (.368); 2—Mike Piazza (.346); 3—Barry Larkin (.319); 4—Kirby Puckett (.314); 5—Frank Thomas (.308); 6—Mo Vaughn (.300); 7—Barry Bonds (.294); 8—Cal Ripken, Jr. (.262); 9—Ken Griffey, Jr. (.258); 10—David Justice (.253)

Page 340
ACROSS: A. 3.7; C. 4.38; E. .55; F. .6; G. .9; J. .57; K. 7.16; L. 4.3
DOWN: A. 3.14; B. 78.29; C. 4.5; D. 8.1; F. .2704; H. 24.3; I. 1.7; J. .36

Page 341
1. $1.55; 2. 23¢; 3. $2.45; 4. 48¢; 5. $12.70
6. $3.51; 7. 32¢; 8. $10.65; 9. 83¢; 10. $2.57

Page 342

Page 343
1. 52; 2. 12; 3. 100; 4. 20; 5. 365; 6. 36
7. 16; 8. 24; 9. 10; 10. 2; 11. 4; 12. 5,280
13. 60; 14. 1,000
Answer: TWENTY AFTER ONE

Page 344
1. scale; 2. ruler; 3. clock; 4. teaspoon
5. thermometer; 6. measuring cup
7. yardstick; 8. measuring tape

Page 345
1. a and e (4); b and c (30); d and g (16)
2. a and d; 3. a, b, and d; 4. 124

Page 346
1. perimeter: 20; area: 9
2. perimeter: 24; area: 13
3. perimeter: 22; area: 11
4. perimeter: 24; area: 15
5. perimeter: 32; area: 23
6. perimeter: 44; area: 48

Page 347
1. eight; 2. acute; 3. perimeter; 4. area
5. square; 6. cube; 7. triangle; 8. circle
9. polygons
Answer: IT ATE MARS BARS.

Page 348
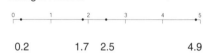

What is the last thing that the trapeze flier wants to be?
The fall guy

Page 349
Children can examine each angle in the letters MATH and determine whether it is right, acute, or obtuse.

Pages 350–351
Tessellate patterns will vary.

Page 352
Taking It Further:

0.2   1.7 2.5   4.9

Scholastic Professional Books

MAPS

Pages 354–355
1. state border
2. Cheyenne
3. Nevada
4. Montana, Idaho
5. Idaho
6. southeast
7. northwest
8. southeast
9. north
10. southwest

Page 357
1. four
2. Southern Hemisphere
3. Prime Meridian
4. north
5. equator
6. It's an imaginary center line on which Earth turns.
7. North America, Asia, Europe, or Africa
8. Asia, Australia, Africa, Europe, and Antarctica

Page 359
1. A world map is flat, a globe is round.
2. Mercator
3. Robinson
4. Mercator
5. Robinson; answers will vary.

Pages 360–361
1. Washington Monument
2. D1
3. Virginia Avenue
4. D1, E1, E2
5. Potomac River
6. E2
7. B2
8. State Department
9. B3
10. A2

Pages 362–363
1. Anchorage
2. 30° N
3. Brasilia
4. equator
5. Nairobi
6. Addis Ababa
7. northern latitudes
8. About 10 degrees
9. 35°N and 35°S
10. 70

Page 364–365
1. north to south
2. west
3. Manaus
4. 30°E
5. Kinshasa
6. Prime Meridian
7. It is on the other side of Earth.
8. 15°W and 45°E
9. false
10. true
11. true
12. true

Pages 366–367
1. a
2. b
3. b
4. a
5. 300 miles
6. 300 miles, about 500 kilometers
7. about 450 miles
8. 400 kilometers
9. about 800

Pages 368-369
1. 1 mile
2. 2 miles
3. 2 1/4 miles, 4 1/2 miles
4. Map A
5. Map B
6. Map B
7. Map A: 300 miles; Map B: 150 miles
8. Map B just shows part of Texas.
9. Beaumont, Fort Worth
10. 300 miles
11. Map A

Page 371
1. desert
2. northern part
3. Small; it would be hard to live in the desert.
4. light green
5. mostly woodland and shrub
6. Algeria, Egypt

Crossword Answers

Pages 372–373
1. volcano
2. mountain
3. hill
4. plain
5. valley
6. plateau
7. canyon
8. isthmus
9. cape
10. peninsula
11. gulf
12. bay
13. strait

Pages 374–375
1. 1,000–2,000 feet
2. Cougar Ridge; 5,000 feet
3. green
4. about 4,000 feet
5. about 2,500 feet
6. the north side; 5,000 feet
7. at 2,500 feet
8. the east side, 4,000 feet
9. Answers will vary.

Page 376
1. 0 to 1,000 feet
2. Hawaii
3. mountains
4. 0-1,000 feet
5. Nihau, Molokai, Lanai, Kahoolawe

Page 377
1. Haiti, Dominican Republic
2. green
3. Dominican Republic; mountains
4. 0 to 1,000 feet
5. 1,000 to 5,000 feet
6. northwest

Page 379
1. false
2. true
3. true
4. false
5. true
6. true
7. true
8. true

Pages 380–381
1. Harness and Saddlemaker, C4
2. Apothecary, I3
3. Cooper, E2
4. Printer, F3
5. Windmill, E2
6. Wetherburn's Tavern, G4
7. Milliner, G3
8. Blacksmith, F4
9. Bake Shop, H3
10. Silversmith, H3

Pages 382–383
1. 80
2. 380
3. Missouri, South Dakota
4. state or county road
5. 3 or 20
6. 30 and 35
7. Des Moines, Ames
8. Possible answer: 29 north to 80 east to 35 north to 18 east

Page 385
1. southeast
2. 50s
3. Minneapolis
4. Los Angeles, Miami
5. Possible answer: warm coat
6. rain and a cold front
7. San Francisco
8. yes

Page 387
1. Warm or hot summers, cold winters; Wet
2. Southeast; Pacific Coast; Hawaii
3. three
4. Cool summers, cold winters; Wet. Cool summers, cold winters; Very dry. Cool summers, mild winters; Wet.
5. Hot summers/mild or warm winters; Wet
6. Cool summers, cold winters; Wet
7. drier
8. Answers will vary.

Pages 388–389
1. northwest
2. red dot
3. Supe Valley
4. Andes
5. inland
6. Thailand, Laos; Vietnam
7. Siem Reap
8. northwest
9. about 150 miles
10. Tonle Sap

Pages 390–391
1. Montana, Wyoming, Idaho
2. five
3. west
4. Yellowstone River
5. Yellowstone Lake
6. about 50–60 miles

Pages 392–393
1. Michigan, Wisconsin
2. WV
3. Atlantic Ocean
4. Cornhusker State; corn
5. Washington; Maine
6. Louisiana
7. because it has a sunny climate

Page 394
1. 0°
2. Ecuador, Colombia, Brazil
3. Southern Hemisphere
4. 80°W
5. woodland and shrub
6. along the western coast
7. forest and farmland
8. near the Amazon River

Page 395
1. 1,000 to 2,000 feet
2. 500 to 1,000 feet
3. Harney Peak in the western part of state
4. 2,000 to 5,000 feet
5. higher
6. 0 to 500 feet

Page 396

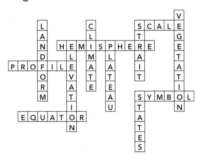